KINGSTON, JAMAICA

Urban Development and Social Change, 1692–1962

Downtown Kingston in 1961 showing the outline of the original grid, the Parade, the finger piers, the central business district, and the densely built-up area of tenements on the periphery of the eighteenth-century settlement.

KINGSTON, JAMAICA
Urban Development and Social Change, 1692–1962

COLIN G. CLARKE

UNIVERSITY OF CALIFORNIA PRESS

Berkeley   Los Angeles   London   1975

University of California Press
Berkeley and Los Angeles, California

University of California Press, Ltd.
London, England

Copyright © 1975 by The Regents of the University of California
ISBN: 0-520-02025-1
Library of Congress Catalog Card Number: 70-153544

American Geographical Society Research Series
Number 27

Printed in the United States of America

To my father and mother

CONTENTS

Preface

Several social scientists have recognised the need for urban research in the Commonwealth Caribbean, but no one as yet has made a detailed study of any of the major settlements. In 1945, while assessing the potential contribution of geographers to an understanding of the problems of the West Indies, Gilbert and Steel reminded colleagues that "geographical work in the towns is especially needed as their growth has been startling and the percentage of urban dwellers continues to increase rapidly."[1] Broom, writing in the early 1950s, described the urbanization of agricultural populations and the progressive concentration of people in the major city of each island as "the most significant social trend in the Caribbean today. These processes are associated with drastic changes in employment, in the nature of the economy and in every aspect of the way of life of the people. Unfortunately, very little work has been done on this topic thus far."[2] It is appropriate therefore that this study should be concerned with Kingston, the capital of Jamaica, a city of more than 500,000 inhabitants in 1970 and the largest settlement in the non-Hispanic Caribbean.

Together with most of the towns in the developing world, Kingston has grown rapidly since the end of the Second World War. In the intercensal period 1943 to 1960 the population increased by 86 percent, and though the growth rate has subsequently decelerated, more than a quarter of the Jamaican population is now living in the city. Kingston's rapid population growth has been owing to the high rate of natural increase and to massive transfers of people from country to town and has exceeded the absorptive capacity of the city in terms of both employment and housing. Social and economic forces have been gravely out of harmony, or at least poorly articulated.

The management of social and economic tensions is complicated by the social structure of the city. Kingston's population comprises persons of European, Jewish, Syrian, African, Chinese, Indian, and mixed descent, and while it is by no means unique in its heterogeneity, it is unusual in that none of these elements is indigenous. Racial differences are accompanied by cultural differences, but if cultural changes have occurred in Kingston, so too have race relations. Thirty years ago the whites were dominant in Jamaica. Now certain sections of the Negro and coloured population are in the political ascendant. The independence of Black Africa, events in the Congo, the black power movement in the United States, and race relations in Britain have had a profound effect in Kingston, where the demand for racial and socio-economic equality has been most persistent.

The role played by race and colour in West Indian societies has been keenly debated by sociologists and anthropologists. Although there is general agreement that the larger Creole societies are composed of hierarchically organized strata, some observers contend that these are based on colour-class distinctions[3] or, in the case of Haiti, on a colour-caste system.[4] A different interpretation has been offered by M. G. Smith who argues that the West Indies are characterized by social and cultural pluralism, that the major social strata are culturally distinct, and that each stratum possesses a different institutional system with regard to family and kinship, education, religion, property, economy, and recreation.[5] He distinguishes between sections and classes. In his view, social classes possess a common system of values and are "differentiated culturally with respect to non-institutionalized behaviours, such as etiquette, standards of living, associational habits, and value systems which may exist as alternatives on the basis of common values basic to the class-continuum."[6] Cultural sections possess their own value systems, but each may be internally divided by social class. Smith relegates race to a relatively minor position among the variables that affect the structure of West Indian societies. Colour-class is responsible for stratification within the cultural sections, but it is culture that determines the boundaries of the major strata.

The plural model contradicts the premise adopted by most sociologists, that a common system of values is essential to the stability in social systems and that without it societies cannot exist. Smith argues that in plural societies, where minority cultures are socially and politically dominant, consensus is replaced by force.[7] Critics of Smith's model claim that it emphasizes cultural differences and neglects the importance of shared values[8] and contend that racial differences are in themselves highly important.[9] Moreover, R. T. Smith, referring to the problem of institutional analysis, has enquired at what point "variations within one institutional sub-system become great enough to warrant our identification of two separate sub-systems."[10] The principal objective in my study however, is not to provide a rigorous testing of the plural model but to use it as a frame of reference for analyzing social structure and social change in Kingston.

This book examines two interconnected themes. The first is concerned with the analysis of the city's spatial, demographic, and economic growth and explores the relationship between social and economic change; the second refers to the social structure of the city and, in particular, to the changing relationship between race, culture, and status. The historical context is supplied by the British colonial period stretching from the founding of Kingston in 1692 to the independence of Jamaica in 1962. But the objective of the earlier chapters is more to trace the development of the social and urban systems than to supply a background to recent patterns and problems, though they provide this information too. The geography and social structure of Kingston have been reconstructed for three stages in the city's history—the period of slavery, 1943, and 1960. These cross sections are linked by chapters which consider the social and economic changes that occurred between 1820 and 1938 and between 1944 and 1960. The major developments since 1962 are indicated in the conclusion.

Although emancipation was achieved in 1834, the chapter dealing with slavery ends in 1820. The changes after that date are best reviewed in conjunction with the post-emancipation period. The availability of census data determined the selection of the years 1943 and 1960 for detailed study. But both dates are close to critical turning points in Jamaican history: 1943 was the last year before the introduction of adult suffrage; 1960 falls just two years short of the end of the colonial period.

This book is similar to a doctoral dissertation accepted by Oxford University in 1967, and is partly based on fieldwork carried out in Kingston between February and October 1961, when I was attached to the Institute of Social and Economic Research at the then University College of the West Indies. The University of the West Indies provided me with a grant toward the cost of a car without which my work would have been extremely difficult. In Kingston the Town Planning Department, the Central Planning Unit, and the Department of Statistics all gave assistance. The last supplied me with a sample of punch cards containing data from the 1960 census and allowed me to tabulate the material to my own requirements. I am particularly indebted to R. H. A. Bailey for his help in programming the tabulator.

Since the initial fieldwork was completed, I have revisited Jamaica three times; for brief periods in 1964 and 1972 and for two months in 1968, during which I was fortunate to be able to work in the Department of Geography at the University of the West Indies as the recipient of an award from the Canada Council. These visits enabled me to check my maps against field conditions, to examine additional documents in the Institute of Jamaica and in the Archives in Spanish Town, and to improve my perspective on the nature of social change in Kingston.

The earliest drafts of this text were written while I was a Leverhulme Fellow in the Department of Geography at the University of Liverpool. My work benefitted considerably from the advice of two of my colleagues in particular—R. Mansell Prothero, and S. Gregory, now Professor of Geography at the University of Sheffield—and from the suggestions of J. M. Houston of the University of British Columbia and of Emrys Jones of the London School of Economics who examined the dissertation on which the book is based. I am also grateful to A. G. Hodgkiss, senior experimental officer, and Joan Treasure of the drawing office, in the Department of Geography at Liverpool for their skill in re-casting my maps, to J. I. Tyndall-Biscoe for the aerial photographs which appear in the frontispiece and in plates 1, 2, and 37, and to the firm of Chas. Goad for the gift of a copy of their Insurance Plan of Kingston which appears, with modifications, in figure 17. My greatest debts of gratitude, however, are to my parents, not least of all for their help with the cost of travel to Jamaica; to my wife for her patience and assistance; to my former supervisor E. Paget, Fellow of Jesus College, Oxford, for introducing me to the West Indies and for guiding my research; and above all to M. G. Smith and David Lowenthal, now at University College London, for their careful criticism of an earlier draft of this book and for their invaluable help over many years. I alone, however, am responsible for any errors of fact or interpretation which appear in the text.

I: Physical Environment

Although the small, mountainous, tropical island of Jamaica is set in the Caribbean Sea, most of its links are with Britain, the United States, and Canada rather than with the other colonial or formerly dependent territories of Middle America (fig. 1). Colonization by, and dependence on, a European power has frequently been the lot of small tropical islands whose proximity to a continent—in this instance South America—made them ideal posts for offshore trading or stepping stones to power on the mainland. However, while both these factors affected the settlement of the West Indies, the value of the islands as sugar producers intensified the competition for their control and generated the centrifugal forces which, in a variety of ways, still effectively divide the area. Separated from its closest neighbours, Cuba and Haiti, by cultural and linguistic barriers, the location of Jamaica in the Greater Antilles also sets it apart from the British territories of the south-eastern Caribbean. Its withdrawal from the then recently formed Federation of the British West Indies in 1961 may partly be attributed to its isolation and parochialism.

Jamaica comprises an area of only 4,400 square miles and is barely the size of the English county of Yorkshire. Shaped planemetrically like a swimming turtle, the island's maximum dimensions are 146 miles from east to west and 51 miles from north to south. Half the land is above 1,000 feet, and elevations exceed 6,000 feet in the Blue Mountains. The relief is highly accidented and provides obstacles to the development of communications and settlement, but in several places the coastal plain expands to form broad embayments. Most of these are cultivated by sugar estates, though a dry embayment on the south side of the island, the Liguanea Plain, is occupied by the city of Kingston. Kingston is situated on the eastern half of the leeward coast of Jamaica and being sheltered from the North-east Trades by the Blue Mountains is admirably situated to act not only as the capital of the island but as the major seaport.

The built-up area of the city covers more than fifty square miles and comprises the parish of Kingston and the suburban section of St. Andrew.

The relief is remarkably uniform, since the fan-shaped Liguanea Plain rises gradually from the sea to a height of 700 to 800 feet eight miles inland and, even in the steepest north-easterly direction, has a slope of less than one degree (fig. 2). Consisting of a bedded series of gravels, sands, loams and clays (fig. 3) the plain is composed of coalescing fans[1] displaced downward and protected from subaerial erosion by movements occurring along the Wag Water Thrust, a fault which underlies its eastern boundary.[2] On the landward side, a crescent of mountains, which rise to more than 2,000 feet, almost encloses the city and the plain (fig. 2 and pl. 1). The northern point of this mountain arc is formed by the 1,250 foot col at Stoney Hill. This col and the embayment below it have provided a route from Kingston to the north coast and in recent years have facilitated the expansion of the city. The col also divides the crescent of mountains into eastern and western horns, whose south-trending tips, comprising Long Mountain and Coopers Mountain in the Red Hills, are set ten miles apart. Long Mountain protrudes north-westwards from the head of Kingston Harbour into the Liguanea Plain. The lowland skirts its northern tip and extends for four miles into the valley between Long and Dallas mountains. A defile, the August Town Gorge, has been cut by the Hope River and continues this valley to the sea. In the west the mountains do not reach the coast, and a gap three miles wide separates the Red Hills from Hunts Bay. The Liguanea Plain extends through this gap and grades into the extensive but less steeply inclined plain of St. Catherine (pl. 2).

Kingston's development as a port can largely be attributed to the Palisadoes Spit, which forms a natural breakwater. The spit consists of a series of cays linked by material supplied by the Hope, Cane, and Bull Bay rivers. Throughout the ten miles of its length, from Port Royal to its junction with the delta of the Hope River (fig. 2), it parallels the arcuate shoreline of the Liguanea Plain, situated two miles to the north. Kingston Harbour, between the plain and the Palisadoes, is regarded as one of the finest anchorages in the world.

The harbour covers an area of almost ten square

miles, and the ship channel requires no dredging to accommodate boats displacing 30,000 tons and drawing up to 30 feet of water. Silt entering the harbour from the gullies of St. Andrew and the rivers of St. Catherine is deposited in Hunts Bay, which acts as a settling basin. The silt is successfully fixed by the red, black, and white mud mangroves (*Rhizophora mangle, Avicennia nitida,* and *Laguncularia racemosa*),[3] and during the last hundred years the shoreline has advanced 700 feet.[4] The formation of mangrove peat and the reclamation of land are also taking place, but at a slower rate, on the harbour side of the Palisadoes.[5] Eventually siltation may have to be checked by dredging if Kingston is to maintain its volume of trade.

Jamaica is regularly subject to seismic disturbances. The Kingston area has suffered two major earthquakes. That of 1692 may be regarded as indirectly constructive, since Port Royal on the Palisadoes was destroyed, and Kingston was founded to replace it. In 1907, however, an earthquake caused great loss of life in Kingston, the commercial area was gutted, and the older parts of the town had to be rebuilt.[6]

The climate of the Kingston area is largely the product of the island's location, but the situation of the city gives rise to important local variations. Kingston records the high annual average temperature of 79°F; the difference between the January and July means is only 5.6°F, whereas the diurnal range in December covers 19.3°F. The higher parts of the Liguanea Plain experience temperatures which are at least 3°F lower than those near the harbour, and this has undoubtedly encouraged the northward expansion of the town. But coastal temperatures are also modified by the sea breeze in the morning and by the land breeze at night. The physiological benefits of the sea breeze have been appreciated since the eighteenth century, when it was known as "the doctor."[7] In contrast, the south-east trade carries dust and smoke from the cement works at the southern end of Long Mountain and deposits them on the eastern suburbs. This provides the main example of air pollution by an industrial plant (pl. 1).

Kingston is sheltered by the mountains from the cold "northers" and the north-east trades. But protection from winds implies a rain-shadow effect, and Kingston suffers from rainfall unreliability and water deficiency. The orographic influence of the Blue Mountains produces an annual average rainfall of 300 inches on the highest peaks, which is in marked contrast with the average of 29 inches recorded in Kingston. Furthermore, rainfall in the capital is concentrated in two seasons, May and October, and the amount has ranged from a low of 8.5 inches in 1914 to a high of 73.5 inches in 1933.[8]

The heaviest precipitation is associated with the passage of hurricanes, which sweep through the Caribbean on a westerly course, bringing gale-force winds and high seas and leaving behind a trail of destruction. During the hurricane in 1933, for example, eight inches of rainfall were recorded in fifteen minutes by the Plumb Point gauge on the Palisadoes.[9] A West Indian adage describes the hurricane season: June too soon, July stand by, August come it must, September remember, October all over. Since 1685 thirty-seven hurricanes have hit Jamaica, but most have passed along the north coast, and Kingston has been affected only twice since 1880.[10] Nevertheless, hurricanes do occasionally threaten the life and livelihood of the inhabitants of the capital, and in 1951 winds associated with Hurricane Charlie caused more than £2 million damage.

The low amount and variable nature of the rainfall at Kingston results in recurring water shortages. Domestic and industrial needs constantly outstrip supplies. This is not a new problem, however, for the original settlement at Kingston had to rely on well water from beneath the Liguanea Plain. The water table lies about twelve feet above sea level, and the concentration of houses near the harbour in the eighteenth century was undoubtedly encouraged by the accessibility of this supply. In the early 1960s, 35 percent of Kingston's annual requirements of 7,400 million gallons was still provided by deep wells on the Liguanea Plain; almost 50 percent was derived from the Hermitage Reservoir in the mountains of St. Andrew, and the remainder came from the Hope River, whose entire flow is abstracted.[11] The wells are critical during the dry season when demand is greatest and supplies from other sources are least. There is no indication that groundwater is being seriously depleted, but the production of the wells cannot be greatly increased, and the Jamaican government is considering a project at Harker's Hall, on the Rio Pedro in St. Catherine, to provide additional supplies for Kingston.

The built-up area of Kingston lies between the Hope River in the east and the Rio Cobre, which forms the parish boundary between St. Andrew and St. Catherine, in the west (fig. 2). The drainage of the Liguanea Plain, however, is confined to a network of gullies, the most important of which, Sandy Gully and Constant Spring Gully, have cut back into the impervious rocks of the north-eastern foot-hills. Sandy Gully reached its present proportions during the storms of 1933 and, with the Constant Spring Gully, forms a catchment area of about twenty-two square miles (pl. 2)

During the wet season floods can occur in the centre of Kingston, and shoppers are occasionally marooned. Edward Long, writing in 1774, observed similar, if more hazardous, conditions.

> The town, thus being commodiously situated in a dry soil, is not incommoded by the lodgement of water in the heaviest rains. ... But although the slope prevents any water from stagnating in the town, it is attended with one great inconvenience, for it permits an easy passage of vast torrents which collect in the gullies at some distance towards the mountains after a heavy rain, and sometimes rushes with so much impetuosity down the principal streets, as to make them almost impassable by wheel carriages, and cause a shoal of water at the wharves, depositing accumulations of rubbish and mud; ... an entire street having been built on the soil thus gained from the harbour since the town was first laid out.[12]

Flash floods in the big gullies have frequently caused loss of life, and the shifting channels have destroyed homes and imposed a limit on the expansion of the suburbs. Since the late 1950s the Jamaican government has embarked on a comprehensive engineering scheme to cope with flood water in Kingston. The Sandy Gully Scheme represents one of the biggest engineering tasks undertaken in Jamaica. At a cost of more than £5 million, it has accounted for a substantial proportion of Jamaica's development funds.

While some of the physical elements in the Kingston area simply provide a backdrop for the city's development, others have played a more vital role, and their influence is reflected in the townscape. Hurricanes and earthquakes have had an inhibiting effect on the layout of houses and explain why few exceed one story in height, and why most new buildings are constructed of reinforced concrete. Until recently the law prohibited elevations greater than sixty feet, and the monotony of the urban sky-line in many areas is broken only by the gentle slope of the Liguanea Plain. Hurricanes and earthquakes have also been important agents in slum clearance and urban renewal. But they are indiscriminate in their choice of victims and have also destroyed many of the fine, double-storyed, colonial houses which formerly graced the north-eastern parts of the old city (pl. 3).

Climate affects the architecture of the more prosperous areas of Kingston in a variety of ways. The sturdy buildings of Britain with their maze of chimney-stacks are replaced by bungalows surrounded by deep verandahs (pl. 4). Carports replace garages and flat concrete roofs are common, though rather poor insulators. Rough-cast gives way before colour-wash, and louvres and jalousies are frequently substituted for windows (pl. 5). Every effort is made to create a flow of air, and the best effects are usually achieved in the older, wooden, shingle-roofed houses whose louvred sides can be opened up like Chinese lanterns. Pedestrians are continually aware of the tropical heat. Shoppers gratefully enjoy the comfort of the piazzas which line the thoroughfares of the city centre (pl. 6) and are eager to use the western or shady side of the streets.

The physical features of the Kingston area are significant for the social values that have been placed on them at various times during the last three hundred years. Two trends have remained fairly constant; a desire to live in the cooler, wetter, and more healthy parts of the upper Liguanea Plain and the avoidance of the marshes which formerly extended from Hunt's Bay to Kingston. The first trend developed after the middle of the eighteenth century, when the availability of cheap well water became less significant for the richest inhabitants. During the present century the private motor car and public transport have facilitated the expansion of the residential areas into the foothills of the mountain rim. But while the marshes have been reclaimed by drainage and filling, they have retained their unattractive associations. These western districts are now among the most densely populated parts of the capital and house persons of the lowest social status. Conversely, the inhabitants of the upper Liguanea Plain stand at the apex of the social scale. However, even on the upper Liguanea Plain the land flanking dangerous gullies is invariably inhabited by squatters and poor tenants (pl. 7). Social patterns therefore tend to reflect physical conditions throughout the urban area.

II: Kingston During Slavery, 1692 to 1820

Kingston was founded in 1692, thirty-seven years after Jamaica was captured from Spain. It was neither the first nor for many years the most important settlement in Jamaica, and its predecessors included St. Jago or Spanish Town, Port Caguay or Port Royal, and the village of Half Way Tree in the parish of St. Andrew (fig. 4).[1] St. Jago, the capital of the island, had been established by the Spanish in 1534 and was situated in a defensive inland position six miles to the west of Kingston Harbour. Port Royal, located at the end of the Palisadoes, was the first town created during the British colonial period, and it provided the colony with its vital maritime link with the mother country.

The thriving economy of Port Royal, which until 1680 was largely derived from the successes of its privateers, enabled it to outstrip Spanish Town in population growth and to become the quasi capital of the island. Port Royal had 8,000 inhabitants in 1668,[2] most of whom were merchants, warehouse-keepers, vintners, and retailers of punch,[3] and it ranked with Santo Domingo, Havana, and Panama City as one of the four principal towns of the Caribbean. But in 1692 an earthquake destroyed Port Royal, killing hundreds of the inhabitants. The survivors fled to the Liguanea Plain, where an even larger number died from exposure and disease. At the end of 1692 the death roll numbered about 3,000.[4]

The central location of the Liguanea Plain relative to the distribution of the population of Jamaica and its size, coastal situation, and proximity to Port Royal made it ideal for resettling the refugees. Consequently, when the Council of Jamaica decided that a permanent replacement for Port Royal was required, they examined the Liguanea Plain for suitable sites. Having rejected Delacree Pen, where the ferry connecting Port Royal to the Liguanea Plain and Half Way Tree deposited passengers in a marshy, unhealthy tract, they selected a hog crawl farther to the east which had access to the deep water of Kingston Harbour, and this site was purchased from Colonel Beeston, an absentee proprietor, for £2,000.

At first the resettlement scheme was undertaken with some urgency, and the actual name of the new settlement, Kingston, appeared in the Council minutes within six weeks of the destruction of Port Royal. But although the Council decided that the town should be developed as rapidly as possible, and that every purchaser of property would have to build within three years a house worth £50,[5] a faction representing the merchants preferred the revival of Port Royal to the establishment of Kingston. This group was highly successful in its intrigues.

By the end of 1692 plans for the new town lay dormant, and the island's secretary and several other officers returned to Port Royal.[6] The development of the new town therefore depended on the influence of Beeston, the original owner of the site. When he returned to Jamaica as lieutenant-Governor in 1693, he was in a unique position to introduce legislation for the recognition and encouragement of the town. Kingston became a legally constituted parish in that year, and the receiver general, the island secretary, and the naval agent, or their deputies, were compelled to transfer their offices from Port Royal to the new settlement.[7] Kingston's position as the commercial capital was confirmed in 1703, when Port Royal was gutted by fire. The refugees fled to Kingston, where the house tax was remitted for a period of seven years in an attempt to encourage them to settle.

The eclipse of Port Royal made Kingston not only the commercial centre and principal port of Jamaica, but also the main rival to Spanish Town, the political capital of the island. Although the Court of Common Pleas and the Jamaica Assembly met in Kingston as early as 1704, it was not until 1755 that the influence of the merchants was sufficient for them to outmanoeuvre the planter-legislators in Spanish Town and to transfer the capital to the larger settlement in Kingston. Kingston's reign was of short duration, however, and the seat of government was returned to Spanish Town in 1758 at the instigation of the King-in-Council.

In spite of these intrigues, the regional functions

of Kingston were slowly established during the eighteenth century. It became the county town of Surrey, which comprised the entire eastern end of the island, and the quarterly assizes were held there. The prosperity of the settlement during the second half of the eighteenth century is indicated by the poll tax of 1768, which showed that "the town of Kingston in Surrey pays about two-thirds more than the other two counties in the articles of house, wheel and rum tax, country houses not being rated."[8] Kingston contributed £83,250 annually to the exchequer, or 54 percent of the colony's income from urban rateable values. From the point of size alone it dominated the urban hierarchy of Jamaica, possessing 1,665 houses in 1772, or four times the number recorded in Spanish Town, its closest competitor.[9] In recognition of its position as the principal city of Jamaica, Kingston was granted the privilege of a mayor and corporation in 1802, and it was the first settlement in the island to be permitted this degree of autonomy in its affairs.

POPULATION GROWTH

The population of Kingston increased from about 5,000 in 1700 to 25,000 in 1790, 30,000 in 1807, and 35,000 in 1828 (table 1). While these figures represent little more than informed guesses, their reliability increases chronologically. If the 5,000 deaths caused by the cholera epidemic of 1850 to 1852[10] are taken into account, the estimate for 1828 bears comparison with the figure of 27,400 enumerated in the first parish census of 1861. The statistics for the eighteenth century are inaccurate in detail, but reliable enough to suggest trends in the growth of the population.

A gradual population increase occurred in Kingston between 1700 and 1775; the rate doubled between 1775 and 1800; and dropped to the earlier level between 1800 and 1820. These three phases reflect demographic changes which occurred throughout Jamaica. During the period covered by this chapter Kingston contained between 9 and 10 percent of the Jamaican population.[11] The ability

of the town to maintain this proportion is easily explained. The growth of Jamaica's population was geared to the labour requirements of the sugar plantations, and Kingston was intimately involved in the import-export trade which formed the basis of the island's economic development.

RACE AND LIBERTY

Throughout the eighteenth and early nineteenth century the population structure of Kingston was affected by two important and interrelated features—racial complexity and slavery. The relationship between the two main groups, the Negro slaves and their white masters, was one of subservience exacted through force. The slave system did not develop in the town but on the sugar plantations, where slavery provided the means of supplying and controlling the labour force. Nevertheless, its influence, though modified, extended beyond the plantations to the towns and especially to Kingston. But by no means were all white people in Kingston masters, or all Negroes enslaved.

As late as 1768 one-third of the white inhabitants of Jamaica were indentured servants, who were introduced under the deficiency laws in an attempt to enlarge the white, arms-bearing population and to ensure that strategic trades did not fall into the hands of Negro artisans.[12] Their loss of liberty, which was usually accompanied by hardship and brutal treatment, lasted for at least four years, at the end of which they were accepted into the ranks of the lower class of free white people. In addition, a small group of free Negroes developed as a result of manumission, while runaway slaves effected their own release, either by joining the Maroons[13] in the mountains of the interior or by hiding in Kingston.

The relationship between race and freedom became increasingly complicated after the middle of the eighteenth century, when miscegenation led to the emergence of the coloured people (table 1). While the illegitimate offspring of lower class whites were condemned to the servile status of their mothers, wealthy white fathers were expected to manumit their coloured children.[14] As a result of their patrilineal links with the white population, the coloured people enjoyed a much greater chance of obtaining freedom than the Negroes. In addition, a few coloured people who had been "regularly baptised and properly educated"[15] were manumitted by private acts of the Jamaica Assembly. Although this particular manumitted group enjoyed all the rights and privileges of the white inhabitants, they were excluded from political activity and from holding public office.[16]

NATURAL INCREASE, MIGRATION, AND SEX RATIOS

The population of Kingston experienced a sixfold expansion during the eighteenth century, but this rapid growth was not due to a high rate of natural increase; in fact, the population failed to reproduce itself throughout the period. In 1771, a typical year, 998 children were born in Kingston, while 2,085 persons died.[17] The high mortality rate can be attributed to excessive drinking and improvidence on the part of the whites; to the brutality to which the slaves, including pregnant women, were subjected; and to the inability of the medical services to cope with tropical diseases, especially yellow fever, which pervaded the marshes on the western side of Kingston. Such was the mortality that in 1817 few slaves were over thirty years of age.[18] Furthermore, the birth rate among slaves was extremely low, owing both to the general shortage of females and to the reluctance of Negro women to bear children into slavery.

Masters mated with Negro women, making the appearance of a coloured group inevitable. This group alone was entirely the product of natural increase, and it made a substantial contribution to the growth of Kingston after 1800. Among the slaves, however, natural decrease continued well into the nineteenth century, and it was not until 1817 that the whites adopted a pro-natalist policy toward them.[19]

Population increase in Kingston resulted from two streams of migration: immigration from Europe and Africa and the in-migration of both whites and non-whites from the sugar plantations. The latter movement was only partly governed by the demand of the town's economy and the desires of the rural population. Whereas free whites were able to live anywhere, slaves and indentured servants were confined to the sugar estates unless their owners resided in Kingston or gave them permission to move there. In contrast, the free coloured people and free Negroes were encouraged to live in the towns.[20] Since it was thought that they would incite the slaves to rebellion, they were usually denied employment on the plantations.

The mobility of slaves was severely restricted by law, and even those who attended the Sunday Market in Kingston were supposed to carry a pass or ticket signed by a white person.[21] Although this legislation was rarely enforced, it undoubtedly restricted movement to Kingston and transformed the plantations into more easily controlled social cells. Nevertheless, the only sizeable group of mobile slaves, the runaways, frequently concealed themselves in the town, where the regimentation of the plantation was replaced by a more confused and liberal social order.[22]

It is impossible to say precisely how differential migration affected the sexual composition of the three social strata and, consequently, whether the sex ratio in Kingston differed greatly from that obtaining throughout the island. However, it is probable that the sex ratio in all three strata was much more balanced in the town than on the plantations, where African males were constantly added to the labour force, and white book-keepers were discouraged from marrying white women.[23] Furthermore, coloured women were in great demand as housekeepers for the whites in Kingston, and it seems quite likely that they outnumbered coloured men. Probably in 1800 this was the only social group with a surplus of women, though female slaves seem to have been well represented in service occupations, and certainly they outnumbered men by the ratio of 1,000 to 780 before the end of the period of slavery.[24]

Migration affected not only the overall growth of Kingston, but also the proportions of the three social strata. The social composition of Kingston was therefore rather different from that of the colony as a whole. In 1788, 9 percent of the total population lived in Kingston, while 6.7 percent of the slaves, 21.8 percent of the whites, and 32.8 percent of the free Negroes and coloured people did so. Whites comprised about 25 percent of the town's population of 16,659 in 1788, the free coloured people and the small group of free Negroes 12 percent, and Negro and coloured slaves 63 percent (table 1).

Differential migration within the three social strata explains why slaves comprised 86 percent of the population of Jamaica, but only 63 percent of the population of Kingston; why whites were two and a half times as numerous in the town as they were in the island as a whole; and why free Negroes and coloured people were almost four times as numerous in the town. By the end of the first decade of the nineteenth century the concentration of whites and free non-whites in Kingston had increased still further, and free Negroes were almost as numerous as the free coloured population.

THE TOWN PLAN

Unlike Port Royal, whose growth had been spontaneous, Kingston was planned. It was, furthermore, a transplanted European town, designed by the white elite to fulfill its own requirements. Responsibility for the layout of Kingston has usually been attributed to Christian Lilly, though evidence in the Minutes of the Council of Jamaica indicates that John Goffe devised the scheme.[25] But Lilly's Plan of Kingston, dated 1702 (fig. 5), provides the earliest cartographic evidence for the town.

The plan of Kingston was geometrical and took the shape of a parallelogram. Measuring three-quarters of a mile in length from north to south and half a mile in breadth, it covered 240 acres and was capable of accommodating many more persons than the 5,000 refugees from Port Royal. The focal point of the town plan was provided by the central Parade, an open space which served as a meeting place for the inhabitants. Straight streets cut one another at right angles and divided the parallelogram into a grid or chess-board pattern. The rectangular street blocks were 320 feet wide and were bisected by lanes which ran from north to south. The depth of each building lot was 150 feet and the frontage 50 feet. These lots formed the framework around which the settlement pattern crystallised, and their influence is still seen in the morphology of modern Kingston (frontispiece).

The town plan had to provide the physical basis for a resettlement scheme and accommodation for the commercial economy of the port. In 1692 the lots on the north side of Harbour Street had direct access to the three finger wharves, and warehousing and trading, generally, were confined to this area. The town plan was modified to provide for these special requirements. The lots between Harbour Street and Water Lane were smaller than average and faced north-south rather than east-west, as the majority did. Their relatively small size reflected the value of a sea frontage, and their alignment was essential for the division of the coast into the maximum number of properties. Other examples of lots orientated north-south occurred on East Queen Street and West Queen Street, on the south side of North Street, and on the north and south sides of the Parade. Those on the Queen Streets were probably designed for commercial reasons, and the others to ensure a balanced layout. Differences in the width of the roads may also be attributed to commercial requirements. The major intersections at the Parade, King Street, and East and West Queen Streets were 66 feet wide, or 16 feet broader than the standard and were designed to carry traffic between the port and its hinterland.

A small but crucial addition was made to the town's layout in 1702 and is shown on Lilly's plan (fig. 5). As early as 1693, Beeston, the Lieutenant-Governor, had obtained control of the mud accumulations which were being deposited on the south side of Harbour Street. Although he had assured the settlers that "the said called Harbour Street should be always used as a Public Street, wherein the Inhabitants might ship off and land goods at all times to come,"[26] he subdivided this new land on resigning the governorship and sold or rented the lots to merchants and warehouse-keepers, many of whom had been established at Port Royal until the second disaster of 1703. The livelihood of the merchants on the north side of Harbour Street was jeopardised by this scheme, and an act was eventually passed in 1712 ordering the demolition of the premises which had been built and the return to the Crown of the land and shoal water which were in dispute. This was disallowed by the King-in-Council, and legal recognition was given to the thoroughfare located on the reclaimed land and appropriately named Port Royal Street.

Only four more additions, three of them quite minor, were made to the town plan before 1820. Evidence for these is provided by Hay's undated map (fig. 6), dedicated to Trelawny, who was Governor of Jamaica between 1738 and 1751. This map shows that lots had been surveyed on the reclaimed land adjoining Port Royal Street and on the St. Andrew side of both North and West Streets. To the east of town, however, the extension was much larger and completely altered the geometrical outline: Hanover Street was laid out, together with a series of lots which covered the low ground between the harbour and the Windward Road. With this addition the shape of the town resembled the letter "L," but the new lots were identical in size, shape, and alignment to those in the original plan, so that the new was integrated with the old. The marshes at Delacree Pen and Greenwich Farm deterred the expansion of the town to the west, and none of the urban properties extended to the west of Princess Street. In all, this plan covered 340 acres, 100 more than that of 1702, and provided the guide-lines for the growth of Kingston until 1820.

DISTRIBUTION OF POPULATION

Although the Council of Jamaica had originally decided that land should be allocated to the white refugees from Port Royal as compensation for their losses, this policy proved abortive.[27] In 1693 Beeston successfully challenged the Council's right to purchase property, and the land at Kingston reverted to his ownership.[28] He abolished the regulations for distribution and started to sell the lots, asking £5 for each one, £3 10s. more than the sum suggested by the Council. Beeston's investment in real estate was therefore undoubtedly his main reason for encouraging the town's development.

The names of at least half of the earliest proprietors in Kingston and the lots which they had purchased by 1702 are marked on Lilly's plan (fig. 5). The plan indicates that only 274 of the original 809 lots had been purchased by the end of the first decade, but the actual number sold was probably greater than 500.[29] The 274 lots sold were unequally distributed throughout the town and unequally apportioned among owners: 147 had one lot each, 37 persons possessed 127 units, and several merchants on Harbour Street had adjacent properties. Lots on which buildings had been constructed were marked in red on the engraving of Lilly's plan, but the original can no longer be consulted,[30] and the information is concealed on reproductions. It is therefore impossible to discover, in detail, which parts of the town were settled first, though it is known that the earliest bill of sale was made out to John Duesbury, who purchased the lot on the corner of King and White (now Tower) Streets on 30 March 1693.[31] By 1702 the population of about 5,000 was concentrated in the southern half of the town, in the area bounded on the north by the Parade and the south by Harbour Street.

The compactness of the settlement was in response to a number of factors. A short journey to work was essential to the economic efficiency of the settlement, for the livelihood of the inhabitants depended on the port, and communications were slow and confined to horse-drawn vehicles, walking, and verbal contact. Furthermore, nucleation was encouraged by two physical factors. Kingston relied on groundwater which was most easily and cheaply tapped near to the shore; the area to the west of the town was marshy and unhealthy and set a sharp limit to expansion in that direction. Between 1702 and the middle of the eighteenth century, the number of lots in the town was increased from 809 to 1,422 (compare figs. 5 and 6). Although the population doubled during this period, it came no nearer to occupying the entire town plan in 1750 than it had been at the beginning of the century. Only 467 lots had buildings on them, and no more than forty-five of these were located to the north of the Parade. Many more, however, may have been owned but not developed, and speculation may have encouraged the eastward extension of the town. Almost 40 percent of the houses and a similar, if not higher, proportion of the total population were concentrated in the area bounded by Church Street, Harbour Street, Orange Street, and the Parade. The end of the lots facing the lanes were covered with huts and rude houses, and high building densities were achieved throughout the settled area, though this comprised only 110 acres, or one-third of the town plan.

Settlement to the north and east of the Parade was dispersed and the population sparse. These properties accounted for less than 10 percent of the dwellings in the town, but most were quite extensive, covering three, four, or more lots. Magnificent town houses, resembling the double-storeyed Georgian mansions shown on the border of the map dedicated to Trelawny (fig. 6), were sited on East Queen Street, East Street, and Hanover Street. They were constructed of stone or brick and displayed high-pitched shingle roofs and shuttered windows. Verandahs supported by slender columns or wooden pillars shaded the rooms on the ground floor (pl. 8). The slow and selective movement of population into this area indicates that a cheap and easily accessible supply of water was less important for the location of houses belonging to the most prosperous white inhabitants. The poorer people, however, were confined to the lower parts of the town and to the areas adjacent to the Parade, where Dicker's Wells provided a public supply of water.

At the beginning of the nineteenth century, Kingston was still a small, compact town of between thirty and thirty-five thousand inhabitants. It was large by Jamaican standards, however, and already had a population greater than all but three of the towns recorded in the 1970 census. Although Jones's map showed that by 1756 some houses had been built in the east, adjacent to the Windward Road (fig. 7), Long referred to "the upper part of the town where a large square is left,"[32] indicating that the Parade still marked the northern limit of the densely populated area in 1774. It is probable that by 1807, when Renny estimated the population at 30,000 and placed the number of houses, exclusive of accommodation for Negroes, at 3,000,[33] the population was still being housed in the south-eastern extension.

The town generally, and the lower parts in particular, were characterised by "a wretched mixture of handsome and spacious houses with vile hovels and disgraceful *sheds*,"[34] the latter occupying the rear of the lots. But many merchants had already evacuated the accommodation near the waterfront in favour of the area to the north of the Parade, where they built spacious wooden houses. It was claimed that "many vie in point of magnificence with those of any capital in Europe."[35]

Scott has left an interesting, though romanticized, description of the architecture of Kingston and particularly of the elite suburb at the beginning of the nineteenth century (pl. 8).

The appearance of the town itself was novel and pleasing; the houses chiefly of two stories, looked as if they had been built of cards, most of them being surrounded by piazzas from ten to fourteen feet wide, gaily painted green and white and formed by the roofs projecting beyond the brick walls or shells of the houses. On the ground-floor these piazzas are open, and in the lower part of the town, where the houses are built contiguous to each other, they form a covered way, affording the most graceful shelter from the sun, on each side of the streets, which last are unpaved, and more like dry river courses, than thoroughfares in a Christian town. On the floor above, the balconies are shut in with a sort of moveable blinds called "jalousies," with large-bladed Venetian blinds fixed in frames, with here and there a glazed sash to admit light in bad weather when the blinds are closed. In the upper part of the town the effect is very beautiful, every house standing detached from its neighbours in its little garden filled with vines, fruit-trees, stately palms and cocoa-nut trees, with a court of negro houses and offices behind, and a patriarchal draw-well in the centre, generally overshadowed by a magnificent tamarind. When I arrived at the great merchant's place of business I was shown into a lofty, cool room, with a range of desks along the walls, where a dozen clerks were quill-driving.[36]

PERIURBAN ZONE

Throughout the eighteenth century, the boundary of Kingston Parish skirted West Street and North Street and then ran eastwards to the head of Kingston Harbour (fig. 7). However, by 1750 the population pattern associated with the town extended into St. Andrew, and five distinct elements can be distinguished in the settlement of the periurban zone at the beginning of the nineteenth century.

As early as 1744, Kingston was surrounded by a discontinuous scatter of huts where free Negroes and runaway slaves found shelter. By the beginning of the nineteenth century at least 2,000 runaways were estimated to be living in Kingston.[37] In an attempt to control this unwanted population and to facilitate searches by the authorities, huts were required by law to have no more than one door; and where more than four huts were built together their inhabitants were compelled to build a seven-foot fence round them and to provide only one entrance to the compound.[38]

During the 1790s French refugees, both white and coloured, who had fled from the revolution in St. Domingue, or Haiti, took up land on the periphery of Kingston. By the beginning of the nineteenth century they monopolised market-gardening and were described as a respectable and industrious class of people.[39] As the decades passed the French language was abandoned and the groups merged with the white and coloured Kingstonians.

Beyond the peripheral zone of small settlements, the dry, lower part of the Liguanea Plain was devoted to cattle farms, or pens, which numbered about fifty in 1763 (fig. 7). Most of the boundaries of the pens were discordant with the road network and confirm that rural settlement antedated the planning of Kingston and the establishment of its communications. Only the Pound Road (now Maxfield Road), running from Half Way Tree to the ferry near New Greenwich, followed field boundaries. The sugar estates of St. Andrew were confined to the higher, wetter part of the Liguanea Plain. North of Half Way Tree, the road ran through "lively fields of canes intermixed with elegant villas and pastures."[40] In 1790 there were eighteen sugar plantations in this area.

Half Way Tree, lying at the junction between the areas devoted to sugar estates and to cattle pens, was admirably situated to act as the main settlement of the parish of St. Andrew. Its functions, however, were gradually usurped by Kingston, and although it stood at the intersection of roads leading to Spanish Town, to St. Mary, and to St. George on the north coast, it contained in 1790 "no more than sixteen or eighteen houses."[41]

The urban influence of Kingston spread outward to embrace the Negro and French settlements, the cattle pens, the sugar estates, and Half Way Tree. By 1774 the Liguanea Plain was being drawn into a potentially suburban relationship with the town,[42] and in 1808 Kingston was described as "a hot, and at times a very unhealthy place. Many of the gentlemen there have pens or country seats, particularly in the Liguanea Mountains, to which they occasionally retire, and where they breathe for a while a more pure and salubrious aire."[43] Before the end of the next decade, merchants were commuting between the Liguanea Plain and their offices and stores in the city.[44]

LAND USE AND ECONOMY

The use of land for non-residential purposes can be analysed under three headings; namely industry, commerce, and various public buildings. It would, however, be misleading to suggest that the specialised use of land for clearly defined purposes characterised Kingston during the period of slavery.

INDUSTRY

Although it is known that a lime kiln and two brick kilns were on the eastern side of Kingston in 1798 and it seems probable that the noxious tanning industry was located to the west, where the Spanish Town Road skirted the mangrove swamp, most of the small industries which developed during the eighteenth century were scattered throughout the commercial and residential parts of the southern half of the town. Sites were rarely used solely for manufacturing purposes, and artisans both worked and lived in buildings located on the lanes.

The dearth of industries may be attributed in part to the absence of natural resources such as coal and iron ore. Furthermore, Jamaican capital and entrepreneurial skill were devoted almost exclusively to sugar production and overseas trade, while the domestic market for manufactured goods was limited by the small size of the population and the high proportion who were slaves. In addition, the British Government discouraged both the growth of towns and the development of manufacturing industry. In 1714, for example, the customs commissioners grudgingly approved the creation of several new ports on the north coast of Jamaica, on the understanding that

the said Act will not encourage the Inhabitants to reside in Townes, and there sett up Manufactures for the Supply of their own Necessities, without Assistance from hence, wch will not only discourage the trade carried out from this Kingdom, as well as our own Manufactures, as by the Reexportation of East India Goods and other Forre[n] goods from hence, but will also take off their hands, wch might be employd more to the Benefit of this Kingdom, in planting and raising Sugars, and other commodities of that Island to be shi'p'd for the supply of our own Forre[n] Markets from hence, to the prejudice of the Trade and Navigation of the Kingdom.[45]

It is hardly surprising to learn from an observer writing in 1807 that "Jamaica receives from Great Britain almost every article and necessary of life."[46]

By far the most important manufacturing industry in Jamaica during the period of slavery was the grinding of sugar cane. Sugar mills were confined to the rural parishes, for cane had to be ground on the estate where it was cut, since sucrose content rapidly diminished after harvesting. Sugar refining, however, was an urban industry that might have been established in Kingston except for the deterioration of refined sugar in transit and the discriminatory British tariffs. Consequently, in 1774 the sugar industry in Kingston was confined to two refineries producing solely for the local market.[47]

British monopoly, Jamaican apathy, and capital inertia perpetuated the economic system and made industrial development in Kingston extremely difficult to effect. Nevertheless, several small industries were developed through the endeavours of local craftsmen. One of the earliest and most successful of these industries was owned by John Reeder who, in 1771 "established a foundry in Kingston and was chiefly employed in casting the various utensils required on sugar estates. Ten years after, it produced a clear annual income to its proprietor of £4,000."[48] Unfortunately, in 1782, during the War of American Independence, it was considered advisable to dismantle the foundry, "lest it should prove serviceable to the enemy then daily expected."[49]

Shortly after the turn of the nineteenth century a number of other domestic industries were developed in Kingston. Joel Evans manufactured leather goods, including boots, harnesses, and carriage tops, and George Ashridge devised an ingenious method for manufacturing a stone which could be used for building walls and roofing houses. On the eve of emancipation, furniture was beng made from local woods by a manufacturer called Turnbull, who employed sixty journeymen and apprentices.[50] In all probability only Turnbull's enterprise resembled a factory. By the end of the period of slavery, cabinet making was a recognised craft in Kingston, the city boasted two foundries, and a certain John Connery was establishing himself as "a manufacturer of very good pottery for which some of the clays in the island are well-suited."[51]

Extractive industries and processers of raw materials were also located in Kingston and its neighbourhood. After the lead mine on the Hope Estate in St. Andrew failed in 1770,[52] extractive industry was confined to lime quarrying on Long Mountain. Some lime was used locally for building stone, but most was processed in the town's lime kiln or sold to the slavers for ballast. One of the most successful industries was tanning, which was based on bark from the mangroves and hides from the cattle pens of the Liguanea Plain. The leather was not only of excellent quality but cheaper than the imported article.[53]

COMMERCE

Overseas Trade

The import-export trade represented the most significant use of land in Kingston throughout the period of slavery. Wharves and warehouses were confined to the area south of Harbour Street, though their hinterland embraced virtually the entire island, and their overseas connections included Europe, Africa, North America, and Spanish America. But if Jamaica's colonial status resulted in the discouragement of industrial development in Kingston, links with the mother country provided an alternative and, temporarily, more satisfactory economic basis for the town's economy.

The economic development of the British West Indies was dictated by the imperial policy of mercantilism. And while the objective of this system was to stimulate British manufacturing and overseas trade and to secure this trade for British shipping under conditions prescribed by the Acts of Navigation, it also assured the commercial growth of Kingston, which was one of the apexes of the triangular trade that linked Britain, West Africa, and the West Indies. Cheap articles manufactured in Britain were exported to West Africa and exchanged for Negroes, who were carried across the infamous Middle Passage to the British West Indies, where they were sold into slavery on sugar estates. Sugar was then exported to the British market. Kingston's role was the import, storage, and despatch of slaves and British manufactured goods to the sugar estates and the collection, storage, and export of sugar to Britain. The growth of Kingston's economy was therefore geared to the growth of the island's economy. The latter can be measured by the increase in the number of slaves and by the amount of sugar exported.

The number of slaves in Jamaica almost doubled between 1703 and 1734, from 45,000 to 86,500. This increase resulted from the labour demands of the sugar estates, which grew in number from 70 to 492 between 1670 and 1739.[54] During the same seventy-year period sugar production rose from 1,333 hogsheads to 33,000.[55]

The economy of Jamaica reached its pre-emancipation peak during the last three decades of the eighteenth century, when Kingston was experiencing its second and most rapid stage of population growth. "As wealthy as a West Indian" was the popular saying in London, where the Jamaican immigrants and other absentee proprietors from the British Caribbean purchased rotten boroughs and, with the merchants of Liverpool, Bristol, and London, wielded considerable power in the House of Commons.

Jamaica's prosperity depended on the increasing demand for sugar and the West Indian monopoly of the market of the British Empire. Both were assured by the Sugar Act of 1739 and the Molasses Act of 1733, which were engineered by the West India interests in London. The number of sugar plantations increased from 492 in 1739 to 700 in 1772 and 769 in 1791.[56] A fourfold increase in the number of Negroes accompanied this development and enabled sugar production to grow from 33,000 hogsheads in 1739 to 75,000 hogsheads in 1772, and to average 92,000 hogsheads a year between 1794 and 1800.[57] In 1800 the Bourbon cane was introduced and in 1805 a record output of 150,000 hogsheads achieved.[58]

At the end of the eighteenth century sugar accounted for 90 percent of the measurable value of Jamaican output.[59] By no means all this sugar was exported through Kingston. Outports such as Montego Bay, Savannah La Mar, Lucea, St. Ann's Bay, Morant Bay, Port Antonio, and, later, Falmouth expanded with the sugar trade, and for a while their combined traffic equalled 88 percent of that of Kingston.[60] Nevertheless, Kingston remained the commercial capital of the island, receiving most of the imports and engrossing the trade with the Americas.

Despite the constraints of British economic policy, Kingston maximised its returns from certain other trading links. By adding to the triangular run the trade of the thirteen British colonies in North America, variety was introduced into the commodities handled by Kingston, and the volume and value of its trade were increased. In theory this did no violence to mercantilist philosophy, since Jamaican molasses could be exchanged for the lumber, casks, flour, and ground provisions of the North American colonies. But the North Americans found it more profitable to sell their goods in Jamaica for coin, which they later exchanged for the cheaper molasses of the French, Danish, and Dutch West Indies.[61] The merchants of Kingston also conducted an illegal but lucrative trade with the French territory of St. Domingue, whose sugar and rum they shipped to Britain disguised as Jamaican produce.[62]

A further stimulus to the economic growth of Kingston was the entrepot trade with the Spanish colonies in Latin America. Started by the buccaneers from Port Royal, it developed steadily in spite of opposition from the Jamaican planters who claimed that the best slaves were re-exported and sold to the Spaniards. Unlike the planters, the Spaniards made their payments in bullion and required no credit. So lucrative were these transactions that as early as the 1690s merchants shipped the equivalent of £100,000 from Kingston to Britain, where the money was desperately needed for the East India trade.[63] The British Government could have found no better reason for breaking the rules of mercantilism, and the legalisation of the trade by the Spanish at the Treaty of Utrecht in 1713 was regarded as a major diplomatic and commercial success.

The *Asiento*, which guaranteed to Britain the monopoly of the slave trade with Spanish America and the right to send one shipload of manufactured goods annually to the Main, was granted not to the Jewish merchants of Kingston who had established the entrepot trade but to the South Sea Company based in London. The latter, however, established its depot at Kingston and helped to expand the town's economy during the 1720s and 1730s. During these two decades the re-export of slaves averaged 2,000 a year.[64] Soon the antagonism between planter and merchant flared up, and in an attempt to increase their labour supplies, the planters in the Jamaican Legislature imposed a duty on exports of slaves. The traders operating under the Asiento avoided the tax by transferring their activities to the cays at the mouth of Kingston Harbour.[65]

Protected by British naval supremacy in the Caribbean, Kingston's trade rapidly increased during wars between the European powers. The destruction of estates on the French islands increased the demand for Jamaican sugar, while the confusion created by warfare and blockade opened new opportunities for the illegal trade in manufactured goods. After the outbreak of the War of Jenkins' Ear in 1739, the illegal trade with the Spanish Main was maintained by the Jewish merchants in Kingston.[66] Their activities were vital not only to British enterprise but also to the economy of Jamaica, where their imports of bullion offset the drain on local currency created by the North Americans. An account in the Rockingham Papers describes the key position of Kingston in the system of trade which evolved out of buccaneering and smuggling.

Soon after the taking of Porto Bello in 1740, sloops and brigs from 50 to 120 tons were fitted out with cargoes of Dry Goods ... and Provisions from 5 to 1,500 sterling each, which they carried to different parts of the Continent from Porto Bello down to Truxillo, and also to the islands of Cuba and Hispaniola. The returns were in bullion and some mules from Rio de la Hacha.[67]

This illegal trade in manufactured goods made a significant contribution to the economy of Kingston between 1740 and 1760. Moreover, the proportion of re-exported to imported slaves was maintained at above 25 percent.[68]

Trade with Spanish America remained one of the

mainstays of the economy of Kingston throughout the remainder of the eighteenth century and increased in importance after 1800. In an attempt to regulate and stimulate this trade the British Government passed the Free Port Act in 1766, the main effect of which was to "admit small foreign vessels from neighbouring foreign colonies into certain ports of the British West Indies with the privilege of importing and exporting certain types of goods."[69] By 1770 Kingston was earning between £300,000 and £400,000 annually from its trade with North America and the Spanish Main,[70] while smaller sums accrued to the free ports at Montego Bay, Savannah la Mar, and Lucea.

Although the island was generally prosperous at the end of the eighteenth century, the economy of the port was subject to depressions which coincided with periods of peace. Furthermore, even wartime became less profitable after 1782, when the thirteen British colonies in North America achieved independence, disrupting the balance of power and pattern of trade in the New World. By 1808, when the slave trade had been abolished and the vendues in Kingston were closed, Britain was embroiled in the Napoleonic Wars, and the output of Jamaican sugar had decreased to 117,000 hogsheads.[71] The free port trade then became the mainstay of the urban economy. Indigence was widespread; but merchants meeting in Kingston, a town of 30,000 inhabitants, agreed that the entrepot trade "defeats the grand aim of Buonaparte, to prevent the use of British manufactures. In the present distressed state of all West Indian concerns it is almost the only trade of consequence left to the city, on which its existence may be said to depend."[72] In 1813 some 577 vessels entered the free ports of Jamaica, and more than 400 visited Kingston; in 1817 Kingston was exporting almost $9 million worth of manufactured goods a year.[73]

Although the economy was precarious at this period, the benefits to the town were considerable. The Spanish trade was partly in the hands of local storekeepers and Jewish entrepreneurs, whereas the export of sugar was monopolised by merchant houses that repatriated to Britain much of the wealth that was created. Indeed, commerce re-

placed manufacturing as the basic activity. Its impact on Kingston at the height of the free port trade at the beginning of the nineteenth century has been described by Scott:

> The harbour was full of shipping ... Everything appeared to be thriving, as we passed along, the hot sandy streets were crowded with drays conveying goods from the wharfs to the stores and from the stores to the Spanish Posadas. The merchants of the place, active, sharp-looking men, were seen grouped under the piazzas in earnest conversation with their Spanish customers, or perched on top of bales and boxes just landed, waiting to hook the gingham-coated Moorish-looking Dons, as they came along with their cigars in their mouths, a train of Negro servants following them with fire buckets on their heads filled with *pesos fuertes.*[74]

Internal Trade

Lack of specialisation, so characteristic of land use in pre-emancipation Kingston, also epitomised the internal trade of the town. Retailing was closely identified with the wholesale trade and was confined to Harbour and Port Royal Streets and, to a lesser extent, to King Street. In 1780, for example,

> the business done by the merchants was, as a rule, of an extensive character, but retail shops were unknown. Drapery goods could only be bought by the piece from the stores. Pedlars travelling on their own account, or [who were] the slaves and servants of free coloured people, did almost the only retailing business then transacted. The proprietors of estates procured most of the articles required by their families direct from England. Provision stores and spirit shops were more common. From 1779 to 1780 the sum paid for licences averaged £8,000 per annum, of which three-fourths came from Kingston.[75]

Conditions of near perfect competition obtained, and although by 1820 retailers could often be distinguished from wholesalers, specialisation by commodity was still rare.[76] Notable exceptions to the lack of specialisation, however, were the two slave vendues which, until 1807, were located on Harbour Street and on Barry Street.

The harbour was the centre for almost all commercial activities, and even the Negro, or Sunday, market was held at the foot of King Street. Conditions in the market in 1819 were described by the Reverend Bickell:

It was on a Sunday, and I had to pass by the Negro market, where several thousands of human beings, of various nations and colours, but principally Negroes, instead of worshipping their maker on His Holy Day were busily employed in all kinds of traffic in the open streets. Here were Jews with shops and standings as at a fair, selling old and new clothes, trinkets and small wares at cent per cent to adorn the Negro person; there were some low Frenchmen and Spaniards and people of Colour, in petty shops with stalls; some selling their bad rum, gin, tobacco, etc; others sought provisions, and small articles of dress; and many of them bartering with the slave or purchasing his surplus provisions to retail again; poor free black people and servants also, from all parts of the city to purchase vegetables, etc., for the following week.[77]

From the economic point of view the slaves were not entirely passive agents, destined solely to labouring on the plantations. They were allowed to cultivate the mountainous backlands of the estates, which became known as Negro grounds, and produced a variety of goods including gums, arrowroot, castor oil, and oil nuts. These entered the internal marketing system and were frequently exported by local entrepreneurs.[78] With their profits, the slaves purchased clothes, household wares, and other articles not provided by their masters. By 1774 they owned most of the coin that was circulating in the island[79] and were largely responsible for the growth of the markets in Kingston and the smaller towns.

At the beginning of the nineteenth century, 10,000 people were attracted to the Negro Sunday market in Kingston,[80] many coming from the surrounding area. This market was an immensely important element in the economy of the town, and stores opened on Sundays to benefit from the crowds which it attracted.[81] Poles apart, socially, the white wholesaler and enslaved market seller were therefore closely associated economically. The

wholesale houses resembled bazaars, while the system of barter, which was widely practiced in the Negro market, was also used in the commercial transactions of the planters. The latter were frequently forced to substitute rum for currency, because there were no banks and coin was in short supply.[82]

PUBLIC BUILDINGS

The first public building in Kingston was the parish church, which was built before 1702 on the south-east corner of King Street and the Parade. Although located at the centre of the town plan, the church was eccentric to the initial settlement pattern. Because of the port, Harbour Street was a more attractive site for public buildings, and both the playhouse and court-house were built there. As the town expanded during the second half of the eighteenth century, the centre of gravity shifted inland. The playhouse moved to a site adjacent to the Parade in 1783,[83] and by 1800 only the court-house, standing on the south-western corner of Hanover and Harbour Streets, provided a vestige of the former pattern of land use. But the court-house was rarely used, and as early as 1774, it was noted that "a building erected for a free-school, situated in the upper districts of the town, being found more airy and commodious, is now made use of for holding the quarterly assize-court for this county."[84]

An increasing number of public buildings were concentrated on or near the Parade, giving rise to one of the most marked forms of land use in the town. The county gaol, free school, and hospital for transient sick and poor were situated nearby, though the military hospital was located in the marshes at Greenwich, where the death-rate, inevitably, was high. At the beginning of the nineteenth century the Methodist Chapel was built on the east side of the Parade, and the barracks stood on the north side in 1774. The Parade served both as the drilling ground for the local militia and as a promenade for the townspeople. It retained military importance long after the 1780s when Up Park Camp was purchased by the Crown to accommodate British troops.[85]

Kingston possessed fewer public buildings than a port of 30,000 inhabitants warranted, however. This was largely due to the legislators in Spanish Town, who systematically deprived the settlement of an efficient administration, since they feared Kingston might then become the capital. Long commented:

No public buildings have yet been erected for the officers of the customs and the receiver general of the island; their offices are kept in private houses, situated in different quarters of the town; which is a very great inconvenience to the trade. Every vessel that arrives is obliged to be entered at the post office, the secretary's, the collector's, controller's, naval and receiver general's. These being all detached and at a distance from one another, the captains of ships are forced to make a tour of the whole town when they attend these offices either to enter or clear. The east side of the Parade or square in line with the barracks, would be a very proper spot for erecting a range of buildings to include all these offices; but such an undertaking is thought too expensive for the town, or the county of Surrey; and the other two counties are supposed to have opposed such a scheme from the apprehension and jealousy that it might one day be converted into a place of residence for the commander-in-chief [that is, the Governor].[86]

Even the Kingston Council, which was established in 1802, adopted a negative attitude to the provision of public amenities. No attempt was made to prevent the streets from becoming extensions to the system of gullies that crossed the Liguanea Plain or to provide the piped water that was needed both to replace the wells, which had become brackish, and to supply the northern and eastern extremities of the town. As late as the 1830s the poorer inhabitants depended on the water-cart,[87] and this alone released the population from the controlling factor of well water.

The systems of burial, sewage disposal and road repair were also primitive and insanitary in the extreme.

There are some other remarkables in this town, which so far as they appear inconsistent with the general health, deserve to be noticed. The first is, the practice of cramming so many corpses into a small church-yard in the centre of the town; instead of providing a proper cemetery at a distance to leeward of all the houses. The second is, a filthy custom of using tubs and empty butter firkins, instead of vaults; and exonerating them of their contents every day at the wharves; by which incessant accumulation of putrid matter, the mud of those parts is rendered still more offensive and injurious to the health of those who inhabit the lowest, which is the hottest quarter of the town. The third is, a strange method of repairing their streets with the offals and nastiness raked from all the dunghills about the town; instead of gravel, or fresh wholesome soil, of which there is a great plenty in the environs.[88]

The protected status of the scavenger bird, the John Crow, represented one of the few public health measures.

In view of the general indifference to hygiene it is hardly surprising that deaths exceeded births in Kingston throughout the eighteenth century. By 1800 the situation had improved somewhat. Gauld's map of the harbours of Kingston and Port Royal (1798) shows that a scheme had been put into effect to drain the swamps on the western fringe of the town, and in 1807 Renny noted that Kingston was "no more unhealthy, nor the mortality greater than in towns which possess an equal population in Europe."[89] Nevertheless, the elite continued to leave the unhealthy areas near the harbour for the cooler suburbs to the north.

In contrast with the dearth of public buildings and amenities, places of entertainment for the white elite were in good supply. By 1783 a race course had been laid out to the north of the built-up area. Two taverns, called Ranelagh and Vauxhall after the pleasure gardens in London, were especially popular. The Ranelagh "was so situated as to command an extensive view of the town and harbour"[90] and was probably patronised by the wealthy inhabitants.

The focal point in Kingston during the period

of slavery was not a central business district but the Parade, on or near to which were located the town's religious and administrative buildings. In the lower part of town, merchant houses adjoined the Negro market, and the social and economic atmosphere of this commercial district was similar to that of the bazaar. Almost no distinction was made between workplace and residence and, with the exception of the mansions of the elite, houses were used as homes, workshops, or places to conduct public and commercial business. While the concentration of public buildings on the Parade represented one of the most specialised forms of land use, the Parade itself was used for recreation, military purposes, and hangings. The ascriptive nature of the social structure, the association of commercial transactions with higgling and with barter, and the confused system of coinage in which Spanish dubloons and French pistoles were legal tender combined to produce an economy and land-use system very different from that of modern Western cities.

DISTRIBUTION OF RACES

The distribution of races in Kingston was related to the patterns of urban growth and land use and to the density of population. Increased segregation accompanied the expansion of the town and the slow trend towards specialisation in land use. The growing white elite displayed their prestige and power by moving from the harbour area to the most attractive and sparsely populated parts of Kingston and St. Andrew. In particular they built homes in the area north-east of the Parade and purchased cattle pens on the Liguanea Plain.

Some wealthy coloured people and Jewish merchants also inhabited these elite areas, but the majority of Jews were concentrated in the western part of the town where they developed their own quarter. The Portuguese Jews (Sephardim) were granted freedom of worship at the end of the seventeenth century, and they built a synagogue on the corner of Princess Street and Water Lane

in 1750; the Ashkenazi sect erected another on Orange Street in 1789.[91] The segregation of the Jews was indicative of their status as a disprivileged minority group, while their location in the western section of the commercial area linked them both with the less attractive, marshy parts of the town, and with the economy of the port.

The densely populated streets and lanes to the south of the Parade were characterised by the greatest racial mixture. Some of the larger houses were occupied by wealthy coloured people and by members of the white elite, but the "vile hovels and disgraceful sheds are inhabited by free people of colour who keep petty huckster's shops and by low white people who vend liquors and give rise to many disorderly and indecent scenes."[92] Indentured servants, also, lived in this area of mixed land use, but their numbers declined rapidly during the second half of the eighteenth century. The deficiency laws that had required certain employers to retain a specific number of whites fell into abeyance, and the financial penalties for non-compliance were increasingly treated as taxes.

The most homogeneous of all racial groupings was located towards the edge of the town where free Negroes and possibly some slaves and runaways occupied shanties. By the middle of the eighteenth century Negro yards were recorded on Duke Street, Barry Street, East Street, and Rosemary Lane[93] on the eastern limit of the built-up area, and at the beginning of the nineteenth century free artisans and jobbing slaves were established at Kingston Pen, to the west.[94] The free Negroes must have found it extremely difficult to purchase property, and the peripheral location of many of their settlements is symbolic of their outcast status. However, the distribution of French refugees, who were located in the west of the town, was more a response to their economic requirements, namely the availability of land for market gardening, than the result of discrimination against them as Catholics.

The slaves were the most dispersed group of all. They were numerous in both the elite and Jewish areas of the town, where their status was unmistakably that of chattels. The greatest concentration of slaves was in the streets and lanes adjacent to Harbour Street.

RELATIONS AMONG THE SOCIAL STRATA

The relations among the three social strata in Kingston—the white, brown, and black—were largely determined by slavery and by the laws of Jamaica. Social and economic roles were apportioned by the white elite, whose power was derived from their monopoly of the legal system and the machinery of government. Furthermore, the formal, or legal, relationships between the strata, which were originally prescribed by the laws of the island, were reinforced by a variety of informal social sanctions. Only white, Christian free-men who possessed a freehold worth £10 per annum qualified for the vote, and representatives to the semi-autonomous Assembly were required to own a freehold of £300 per annum or a personal estate of £3,000.[95] Thus, although many of the whites were enfranchised, membership of the legislature was confined to the elite.

MASTERS AND SLAVES

The relationship between masters and slaves was legally defined in two major slave laws, the *Code Noir* of 1696, to which certain amendments were later made, and the Consolidated Slave Laws of 1792. Although they defined the obligation of masters to feed and clothe their slaves and to release them from work on Sundays, established limits to the mobility of slaves, and proscribed slave gatherings, the protective clauses, which forbade such excesses as mutilation, were rendered nugatory by the very existence of the master-slave relationship —for not only did the whites frame the slave laws but they also administered them in the courts. Furthermore, slaves were prevented from testifying against white persons, though they themselves could be convicted on the evidence of other slaves. The punishment meted out to masters and slaves

who were found guilty of the same offense was grossly disproportionate; "self-defence was a capital crime in a slave—and murder a fifteen pound penalty in the oppressor."[96] In Kingston, as in all the other parishes, a council for the protection of the slaves was set up, composed of the justices and members of the vestry. The vestry was a replica in miniature of the Jamaica Assembly and comprised elected white freeholders and the head of the magistracy, or *Custos Rotulorum*. In their roles as councillors and justices the whites were asked to defend the slaves from the very misdeeds which they, as masters, had committed. Despite laws to the contrary, therefore, slaves were dismembered, pregnant women punished, and imported Africans arriving as family groups were broken up.

Although the slaves held rights *in rem* against all other slaves and were permitted to barter in the Sunday Market, and occasionally owned slaves of their own,[97] as chattels they were liable to be seized in payment for their owner's debts. The only rights they held *vis-à-vis* their master or his agent were rights *in personam*, which guaranteed them usufruct, medical treatment, holidays, and limited amounts of food and clothing. Slaves regarded rights *in personam* as payment for their labour and refused to concede that their master held rights *in rem* against them with respect to material possessions.[98] Consequently, while the slave argued, "what I take from my master, being for my own use, who am his slave or property, he loses nothing by its transfer,"[99] the whites tended to regard all Negroes as thieves. Misunderstandings of this kind were prevalent and developed automatically out of the master-slave relationship.

THE WHITE AND FREE COLOURED POPULATION

The legal and social status of the free people of colour was intermediate between the masters and the slaves. Slaves bore the brand-marks of their owner, but the coloureds were compelled to carry certificates of freedom and to wear a blue cross on their right shoulder.[100] Originally a distinction before the law was made between persons who were born free and those who were manumitted, but by the middle of the eighteenth century both groups were allowed to bear witness against a white person, provided they had been baptised and had been free for at least six months.[101] But free people of colour were allowed to testify only in civil cases; in criminal suits their evidence was never accepted,[102] for these were crucial to the social supremacy of the whites.

Although the whites were responsible for the growth and manumission of the coloured population, they became increasingly alarmed at their rising numbers and fortunes. In 1762 it was estimated that the 3,400 free coloured people in Jamaica owned property worth £250,000,[103] and an act was passed restricting to £2,000 the value of real estate which could be transmitted by whites to coloured people or Negroes.[104] Even so, this legislation could be circumvented by special acts of the Jamaica Assembly. The attitude of the whites to the free people of colour was essentially ambivalent. While individually they were prepared to baptise and to educate their illegitimate coloured children and to send them to English public schools, they were not as a group prepared to accept them into their society. The whites introduced their coloured dependents to European culture but, because they were not white, refused to allow them to reap its rewards. Although the coloured people continually attempted to make themselves culturally "white," they were frustrated in this aim and gradually formed "a separate society of themselves."[105]

THE WHITES AND FREE NEGROES

The legal basis for the relationship between the whites and the free Negroes was the same as between the whites and the free people of colour. But the ambivalence that typified the attitude of the whites to the coloured contrasted with their open hostility to the free Negroes,[106] whom they regarded as prototypes of the emancipated slave. Free Negroes were expelled from the plantations because it was feared they would instigate revolts,[107] yet

they were abused by the whites for shunning state labour and for their idleness and inefficiency as urban tradesmen.[108] The poorer members of the free coloured population received similar treatment.[109]

WHITES AND JEWS

The legal standing of the free people of colour was shared by the Jews. But while the free coloured were discriminated against because they were not white, the Jews, who were European and ranked high in the colour spectrum of the society, were penalised for not being Christian. However, their disabilities were less onerous in Jamaica than elsewhere, and they were permitted freedom of worship.[110] The Jews were able to own property and to undertake trade, but they were criticised for inducing people to live above their means.[111] In times of economic hardship or political unrest the whites used them as scapegoats and charged them with receiving goods stolen by the slaves, siding with the free coloured people and Negroes, and selling ammunition to the Maroons.[112]

Their attitude to the whites was more positive and independent than that of the free coloured people. This stemmed from their ability to identify themselves racially with the whites, from their cohesion as a religious group, and from their economic independence. They achieved a live-and-let-live relationship with the whites, accepted their subordination, immersed themselves in commerce where they were their own masters, and enjoyed their freedom from administrative responsibility.

FREE COLOURED PEOPLE AND SLAVES

The eagerness with which the coloured population, and the free people in particular, attempted to identify themselves with the whites was equalled by their determination to dissociate themselves from the slaves, and especially the Negroes. Edwards described their behaviour in front of whites as "humble, submissive, and unassuming. Their spirits seem to sink under the consciousness of their condition. They are accused, however, of proving bad masters when invested with power; and their conduct towards their slaves is said to be in a high degree harsh and imperious."[113] While coveting the appearance of the coloured people, the Negro slaves, for their part, vilified them as hybrids[114] and usually preferred white masters;[115] their objection to free Negro masters was equally strong.[116]

The free people of colour and the slaves expressed their frustration in mutual hostility. They never mixed on terms of equality, and in Kingston even the Set Girls at the New Year celebrations were segregated into bands of different colours. "There were brown sets, and black sets, and sets of all the intermediate gradations of colour. . . . But the *colours* were never blended in the same set—no blackie ever interloped with the browns, nor did the browns in any case mix with the sables—always keeping in mind—black *woman*—brown *lady*."[117]

In a society preoccupied with considerations of slavery, status, and colour, it was impossible for the free people and slaves to form a common front against the white population. The free people of colour, like the Jews, were concerned solely with their own disabilities.[118] As slave owners themselves, many held the same view of slavery as the white population, treating it as an evil but essential institution.[119]

SOCIAL STRATA AND OCCUPATIONS

Trade provided the basis of Kingston's economy, and most were employed in either commerce or the services. However, the three major social strata were largely confined to different pursuits, and each stratum was divided by occupation into socio-economic classes.

Free whites were employed in two basic occupational categories composed of merchants, mercantile attorneys, surveyors, lawyers, clergymen, doctors, and army officers, on the one hand, and storekeepers, wharfingers, manufacturers, clerks, and soldiers on the other. Many of the first group earned between £2,000 and £4,000 a year.[120] Their ranks comprised immigrants trained in the professions and the armed services and Creole merchants who participated in the export trade with Britain. This group formed the elite and was distinct from the lower class of whites, who were mostly poor Creoles or recent immigrants. A distinction was therefore made between established immigrants and newcomers, as well as between immigrant and Creole whites. A European Club was formed in Kingston, the qualification for full membership being thirty years residence in Jamaica.[121]

Beneath the lower class and slowly merging with it was the lowest rank of immigrant whites, the indentured servants. They were employed either in trades such as carpentry or bricklaying at which they were almost invariably inept or in menial tasks in the retail sector.[122] For the deficiency laws decreed that "tavern keepers, retailers of rum, sugar or rum punch, or keepers of billiard tables in or within six miles of any town should respectively keep one white man such as the commander of the militia may approve as able to bear arms under penalty of £26 a year."[123]

The white population monopolised the official institutions in Kingston; the law courts, the militia, and the established church. This had structural as well as functional implications. The law courts and militia acted as agencies through which the slaves and free people of colour could be controlled and as the means whereby the elite could express its superiority over the lower classes of whites. The white elite were preoccupied with status and dignified titles; "one man sometimes holds the different situations of Major-General of Militia, Assistant-Judge of the Grand Court, and Custos Rotulorum and Chief Justice of the Court of Common-Pleas, *without being either a soldier or a lawyer*."[124] Patronage was in the gift of the town's elite, and they determined the social mobility of the lower classes of whites, appointments in the church, promotion in the business houses, success in the professions, and rank in the militia.

The free Negroes and people of colour were restricted by law to urban occupations and were prevented from voting, from holding political or administrative appointments, and, until 1816, from driving carts.[125] It was extremely difficult for them to find jobs, and the poorer ones had to become self-employed. Emulating the lower class of free whites and the Jews, they usually opened petty huckster's shops, or sold in the Negro Market. Some who were slightly better provided for lived off the earnings of their slaves, whom they hired out as jobbers; others accepted a percentage of their slaves' earnings and allowed them to find their own work as journeymen.[126] But while the income of the free coloured people placed them on a financial footing similar to the lower class of free whites, wealthy coloured people, who inherited money or property from their white fathers or who were successful in business on their own account, ranked economically, though not socially, on par with the white elite.[127]

The division of labour among the slaves in Kingston probably reflected the pattern that had developed on the plantations. Manual jobs in the port were reserved for small gangs of Negroes, especially Africans, and the less onerous domestic and jobbing tasks were for the coloured slaves. Slave women sold dry goods on behalf of their coloured owners, though domestic work was probably the largest employer of female labour. However, while slavery graded into metayage, metayage was frequently synonymous with prostitution, and many slave women were expected to supply their owners with earnings proportional to their beauty.[128] Nevertheless, the position of the slaves in Kingston was generally better than in the rural areas. Many were still maltreated, but since they were usually owned in groups of fewer than six,[129] they were spared the conditions of the slaves on plantations. Furthermore, the system of metayage enabled provident slaves of all shades of colour to save money for their own use, accommodation, or manumission.

The Jews also were divided by occupation and wealth into two social classes. The upper class, comprising merchants who were involved in the free-port trade with Spanish America, frequently undertook financial schemes as a group. Through the co-operation of members and their ability to produce cash when no one else could do so, this element frequently made great bargains in its transactions.[130] They were acutely aware of their social and cultural identity as Jews, and wealthy ones usually attempted to help the poorer. Some of the lower class of Jews were established in commerce and traded "among the negroes chiefly in salt-fish and butter, and a sort of cheap pedlary wares, manufactured by their brethren in Jamaica."[131] Yet despite their contribution to the economy of the town, the Jews were disenfranchised and excluded from political and administrative posts in the colony.

LABOUR EFFICIENCY AND UNEMPLOYMENT

Labour was remarkably inefficient throughout the period of slavery. Whether the slaves malingered or worked hard, the benefit of their endeavours was passed on to their masters, and the notion of profit-sharing was virtually confined to Kingston and the other towns. Metayage was rejected by the planters as a threat to the established order, but it provided many of the landless inhabitants of Kingston with their sole opportunity for capitalising on their slaves. The very existence of slavery discouraged innovation, and the Negroes in Kingston were taught practically none of the mechanical skills that would have made their labour more effective.

It was impossible for unemployment to develop among the slaves in Kingston, for they could be bought, sold, and deployed in accordance with the requirements of the labour market. Furthermore, although slavery condemned the greater part of the population to a low level of living, it provided a rudimentary system of social security. The concept of unemployment is meaningful only where conditions of free labour obtain. The fact that unemployment only affected the free population in Kingston is therefore less paradoxical than it might otherwise appear. While the Jews provided one another with financial support and probably avoided the worst effects of the trade depressions, unemployment affected the white population at the end of the Napoleonic Wars. Unemployment among this group was largely caused by the rigid occupational structure of the town, for the whites simply refused to undertake tasks which they considered beneath their social station.

Denied the social security of slavery and discriminated against when seeking employment, the free coloured people and Negroes frequently became indigent. Some had been manumitted because their owners refused to support them in old age; most had the greatest difficulty in selling their labour in a market which had no use for them. Unemployment certainly affected this group, and after 1774 masters manumitting a slave were required to deposit bonds worth £100 with the church wardens as a security against vagrancy.[132] By the end of the eighteenth century an asylum had been established in Kingston to provide for abandoned slaves.[133] The population of the town grew faster than its economic development warranted. The increasing free-coloured and free-Negro population, expelled from the country, outstripped the capacity of the town for employing them.

FAMILY AND COLOUR

Although the legal division of the society into three hierarchial strata was originally associated with genealogy, phenotype became a major determinant of social status within both the enslaved and free sections of the population in Kingston. Gradations from the "bad" features of the Negro to the "good" features of the European, exemplified by mulattoes, quadroons, mustees, and "retrograde" groups like the sambos, formed stages on the way to whiteness and higher social status. Phenotypical colour provided the basis for a miniature social hierarchy which Monk Lewis, with great exaggeration, has compared unfavourably with the Hindu caste system.[134] The possession of a white skin, aquiline nose, straight hair, and thin lips became a badge of status. To approach this ideal white women avoided sunburn, and coloured people powdered their faces.[135]

In addition to the white bias, there was a legal incentive to improving the colour. For although free mulattoes, quadroons, and mustees were de-

nied full civil rights, all who were "three degrees removed in lineal descent from the negro ancestor were permitted to vote in elections and enjoy all the privileges and immunities of his majesty's white subjects in the island."[136] The Jews could achieve mobility through conversion,[137] but for the non-white population opportunities for improving the colour were vitally important: to the slaves who hoped to obtain their freedom or their children's freedom through the intercession of a white father; and especially to the free people of colour who hoped to improve their social standing and provide their children or their children's children with an almost European appearance.

Males of the white elite took coloured mistresses, euphemistically called "brown girls," and by preference those who were free. The lower class of whites were invariably too poor to qualify for the attentions of coloured women, and their mistresses were usually Negro slaves. These unions were impermanent and never confirmed by marriage. It was generally agreed that "for a white man to marry a mulatto would be a degradation which would forever exclude him from the respectable company of his own colour."[138] In view of the instability of their unions, coloured concubines of the elite usually required large sums of money to be settled on them as a form of insurance, while those with wealthy fathers were often given a kind of dowry to ensure their financial independence.[139] Nevertheless, coloured women treated the keeper relationship as marriage and seem to have preferred associations with the whites to legal unions with men of their own colour.[140] Coloured men therefore took Negro concubines, in the same way as the lower class of whites. The latter were particularly attractive to Negro women, and slaves frequently tried to persuade young immigrants to accept their daughters as mistresses.[141]

Although mating between the races followed a pattern that was structurally hypergamous, it was essential only for males of the lower class of whites and for free people of colour. Among the other groups alternative forms of union with members of the same racial group were possible. Males of the white elite married women of their own colour, the union being solemnized by the Anglican Church. The Jews, likewise, practised both monogamy and concubinage.[142] Unions between coloured people were rare. When they occurred, they seem to have involved the former mistresses of white men and were usually legalised by marriage. Long asserted that mulattoes were mules and could not breed together.[143] Refuted by Lewis at the beginning of the nineteenth century,[144] this claim nevertheless illustrates both the extent to which coloured women associated with the whites and their determination to improve the colour of their children.

Mating among the slaves was regulated neither by the Christian Church nor by any form of African code. House-building and feasting accompanied a girl's first mating,[145] and unions were dissolved by cutting a cotta, or pad used for supporting loads carried on the head;[146] these ceremonials were at the most vestigial and in no way associated with life-long monogamy. Liaisons between the slaves were essentially polygamous, providing a basis for economic co-operation between the sexes. But whereas most unions were described as "temporary connexions which they form without ceremony and dissolve without reluctance,"[147] slaves who were past "the fickleness of youth" frequently formed durable relationships.[148] Concubinage was the norm, though marriages are recorded among baptized slaves in Kingston at the beginning of the nineteenth century.[149] An interesting aspect of the "white bias" and the inability of the slaves to comprehend the part played by cultural factors in mating is revealed by their attitude to concubinage and matrimony: slaves invariably expressed a preference for marriage—provided their spouse was white.[150]

Although mating in Kingston followed a developmental pattern, the sequence applied to individuals and not to household units themselves.[151] Slaves mated extra-residentially but adopted consensual cohabitation in later life. Coloured women practised consensual cohabitation or mated extra-residentially with members of the elite, though some eventually married coloured men.

Extra-residential mating was widespread among the slaves, whose domestic units comprised single males or groups of males, or matrilocal households in which women supported children conceived from different fathers. Geographically separate, these two sets of domestic units among the slaves were socially and biologically complemetary. Half siblings led to the proliferation of loose ties of kinship, both in these matrilocal units and in those formed by consensual cohabitation. Consequently, the concepts of legitimacy and illegitimacy, which were so important to the whites, were meaningless to the Negroes. These mating patterns and family forms were related more to the social structure of the island than to the matriarchal and matrilineal character of West African and above all, Ashanti, society.

The "white bias" and drive toward "improving the colour" formed one aspect of inter-racial mating, but unions that were structurally hypergamous also possessed an element of sexual plunder. Men from the higher social strata dispossessed their male subordinates, and even the parental role of the male slaves was alienated by their masters. Although personal property was inherited patrilineally among the slaves,[152] the family remained matrifocal.

RELIGION AND MAGIC

It was in the realm of religious belief and practice that African cultural traits were most markedly preserved among the Creole slaves, and the town's social strata were most sharply distinguished from one another. With few exceptions, the whites were nominal members of the Anglican Church, though congregations were small and the sacrament rarely administered. Priests of the established church included "the most finished of debauchees" who were usually apologists for, or advocates of, slavery.[153] The *Code Noir* of 1696 made it obligatory for masters to instruct their slaves in the Christian faith, but little or no attempt was made to baptise or educate them until the beginning of the nineteenth century.

The Anglican Church neglected the free people of colour, and many of them were attracted to the Wesleyan Chapel by Dr. Coke, a missionary who visited Kingston in 1792. By 1817 there was a large Methodist congregation in Kingston, one-third of whom were coloured.[154] This church became a major agent promoting the acculturation of the coloured people.

Among the slaves, the most important cultural group was the Coromantins from Ashanti in what is now Ghana. Their pantheism and ancestor cults were gradually incorporated into the beliefs of the entire slave population.[155] Slaves lived in fear of the spirits of the dead, and often engaged obeah men to manipulate malevolent duppies.[156]

Obeah was employed against slave owners as well as in disputes among the slaves themselves. Many attempts were made to poison whites, mostly without success. Eventually, the elite became convinced that obeah was used to create solidarity among the slaves as a prelude to rebellion, and in 1760 practitioners of black magic were punished by death. It has also been argued that oath-taking was associated with myalism or "white-magic."[157]

Creole slaves attempted to engineer their advancement through the practice of obeah, but the Africans, believing that they would return to their homeland when they died, were liable to commit suicide. Conversion to Christianity fitted into the Creole system of belief. Baptism was conceived as a protection against black magic and soon became an end in itself.[158] This presented a major obstacle to the non-conformist missionaries at the end of the eighteenth century. Furthermore, Negro bible-class leaders channelled slaves into unorthodox beliefs and often established break-away cults.[159] In Kingston many slaves were attracted to the Native Baptists led by George Lisle and Moses Baker, both of whom were American Negroes. Baker established a church near the Windward Road on the eastern outskirts of Kingston, and by 1816 had a following of about 2,000 people.[160]

An amalgam of Christian belief and the superstition of the slaves, the Native Baptists, like the cult groups, stressed emotional stimulation, possession, prophecy, and healing. But in some cases acculturation in religious belief and behaviour went a stage further. By the beginning of the nineteenth century many Negroes were attending the Anglican church in Kingston to celebrate the most important stages in the life cycle: "they flock to be baptised in great numbers, and many have lately come to be married; and their burials and christenings are performed with great pomp and solemnity."[161]

EDUCATION

Education reflected and reinforced the patterns of culture developed by the various groups in Kingston. Among the whites, the teaching profession was "looked upon as contemptible,"[162] and the funds of the town's educational charities were often misappropriated. Yet considerable sums were spent on sending white children to English public schools and universities, and in the late eighteenth century about three-quarters of the offspring of the elite were educated in this way.[163] However, girls were often kept at home, and rapidly adopted the speech and manners of their Negro nurses. Less than two-thirds of those who were sent to Britain for schooling returned to the island, and a chronic shortage of local leaders developed.

During the second half of the eighteenth century Woolmer's on the Parade was the only secondary school in Kingston, and its pupils were almost entirely Jews and free people of colour.[164] Some illegitimate coloured sons of the white elite were educated at English public schools, where they rapidly assimilated British culture and manners. By the beginning of the nineteenth century a few of these English-educated men of colour had been admitted to the highest ranks of society in Kingston, though coloured women were still excluded from formal gatherings.[165]

The education of the slaves was informal rather than formal and was conditioned by two factors. Many whites regarded them as intellectually inferior and incapable of improvement.[166] Furthermore, the economic system required subservience and tolerance of heavy work. The slaves received no formal education unless it was imparted by the missionaries. They remained a pre-literate group whose folk-hero was Anansi—the spider man—the trickster of Ashanti legends, and their skills were essentially manual ones.

SOCIAL STRUCTURE

During slavery, the social structure of Kingston comprised three major strata. The upper stratum was exclusively white, and included both an elite and a lower class. Although these two groups had different life-styles, their social and cultural values were identical. The principal objective of lower-class whites was to adopt those aspects of the elite culture from which they were barred by their low socio-economic status. In contrast, the slaves practised neither monogamy nor orthodox Christianity, were prohibited from owning land, and denied the benefits of a formal education. The matrifocal family, the pattern of extra-residential mating, the deferment of faithful concubinage and marriage until later life, the retention of "African" beliefs and their synthesis with Christian concepts and forms of worship, and the oral tradition of its members—all indicate that this stratum was only partly acculturated. The median stratum, generally coloured but with a few blacks, practised institutions peculiar to itself as well as those assimilated from the other groups. While its members were limited in their ability to inherit property from the whites, their educational and religious institutions were derived from the upper stratum.

The distinction between the two higher strata and the lower was marked; but the institutional practices of the two upper groups also differed from one another in terms of organisational framework, status, and function. Each system of institutions was internally integrated, and the three strata were arranged hierarchically and associated respectively with people who were white, brown, and black.

In general, there was a close association between colour, culture, and legal status, and this was clearly expressed in the hierarchical arrangement of free whites, free people of colour, and Negro slaves; these formed the major strata. Among the remaining groups, which were numerically small, the discrepancies between colour, culture, and legal status were considerable. Indentured servants, though white, were, like the Negro slaves, unfree; but from the cultural standpoint were similar to the lower class of whites with whom they eventually merged. The Jews enjoyed a social and legal position identical with the free coloured population, though they were different from the whites only with respect to religion. While free Negroes ranked on a par with free people of colour, coloured slaves were associated with the mass of the unfree Negro population.

Despite the discordance between the legal and cultural boundaries which cut across the various racial groups, relations of an egalitarian nature rarely if ever developed between members of different social strata. Furthermore, misfits like Jews, indentured servants, coloured slaves, and Negro freemen formed isolated cellular groups that were hostile to, or reviled by, the other elements in their stratum.

The legal barrier to mobility placed a premium on "improving the colour" as a means of manumission and, above all, of entry into the dominant group. Although race and colour were by no means the most important determinants of social status, they were the principal qualification for membership in the highest echelon. Furthermore, colour, together with occupation, contributed to the stratification of both the middle and lower strata. The close association between colour, culture, and legal status was indicative of the rigid and static nature of the social structure of Kingston and illustrates the part played by race in defining social status both in reality and symbolically. It is hardly surprising that many white extremists eventually turned to racism as a justification for slavery and the social system as a whole.[167]

FISSION AND FUSION

Although the "white bias" conditioned many of the non-whites to accept the notion of white superiority, to undervalue their own capabilities, and to accept the *status quo,* the maintenance of the social order depended even more on the solidarity of the upper social stratum and its ability to exploit divisions between and within the others. The white elite possessed both the ability and will to control the social system, and though a debating society in Kingston in 1774 approved Thomas Hibbert's motion that *"the trade to Africa for slaves was neither consistent with sound policy, the laws of nature nor morality,"*[168] in practice their policy of enslavement never wavered. The roots of the social structure lay in the economic demands for labour, but slavery became the basis for a "status economy" and for grave social and economic injustice.

Preoccupation with social status ultimately provided the major obstacle to change in the social order, for the whites feared that any alteration in the relationship between the three legally defined strata would threaten the stability of the society.[169] Consequently, advocates of emancipation were denounced, non-conformist clergymen obstructed, and white and coloured liberals ostracized or driven into exile. In the final analysis the cohesion of the urban community depended on force or the threat of force. The political and legal supremacy of the whites was reinforced by the whip, by the British military detachment, and by the local militia. In 1802 the foot militia in Kingston comprised "two companies of artillery and grenadiers, besides 6 companies to each batallion of light infantry—the 2nd Co. was composed of Jews, the 3rd of mulattoes, the fourth of quadroons, and the fifth and sixth of blacks—all officered by white men."[170] Free coloured people were usually promoted to the rank of non-commissioned officer, and the militia was a replica of the social structure of the town.

The instabilities of this segmented community arose from the fierce opposition of the Africans to slavery. Twenty-nine rebellions occurred in Jamaica during a period of 150 years,[171] and many, both in Kingston and the country, were led by the Coromantins. One of the most dangerous took place in 1760.

> In Kingston a wooden sword was found of a peculiar structure, with a red feather stuck in the handle; this was used among the Coromantins as a signal for war; and upon examining this, and other suspicious circumstances to the bottom, it was discovered that the Coromantins of that town had raised one Cubah, a female slave belonging to a Jewess, to the rank of royalty, and dubbed her *queen of Kingston*; at their meetings she sat in state under a canopy, with a sort of robe on her shoulders, and a crown upon her head.[172]

Invariably the different African tribes refused to join together against the whites, and the Creole slaves, who called the Africans "salt-water Negroes" and regarded them with "the utmost contempt,"[173] steadfastly rejected rebellion as a solution to their enslavement and frequently exposed the plots. In 1769, for example "a black girl who was kept by a Jew at Kingston, gave information of a conspiracy among the negroes in that town, to burn it and massacre the inhabitants. The colonel of the militia proceeded with his men, to the place of the *rendezvous*, where he surprised 300 armed negroes and made several of them prisoners, many of whom were afterwards executed."[174] As Gardner later observed, "the city must have been sadly deficient in all supervision when twenty or thirty so-called Negro dukes and generals . . . could meet in the suburbs to discuss their plans, and practise pistol-shooting at trees every Sunday afternoon."[175]

As the free coloured population grew in importance it became increasingly common for white liberals to recommend that they should be promoted to legal equality.[176] Long, the historian, and by no means a liberal, went so far as to recommend the enfranchisement of the free people of colour, in the mistaken belief that "they would then form the centre of connection between the two extremes."[177] But although this scheme required a minimum amount of social change and allowed the retention of slavery, it was rejected for at least fifty years on the grounds that change, however modest, would be catastrophic. Nonetheless, demands for social change, for removal of civil disabilities, and even for emancipation were increasingly heard after 1800. The abolition of the slave trade in the British Empire in 1808 was an augury of what was to follow. For it suggested that if the local whites were unprepared to change the social order, the British Government not only had the right of veto in Jamaica's affairs but the power to intervene and perhaps the will to do so.

III: Social and Economic Change, 1820–1938

By 1820 Kingston was by far the largest and most prosperous city in the British West Indies but its society, economy, and functions were soon to undergo radical change. In the face of strong local opposition the legal framework of the social structure was slowly dismantled. Free Negroes, people of colour, and Jews were all granted full civil rights and suffrage by 1832, the slaves were emancipated in 1834, and their period of apprenticeship brought to an end in 1838. In 1845 Britain started to equalise the duties on its sugar imports, and an era of free trade gradually was entered. Stripped of the imperial supports that for more than half a century had shored-up the inefficient sugar industry, Kingston's overseas trade and entrepot functions sank into a deep decline. Nevertheless, although many patterns and trends that had been established during slavery ended or were reversed, other social and economic structures in Kingston remained firm.

The period between 1838 and 1865, which Hall has called "the dark age of Jamaican history,"[1] concluded with the Morant Bay rebellion. In that year also the Jamaica Assembly abdicated in favour of Crown Colony Government, and the corporation of the city of Kingston was dissolved. A greater emphasis was immediately placed on economic and administrative efficiency, and in pursuit of this policy the capital was transferred from Spanish Town to Kingston in 1872. The growth of population in Kingston soon presented a new set of administrative problems. As early as 1867 the boundary of the parish of Kingston was extended northward to approximately its present location, and the race course and the new suburbs of Smith Village, Hannah Town, and Fletcher's Town transferred from St. Andrew to Kingston parish (fig. 17).[2] The Corporation of Kingston was reinstated in 1885, but by 1921, when the combined population of Kingston and the adjacent parish of St. Andrew reached 117,000, the expansion of the city and its suburbs had outrun the organisational capacity of the local authorities. In 1923, therefore, the functions of the Mayor and Corporation of Kingston, the Kingston General Commissioners, and the St. Andrew Parochial Board were amalgamated and placed under the direction of the newly formed Kingston and St. Andrew Corporation.

During the post-emancipation period, Kingston's growth was due to natural increase and decrease and to the internal movements of the population; but most of the other changes that took place—the granting of civil rights, emancipation, the adoption of free trade, and the removal of the capital—were effected by the British Government. Thus from the Jamaican viewpoint the period from 1820 to 1938 consists of a series of reactions to imposed change. Yet this interpretation is only partly true, for persons of low status were by no means passive. Emancipation in 1834 followed the slave revolt of 1831; the establishment of Crown Colony Government and the transfer of the capital to Kingston came after the Morant Bay rebellion of 1865; and the granting of universal adult suffrage in 1944 was preceeded by the riots of 1938. Discontent was widespread in the slums of Kingston, and many of the inhabitants of the capital played an active part in the political awakening that brought the post-emancipation period to a close.

POPULATION GROWTH

The population of the parish of Kingston expanded from about 35,000 in 1828 to 62,700 in 1921—an increase of 79 percent. Yet Kingston's growth during this period was most uneven. Between 1830 and 1840 the population failed for the first time to increase (fig. 8). This period of near standstill continued until 1850 when the cholera epidemic and, subsequently, the emigration of male workers to Panama, caused a rapid decline. Between 1860 and 1920 the population again increased with fluctuating rapidity. The pattern of growth in St. Andrew reflected that in Kingston, the similarity being especially close after 1881. However, St. Andrew's rate of increase, from 14,500 inhabitants in 1836 to 54,600 in 1921 was much higher.

The intercensal period 1911 to 1921 was characterised by very small increases in Kingston, St. Andrew, and Jamaica as a whole. This, however, proved to be simply a breathing-space before the population explosion which occurred during the third and successive decades of the twentieth century. A massive increase took place in Kingston between 1921 and 1943, and the number of persons living in the corporate area grew from 117,000 to 237,000, a rise of 101.8 percent. The overall growth of the population was accompanied by differential increases in various sections of the city. Kingston recorded an intercensal increase of 72.7 percent, St. Andrew of 134.7 percent, and Liguanea (suburban St. Andrew) of 347.6 percent. The population of St. Andrew overtook that of Kingston in about 1935 and by 1943 exceeded it by 19,000. Moreover, the population of Kingston (109,000) was almost equalled by suburban St. Andrew (92,000) in 1943, by which time the modern city and its suburbs had already taken shape.

MIGRATION

Although the slaves were emancipated in 1834 and became "full free" in 1838, no massive migration to Kingston developed immediately. Where their former owners were able to pay regular wages, the ex-slaves remained as plantation labourers. But gradually an increasing number of the more enterprising Negroes "burrowed into the interior" and occupied the mountains, including those of St. Andrew. There they established themselves as peasants and small farmers growing and marketing ground provisions and other crops. By 1902 holdings of less than five acres numbered 109,000.[3]

The growth of the peasantry both deflected many potential migrants from Kingston and accelerated the decline of the sugar industry. Former slaves who were too poor to purchase land rented plots or squatted in the forests which covered the mountainous backbone of the island. Most of the early settlements were organized by the non-conformist missionaries, especially the Baptists, and formed part of the free village movement. After 1865, however, the government became the main agency sponsoring land settlement.

Since births exceeded deaths in Jamaica by the low margin of only 52 to 40 per 1,000 population during the intercensal period 1844-1861, and deaths from cholera in Kingston numbered 5,000 between 1850 and 1852, the slow growth of the city in the first four decades after emancipation is easily explained. Soon after the transfer of the capital to Kingston, however, there is evidence of considerable migration to the city. The parish's intercensal growth between 1881 and 1891 was 9,900, despite the slight excess of deaths over births.[4] This pattern of high mortality accompanied by heavy in-migration was reminiscent of the situation which obtained throughout the eighteenth century. During the intercensal period 1891-1911 Kingston parish grew by 11,200 only 6,900 of which was accounted for by natural increase.

In contrast, the natural increase recorded by St. Andrew between 1881 and 1891 was 4,200, but the addition to the population only 2,900. While the suburbs on the Liguanea Plain were slowly growing, the rural section of the parish was experiencing out-migration, some of which was probably directed to the adjacent parish of Kingston. During the intercensal period 1891-1911, however, St. Andrew's growth (14,900) greatly exceeded the natural increase (7,900), both figures being larger than those for Kingston. By the beginning of the twentieth century, therefore, almost half the population growth in Kingston and St. Andrew was due to in-migration, though some of the increase in St. Andrew can be attributed to out-migration from Kingston.

After 1865 the immigration of indentured labourers from the Indian sub-continent coincided with the arrival of British officials employed in the Colonial Service. During the last two decades of the nineteenth century, however, immigration was overshadowed by the much larger volume of emigration. Between 1881 and 1921 net emigration from Jamaica was 146,000, 46,000 going to the United States, 45,000 to Panama for work on the canal, at least 20,000 to Cuba, and 43,000 to other areas.[5] This movement accounted for the slower growth of the population at the turn of the century. Between 1911 and 1921 alone, 77,000 emigrated from Jamaica, 10 percent being residents of the capital.[6]

The establishment of a free peasantry coupled to heavy emigration between 1881 and 1921 drew many potential migrants away from Kingston. However, both these magnets disappeared after the First World War, and the growth of the population of the corporate area between 1921 and 1943 was due largely to migration from the rural areas and, to a lesser extent, to returning migrants. With improvements in curative and preventive medicine, the rate of natural increase almost doubled between the intercensal period 1844-1861 (8 per 1,000 population) and 1921-1943 (15.3 per 1,000 population). The birth-rate dropped from 40 to 33 per 1,000, but the death rate, which originally stood at 32 per 1,000, was more than halved.[7] Nevertheless, by 1943 no more than 43.5 percent of the residents of Kingston parish and 49.1 percent of those of St. Andrew were natives.

Between 1921 and 1943 Kingston lost 3,200 persons through net overseas migration, but St. Andrew gained 15,500, most of them returning migrants. Kingston parish was the main goal of rural migrants prior to 1891, but by the beginning of this century the focus had moved to St. Andrew. Between 1921 and 1943 rural-born migrants in Kingston numbered 21,500 and in St. Andrew 36,000.[8] In-migration at this period was therefore a major contributor to urban growth in general and to suburban expansion in particular. It vastly exceeded the measurable movement of population from Kingston to St. Andrew which comprised 11,300 persons between 1921 and 1943.

FACTORS AFFECTING MIGRATION TO KINGSTON

Although the mountains were a major pole of attraction for the emancipated slaves, there is evidence that a small number moved from the rural areas to Kingston prior to 1880. A report on the condition of the juvenile population in 1880 noted that "there is a tendency amongst portions of the rural population to gravitate towards the towns and Kingston especially. The class to which we refer are moved by a desire to obtain their livelihood by other means than agricultural labour, and by the hope of that casual employment at high rates which is often to be obtained in towns."[9]

The content and language of this quotation indicates the attitude of the Jamaican whites to the emancipated Negro. It was widely felt that the Negro should be prepared to work "steadily and continuously, at the times when his labour is wanted, and for so long as it is wanted."[10] According to this view, both the migrants to Kingston and the peasantry had betrayed the planters in abandoning the sugar estates; salvation of the colony's economy therefore required imports of labour from India to cultivate what remained of the plantations. In fact, the attraction of high wages in Kingston, illusory though they often proved, supplied a pull factor in the migration process. Among the push factors can be discerned the poverty of the planters and their constant recourse to coercive measures.

At the beginning of the twentieth century push factors were assuming even greater importance. By 1911 the areas which were available for peasant cultivation were well on the way to being fully occupied, and modernisation in the declining sugar industry had reduced the demand for rural labour.[11] Furthermore, the banana industry, which had become the mainstay of the export economy during the last quarter of the nineteenth century, was essentially labour extensive. Simultaneously, changes in the aspirations of Jamaican women completely altered the pattern of employment. They withdrew from the agricultural work force, their numbers falling from 133,700 in 1891 to 45,600 in 1943, and transferred part of their labour to the domestic service industry where numbers expanded from 21,400 to 51,200.[12] This change from agriculture to domestic work also reflected a change of residence, a move to the towns.

These push factors operated within the general context of a growing population and, after 1920, of limited opportunities for emigration. Furthermore, the Negro increasingly tended to associate agriculture in general, and not solely plantation labour, with the degradation of slavery. Soon after 1921, therefore, increasing numbers of newcomers arrived in the capital. Some migrants, however, were deflected to the coastal parishes of St. Mary and Portland, where the successful banana industry was located, and others were drawn to Westmoreland, Clarendon, St. Catherine, and St. Thomas, where the rise in market prices caused by the First World War had stimulated a modest recovery in the sugar industry. During the economic depression of the 1930s, however, Kingston provided the sole attraction. Writing at this time, Olivier described the city as "the sink of the landless, casual labouring folk of most of the island."[13]

Between 1921 and 1943 more than 2,000 rural-born Jamaicans were arriving in Kingston each year. By 1921 the capital was ten times the size of Spanish Town, whereas it had been only five times as large sixty years earlier. While the number of towns recording a population of more than 1,000 had increased from ten to thirteen during this period, and their proportion of the Jamaican population had risen from 11.2 to 14.8 percent, Kingston's share of the urban dwellers had increased from 55 to 69 percent. In Jamaica the term "urbanisation" was already shorthand for the migration of the rural population to Kingston.

SEX RATIO AND
AGE STRUCTURE

A major change in the sex ratio accompanied the abolition of the slave trade. Women, who had been in the minority in Jamaica before 1800, comprised half the population by 1820 and actually outnumbered men in 1861 (table 2). In 1861 the sex ratio in Kingston was 671 males per 1,000 females, indicating that there had probably been an influx of women both before and after emancipation, though the vast preponderance of females at this particular time was largely due to the migration of males to Panama in 1853-1854.

The excess of women over men became an enduring feature of the population of Jamica and, in particular, of Kingston—St. Andrew. Island-wide fluctuations in the sex ratio between 1881 and 1943 may be attributed to the outward and inward currents of migration. Furthermore, the constant improvement in the sex ratio for Kingston since 1861 (excluding only the intercensal period 1911-1921 when there was heavy migration from the capital), reflected the in-migration of both foreign and local-born males. Meanwhile, the ratio of males to females in St. Andrew widened after 1881. This reflects the increasingly urban nature of the parish and reveals the contribution made by female migrants to the growth of the suburbs.

The demographic features associated with the expansion of the population of Kingston are summarised by the age-sex structure of the city in 1881 (fig. 9). Kingston possessed the profile typical of a city in an underdeveloped territory. Above the relatively narrow base representing the age groups 0-14, an asymmetrical bulge occurred, indicating that population growth depended largely on the in-migration of young adults. Mortality rates were high, however, and resulted in the rapid tapering of the population in groups over age 40. In every age group in Kingston women outnumbered men.

CHANGING RACIAL
COMPOSITION OF THE
POPULATION

The racial composition of the population of Kingston was altered during the post-emancipation period both by the differential growth of the Negro, white, and coloured population and by the introduction of three new nationalities, East Indian,[14] Chinese, and Syrian (figs. 10, 11, 12).

The Negro population of Kingston declined slowly after emancipation in keeping with the trend which developed throughout the island as a whole. The decline was, of course, greatly exaggerated by the cholera epidemic, and by 1881 Negroes comprised only 49.7 percent of the inhabitants as compared with 63 percent in 1788 (table 3). However, heavy cityward migration between 1881 and 1943 lifted their contribution to the population of the capital to more than 60 percent and increased their concentration in the corporate area from 4.3 to 15.6 percent (table 3).

The spectacular growth of the coloured, or brown, population during slavery continued throughout the first forty years of emancipation. They surpassed the white population of Kingston in 1838, and by 1871 threatened to become the largest racial group in the city (fig. 10). Between 1788 and 1881, for example, their contribution to Kingston's population increased from 12.4 to 36.4 percent (table 3). Their rate of growth decreased after 1861, however, and although they were well represented among rural migrants at the turn of the century, they were overshadowed by the Negroes in the movement to Kingston. By 1943 the coloured population comprised 30.7 percent of the inhabitants of the capital. Care is required in interpreting these figures since many Negroes probably tried to pass as coloured in the census, and coloured people, in turn, preferred to be enumerated as white. In 1788 just over 30 percent of the coloured population was concentrated in Kingston, 13 percent in 1881, and 30 percent in 1943. These fluctuations reveal the magnetic attraction of Kingston during slavery, when the free coloured population was denied employment on the plantations, and again after 1881, when the city began to develop the functions associated with a capital.

During the period 1834 to 1943, the white population of the city declined from about 6,000 to 1,800. This overall reduction masks a rise which started soon after 1861 and lasted until 1911, and also conceals the slight increase recorded between 1921 and 1943. Nevertheless, the contribution of the whites to the population of Kingston fell from 24.6 percent in 1788 to 2.8 percent in 1943 (table 3). In marked contrast, the concentration of this group in Kingston increased from 21.8 percent in 1788 to 60.4 percent in 1943. The decline in the white population and its increasing segregation reflected the contraction of the sugar industry and commerce as a whole and the disruption of the white oligarchy. But the increase which occurred during

the last quarter of the nineteenth century marked the establishment of Crown Colony government, the transfer of the capital to Kingston, and the arrival of a white-collar group of expatriate Englishmen.

The decline in the absolute number and relative proportion of whites in Jamaica, coupled with the changes in their economic and political roles, perpetuated a pattern established during slavery, whereby minority status was associated with residence in the capital. Another trend which had been formed during slavery increased in significance after 1860. The white population of St. Andrew rose consistently (fig. 11) and continued to do so even after 1911, when the white population of Jamaica and Kingston parish in particular (fig. 10) began to decline. This shift in the distribution of the white population within the corporate area is most important, for it indicates the large number of persons of this racial group who were moving from the parish of Kingston to the suburbs and, to a lesser extent, from England directly to St. Andrew. A similar trend occurred among the coloured population. These cross-town movements led to a decline in the contribution of Negroes to the population of St. Andrew between 1911 and 1943.

Although East Indians were first brought to Jamaica in 1845, it was not until 1860 that a migratory flow of indentured labourers developed. Like the slaves before them they were destined mainly for the sugar estates. At the end of their indenture, they could re-enlist as labourers, return to India, or settle as free men in Jamaica. By 1850 a small group had apparently moved to Kingston[15] but the 1881 census which enumerated 200 East Indians is the first to record them. The number in the city rose to 900 in 1891, but declined to 750 in 1911 (fig. 10), by which date their contribution to the population of the island as a whole exceeded that of the whites (fig. 12). Soon after 1911 the East Indian population of Kingston started to grow rapidly. In spite of the end of indentured immigration in 1917, between 1921 and 1943 the number of East Indians in Kingston rose from 1,700 to 4,000 (fig. 10) and an even more rapid rate of increase was recorded in St. Andrew. By 1933 they surpassed the white population of Kingston parish. This figure, however, includes the East Indian coloured population and a small group of Bombay businessmen who arrived immediately after the First World War. Although their contribution to the city's population increased from 0.5 percent in 1881 to 2.60 percent in 1943 (table 3), the East Indians remained the least important of the minority groups in Kingston. Their numerical strength continued to lie in the sugar and banana areas, and only 20 percent were located in the capital in 1943. Even in the corporate area they were originally associated with agricultural work, and their decline in St. Andrew between 1881 and 1891 faithfully reflects the abandonment of the sugar estates on the Liguanea Plain.

The Chinese, also, were originally introduced into Jamaica as indentured labour. The first attempt in 1854 "was a failure, for mortality was high and the Chinese proved sickly and unwilling workers,"[16] while the second attempt, in 1884, revealed that they were "intractable and preferred exorbitant demands for wages which could not be complied with."[17] They numbered only 99 in 1881, but 84 of them were residents of Kingston, where they comprised 0.2 percent of the population (table 3). The Chinese population increased steadily until 1911 (fig. 10), when free immigration developed. Between 1921 and 1945 the Chinese contribution to the population of Kingston increased from 1.3 to 2.6 percent, and by the latter date 50 percent of the Jamaican total were living in the corporate area. The population, including Chinese coloureds, slightly exceeded the number of white inhabitants in Kingston parish in 1943, though in St. Andrew they were still fewer in number than the white population (fig. 11).

Of the three new immigrant groups only the Syrians were completely untainted by indentured labour. The first Syrians in Kingston came for the Jamaica Exhibition of 1891. Some of them settled in the island and were joined by other immigrants. In 1943, the first census in which they were enumerated as a separate group, the Syrian and Syrian coloured population of Kingston numbered almost 600. They comprised only 0.3 percent of the inhabitants of Kingston, though 61.7 percent of their total population were found there.

URBAN GROWTH AND THE TOWN PLAN

Kingston's growth of population was accompanied by the expansion of the built-up area. A policy of laissez-faire was maintained, and it was not until 1907 that the government once more intervened to promote urban development and then only because of circumstances which could not be ignored. In that year an earthquake destroyed buildings throughout the southern and eastern sections of the city, and a fire gutted the entire commercial area to the south of the Parade. A grant of £150,000 and a loan of £800,000 were secured from the British Government, and shared among the property owners, who were responsible for their own redevelopment. Residences as far north as Half Way Tree in St. Andrew (fig. 13) had to be reconstructed, but the most comprehensive rebuilding was undertaken in the commercial area.

During the post-emancipation period private and speculative builders added two suburban zones to the L-shaped settlement which had been developed during the eighteenth century. Areas that were built before 1890 were laid out in geometrical designs reminiscent of Goffe's original town plan. By 1848 new houses had been constructed in the west, north, and east (fig. 14), and major settlements developed at Rae Town, Brown's Town, Lindo's Town, Hannah Town, and Smith Village.[18] To these were added, between 1848 and 1889, the suburbs of Fletcher's Town, Kingston Gardens, Allman Town, Franklin Town, and Passmore Town (figs. 13, 17). By 1920 several of these districts were composed of densely populated tenements, and the continuously built-up area had spread across the parish boundary into St. Andrew, reaching Up Park Camp, Jones Town, and the Mental Hospital in the north, west and east respectively (figs. 13, 14). As yet, however, little development had occurred along the Spanish Town Road in West Kingston.

The second zone of more sparsely populated

suburbs developed after 1890. It expanded rapidly between the First and Second World Wars, as the population of the capital doubled and the inhabitants of some of the older parts of Kingston moved into St. Andrew. By the 1940s the built-up area extended eastward to Long Mountain, north-east to Matilda's Corner, north to Cross Roads, Half Way Tree, and the Sandy Gully which it crossed in the area adjacent to the Constant Spring Road and westward to beyond the Hagley Park Road. Unfortunately, the growth map (fig. 14) cannot reveal all the complexity of this expansion. It does not indicate areas in which rebuilding had taken place nor those in which older settlements had acted as fixation points for the growth of the suburbs.

From the late eighteenth century until approximately 1890, the Liguanea Plain existed as a quasi-suburb of Kingston. Its agricultural character declined with the eclipse of the sugar industry, and by 1890 only the Mona Estate remained in production. The cattle pens and former estates increasingly became the residences of business men; Cherry Garden, for example, was the home of George William Gordon, famous for his association with the Morant Bay rebellion. As late as 1872 the plain was divided into a large number of estates (fig. 15). Considerable building had already taken place at Cross Roads, and ribbon developments on the Slipe Road linked it to Kingston. Moreover, Half Way Tree, Mary Brown's Corner, Constant Spring, and Matilda's Corner existed as subsidiary commercial centres of varying importance. Half Way Tree, of course, was still the main settlement of the parish of St. Andrew.

Two important features are disclosed by the map of 1872. Following the transfer of the capital to Kingston, the residence of the Governor of Jamaica, King's House, was located in the central part of the Liguanea Plain to the north-east of Half Way Tree. King's House provided a further stimulus to the growth of the suburbs and confirmed the high social satus of the surrounding district. Simultaneously a movement of a completely different order was taking place, a reminder perhaps of the widespread changes that were occuring in rural Jamai-

ca. Small settlers were making in-roads into the pens, notably near King's House, in east Kingston and on the Spanish Town Road (fig. 15).

In 1897, at the end of the first decade of true suburban growth, settlement on the Liguanea Plain took the form of a series of ribbon developments (fig. 16). The main arteries radiating from Half Way Tree and Cross Roads, and especially the Half Way Tree Road, Hope Road, Old Hope Road, and Constant Spring Road, were flanked by large houses, each standing in its own grounds. Although there is evidence that small settlements had been established by the 1870s on Spanish Town and Windward Roads and in the north of the Liguanea Plain, open spaces abounded between the loose network of roads and houses. The entire south-western quadrant of the plain in particular, including the properties of Trench Pen, Maxfield, and Tower Hill Pen, and running from them down to the shore, was undeveloped (fig. 16). The occupation of this marshy and once unhealthy area and the infilling of the interstices between the ribbon developments in the suburbs north of Cross Roads took place after 1920. Yards, or compounds, were constructed along the Spanish Town Road, and the ground lots were often rented, huts and houses being constructed by the tenants. Sometimes the huts, too, were rented as if they were rooms.

DISTRIBUTION AND DENSITY OF POPULATION

In 1891 the urban area contained a population of 56,400, 65.5 percent of whom were living in central Kingston, 17.0 percent in the inner suburbs,[19] and 17.5 percent on the Liguanea Plain beyond the continuously built-up area. By 1921, however, when the city's population was 89,400, central Kingston's share had declined to 46.1 percent, and the proportion contributed by the inner suburbs and the Liguanea Plain had risen to 24.1 and 29.8 percent respectively. While the population of the urban area as a whole increased by 58.4 percent during this period, central Kingston grew by 11.6 percent, the inner suburbs by 126.0 percent, and the Liguanea Plain by 170.8 percent. Between 1891 and 1921, 11,900 additional people inhabited the inner suburbs, accounting for one-third of the total increase experienced by the urban area as a whole. Although this figure was less than that achieved in the outer zone in St. Andrew, the small size of the area covered by the older, compact suburbs gave them a density of population close to that recorded in central Kingston.

Growth patterns within the main suburbs varied both with time and place. In 1881, Fletcher's Town on the southern boundary of the race course, Brown's Town, and Rae Town near the penitentiary were the largest of the inner suburbs, all with populations above 600. At this date, unfortunately, Allman Town was the largest suburb, with a popu- were combined in the census tabulations. By 1891 Allman Town was the largest suburb with a population of almost 2,000. All the other suburbs with the exception of Brown's Town grew rapidly during this intercensal period.

At the end of the nineteenth century the areas which had housed the smallest number of persons in 1881 were growing most rapidly. Notable among these were the western settlements of Smith Village and Hannah Town (fig. 17). One of the slowest increases was recorded in Kingston Gardens, which, unlike the remainder, was an area of high social status. By 1921 the tenements in Allman Town, Hannah Town, Fletcher's Town, and Smith Village had a population of more than 2,500, and so did the new development along the Windward Road in East Kingston.

Between 1891 and 1921, slightly more than half the increase in the city's inhabitants was contributed by the settlements on the Liguanea Plain. The development of this loose network of settlements was made possible by the tramway system which was opened in 1876. In the 1880s track extensions were made to May Pen Cemetery on the Spanish Town Road and to Constant Spring in the north (fig. 16). By 1884 over one million passengers were carried each year.[20] Later the system was extended along the Old Hope Road to Papine and eastwards along the Windward Road to the head of Kingston

Harbour. However, although the inhabitants moved farther and farther out towards the foothills, the overall pattern of the distribution and density of population was modified but not destroyed. In 1921, as in 1891, the city core was still, in general, densely populated, and the inner suburbs were only slightly less so. The Liguanea Plain, however, was characterized by lower densities of roads, buildings, and people. Two trends were taking place. Population was spreading thinly but continuously across the Liguanea Plain, and the tenements in the inner suburbs were slowly approaching central Kingston in density.

CHANGING TRADE PATTERNS

EXTERNAL TRADE

In contrast with the eighteenth century the first five decades after emancipation were characterized by economic decline. It was within this context that changes in land use were first effected. The following description of Kingston given by Bigelow on the eve of the cholera epidemic is therefore at variance with Scott's account[21] written at the beginning of the nineteenth century.

The city is well enough situated, but a most undesirable residence. The streets are narrow. ... The houses are partially dilapidated and, of course, old. Though I have been through nearly every street, I have not seen a single house newly erected, save an insane asylum, which, by the way, has been suspended for want of funds. A terrible fire laid a large portion of the city in ruins (in 1843) and only a portion of the houses have been rebuilt. These are commonly only one storey high and very mean. In the busiest parts of the city, and on every block, may be seen vacant lots, on which are crumbling the foundation walls of houses long in ruins. Rents are exceedingly low—less than half a fair interest on the cost of buildings alone—while the vacant lots cannot be said to have any market value, there being no sales. There are several fine houses yet extant here, but they were all built years ago, when the island was prosperous, and few of them are in repair.

Though Kingston is the principal port of the island, it has but little of the commercial city. One looks and listens in vain for the noise of carts and the bustle of city men; no one seems to be in a hurry; but few are doing anything, while the mass of the population are lounging about in idleness and rags. Here are no merchants or mechanical operatives, such as abound in the larger cities of the north. Nearly all who do not traffick, wait upon those who do, or lead a life of comparative indolence. The professional men are about the only exceptions.[22]

The white citizens of Kingston attributed their impoverishment to two events: the emancipation of the slaves and the equalization of the sugar duties. But Jamaica's production of sugar had fallen continuously after 1805, while the indebtedness that was already noticeable at the end of the eighteenth century was rampant after 1800.[23] Ragatz has attributed the decline in the sugar industry to monoculture, slavery, and absentee ownership,[24] all of which contributed to economic inefficiency. The prosperity of the industry during the late eighteenth century may be explained by protective tariffs and by the Haitian revolution which destroyed, economically, a rival whose production equalled that of the entire British West Indies. The gradual equalization of the sugar duties after 1846 revealed the true state of Jamaica's economy. It is in the light of these factors that the decline in sugar production from 1,363,000 hundredweights in 1828 to 592,000 hundredweights in 1850 should be interpreted,[25] and it is to this decline that Kingston's depressed condition may largely be related.

Although sugar was the mainstay of the Jamaican economy during slavery, Kingston's viability at the beginning of the nineteenth century was principally due to the free-port trade. This, also, was in decline long before emancipation. In 1815, at the end of the Napoleonic Wars, improvements in international relations in the Caribbean and, above all, the break-up of the Spanish-American Empire enabled businessmen from Jamaica to establish trading posts on the Pacific Coast of the Isthmus of Panama.[26] Kingston's strategic position

became dispensable, for clandestine trading was no longer necessary, and in 1822 the Free Port Acts were repealed. Yet as late as the 1830s the entrepot trade in Kingston earned the annual sum of £450,-000 and accounted for one-sixth of Jamaica's exports.[27] This proportion slipped to 14.6 percent in 1850, by which time steam ships were replacing sail, and cargo was being sent directly from Europe to the mainland of Central America; it dropped further to 7.8 percent in 1870; and to 1.3 percent in 1890.[28] After 1870 the entrepot trade with Latin America was completely dead, and re-exports were directed to the Lesser Antilles.

During this period when contact with Africa and Latin America was lost new links were established with the United States. The British share of Jamaican exports fell dramatically from 78 percent in 1870 to 19 percent in 1910, the United States and Canada receiving the remainder.[29] The sources of imports were almost identical. By the beginning of the twentieth century half the value of domestic exports was contributed by the banana trade centered in Port Antonio.[30] Nevertheless, Kingston remained the import centre for virtually all consumer goods. These imports increased in value by almost 400 percent between 1830 and 1930, the rise being even more rapid between 1850 and 1930.[31]

INTERNAL TRADE

Despite the decline in the commerical activities of the port, freedom of movement, freedom of production, and the adoption of a cash economy stimulated the internal trade of Kingston. A small shopping centre developed between the Parade and the warehouses that fringed the harbour. Harbour Street formed the main commercial axis, and although several stores were located on King Street in 1850 (pl. 9), it was not until after the earthquake and fire of 1907 that it became the main area for retailing. By the beginning of the twentieth century the retail trade had been largely divorced from wholesaling, and three main branches were in evidence; namely, provision markets, groceries, and dry goods stores. Each category was marked by lack of specialization and by association with a distinct racial enclave.

The Negro peasants were predominantly subsistence agriculturalists, but a certain proportion of their produce was sold in the markets. In Kingston, the Victoria and Sollas markets were the most important; the former was located at the foot of King Street on the site of the old Sunday Market, and the latter on West Queen Street, where Jubilee Market now stands. Lack of specialization by commodity also characterized the dry goods and grocery trades. The dry goods trade was in the hands of the Syrian immigrants, most of whom launched themselves in business by peddling, as the coloured people and Jews had done during slavery. The monopoly of the dry goods business by the Syrians was soon challenged by Bombay merchants who settled in Kingston after 1920. They obtained several shops on King Street and sold both oriental and Western articles. The grocery trade was introduced by the Chinese at the beginning of the twentieth century. Groceries were rapidly built throughout the corporate area, though both retailing and wholesaling were especially well-developed in central Kingston. By 1920 a China Town was being created between King Street and West Street on the edge of the central business district, and the Syrians were forming a similar centre slightly to the north in the area adjacent to South Parade.

INDUSTRY

Although mercantilism was gradually replaced by free trade after 1845 and the Acts of Navigation were finally repealed in the 1850s, these policies had conditioned the economy of Kingston during its formative period and continued to influence its development after emancipation. There were few factories even at the beginning of the twentieth century, and manufacturing was largely confined to the skilled trades practised in the lanes of central Kingston.

Lack of mineral and power resources remained obstacles to industrialisation. The harnessing of water power was uneconomic, and up to 1930 only one company had developed hydroelectricity, which was used to operate the tramway and to supply electric light to Kingston and lower St. Andrew. Local merchants and landed proprietors had no training and little more than an ephemeral interest in manufacturing and frequently no risk capital. Moreover, the British investors had turned to the independent states of Latin America, neglecting the minute, derelict islands of the Caribbean. In addition, the legislature in Jamaica did nothing to encourage import substitution, and by 1865 had imposed an identical duty (12 1/2 percent) on both raw materials and manufactured articles.[32]

Many of the manufacturing enterprises which had been established in Kingston during the later years of slavery disappeared after emancipation. According to Sir Charles Grey the articles manufactured during the late 1840s consisted of sugar and rum, "and I believe a little tanning and dressing of leather."[33] In 1855, George Willis, the stipendiary magistrate in Kingston, reported that "the only pursuits of industry coming within my observation are the mere handicrafts, as Carpenters, Masons, Shoemakers, Tailors, Tinmen, Cigar Makers and such like; most of which, as carried on, hardly deserves the name of industrial pursuits."[34] Factory enterprise was confined to foundry yards, two manufacturers of perfumes and cosmetics, and a firm of engravers.[35] Despite the decline in the population, Willis also noted that the labour supply exceeded demand.[36] By the early 1860s it was claimed that large numbers of persons in Kingston "eke out a miserable existence as tailors, shoemakers, straw hat platters, cigar makers etc; and who in the country would do much better for themselves, did they not look down upon agricultural labour with contempt."[37]

This information supports Bigelow's description of Kingston and partly accounts for the decline in the city's population during the first two decades after emancipation. It is clear also that migration to Kingston was inspired by the rejection of agricultural labour and that the number of migrants, small though it was, outstripped the capacity of the city for employing them. It is hardly suprising therefore that between 2,000 and 3,000 adult males left the city in 1853 and 1854 to work on the railway which was being built across the Isthmus of Panama.[38]

The economic climate remained basically unconducive to industrialisation throughout the remainder of the nineteenth century. According to Livingstone, writing in 1899,

> without manual education it was useless to expect a body of competent mechanics and tradesmen to grow up in the colony. To this subject the Government has not yet given any large consideration. Neither has it attempted to foster the scanty trades that have been struggling to exist, and local manufactures are more and more being made impossible by the importation of cheap goods from abroad. These range from babies' shoes to ready-made houses which are run-up with a few blows of the hammer; and they ... filch all opportunity from the negroes disposed to cultivate whatever skill they possess.[39]

Towards the end of the nineteenth century, however, several new manufacturing enterprises were established using agricultural raw materials and sometimes depending on import substitution— a situation reminiscent of the last decade of slavery. A furniture factory was started in 1870, and in 1885 ice, bay rum, carbonated beverages, bread, and pharmaceutical goods were being manufactured.[40] By the 1890s factories were producing beer, tobacco, and matches.[41] The most important tobacco firm belonged to the Machado brothers who had migrated from Cuba in the 1860s to found one of Jamaica's most famous export industries. According to Goad's Insurance Plan of Kingston, in 1894 the most important manufacturing concerns were cigar factories, bakeries, furniture factories, printeries, foundries, and mineral-water factories. These were scattered throughout the business area, though except for the Machado's cigar factory, Harbour Street contained few. Furthermore, the tendency was for the larger concerns to locate on main streets in preference to back lanes; King

Street, for example, possessed one establishment manufacturing cigars.

Between 1890 and 1910, a large number of new enterprises were opened, but almost all produced the limited range of items described above. In 1910, sixty-two factories were operating in Jamaica, and most were probably located in Kingston. Of these, tobacco works and tanneries accounted for seventeen each, factories producing mineral waters for eight, and beer and ale for seven, while the remainder consisted of match, dyewood, banana, and cassava starch concerns. Eisner's comments on the changes which later affected these factories are pertinent.

> It appears, however, that many of these factories were uneconomically small. We can see this from their rate of survival. Between 1910 and 1929, the number of tanneries was reduced from seventeen to four and that of tobacco factories even more sharply from seventeen to one. Since this reduction was not accompanied by a loss of total output ... we conclude that it must have been due to the amalgamation of factories. Scale of operation seems to have been less important in the case of factories producing beer and ale and mineral waters because in their case the number was reduced by only four from fifteen in 1910 to eleven in 1929.[42]

While amalgamation took place between many of the existing firms, several new establishments were opened after 1910. In 1911 the first biscuit-making plant came into production, and at about the same time an industry manufacturing sugar machinery and spare parts was founded.[43] The industrial sector of the economy underwent a relatively rapid expansion during the period succeeding the First World War and by 1940 the following additional articles were being produced: confectionery, optical products, neon signs, tiles, blocks, leather, footwear, washing soda, ice-cream and frozen products, matches, alimentary pastes and powders, condensed milk, cigars and cigarettes.[44] Almost all the enterprises were engaged in processing rather than in manufacturing. Furthermore, the majority depended on local supplies of raw materials—usually of an agricultural nature—and almost all sold on the home market.

For industrial development 1923 was a key year; the Jamaica Public Service Company, the subsidiary of a Canadian firm was incorporated and took over the generation and distribution of electricity from the West Indies Electric Company, which had started operations in Jamaica in 1918. After 1924, when the new firm generated 4,700 kilowatt hours of electricity and supplied almost 4,000 customers,[45] power was made increasingly available for industry. It removed from factories the burden of generating their own requirements and led to a reduction in the capital outlay which was required when new enterprises were started.

While the development of the infrastructure was left to private capital, the government became tentatively, but increasingly, involved in industry. During the 1930s protective legislation was introduced to bolster selected concerns, but no encouragement was given to the establishment of new industries. Although it had no immediate bearing on manufacturing in Kingston, the Coconut Industry Aid Law of 1931, which prohibited the imports of edible oil, was ultimately of prime importance. It represented the first departure, so far as industry was concerned, from the laissez-faire policy which had dominated the post-emancipation period. Soon afterwards, government commitment to industrial stabilisation increased, for the Jamaica Match Industry, Ltd., a company incorporated in 1932, was granted a virtual monopoly of the domestic market.[46] The safeguarding of Local Industries and Trades Law which was passed in 1935 prohibited the manufacture of matches without a licence from the government.

Jamaican products were held in low repute, and almost all the consumer goods purchased by the upper and middle strata were imported from Britain or North America. Consequently, those who accumulated capital continued to invest in property, agriculture, and trade rather than manufacturing. "If Jamaica had had capitalists interested in developing local industries they would have influenced the Government to build schools, to impose higher tariffs, to improve the public utilities, or whatever else they felt to be the deficiency. These things did not happen because Jamaicans did not think in terms of developing industrial employment."[47]

During the 1930s Kingston's economic problems were compounded by the effects of the depression. National and per capita income declined for a decade. When the former rose again in 1938, per capita income stood at £17.8, or £1.3 less than in 1930.[48] Poverty is hardly an incentive to industrialisation, but demand was not uniformly low. In 1930, for example, "about 12 percent of the national income was spent on imported consumer manufactures, of which over 40 percent was textiles."[49] The failure of entrepreneurship in the face of rising population was critical. "Where neither local supplies nor heavy freight charges on imports provided inducements to local enterprise no development took place. The presence of an abundant supply of labour, by itself, was insufficient. Most of the industries established drew on only a negligible number of workers. Even the industry with the largest labour force—the tobacco factory—employed only 400 workers in 1931."[50] Excluding the second and third largest factories, neither of which were in Kingston, the remainder employed on the average only 21 workers apiece. By the end of the post-emancipation period, therefore, Kingston was a crowded capital with an essentially non-industrial economy.

PUBLIC BUILDINGS

Two major factors affected the growth and distribution of government buildings: the transfer of the capital to Kingston in 1872 and the earthquake and fire of 1907. During the second half of the nineteenth century King's House was located in St. Andrew, to the north of Half-Way Tree, marking not only the tentative beginning of true suburban development on the Liguanea Plain, but the penetration of St. Andrew by users of land associated directly with the central government. The public buildings, which Long had hoped for, were never constructed on the Parade. Headquarters House, the seat of the legislature, was situated on Duke Street, in the north-eastern sector of the original town plan, and occupied the mansion which had formerly belonged to the Hibbert family. The Parade actually declined in importance as the focus of the city. Its military facilities were replaced by more discrete, and perhaps more effective, installations at Up Park Camp. The barracks were closed, and even the new court house (fig. 17) was rivalled by the older building located on the corner of Duke and Harbour Streets. At the beginning of the twentieth century the Parade was converted into the Victoria Park.

The earthquake of 1907 provided an opportunity for rationalizing the pattern of public buildings along the lines suggested by Long. Land was acquired not on the Parade, however, but on both sides of King Street, between its intersections with Barry and Tower Streets. Comprising one block on either side of the main street, these buildings maintained the pattern of land division effected after 1692 and accommodated a variety of public offices which had previously been scattered throughout the downtown area. Changes in the provision of public buildings in Kingston were also affected by technological developments. The Public Works Department was situated on the Parade, and the Railway Depot was sited in West Kingston, from which point the city was linked to Spanish Town and ultimately to both Port Antonio and Montego Bay. However, the railway had relatively little impact on the functions of Kingston.

The increase in the number of churches between the latter half of the period of slavery and 1894 reflected the importance of Jamaica as a mission field during the post-emancipation period. Churches were highly concentrated in the eastern part of the old city. The Jewish synagogue was relocated in the eastern section of the original town plan, and not in the west, as it had been during slavery. Indeed, figure 17 shows only two religious buildings located in the low class, unhealthy area to the west of King Street. One of these, the Ebenezer Church, on the south side of the Spanish Town Road, belonged to the Methodists and was later to play an important role in the social development of West Kingston.

The schools and the only hotel were located in the eastern half of the city; so, also, were the penitentiary and the lunatic asylum. Few hospitals were situated in West Kingston, but one of these specialised in smallpox. It is clear that, in general, East Kingston enjoyed a higher social status than West Kingston both during slavery and the post-emancipation period.

The pattern of buildings associated with entertainment changed relatively little after emancipation. The theatre remained adjacent to North Parade, while the race course and Parade itself provided open spaces for the enjoyment of the citizens. Although, generally, there was a tendency towards specialization in all forms of land use, the major elements inherited from slavery were preserved or only slightly modified.

RESIDENTIAL LAND USE

In 1894 the areas to the north, west, and east of the Parade were all residential, and poor dwellings were within the central part of the city which was generally commercial. Goad's Insurance Plan divided buildings into poor, mixed, and better class (fig. 17). The last two categories were confined to the northeastern section of the original town plan, as they had been during slavery, and to some of the new suburbs. Few of the buildings located to the west of King Street were described as better class, though a mixture of poor and better-class buildings characterized southeastern Kingston and those parts of West Kingston which lay adjacent to King Street. On the periphery of the city in general and near the city rubbish heap in West Kingston, the majority of buildings were described as poor.

By the middle of the nineteenth century a large proportion of the dwellings of the poorest inhabitants, especially on Bond Street, Oxford Street,

Regent Street, Tulip Lane, and the Spanish Town Road in West Kingston, were described as

> filthy and miserable; and yet most of them are, as I was informed, occupied by petty freeholders exercising the right of elective franchise. In the outskirts of the city in different directions, there are groups of such hovels, with a few of a somewhat better description interspersed among them. Of this description are Hannah's Town, Altman's Town [Allman Town], Smith's Town [Smith Village], Rae's Town, etc.[51]

In 1894 most of the buildings were described as detached. Only in the area immediately west of the Parade were many of the lots covered by premises which were less than eight feet apart. Scattered dwellings occurred under two quite different conditions. In Kingston Gardens and the surrounding area the term referred to properties standing in their own grounds. When applied to the poor areas near the Smallpox Hospital, however, the connotation was quite different; these were undoubtedly shanties. Milroy has indicated that the houses of the majority of the urban population had reached a deplorable state by mid-century.

> Often no proper foundation is made, the joists are laid down upon the bare, undrained soil, and the boarding placed upon them. They consist of but one floor, a little raised above the ground, and are ill-suited for a climate where a free perflation of air is so much required. ... The kitchen, which is always detached in the court yard, is the only building ever provided with a chimney.[52]

It is clear that subtler shades of social differentiation were incorporated in the geographical patterns than the dichotomy between East and West Kingston alone would suggest. An elite residential area was retained in north-east Kingston until at least the end of the nineteenth century, while the periphery remained the home of the most depressed social groups. Both patterns of residence dated back to slavery.

PUBLIC HEALTH, SOCIAL DISEASE, AND HOUSING

During slavery masters had been responsible for their Negroes' health. After emancipation, however, the ex-slaves had to provide for their own well-being—and usually under the most difficult circumstances. Even in Kingston there were few public hospitals, doctors were rare, and medical fees frequently exorbitant. Consequently, "when advice was sought, it was the obeahman, or the bush doctor, or some old woman of repute, that was consulted."[53] By the middle of the nineteenth century conditions were as bad as, if not worse than, during slavery, and tuberculosis, stomach disorders, yaws, and leprosy were all on the increase.

> Quarantine was a farce. In the towns the state of sanitation did nothing to hinder the outbreak of diseases. Refuse was left to decay in the streets and no regulations existed to enforce the safe disposal of sewage, or for the supervision of markets, water supplies and cemeteries. Graveyards were numerous in Kingston and located near residential areas. The handling of food for human consumption also left much to be desired. The office of Clerk to the Markets existed but, instead of being used to supervise the sale of food, was regarded as a mere sinecure. Open swamps were also a constant source of malaria and while a number of private water companies had existed for some time providing an indifferent service, the bulk of the population depended on wells and ponds of questionable purity.[54]

Yellow fever was endemic, and smallpox a frequent occurrence.

Both preventive and curative medicine were therefore in a state of neglect when cholera broke out in 1850. Milroy's comments on the outbreak are germane both to the social geography of Kingston at this time and to the relationship between social conditions, social structure, and disease. The cholera was traced to a fisherman in Kingston called Phipps, "living within one of the ordinary close and filthy yards at the upper end of Oxford Street at the north-west end of the town."[55] The first two cases were both on Oxford Street, and the third on Salt Lane near the Spanish Town Road. According to Milroy, "several other cases speedily occurred in this locality." Initially, therefore, "its chief stress fell upon the west-end districts, which were at all times and in all seasons ... the most unwholesome part of Kingston."[56]

The cholera soon developed into an epidemic. "In Kingston no part or district escaped the ravages of the pestilence wherever the people were living in filth and huddled together. It was particularly severe in Harbour Street and other low-lying parts of the town. From a single house at the east end of this street, nineteen corpses were carried out in the course of six-and-thirty hours. The inmates were chiefly women of bad character, and amounted to forty when the disease broke out. All the clusters of Negro dwellings in the suburbs of the town were devastated."[57] Milroy's final statement is, however, most revealing. "While death was thus raging in every direction among the great mass of the people, the well-conditioned classes all but escaped; not above two or three in a thousand perished."[58]

Although Milroy's analysis of the situation apparently led to improvements in Rae Town, elsewhere the appalling conditions persisted into the twentieth century. Nevertheless, the establishment of Crown Colony Government in 1865 at least ensured an improvement in health and hygiene and created a social environment that was more conducive to the natural increase of the population. A public medical service was formed in 1869, and to it were latter added almoner facilities, the public hospitals, and the lunatic asylum. In the port, quarantine regulations were enforced, and in 1874 May Pen Estate in West Kingston was turned into a cemetery, and burial grounds in the city were gradually closed.

During the 1870s the government also took over and began building on its own initiative a number of public utilities. In 1871 the Kingston and Liguanea water works were bought. Completely new works had to be built to ensure an adequate supply of water for the town at sufficient pressure to extinguish fires—a calamity with which Kingston was frequently afflicted. Unlike the old supply, the new works provided filtered water. In 1899 Kingston suburbs were supplied.[59]

The city slaughterhouse was opened in 1876, and after 1899 the sale of fresh meat, poultry, and game was confined to the official markets. The spate of tardy but essential legislation was concluded by the appointment of the Kingston Commissioners with responsibility for the collection and discharge of sewage. "Five years later the town had been equipped with street sewers and work had begun on linking them with private premises."[60] By 1905, 1,896 houses had been connected, though they probably comprised no more than one-sixth of the dwellings in Kingston parish.

Many of these improvements still failed to touch the mass of the citizens of Kingston. As late as 1899 it was observed that "the official medical system continues to work well within the field it covers, but that is limited, while resort is still had to the bush doctors."[61] Moreover, there was "no inspection of domestic sanitation, or effort to prevent overcrowding."[62] The housing situation improved at the beginning of the twentieth century; the average number of persons per dwelling in Kingston parish fell from 7.2 in 1881 to 4.0 in 1921. Unfortunately, the impact of this change was vitiated by the proliferation of one-room dwellings as the tenement areas were rapidly built-up. Single rooms accounted for 52.6 percent of the accommodation in 1911, and for 60.9 percent in 1921.

DISTRIBUTION OF RACES

Although the pattern of racial distribution in Kingston during the post-emancipation period was changed by the introduction, growth, or contraction of the various groups, the overall system of social areas like the pattern of non-residential land use was not radically altered. West Kingston and the outskirts were still associated with low status, east and central Kingston with median status, and northeast Kingston with high status, while the new suburbs of central St. Andrew represented a northward extension and infilling of the elite areas that had been formed during the eighteenth century. The distribution of each race in relation to these social areas was fairly indicative of its standing in the community.

The white inhabitants continued to withdraw from the densely populated and increasingly commercial areas of central Kingston. By 1860 hardly any Europeans, or even white Creoles, lived in the town.[63] The white population of Kingston parish expanded after the capital was transferred from Spanish Town. Kingston Gardens was built during the last quarter of the nineteenth century to house members of the elite. Although this suburb was situated in Kingston parish, it was sandwiched between the boundary with St. Andrew and the elite district that had been developed during slavery. While giving ready access to the downtown area, it conformed to the dominant trend in suburban growth. In 1900 three times as many whites were living in Kingston as in St. Andrew, but parity was reached soon after the First World War. During the 1920s the exodus, which originally affected only the growing commercial centre, extended to the whole of Kingston parish. By 1930, almost three times as many whites were living in St. Andrew as in Kingston, and out-migration had affected even Kingston Gardens. Furthermore, the whites were both the creators of the modern suburbs and the initiators of the inner ring of "towns" which developed during the nineteenth century. To them, therefore, may be attributed most aspects of the city's morphology.

During the first fifty years after emancipation the major concentration of Jews remained in Kingston parish. In 1881, for example, they numbered 1,087 in Kingston and 77 in St. Andrew. Within the older part of the town, however, a radical change in their distribution took place. After 1840 the addresses recorded for prominent Jews were situated on lower King Street, East Queen Street, lower Hanover Street, upper Duke Street, upper Hanover Street, and East Street.[64] The move from West to East Kingston after emancipation reflected the improvement in their social status. By 1910

all the synagogues were located in East Kingston, and the Jewish evacuation of the western part of the eighteenth-century grid was almost complete. The Jews penetrated the older, white elite area and, after 1900, the growing settlement in central St. Andrew. In 1921 three-quarters of the Jewish population of Jamaica was concentrated in the city—613 in Kingston parish and 260 in St. Andrew. On both the macro- and micro-scale, therefore, they tended to emulate the white population with whom they became increasingly associated.

Changes in the distribution of both the coloured and Negro population are difficult to reconstruct. It is known that in 1850 Negroes were clustered on the fringe of the city, as they had been during slavery; and it is clear that the growth of the tenements in the inner suburbs at the end of the nineteenth century was due principally to the in-migration of rural-born Negroes. Furthermore, they made a major contribution to the growth of the yards in the western section of the city after 1920, and by 1935 the Negro population of St. Andrew exceeded that of Kingston. With a total population of about 120,000 in the corporate area at this date, Negroes were still the most ubiquitous of all groups. Their association with areas of low status and high population density was partially offset spatially, if not socially, by their employment as servants in the most exclusive areas.

There is no descriptive information relating to the distribution of the coloured population, but certain trends may be inferred from census data (figs. 10, 11). The coloured population of Kingston parish continued to grow steadily throughout the post-emancipation period, but the gains in St. Andrew occurred between 1891 and 1911 and between 1921 and 1943. These time periods coincided with the extension of the inner and the outer suburbs. It is probable that the coloured population was associated with two residential patterns, one which approximated the distribution of the whites, and another which was more akin to the location of the Negroes.

The Chinese are the best documented among the groups that appeared in Kingston for the first time during the post-emancipation period.[65] By the end of the nineteenth century they had established groceries on Pechon, Orange, Beckford, and Barry streets where Chinese immigrants were replacing the original Jewish inhabitants. In 1930 there were four hundred Chinese groceries in the corporate area, many located in St. Andrew.

Information about the residence of Syrians is scanty, though it seems that many were living over their stores in central Kingston at the beginning of the twentieth century. By 1940 they were, like the whites, largely suburban in location.

The whites remained the dominant element in the city, deciding both informally and through the government the pattern of urban growth and morphology. Other groups accommodated themselves as best they could to the trends and tastes created by the whites. The least independent of the other groups were the East Indians. Milroy in his report on the cholera epidemic illustrates the attitude of the white and coloured groups toward them, and their close association, as an impoverished element, with the west end of the city.

> It is also worthy of note that very few coolies amounting to upwards of 300 about Kingston fell victim to the pestilence. At its appearance they were living in some wretched hovels at the west extremity of the town near the terminus of the railroad. By order of the city authorities they were driven out of the spot, and their dwellings burnt down. Most of them, it was believed, lived and slept in the open air.[66]

The East Indians who were living in Kingston in 1850 had presumably served their period of indenture, but by 1891 two other groups who were unfree were located on the Liguanea Plain. One was situated near Sandy Gully to the northeast of King's House, and the other at Papine, adjacent to the Mona sugar estate.[67] These, like the slaves before them, were confined to the property to which they had been indentured. After 1920, however, the rapid expansion of the East Indian population of the city was increasingly concentrated in St. Andrew, and an absolute decline in numbers occurred in Kingston parish during the late 1930s.

LEGAL CHANGE AND THE SOCIAL STRUCTURE

The first improvements in the position of the free coloured people were achieved in 1813, when, despite the opposition of the whites in Kingston,[68] their testimony was permitted in both civil and criminal suits. They were also allowed to save deficiency, and the restrictions on their ability to inherit property were withdrawn.[69] However, the most crucial changes took place after 1820. These were brought about through their agitation under the leadership of Edward Jordan and Robert Osborn and by the intercession of the British Government on their behalf.

During this period, many whites were concerned about the growing size of the free group due both to natural increase and manumission and were alarmed by their financial power, cohesion, and outspokenness. More and more whites felt it necessary to "place the browns gradually on a footing with ourselves, to create a defensive alliance which may prove a security to us in our hour of need."[70] In 1826, therefore, at the time when the Jews were freed from their various disabilities, the free Negro and coloured population were no longer required to live in towns. In 1830 they likewise were admitted to full civil rights, and in 1832 together with the Jews, were enfranchised. By the end of the period of slavery the division between free and unfree people was greatly simplified but nonetheless emphatic. Moreover, it is significant that the suffrage was extended only at the end of a period of social stress which culminated in the slave revolt, or Baptist War, of 1831.

Soon after the abolition of the slave trade in 1808, demands were increasingly made in Britain for improvements in the slaves' condition. The two features of slavery which most shocked British susceptibilities were the selling of produce by slaves on Sundays and the lack of marital unions among them. In 1816, therefore, the Jamaica Assembly introduced a new slave law prescribing holidays and making small improvements in the lot of the Negroes. In 1823 a more liberal policy of amelioration was established by Canning. He demanded that the anti-sectarian clauses in the law should be removed, that slaves should have legal protection, and that females should be spared punishment by flogging.[71]

The whites paid only lip-service to these changes. They obstructed amelioration at every turn and viciously attacked the sectarian missionaries. The Jamaica Slave Act of 1826, which was eventually disallowed by the British Government, is replete with evidence of their resistance to any form of change. In view of the failure of the whites to ameliorate, demands in Britain gradually became more radical, and the possibility of emancipation was discussed. At this stage the Jamaican whites embarked on an extreme course of action. Falling back on the constitutionalist argument which had raged at the end of the seventeenth century, they claimed their legislature was autonomous and that Britain had no right to intervene in their affairs.

In 1831 the third element, the slaves, entered the struggle by breaking out in open but abortive rebellion. In Kingston, ships were moored at the end of the north-south streets along which they could have directed their fire had their intervention been necessary to contain the disturbance.[72] The whites blamed the rebellion on the non-conformist missionaries; the missionaries claimed that the slaves had risen because the whites were known to oppose British plans for emancipation. Secretly, no doubt, many whites were delighted that the rebellion had embarrassed the British Government and the Emancipationists.[73] For their part, the slaves believed that their freedom had been granted by Britain only to be withheld by their masters.

The reaction of the whites to the rebellion was, predictably, extreme. The Colonial Church Union, an ultra-conservative organization, was formed by the lower-class whites to "resist by all constitutional means the encroachment of their enemies."[74] One of the main activities of the union was the burning of non-conformist chapels, but in Kingston these schemes were defeated by the free coloured population "who night after night kept guard over them."[75]

Simultaneously a secessionist movement gained strength. Some whites talked about rebelling against the Crown,[76] while others made overtures to the United States to discuss the possibility of a political union.[77] This impass was eventually resolved by the reformed House of Commons in Britain. The Colonial Church Union was declared illegal, and proposals were made to emancipate the slaves in 1834. The slaves, however, were not to be "full free" but were consigned to their former masters as apprentices until 1840 (later brought forward to 1838). Furthermore, to compensate for the loss of their slaves, Jamaican owners were awarded an indemnity of £6 million. To these changes the whites, reluctantly and with great forboding, finally agreed.

RACE RELATIONS

Emancipation removed the most critical legal barrier to social advancement, but extreme inequalities persisted among the population of Kingston throughout the post-emancipation period. Indeed, with the abolition of slavery the informal determinants of status increased in importance. The superordinate sections searched for symbols that summarised their distinctiveness and distance from the ex-slaves. Both colour and culture therefore became increasingly important considerations. With the disappearance of the white indentured servants and, to a lesser extent, the lower class of whites, with the granting of full civil rights to the Jews, free Negroes, and people of colour, and with the emancipation of the slaves, many anomalous relationships among colour, culture, and status were gradually removed between 1800 and 1840.

Although the social situation was complicated by the introduction of the East Indians, Syrians, and Chinese, it was to the highly visible characteristics of race and colour that most observers referred when explaining the workings of the social system. The close relationship between colour and status and the role played by segregation are explicit in the observations made by Livingstone at the end of the nineteenth century. "Based on sentiment, colour-caste is by no means so rigid in its application as the religious castes of the world, and society is established on a system of mutual tolerance, which, however, has its well-understood limitations. In many spheres these are still strictly observed, as for example, in some Anglican churches, where the whites occupy the front and the Negroes the rear pews."[78]

WHITES AND NEGROES

During the post-emancipation period the white population of Kingston comprised several semi-endogamous groups: "the pure Creoles of British origin, including the old British aristocracy, surviving still in reduced numbers, the Creoles styled English, but who are the descendants of Jewish immigrants from Portugal and Spain, and of refugees from Royal France."[79] It was the relationship between these whites and the Negroes which was so dramatically changed by emancipation. Yet the change proved more apparent than real. As late as the 1860s, the whites in Jamaica retained 37 of the 47 seats in the Assembly,[80] and by a variety of means, including taxation, they excluded propertied Negroes from the electoral rolls.[81] Constituencies remained rotten boroughs, and when the Jamaica Assembly abdicated in favour of Crown Colony Government in 1865 it was largely to nullify the potential influence of the Negro population on the internal government of the island. As late as 1935, only 5 percent of the population registered for the vote,[82] and the whites controlled local government in Kingston until the end of the Second World War.

A real change in the relations between the races depended on a change of attitude among the dominant element, the whites. This was not forthcoming. Indeed, according to Froude, "the white residents and the negroes had not been drawn together by the abolition of slavery, but were further apart than ever."[83] The elite had anticipated that emancipation would be followed by mass emigration of whites to Britain or by the establishment of military stations throughout the interior of the island.[84] Since neither of these expectations was fulfilled, they fell back on such coercive measures as were permitted by the law, the unpaid magistracy, and the existence of a volunteer militia.

Race relations became particularly tense during the 1860s. It was widely rumoured among the Negroes that the whites were going to reintroduce slavery, while the whites feared the outbreak of a Negro revolt and the creation of a second Haiti. When rebellion broke out at Morant Bay in 1865, it was put down with great brutality by the army and the local militia.

After 1865 the techniques employed by the whites to maintain the social order changed from undisguised coercion to firm paternalism. The movement of Britain to the centre of the Jamaican stage created a truce with which the Negroes were prepared, at least temporarily, to comply. Consequently, when at the end of the nineteenth century it was proposed to reintroduce limited male suffrage, the Negroes of Kingston petitioned against the plan, stating "we are law-abiding people, being fully conscious that without the protection of the Government our fellow Colonists would not allow us to enjoy the breath we breathe."[85] Local commentators concluded that race and colour were "the most powerful influences regulating the destiny of the colony" and noted that the fundamental equality of the Negro "to the white man is denied. It is alleged that there is an inherent antipathy between the two races, and that it is hopeless to expect them ever to live side by side."[86] Furthermore, it was observed that Negroes "never place themselves in any situation that would antagonise the whites, and the easy relations that exist may be expected to continue so long as the humbler race remains as ignorant and self-conscious as it is at present."[87] Despite the electioneering of Dr. Love, a black Bahamian who championed the Negro cause in Kingston at the turn of the century, and the work of Marcus Garvey, who founded the Universal Negro Improvement Association and during the 1920s and 1930s appealed to the Negro in racial terms, these conditions persisted until just before the Second World War.

WHITES AND COLOUREDS

The relationship between whites and coloureds remained ambivalent during the post-emancipation period. Initially the coloured people achieved considerable advancement. In Kingston Edward Jordan became mayor and assemblyman; later he was made a vestryman for St. Andrew, Speaker of the House of Assembly and, finally, Island Secretary.[88] By 1860 when the coloured people comprised 30 percent of the population of Kingston, it was claimed that "they are to be met at the Governor's table, they sit in the House of Assembly; they cannot be refused admittance to state parties, or even to large assemblies; they have forced themselves forward and must be recognised as being in the van. Individuals decry them—will not have them within their doors—affect to despise them. But in effect the coloured men of Jamaica cannot be despised much longer."[89] Such was their success that Trollope criticised the whites for regarding "themselves as the ascendant race. I look upon those of colour as being so, or at any rate about to become so."[90]

Despite their solidarity with the whites during the Morant Bay Rebellion, the changes that followed it effectively reduced the power of the coloured group. Political power was transferred to a white expatriate executive, and as late as 1943, white control over the civil service was so complete that only two of the twenty-five highest officials in Kingston were non-white.[91] Furthermore, "when the Governor of Jamaica arrived in that year, only seventeen per cent of the guest list at his first reception was coloured."[92] The coloured population of Kingston therefore remained an intermediate group distinguished from both the dominant whites and subordinate Negroes.

COLOURED AND BLACK

On the eve of emancipation in 1833, the free people of colour in Kingston declared themselves "the firm and unbending opponents of the present system—the zealous advocates of a change from slave to free labour with due regard to the rights of everyone."[93] This apparant *volte face* must be seen in the context of the rebellious views of the whites and of the loyalist attitude adopted by the coloureds in gratitude for the support they had received from the British Government. In general, however, the hostility and discrimination suffered by the coloureds at the hands of the whites was meted out by them, in turn, to the Negroes.

The coloured people, taking every opportunity to dissociate themselves from the Negroes, talked "contemptuously of niggers."[94] The hostility was mutual, however. One visitor noted, "a Negro as a rule will not serve a mulatto when he can serve a European or a white Creole. He thinks the mulatto to be too akin to himself to be worthy of any respect."[95] Throughout the post-emancipation period, therefore, the relations among the whites, coloureds, and Negroes remained essentially hierarchic and based on distrust, discrimination, force, and British arbitration. The essence of race relations in the Creole community of Kingston was succinctly summarised in a sentence by Trollope: "both the white man and the black dislike their coloured neighbours."[96]

THE NEWCOMERS

As the distributional patterns suggest, the East Indians, Chinese, and Syrians remained to a greater or lesser degree aloof from the Creole society of whites, browns, and blacks in Kingston. The Syrians proved the most adaptable economically and culturally and the most acceptable to the whites from the point of view of race and colour. By the end of the post-emancipation period the Syrians were slowly being assimilated into the white community, though the older Syrian settlers were still subject to discrimination.

Despite, or perhaps because of, their success as entrepreneurs, the Chinese were resented by most sections of the host community. A Committee on Alien Immigration reported in 1931 that "such money as they do not send out of the Island is retained probably for the purpose of propogating gambling schemes. Only a small portion of the money earned by the Chinese is used for the employment of local labour and we do not consider that the population of the Island is sufficiently large to support a continued increase of small traders."[97] In addition to the disparagement of the whites, the Chinese were also subject to the hostility of the Negroes, who criticised their low standard of living and resented their refusal to employ Negroes in their groceries. Despite increasing economic contacts with Creole society, the Chinese remained basically endogamous and somewhat isolated socially.

Unlike the other immigrant groups, the East Indians achieved only a low social status. The Negroes, it was claimed, were "more or less repugnant" to the East Indians.[98] The East Indians endured many uncomplimentary epithets, such as "parsimonious" and "slave coolie," though the Negroes seem to have preferred them to the Chinese.[99] Despite proselytisation on the part of the Presbyterians, Hindus and Muslims remained culturally as well as racially distinct until well into the twentieth century.

RACE AND EMPLOYMENT

The structure of employment in Kingston throughout the post-emancipation period reflected the pattern established during the eighteenth century. Although slavery was abolished, the work force still depended on servicing and the economy of the port. Manufacturing was of little importance, and the typical port industries were non-existent. Furthermore, the relationship between social status, race, and occupation was still basically a rigid one. Census data for 1881 and 1921 (table 4) reveal the increasing concentration of professional people in the capital, the decline of agriculture in the Kingston area, and the growing significance of domestic, commercial, and industrial occupations.

Care is required in interpreting the figures, however. In 1881, for example, when 24.4 percent of the population of Kingston parish were apparently employed in industry, half were milliners, seamstresses, washerwomen, and laundresses, and most of the remainder were carpenters, coopers, and

general labourers. The proportion of the population which was non-productive or of indefinite occupation fell between 1881 and 1921, but this was accompanied by the growth of domestic service. By 1921 almost 40 percent of the gainfully employed females in Kingston were working as servants, and this underlines the dearth of truly industrial pursuits.

The relationship between race and occupation was quite clear-cut. "There are but few white labourers in Jamaica, and but few Negroes who are not labourers. But the coloured people are to be found in all ranks."[100] The whites in Kingston occupied positions of command in the civil service, dominated the professions, and, with the Jews, continued to engross the city's foreign commerce. After 1900 the internal trade in Kingston fell increasingly into the hands of the Asian immigrants.

In 1860, however, when the power of the coloured people was at its height, it was claimed that they were important as shop owners and workers, and prominent both in the professions and public service.[101] Despite the political changes which occurred in 1865, their economic progress continued, and by 1930 it was noted that:

coloured girls are the office workers and shop clerks and school teachers. In large offices in Kingston, employing scores of workers, practically everyone is coloured; as a rule they are a clean, well-dressed, well-behaved and self-respecting group. Many lawyers, doctors, dentists, engineers, actuaries, accountants and other professional men are people of colour, usually brown or lighter. Many of these people are as cultured as white people of the same economic status. There is admittedly a colour line or colour lines, but there is as much caste feeling and caste practice between the light coloured negroes and the full blacks as between the white and coloured groups.[102]

The burden of this caste-like situation fell heavily on the Negroes. Admittedly, by the end of the nineteenth century, some were filling "minor offices in the various public departments." and others were qualifying as physicians, solicitors, and barristers or working as teachers, journalists, and postmasters.[103] Nevertheless, the greater proportion in Kingston were employed in semi-skilled trades, in unskilled labouring jobs, or in domestic service.

UNEMPLOYMENT AND LABOUR EFFICIENCY

Although the planters claimed that emancipation created a labour shortage within the estate sector of the economy, conditions of labour surplus were almost immediately recorded in Kingston. Unemployment was noticeable in the city by 1842 and was attributed in part to the inflow of "idle and disorderly persons from all the out-parishes."[104] Despite the cholera epidemic of 1850 and the subsequent emigration of males to Panama, the problem of unemployment remained endemic. In 1860 when Sewell observed that "the Kingstonians remind one much of the Bahama wreckers,"[105] more than 500 persons depended on a weekly relief of a shilling or two, while many more qualified for assistance but received none.[106] The situation deteriorated still further after the capital was transferred to Kingston and the population began to increase rapidly. By 1877 there was not enough employment "for one quarter of the honest and industrious poor in Kingston who would be willing to work. The idle boys and men of Kingston were supported by their mothers, aunts or grannies, who worked as servants or in other domestic and feminine occupations, or by their women who worked on the wharves, in coaling, or in loading bananas."[107]

Labour inefficiency was associated with the uneconomic deployment of labour. By 1861 there were too many people doing too few jobs.

A stranger in Jamaica and especially an American, who knew nothing of its past history and present wants, would never dream that labour is the great desideratum. He finds, on arriving in Kingston, a dozen boatmen eager to convey him ashore—a dozen porters ready to carry his luggage—a dozen messengers quarrelling to run his errands. He is pestered

with able-bodied men and their offers of assistance for a paltry remuneration. He sees as many attendants in a petty Kingston shop as in a Broadway store, and a government clerk with as many servants as a foreign ambassador. Servants must have under-servants, and agents sub-agents.[108]

These conditions had been inherited from slavery and were maintained and worsened by the impact of in-migration and by the decline in the city's economy. Although town labourers, most of whom were Negro or coloured, were no longer preserved from unemployment by the institution of slavery, they developed, as Sewell has shown, a dependency sub-culture which was attuned to conditions of labour surplus. This sub-culture declined in importance at the turn of the century, as Kingston's economy improved and emigration drew off both city dwellers and potential city-ward migrants.

During the depressed 1930s, however, unemployment once more became characteristic of the labour situation in Kingston. The problem was aggravated by the rapid growth of the city's population, caused by natural increase, rural migration, and the return of Jamaican nationals from Central America. In 1936 a commission was set up to investigate unemployment. It reported that of the 90,000 people living in the "Kingston area," 5,000 were "genuinely unemployed," and that 40 percent of these had been born in rural areas.[109] If we assume an urban labour force of approximately 45,000, it is probable that 11 percent were unemployed at this date. The Times Store in Kingston disclosed that 2,000 men and 187 women had applied for jobs in 1934, but that employment had been found for only ten women and four men. By this time unemployment, though weighing most heavily on the labouring population, was also affecting white collar workers. In view of this white-collar unemployment, the Commission recommended "that a much greater proportion of the education should have a vocational and particularly an agricultural bias, and that government should apply a larger percentage of the educational vote to this end."[110] However, it was to white collar jobs that the coloured and Negro population aspired.

FAMILY AND COLOUR

Family structure in Kingston was characterized by two traits that had also been observed during slavery; namely, the low incidence of marriage, and a rate of illegitimacy that approached 70 percent of all live births. As late as 1921, only 29 percent of the population of Kingston parish above 20 years of age were married; the proportions for St. Andrew and Jamaica as a whole were 40.0 and 33.6 percent respectively. At this level of generalisation, it is possible to contrast the high rates of illegitimacy recorded in the low-class sections of Kingston with the high rates of marriage in the upper-class suburbs of St. Andrew.

Although the "white bias" of the society and inferiority complex of the Negro were inherited from slavery, both features became a continuing part of the social system in Kingston. The Negro despised the coloured people but envied their racial appearance and social status. Furthermore, the Negro continued to accept the superiority of the whites and was "content to starve for a month if he could appear as a white man for a day."[111] "Each remove from the sable hue" meant "a step higher in the social scale,"[112] and marrying light was the principal method of achieving social mobility. Parents made "every effort to unite their children to mates of a lighter shade. Black girls, no matter how handsome and well-educated, are left by suitors of their own class for mulattoes and quadroons, who again seek for higher alliances."[113] This system of "improving the colour" remained crucial for black men who hoped for social advancement.

The mating patterns practised by the upper social stratum became more homogeneous during the post-emancipation period, owing to the reduction in size of the lower class of whites, the increased proportion of white women in the population, and the veneer of Victorian values. Most white men married white spouses though many still maintained outside unions "hidden under the veil of secrecy."[114] Their mistresses were usually fair-skinned, though casual relations were also formed with Negro women. After the middle of the nineteenth century, there was an increasing tendency for coloured people to intermarry, and it was among this group that shades of colour became of the greatest importance.

Mating among the Negroes in Kingston continued to follow a different tradition. Marriage was conceived either as a badge of slavery or as a mark of social status and was rarely embarked on before middle age. Despite the dissemination of Victorian ideas about chastity, many Negroes "entered into illicit unions, produced children and separated after a longer or shorter interval to form other connections of an equally transient nature."[115]

Family forms therefore differed markedly among the three social strata. Marriage and female chastity were norms for the whites, including the Jews and later the Syrians who comprised semi-endogamous cells. These conditions were atypical of the lowest ranking group where marriage was associated with middle age, and illegitimacy was the norm. Among the Negroes, therefore, the family remained matrifocal.

Within the median stratum, the mating and family forms of both these groups were practised. One element embraced the behaviour of the Negroes, while the other, in attempting to identify with the whites, adopted a strict Victorian code. For the Chinese and East Indians endogamy remained the ideal, though both groups entered into either consensual cohabitation or extra-residential mating with Negroes. At first these systems were unavoidable, since the immigrants were mostly men. By the end of the post-emancipation period, when women were well-represented among these groups, they remained as alternative or additional forms of mating.

RELIGION

The representation of religious groups in Kingston during the post-emancipation period is adequately summarised by the census data for 1881 (table 5). At that date approximately one quarter of the inhabitants of Kingston parish were Anglicans, one quarter Methodists, 17 percent Catholics, and 8 percent Baptists. Jews were a notable minority, but pagans, mostly Hindus, were present only in small numbers. The largest denomination was recorded in similar proportions in St. Andrew, though the Christian sects, which accounted for only 18 percent of the population of Kingston parish, comprised more than 40 percent of St. Andrew's inhabitants. However, a distinction must be made between church membership and the frequency of attendance. As late as 1861, half the church-going population of Kingston were Native Baptists.[116] Among the Negroes, church attendance and belief in the power of obeah were by no means mutually exclusive.[117] Despite the disappearance of many purely African beliefs and the infusion of British Victorian values, Afro-Christian cults persisted throughout the post-emancipation period, and the three social strata maintained distinct religious systems.

In general terms, the whites were associated with the Anglican Church, disestablished in 1870. The median stratum was mostly Methodist or Catholic, while the Negroes, in Trollope's cynical words, liked "best that class of religion which allows them to hear the most of their voices. They are therefore fond of Baptists; and fonder of the Wesleyans than of the Church of England. Many also are Roman Catholics."[118] Among the Negroes, however, the development of the missionary movement was paralleled by the growth of Afro-Christian cults. Local preachers or daddies, many of whom were illiterate, continually diverted orthodox converts into informal cults and sects. The impact of the missionaries was further reduced by their campaign against the marriage customs and festivals of the Negroes. In 1841 a riot broke out in Kingston after attempts had been made to suppress the John Canoe celebrations which were held at Christmas.[119] The Negroes began to link the missionaries with the ruling class and to treat them with distrust.

The work of the missionaries also suffered from direct competition. In 1857 a myal outbreak occurred in Kingston, and "the incursions of Africanism reached a climax in the Great Revival of 1860-61, a movement that brought the final surge of missionary hope and final depths of missionary despair."[120] In Kingston the people were so caught up in the religious fervour that they could not be persuaded to go to work, "even if you offer them a pound per day."[121] Moreover the influence of obeahmen remained potent, despite the heavy punishment inflicted on offenders.

So late as 1861, during the revival, as it was termed, a party of young women, in a state of religious excitement, went to the house of a reputed Obeah man, residing in one of the suburbs of Kingston, and brought him, with all the implements of his art, to the parade. His box contained not only nearly all the abominations mentioned, but several lizard- and snake-skins. There was also a bell, said to be used to summon a sort of familiar spirit, and a pack of cards. In the midst of all, sad to say, was a number of class tickets, indicating that he had been a member of a religious body for a great number of years.[122]

During the 1920s a local messianic leader called Alexander Bedward established himself at August Town on the banks of the Hope River, his Jordan, and created a large following from among the poorest sections of the city. He appealed directly to the depressed Negroes by promising physical healing and spiritual redemption in a language reminiscent of Lisle and Baker. After he attacked the supremacy of the whites and failed in an attempt to ascend to heaven, he was tried and placed in a lunatic asylum, where he eventually died.[123] Bedwardism contained a strong element of escapism. It was, however, of a temporary, mystical nature and contrasted with the elaborate plans for Negro emigration to Africa which Marcus Garvey was developing in the United States and Jamaica at the same time. Both movements were responses to the inequalities of Creole society and symptomatic of disaffection among a small group of Negroes within the population.

EDUCATION

The inequalities inherent in the social order were underwritten and perpetuated by the educational system. While the white elite were educated in Britain or, later, in North America, the local secondary schools remained the preserve of the middle stratum, and of the coloured people in particular. By the middle of the nineteenth century, 500 pupils were enrolled at Woolmer's School[124] but few scholarships were awarded[125] and the system of fee-paying virtually excluded the Negroes.

Until the second half of the nineteenth century the education of the Negroes in Kingston was subject to a "pernicious neglect" mitigated only by the efforts of the charities,[126] the missions, and, until 1846, the British Government. In 1861 the legislature voted "less than one shilling for the instruction of each child during the space of twelve months."[127] Among the whites it was widely believed that schools spoiled labour and that the mental capacity of the Negro was defective. By 1864 "elementary education had fallen into a state of sad neglect,"[128] and both the quantity and quality had actually declined since the abolition of apprenticeship.[129] As late as 1883, many of the teachers were regarded as "totally unfitted for the posts they occupy."[130]

According to the 1871 census, only 40 percent of the inhabitants of Kingston parish aged over five were able to read and write. Nevertheless, conditions were infinitely better than in St. Andrew (14 percent) and in Jamaica as a whole (16 percent). The situation had improved immensely by 1921, when the literacy rate reached almost 80 percent in Kingston and 64 percent in St. Andrew. Indeed, in St. Andrew the rate doubled between 1891 and 1921, and this reflected the extension of the suburbs across the Liguanea Plain. For Jamaica as a whole, however, the literacy rate barely exceeded 50 percent. The differential between the capital and the rural areas was due principally to the better educational facilities in Kingston, though migration to the town of well-educated country people also contributed to it.

The literacy rate improved after 1892, when school fees were abolished, but education was not compulsory and attendance remained low. Literacy, however, provides an inaccurate guide to educational advancement in the elementary schools. "The teaching was almost entirely by rote, 'sound without sense.' This so-called education naturally did little to fit its recipients for the most ordinary duties of life, and still less for the advancement in social position which many had anticipated and hoped for as its result; reaction, as might have been expected, set in, gradually producing utter indifference towards education in the minds alike of the labouring population and of the more intelligent classes."[131]

The educational system provided an ideal training ground for the social roles which children were to play as adults. Moreover, it encouraged cultural conservation rather than acculturation. The Negro still depended heavily on the informal education he received at home, and to this were added attitudes and interpretations supplied by missionaries from Britain. But while the educational system fitted the Negro for his social role, it did not prepare him economically. Craftsmanship and the mechanical skills were neglected, and for many years the only source of trained labour was the reformatory at Stony Hill in St. Andrew.

IV: Kingston in 1943

INTRODUCTION

The year 1944 represents a turning point in the social and economic development of Kingston, second in importance only to the year 1834. In 1834 the slaves were emancipated; in 1944 universal adult suffrage was introduced, initiating the movement toward self-government and independence. The first task is to analyse the social geography of Kingston before these changes were affected. Most of the material used in this chapter was provided by the detailed census of January, 1943. It must be remembered, however, that 1943 falls within a period of change bounded by the riots of 1938 and the suffrage of 1944. This period resembled the apprenticeship of 1834 to 1838. Furthermore, it coincided with the Second World War.

METHODOLOGICAL PROBLEMS

Although the corporate area of Kingston—St. Andrew contained a population of 237,000 in 1943, no attempt was made to define a legal city boundary. But the census distinguished between the city and the corporate area and divided the former into ten zones with a population of 201,900. The area covered by these zones has been used here as an arbitrary definition of the city. These ten census zones contained 222 enumeration districts. Material for these districts was never published, though a copy of some of the tabulations was found in a repository in the Institute of Social and Economic Research at the University of the West Indies in Kingston.

The examination of the 1943 census data is based on the following assumptions: that the enumeration districts are adequate units for data collection and representation; that they are homogeneous; and that groupings of enumeration districts may be made so that they, too, are homogeneous within the limits established by the class intervals. The basic technique is to start with the smallest, most detailed units available and build outward by grouping units that are similar with respect to the

factor being mapped. In this way the generalised patterns for the city as a whole are based on the detailed, particular recordings of each enumeration district. This synthetic approach has been widely adopted in geographical studies.

DISTRIBUTION AND DENSITY OF POPULATION

The population of Kingston more than doubled between 1921 and 1943. This growth was accommodated both by the concentration of even larger numbers within the parts of the city which dated back to the nineteenth century and by suburban development on the Liguanea Plain (fig. 14). On the basis of population distribution and density five areas could be distinguished (fig. 18). These were arranged concentrically around the original town plan, most of which was occupied by the central business district. Areas devoted to retailing, administration, commerce, and overseas trade had densities of less than 50 persons an acre, but densities rose to between 100 and 250 persons an acre on the periphery of this zone. The largest concentration was in West Kingston, where densities exceeded 191 persons an acre in the single-story tenements that extended from the Spanish Town Road to North Street and the Kingston Public Hospital (fig. 13), while densities ranging from 9 to 90 persons an acre characterized a belt located on the northern, eastern, and western fringes of this tract. Densities of between 27 and 54 persons an acre were especially widespread in Passmore Town in East Kingston, and in the rent-yards adjacent to Maxfield Road in southwestern St. Andrew. The latter, together with the suburbs south of Half Way Tree, had been important growth areas during the period from 1921 to 1943 (fig. 14). Densities of less than 9 persons an acre prevailed throughout most of St. Andrew and, in particular, to the north of Half Way Tree. However, figures of between 9 and 27 persons an acre were recorded in isolated concentrations in the central part of the suburbs. These settlements were located on the banks of storm-water gullies and formed pockets of poverty within the suburban area. Neverless, throughout three-quarters of the city densities averaged less than 9 persons per acre.

DISTRIBUTION OF MIGRANTS

In the preceding chapter it was noted that in-migration was a vital component of population growth during the period from 1921 to 1943. In 1943 more than 45 percent of the inhabitants of the corporate area had been born elsewhere. By mapping the distribution of migrants to Kingston and St. Andrew it is possible to discover and examine the reception areas.

Migrants whose residence in Kingston parish ranged between one and five years (fig. 19) numbered 19,000. They were concentrated in the tenements on the fringe of the central business district and in a zone in East Kingston extending from the mental hospital to the Alpha Institute. The newcomers accounted for more than 36 percent of the total population in some of the densely populated parts of West Kingston, and for at least 12 percent throughout the remainder, including the central business district (fig. 20).

Recent migrants to St. Andrew, including persons who had formerly lived in Kingston, numbered 27,000. They were concentrated in the tenements and yards close to the southwestern boundary with Kingston, and to a lesser extent in the suburbs spreading northward to Half Way Tree and Cross Roads (fig. 21). The number of migrants decreased in a northerly and northwesterly direction away from Half Way Tree, and was least on the periphery of the city. Throughout large sections of the suburbs these migrants comprised between 20 and 50 percent of the total population, the highest proportions being recorded between Half Way Tree and Cross Roads in the north and the Kingston parish boundary in the south.

The most important movement of population within the city was the outflow of migrants from the parish of Kingston to the suburbs of St. Andrew. Between 1921 and 1943, 11,300 persons left

Kingston for St. Andrew, accounting for 24 percent of the newcomers who settled during this period. This outflow is incorporated in figure 21. Figure 22 shows that the reception areas for these short-distance movers were similar to those for all migrants to St. Andrew. The cross-town movement probably involved two groups of migrants and two different reception areas. The first group comprised persons leaving Kingston for the better, low-density residential suburbs that extended northward to Half Way Tree; the second settled the impoverished yards adjacent to the Spanish Town Road in West Kingston.

SEX RATIOS AND AGE STRUCTURE

The outstanding feature of the sex ratio in Kingston in 1943 was the vast preponderance of women. The sex ratio for the city was lower than for the island as a whole: Jamaica recorded 937, Kingston 775, and St. Andrew 774. Mortality differentials, particularly among infants, together with the emigration of male workers, accounted for the island-wide imbalance. However, the lower sex ratio in Kingston may largely be attributed to the over-representation of females among the migrants to the city. Between 1921 and 1943 the sex ratios of the migrants to Kingston and St. Andrew were 603 and 721 respectively. Although the sex ratio was highest in the sparsely populated yard areas of Southwestern St. Andrew and in parts of central and East Kingston, males outnumbered females in fewer than 5 percent of the enumeration districts (fig. 23). There was a large preponderance of women throughout most of the rapidly growing tenements and the upper-class suburbs: this was particularly marked near Half Way Tree, where most households employed domestic servants and provided the very occupations for which most female migrants were searching.

Analysis of the age structure of Kingston substantiates and amplifies the information about migration (fig. 9). Whereas in 1881 the outstanding features of the population pyramid of Kingston as compared with Jamaica as a whole had been the over-representation of females and under-representation of males, in 1943 three characteristics were noteworthy. These were the under-representation of children aged 0-15, the over-representation of adults aged 20-45, and the under-representation of persons aged more than 50 years.

This three-fold pattern had existed to a slight degree among the male population of Kingston in 1881; among the younger female age-groups it had been quite marked, though aged women were numerous in the city at that date. While the superfluity of young adults in Kingston in 1943 may be attributed to in-migration, the deficiencies of both children and elderly persons were associated with out-migration. Children probably comprised the greater proportion of those who had been born in Kingston but who were residing in the rural parishes; this out-movement comprised 8,000 persons between 1921 and 1943.[1] Despatched to the country by their mothers, these children were usually reared by kin. Furthermore, elderly people retired to the country where they occupied family land.

LAND USE

RESIDENTIAL LAND USE AND HOUSING

A map prepared by the government's Town Planner in 1947 provides the major guide to land use in Kingston at this period. This map identifies only two main categories of use—residential and non-residential. It indicates the limits of the built-up area of the city and the extent to which the Liguanea Plain was occupied by the expanding suburbs (fig. 24). Predominantly residential land was located in three main zones to the east, north, and west of the commercial area. Each zone contained nuclei of older settlement around and between which the newer suburbs developed. These three zones were located in East Kingston to the southeast of Up Park Camp, in West Kingston to the north of the Spanish Town Road, and in

central and northern St. Andrew. The line dividing good from poor housing followed the division between West Kingston (poor) and central St. Andrew (good), but bisected East Kingston.

In East Kingston the tenements were closely associated in form and function with those of West Kingston, while the recent suburbs were morphologically part of the suburban complex of St. Andrew. While poor housing and other signs of poverty affected some of the less densely populated parts of the city, expecially in the western zone, poor housing and high densities conspired to produce massive slums in East and West Kingston. The development and growth of these slums was due to population increases, in which in-migration was an important component. However, conditions in the slums were also affected by the fabric and facilities that were available.

As a result of a survey undertaken in the slums in 1935,[2] several areas in the west, notably Smith Village and Back O'Wall (fig. 25), had been scheduled for demolition, and a rehousing scheme was prepared in Denham Town. The scheme, however, was designed to accommodate only 3,000 people, and it failed to house more than one-sixth of the depressed and most needy inhabitants of Kingston. But it established the principle that the government had a responsibility for improving housing conditions and for providing accommodation at uneconomic rents.

The scheme was confined to short-term, remedial measures that were conceived and implemented on the microscale without reference to other urban problems or to long-term developments in the city. Consequently, when the 1943 census was taken, 22 percent of the dwellings in Kingston were found to be good, 51 percent fair, and 27 percent bad; in St. Andrew the proportions were 30, 39, and 31 percent (table 6). Both parishes had about 35,000 dwellings. St. Andrew recorded more good and more bad dwellings than Kingston, and this reflected its suburban and rural facets. Sixty-two percent of the dwellings in Kingston and 80 percent in St. Andrew comprised single story buildings (table 7). The urban silhouette was extremely low and reflected the building laws introduced after the 1907 earthquake.

Tenements represented the most typically urban form of housing, providing 28.5 percent of the accommodation in Kingston, 15 percent in St. Andrew, and 8 percent in Jamaica as a whole. The ratio of building area to open land was high wherever tenements occurred, and especially so on the fringe of the central business district. Throughout the remainder of the city, and in the suburbs of St. Andrew in particular, single houses of one story prevailed (table 7). More than half the buildings in Kingston and St. Andrew were built of wood, and fewer than 20 percent of concrete.

Building materials used in the city were superior to those employed in rural areas; thatch, Spanish Wall, and wattle were rarely found in the city. Even so, walls were often made of nogging, and the one-room shacks in the yards of West Kingston were invariably built of flotsam. Two interesting features of the fabric of Kingston were the use of brick, a legacy from the nineteenth century, and the growing importance of concrete. More and more roofs were covered with galvanized iron, which rapidly weathered to a rusty ochre. Inflammable but cool Canadian shingles were gradually disappearing, though wood remained in use in the country parts. Most of the floors in the city were made of wood, but wherever walls or floors were constructed of this material the problem of termites was encountered. More than half of the dwellings in Kingston and St. Andrew were infected, and the distribution of poor housing (fig. 24) undoubtedly reflected the incidence of this pest.

The problems posed by the poor fabric of so many of the dwellings were compounded by the nature of many of the facilities. Most of the wooden houses in the city were extremely small—little more than shacks. Some 80 percent of the dwellings in Kingston and 60 percent in St. Andrew were without a separate bedroom, and some were without a kitchen (table 8). In most instances, the kitchen was located outside the main structure of the house. Bathing facilities were better in the city than elsewhere; 9 percent of the houses in Kingston

as compared with 40 percent in St. Andrew and 77 percent in all Jamaica had none whatsoever. The general inadequacy of amenities is exemplified by the lack of toilets. Fewer than two-thirds of the dwellings in Kingston and barely a quarter in St. Andrew were provided with water closets, and pit latrines, which were widespread in rural Jamaica, were common in the poorer parts of the city (table 8). These deficiencies in fabric and facility clearly dated back to the nineteenth century. Nevertheless, they provided the physical environment within which the population explosion of the 1920s and 1930s took place, and the basis from which massive slums could develop.

NON-RESIDENTIAL LAND USE

While the residential areas expanded northward from the Spanish Town and Windward Roads, land for industrial and commercial purposes was largely confined to the low-lying tract near the harbour (fig. 24). During the post-emancipation period, the commercial area, comprising shops, offices, and warehouses, had expanded, and by 1943 it occupied almost the entire area covered by Kingston at the beginning of the eighteenth century. Only the former elite suburb in the north-east of the original town plan was still unoccupied by business houses or tenements. Despite migration to the suburbs, this area and Kingston Gardens to the north had retained their status as good residential districts (fig. 24).

Subsidiary commercial centres were located at Cross Roads, Half Way Tree, and along the Spanish Town Road where the Coronation Market was situated. The latter served as the emporium for West Kingston and to some extent for the city as a whole. It housed dry goods stalls, fish and meat vendors, and higglers who supplied the town with its ground provisions. Shops supplying daily needs were scattered throughout the densely populated parts of Kingston parish and lower St. Andrew, and ribbon developments of retail premises occurred in East Kingston and on the Spanish Town, Maxfield and Slipe Roads. The newest suburbs, especially in the north, were insufficiently supplied with neighbourhood shops at this period, and depended upon the services provided at Cross Roads and Half Way Tree or on the small concentrations of retailers at Matilda's Corner and Mary Brown's Corner.

Despite the small amount of industrial development that took place during the first three decades of the twentieth century, the distribution of manufacturing still resembled the pattern established during slavery. Factories were scattered throughout the commercial area or located on its eastern and western fringes. However, two new locations are worth noting. One of the large tobacco firms had chosen a site to the south of Mary Brown's Corner in upper St. Andrew, while several factories had been built on or adjacent to the Spanish Town Road in West Kingston. In both places large amounts of land were available at low cost, and, in the case of the Spanish Town Road, the premises had relatively easy access to the wharfs and to the other parts of the island.

EMPLOYMENT

By 1943 manufacturing and mechanical industry were the largest employers of male labour in Kingston parish, closely followed by construction, public service, trade, and transport and communications (table 9). The employment structure of the male labour force was therefore typically urban. The pattern for females was quite different. Domestic service was the largest employer, followed by public service, trade, and manufacturing. A similar employment structure existed in St. Andrew, with the notable exception that agriculture was the main employment for men, owing to the rural character of part of the parish. Furthermore, domestic service was of even greater significance among the women of St. Andrew, providing employment for 43 percent of the labour force.

The industrial structure of Kingston differed from that for the island as a whole in the low proportion of persons engaged in agriculture and odd jobs and the high proportion employed in manufacturing, construction, trade, transport, and public service. By island-wide standards, domestic service was slightly under-represented in Kingston and over-represented in St. Andrew. Nevertheless, it provided the greatest opportunity for female employment in both city and country. The industrial structure of Kingston reflected the concentration of functions associated with administration and transport—typical features of capital cities. The contribution of manufacturing to the employment structure, as revealed by the census, was, however, a new departure. In 1943 it employed more persons than did trade, though much of the labour force was undoubtedly concentrated in small workshops and repair yards.

The occupational categories used by the 1943 census were poorly devised and represented little more than refined industrial groupings. Consequently, the pattern of employment is basically similar to that established by the industrial classification. Noteworthy points are the concentration in Kingston of persons employed in clerical, manufacturing, public service, and personal service occupations and the high proportion of males employed as general labourers. More women were employed in manufacturing occupations than in manufacturing industry, and this discrepancy suggests that a large number were probably seamstresses or held similar jobs. The relatively high proportion of males in St. Andrew who were employed in public service indicates that residence in the suburbs was largely associated with persons holding white collar posts in the government.

UNEMPLOYMENT

Although industrialisation was taking place at the beginning of the twentieth century, the high proportion of men who were employed as general labourers, together with the high proportion of females who were engaged as domestic servants, indicated fundamental characteristics of the employment structure of the city. Moreover, during the week ending 28 September 1946, 23,500 persons in Greater Kingston were unemployed, representing 15.5 percent of the total population aged over fourteen.[3] The percentage unemployment for males and females was 17.5 and 14 percent respectively. By this date the number of unemployed was double that estimated in 1938.[4] The 1943 census, however, contains no information about the relationship between unemployment and occupation in Kingston, nor is there any information on unemployment by enumeration district. However, material published by the census indicates that 28.6 percent of the male and 24 percent of the female wage earners in Jamaica were unemployed during the week ending 12 December 1942. Although these figures were probably boosted by seasonal unemployment in the sugar industry, rates exceeded 20 percent among males working in four of the five most important occupational groups in Kingston; namely manufacturing, general labouring, construction, and transport. Unemployment was generally lower for females than for males, though the rate was 18 percent in personal service. However, while unemployment increased in intensity among persons aged between 20 and 50 and affected those very age-groups which, through migration, were over-represented in Kingston, unemployment was also widespread among school leavers. According to a contemporary observer, "unemployment is already the dominant problem; the steady recruiting for its ranks which takes place as the young people leave school is nothing short of disastrous."[5]

The unemployment situation in 1943 therefore represented a perpetuation and intensification of the conditions that had developed during the trade depression of the 1930s. Unemployment, which was originally cyclical or associated with trade cycles, was transformed into a permanent feature of the socio-economic structure of the city. High rates of unemployment were endemic among manual workers and affected even white collar employees. The persistence of unemployment on this scale was

due to structural defects in the economy and to the increase in the population. In Kingston the situation was particularly desperate since it was the focus for cityward migration, and no system of social security existed to cushion the effects of unemployment.

In 1938 the West India Royal Commission reported:

The increase in rural under-employment and the comparatively greater urban wage-increases have intensified the drift to the towns which is a characteristic of the West Indies as of practically all countries in the world. This tendency is most noticeable in Jamaica, where the lure of work at the docks loading bananas, which is carried on all the year round, is potent and evil in its effects. But it is to be found as well wherever there is a centre of population and even the most illusory prospect of casual labour somewhat better paid than that available in the country. . . . This tendency is vicious in its long-term effects. There is no economic possibility for large additional populations to establish themselves in conditions sufficiently stable to enable them to form and perpetuate a healthy community. Further, each influx dilutes the amount of employment available for the original inhabitants and drags down standards of life for others than the newcomers themselves.[6]

This description is reminiscent of conditions in Kingston in the middle of the nineteenth century. The improvements which had occurred by 1900 were due principally to emigration and to the development of the banana trade. By 1938, however, when the riots broke out, these trends had been reversed, and the situation had become highly dangerous and difficult to resolve. "Once town life was adopted, it was, as usual, abandoned with reluctance; in consequence, unemployment and privation existed to a serious degree in Kingston."[7] Orde Browne also noted that "there has thus grown up in Kingston a body of some thousands of persons for whom employment is at best intermittent. The tendency for such people to become unemployable, if not criminal, is obvious. Hence the importance of measures calculated actually to reduce the urban population, and this on a considerable scale."[8]

OVERCROWDING

In contrast with the spacious accommodation provided in the modern suburbs, housing in the tenements and yards was cramped as well as decrepit. The vast majority of the accommodation in Kingston and in St. Andrew consisted of only one room, and more than half the population of the city lived in minute, single-room dwellings with less than 150 square feet, and averaging 2.5 occupants. According to the Royal Commission

it is no exaggeration to say that in the poorest parts of most towns and in many of the country districts a majority of the houses is largely made of rusty corrugated iron and unsound boarding; quite often the original floor has disappeared and only the earth remains, its surface so trampled that it is impervious to any rain which may penetrate through a leaking roof; sanitation in any form and water supply are unknown in such premises, and in many cases no light can enter when the door is closed. These decrepit homes, more often than not, are seriously overcrowded, and it is not surprising that some of them are dirty and verminous in spite of the praiseworthy efforts of the inhabitants to keep them clean.[9]

After examining conditions in Kingston in 1936, the Central Housing Advisory Board defined as overcrowded those premises in which there were "too many persons living in any one room or house," or those occurring in localities where there were "too many buildings on any one given area of land."[10] The board's ideal standard for living space was 4,500 cubic feet per adult, or no more than two persons for every 100 square feet. According to this criterion, overcrowding was extensive by 1943.

As early as 1938, a number of slum areas had been described by the Acting Medical Officer for Health in Kingston and St. Andrew[11] (fig. 25). These were located in a solid wedge in the rent-yards of West Kingston, in tenements to the north

and east of the central business district, and in three areas to the north of Cross Roads and contained a total population of nearly 20,000. Although the most densely populated tenements escaped designation as slums, there was a close relationship between the slum areas and the districts having densities of more than 9 persons an acre (fig. 18) and between both these parameters and the areas containing poor housing (figs. 17, 24). But in East Kingston much of the densely populated poor accommodation had not yet degenerated to slum conditions.

The statistical information collected by the Central Housing Advisory Board is too fragmentary to permit systematic analysis. However, representative selections from the data give emphasis to the discussion. The highest density of persons per room in 1936 was recorded in Fletcher's Land (2.08), one of the oldest of the inner suburbs of the city. In almost all the designated areas in the western tenements and yards the ratio exceeded 1.5, and in certain streets in Smith Village many rooms contained more than six occupants. Sanitary provision was generally deficient, and only a few of the dwellings in Hannah Town and Admiral Pen had water closets; pit latrines were therefore ubiquitous, and the greater proportion in Friendship Lane, Providence Pen, Smith Village, and the areas adjacent to the Spanish Town Road were in bad condition.

Some 60 percent of the premises in Rose Town, Friendship Lane, Hart Lane, Providence Pen, and Admiral Pen were considered bad, as were 50 percent in Fletcher's Land and a slightly smaller proportion in Smith Village. In the previous chapter it was noted that by the end of the nineteenth century the inner suburb of Smith Village was growing rapidly and that by the 1930s it was probably overcrowded. It contained the city dump, or dungle. When it was visited by the Royal Commission in 1938, the village had

large areas covered by ruinous shacks, none of which could have escaped instant condemnation in this country [Great Britain] even under standards long since abandoned. The conditions of squalor almost beyond imagination are accentuated by appalling overcrowding. Whole families—father, mother, and numerous children—have their meals and sleep in one room; such is the pressure of poverty that when a second room is available, it will often be sub-let for the sake of a few shillings which are thus to be obtained each month. Often the only available source of water supply for large numbers of these dwellings is cut off for long periods each day. These properties appear to be neglected by their owners, who spend nothing on even the crudest maintenance.[12]

The poverty of the mass of the inhabitants of the city and the predeliction of capitalists for investing in property meant that renting was widespread in Kingston (83 percent) and to a lesser degree St. Andrew (50 percent). The absence of owners from their property (54 percent in Smith Village) may partly account for the dilapidated dwellings, but pressure on the existing accommodation maintained high rents throughout the slums. Even in the infamous Smith Village, the average charge for a room of 90-100 square feet was ten shillings a month, while 64 percent of the households in Kingston and 50 percent in St. Andrew paid between ten shillings and nineteen shillings rent a month for their dwellings. At a period when the annual per capita income was £32.5 and unemployment affected 15 percent of the adult population, rents of between £6 and £13 per annum were excessive and simply encouraged overcrowding. Whether the overcrowding of buildings led to their being in bad condition is by no means certain. By the late 1930s it was clear that "the urban worker has only a small margin between himself and definite want, while any reduction to part-time pay must make the balancing of the family budget impossible."[13]

Unemployment in Kingston and the high rent charged for even miniscule accommodation led to squatting. The two most prominent squatter areas in 1935 were at Back O'Wall and Facey's Brick Yard in Smith Village (fig. 25). The density of population in Back O'Wall, which was occupied by 988 persons, was only 1.5 per room, the lowest recorded for any of the slum areas. However, this density was high when related to the fabric of the buildings and the amenities available. The dwellings in Back O'Wall consisted of poorly ventilated shacks, and drainage was provided by open trenches; the settlement at Facey's Brick Yard was located on the corporation garbage dump and has been described as unfit for habitable purposes.

Living conditions in Kingston gave rise to a public health problem. Typical of the diseases rampant were tuberculosis, dysentery, and enteric fever, and during the years from 1933 to 1935 most of the slum areas were affected (table 10). Smith Village had the highest incidence of all three diseases. The Royal Commissioners related disease to a host of environmental factors, which typified the slums of West Kingston. "The generally insanitary environment gives rise to malaria, worm infection, and bowel diseases; leaking roofs, rotten flooring, and lack of light encourage the spread of tuberculosis, respiratory diseases; overcrowding, which is usually accompanied by imperfect ventilation, is an important agent in contributing to the high incidence of yaws, tuberculosis, venereal diseases and, to a certain extent, leprosy."[14]

SOCIAL STATUS

High rates of unemployment and overcrowding in Kingston were indicative of population pressure—pressure on the economic resources and social facilities of the city. At least one-sixth of the population were unemployed and, economically speaking, superfluous; so probably were most of those employed in domestic service. To a marked degree high population densities were associated with dilapidated buildings, with the development of slum areas lacking sanitary conveniences, with the high incidence of disease, and with the occurrence of squatting and provided clear evidence of population pressure. Migration, unemployment, and overcrowding were part of a chain reaction. The districts that were adversely affected by population pressure were confined to West Kingston and to parts of inner East Kingston; the suburbs of East Kingston and central and northern St. Andrew remained largely immune.

The distribution of this syndrome of poverty was closely associated both structurally and cartographically with the distribution of social status. The index of occupational status has been calculated for each enumeration district using as a basis the proportional representation of professional people.[15] Areas of high socio-economic status were concentrated around Half Way Tree in central St. Andrew and, in particular, along the Constant Spring, Hope, and Old Hope Roads. Other areas of high status were located at Retirement Pen near Cross Roads, at Kingston Gardens, and near the three institutions which were bounded by the Windward Road and Mountain View Avenue in East Kingston. West Kingston in its entirety, the western fringe of the city, and the tenements in inner East Kingston all recorded scores indicative of low status. So, likewise, did certain of the pockets of poverty in St. Andrew, such as Providence Pen, Mary Brown's Corner, and Long Mountain. Areas of median status formed a buffer zone running southeastward from Half Way Tree to Bournemouth Gardens. Other areas of similar status were located in northern St. Andrew. It is most likely that these northern districts were occupied by persons of high socio-economic status, and that the summary score for each enumeration district was affected by the high proportion of country folk who were living on the fringe of the city.

There was a strong cartographic association between low socio-economic status (fig. 26), poor housing (fig. 24), and the distribution of slums (fig. 25). Likewise, a close connection existed between low socio-economic status and high population densities (fig. 18). With the exception of Kingston Gardens and the suburbs immediately to the east of it, those parts of the city which had been built before 1900 had either been turned over to commercial premises or had been developed into high density tenements. By 1943 the latter were the most important reception areas for migrants and especially for those who were looking for work outside the domestic service industry. Furthermore, these tenements together with the shack yards comprised the worst slums.

Persons of medium and high socio-economic status were associated with low densities of population and good housing, most of which had been built after 1900. By 1943 various social areas were crystallising, and as the city expanded, segregation by social status became increasingly marked. While the Spanish Town Road was synonymous with poverty, the suburbs around Half Way Tree epitomised relative affluence and security. In general terms, population pressure increased from north to south and east to west in step with increases in population densities and decreases in social status. The polarisation of these zones was an expression of social distance.

RACIAL COMPOSITION OF THE POPULATION

According to the 1943 census, the population of Kingston consisted of ten racial groups (table 11). Although 19 percent of Jamaica's population was in the corporate area, only 15.6 percent of the island's black population lived in Kingston, compared with 20.4 percent for East Indians,[16] 30.2 for coloureds, 50.3 for Chinese, 60.4 for whites, 61.7 for Syrians, and 84.5 for Jews. Negroes remained essentially rural in location, whereas the whites, coloureds, and Jews, together with the later immigrants from Asia and the Middle East, were in varying degrees associated with the city. There was a close relationship between the size of the racial group and residence in Kingston. The smaller the minority, the greater its concentration in the capital.

Migration to the corporate area affected urban expansion; it also influenced the racial composition of the population during the period from 1921 to 1943. The white population of Jamaica decreased by 4.6 percent, but the increase in the corporate area amounted to 8 percent. The Chinese population in Kingston increased by 300 percent compared with 235 percent for Jamaica as a whole. The East Indians, however, increased by 260 percent in Kingston, and by only 42 percent in Jamaica. This rapid expansion was due to migration from the rural areas and also to the arrival of Bombay businessmen. The largest absolute increase occurred among the coloured and black populations; they accounted for 32,900 and 78,020 new residents respectively, or 92.5 percent of the city's intercensal growth by both natural increase and migration. Despite the large numbers involved, both these groups recorded rates of growth in Kingston in excess of 100 percent. These were more than double the rates observed for the island and indicate the importance of Negroes and coloured people in the movement to Kingston.

By comparing the sex ratio of each group in Kingston, St. Andrew, and Jamaica the influence of internal migration can also be assessed (table 12). Sex ratios that were lower than the national average—indicating an influx of females into Kingston and St. Andrew—were recorded among the Negroes, coloureds, East Indians, and East Indian coloureds. In all three cases, the sex ratio was lower in Kingston than in St. Andrew. The second pattern that is in evidence is particularly important. Among the whites, Chinese, and Jews, the sex ratio was higher than the national average in Kingston but lower in St. Andrew. The relatively high proportion of men in these groups in Kingston was probably due to the arrival of immigrants who settled in established racial enclaves located in the older parts of the city.

RACE, STATUS, AND CULTURE

In the preceding chapter it was noted that racial distinctions and prejudice remained important features of the social structure of Kingston between 1838 and 1938, and that it was to race that most observers referred when explaining the nature of the social system. The procedure, therefore, has been to map each racial group and to examine its socio-economic and cultural characteristics as defined by cross-tabulations published in the 1943 census.

WHITES

Although the whites accounted for only 2.5 percent of the city's inhabitants, they constituted far less than this proportion in more than half the enumeration districts (fig. 27). The group was highly segregated and confined to central, northern, and eastern St. Andrew and to parts of central and East Kingston. The central business district and the elite areas that had been developed during the eighteenth and nineteenth centuries were still occupied by small percentages of whites. However, most had moved to the suburbs, and by 1943 marked concentrations had been formed near Up Park Camp and, more notably, in the vicinity of Half Way Tree and Constant Spring. In all three areas whites comprised more than 20 percent of the population. The areas they occupied recorded at least median socio-economic status scores (fig. 26), and most of the heaviest concentrations were associated with areas of high rank. Whites were almost completely absent from the slum areas of the city and from West Kingston in particular. The largest of the white enclaves, near Half Way Tree, acted as the principal low-density settling basin for migrants, receiving the cross-town movement of Creole whites as well as immigrants from Britain. Almost all the Negroes who entered this area were domestic servants. East Kingston contained many of the family houses of the local elite, the younger members of which were moving to the suburbs. Furthermore, there is evidence that East Kingston contained not only the older members of the white population but the poorer ones too.

This analysis of the geography of the white population of Kingston depicts a small, segregated, and prestigious minority. Each member, according to Henriques

knows that by virtue of his colour not only will he be welcomed everywhere but that in itself his colour commands respect. Money will enable him to further his education abroad and any career is open to him. An individual of this class may lose his money, but he cannot lose his colour or class position. In other words, he will still be entitled to and will receive the respect due to an upper class person although he may not have the money which usually goes with that position. This results in the surety about life which amounts almost to arrogance. This is in marked contrast to the other classes where there is so much more social and economic insecurity.[17]

The power and prestige of the white group was derived from colour and from control of the legal system and the machinery of government. As a result of the suffrage qualifications fewer than 5 percent of the inhabitants of Jamaica were registered to vote, and the colony was administered by the Governor and the nominated members of the legislature. After 1900 the latter equalled the fourteen elected members of the council who were more often coloured or Negro than white. Moreover, the whites occupied the senior posts in the civil service and also exercised control over the external trade of the colony.

The census contains no cross-tabulations relating occupation and income to race for individual parishes, but it is possible to derive a general impression of the occupational structure of the white population of Kingston by reference to conditions in the island as a whole. The Creole whites in Kingston were basically a white-collar group engaged in the import-export trade, in the professions, and in retailing and manufacturing. Expatriates were similarly occupied, though fewer were self-employed. Office work in the private business houses was essentially a white preserve, but immigrants from the British Isles were especially prominent in the civil service, the professions, and teaching. The correspondingly small proportion of whites who were engaged in manual work, and the relatively low incidence of unemployment, were consistent with the high socio-economic status of the group as a whole. White women were largely confined to the home and rarely took employment.

While the elite occupied posts of command, the lower class of whites were found mainly in clerical and technical positions. Data on incomes substantiate this distinction. Approximately two-fifths of the whites earned more than 100 shillings a week,

though fewer than 2 percent of the total wage earners received this amount. Furthermore, half the wage-earners of Jamaica were given under ten shillings a week, compared with fewer than 3 percent among the whites. Even the lower class of whites, therefore, ranked high in the socio-economic scale, benefitting from the privileges accorded to their colour.

The educational values of the whites had changed considerably since emancipation. Only 3.7 percent of the white Jamaicans were illiterate; the figure for Kingston was 4.8 percent and for St. Andrew 3.6 percent (table 13). By 1943 more than 60 percent of the whites had had or were receiving secondary schooling, pre-professional, professional, or practical training (table 14). White parents were using their incomes to purchase secondary education for their children, without which entry into white-collar employment and the professions was impossible. Privilege was used to perpetuate privilege. Many boys were educated at Woolmer's School or Jamaica College, while those with less ability were frequently sent to country boarding schools. Despite the high quality of the formal education that was by this time available in Kingston, wealthy parents still preferred an English public school for their children. The emphasis, even in Jamaica, however, was on teaching grammatical, non-technical subjects to a potential elite.

The pattern of mating among the whites changed considerably during the post-emancipation period. Christian monogamy became the norm—even among the lower class of whites. By 1943, 35 percent of the white population of Kingston were married and the figure for St. Andrew was 45 percent (table 15). Both rates were double the average recorded for the total population in each parish. Only minute proportions were engaged in common law unions (concubinage), and the number of persons involved in the city as a whole was exceeded by the number divorced. However, certain customs dating back to the period of slavery were retained. Women were confined to the home where their chastity was carefully preserved, though it was by no means uncommon for men to maintain separate households for their coloured or black mistresses.

The 1943 census contained no tabulation for the religious affiliations of the various racial groups. For the city as a whole, however, the Anglicans, Baptists, and Roman Catholics were most important, comprising between them more than 65 percent of the inhabitants. It was claimed that

the great majority of the upper class are members of the Anglican Church. There are a few Roman Catholics, but rarely if ever does the individual belong to any other denomination. "Good" works of the church are supported financially, but if the colour of the parson is "wrong" it may mean that upper class parishioners are absent from church. There is a conventional acceptance of the teaching of the Anglican Church in preference to others but there is no zeal for religion as such in the manner in which it is found in other classes.[18]

NEGROES

Sixty percent of the population of Kingston were Negroes, the largest and most ubiquitous of all racial groups (fig. 28). Nevertheless, segregation was quite marked in parts of West Kingston and in the area adjacent to Half Way Tree; the former was due to over-representation and the latter to under-representation of Negroes in the population. High concentrations were recorded in West Kingston, in separate clusters in East Kingston, and in settlements on the northern and eastern fringes of the city where the urban population graded into the peasant communities of rural St. Andrew. Many Negroes were confined to the slum areas of West Kingston, which had a low socio-economic status, high densities of population, poor housing conditions, and poverty. Although some had established themselves in median and high status areas in East Kingston and in the new suburbs south of Half Way Tree, low proportions were recorded throughout the elite areas of Central St. Andrew. The widespread distribution of Negroes and their ability to penetrate even elite areas was, of course, largely due to their association with domestic service.

The poverty of the Negro is writ large in the census data. Among the typically urban occupa-

tions, general labouring, manufacturing, construction, and personal service were most important for men, followed by transport and communication, professional and public service, and clerical work. Males were largely confined to manual occupations, though a few had achieved white-collar jobs in medicine, law, teaching, and the lower ranks of the civil service. These socially mobile Negroes inhabited between-the-wars suburbs in East Kingston and south of Half Way Tree. It is remarkable that almost none were entrepreneurs or involved in trade or finance. Employment was widespread among Negro women, and personal or domestic service accounted for half the wage earners. Other important occupations were general labouring, clerical work, and trade—the latter reflecting the involvement of women in market selling and higgling.

The low socio-economic status of the Negro is confirmed by income data. In the island as a whole, only 0.3 percent earned more than 100 shillings a week, while an additional 4 percent received between 40 and 100 shillings. Almost 60 percent of Negro wage earners earned less than 10 shillings a week, and the greater part of the population in Kingston suffered from poverty.

During the week ending 12 December 1942, 21 percent of Negro wage earners in Jamaica were unemployed; the figure for men alone was 20 percent. Similar rates undoubtedly applied in Kingston. Underlying and reflecting this poverty was their poor educational standard; 10 percent of the black population of Kingston were illiterate, as were 15 percent in St. Andrew (table 13). The Negro was caught in a vicious circle in which poverty prevented him from buying a secondary education for his children and from keeping them at school for regular intervals, while illiteracy and lack of grammatical and technical training condemned the lower stratum to an existence circumscribed by poverty. In 1943 fewer than 2.5 percent of the Negroes in Kingston had received or were receiving secondary schooling, and the figure decreased to 1.4 percent for St. Andrew and to 0.6 percent for Jamaica as a whole (table 14). Those in the city benefitting from practical, pre-professional, and professional training were negligible, though higher than for the entire island. Although Kingston offered better opportunities for education than the rural parishes, it seems likely that the rural areas lost their best-educated Negroes to the city.

The social system was largely regulated by the educational institutions of the colony. Consequently, the financially well-entrenched white minority could easily dominate the social and economic scene, while insisting that a free society existed without a legal basis for racial discrimination.

Mating patterns and family forms among the Negroes continued to distinguish them culturally from the white population. Marriage rates were less than half those recorded among the whites (table 15). Furthermore, the common-law union, which ironically has no standing in law, was widespread among Negroes, accounting for more unions than marriage in Kingston parish. There were several reasons for the prevalence of concubinage. The most important were

> the fear of a woman changing her behaviour, and the actual cost of the wedding. ... The female's fear of marriage is not so strong as the male's. It is a negative reaction rather than a positive one. But the feeling that a man may ill-treat her once he is her husband exists quite strongly. The woman has her independence guaranteed by concubinage. She can leave the man at any time, and he feels the same. In practice this does not take place but it is clear that the feeling of freedom, which is absent in marriage, is a powerful force in keeping such unions together.[19]

While concubinage and marriage among the Negroes in Kingston produced nuclear families similar in form to those of the whites, they were very different in content. Marriage became widespread only among the middle-aged, and households tended to be made up of half-siblings and other collateral kin. Extra-residential mating or visiting also remained important and provided an alternative to concubinage or marriage. In 1942 almost 70 percent of live births were illegitimate; the figure for Negroes alone presumably was higher. According to the census, more mothers were single than married or in concubinage. This illustrates the importance of visiting in initiating a girl's mating history and explains the prevalence of households headed by women.

It is clear, however, that more children had been born to married women than to either single mothers or to women in common-law unions. Since changes in mating patterns were associated with changes in the life cycle, these differences may be attributed partly to age and partly to the irregularity of sexual relations between persons engaged in visiting unions.[20] The orthodox clergy denounced this behaviour as immoral, failing to appreciate that "the black people have an entirely different conception of sexual morality from the coloured and white sections."[21] The Royal Commission, too, misguidedly attributed concubinage and illegitimacy to bad housing and overcrowding,[22] instead of seeing them in their cultural context.

Although Negroes were well represented in the congregations of the orthodox churches, the majority of these were persons who aspired to a high social rank. Orthodox churchgoing was one method of demonstrating status, but "to appear in a congregation badly dressed" was "to admit lack of respectability."[23] Many Negroes in Kingston, therefore, belonged to unorthodox sects which stood in direct line of cultural descent from the Native Baptists. According to Henriques, the "native" as opposed to the orthodox religious groups, relied "entirely on lower class support, and are served by a black "clergy." In origin they may be Jamaican, as in the case of the Bedwardites, or American, as the "Church of God"; in ritual they approximate more to the cult groups than to the orthodox churches."[24]

In 1953 Simpson carried out a study of revivalist cults in West Kingston, concentrating on districts lying within or adjacent to the slum areas depicted in figure 25.[25] These cults in decreasing order of age and preservation of Africanisms were Cumina, Pocomania, Revival, and Revival Zion. Cumina has been traced back to the period of slavery,[26] but while Revival and Revival Zion were no doubt continuations of the Native Baptist movement,[27] the source of Pocomania remains obscure. All these groups were characterized by their small size, rapid dissolution, and search for mystical experience under the guidance of a local leader. Although many low-status Negroes also belonged to the sects or orthodox churches, the cults were undoubtedly much larger than census data suggest; for cultists were widely condemned in Kingston for their anti-social behaviour and for their supposed association with obeah. It is likely, therefore, that many concealed their affiliations when interviewed by census enumerators.

The system of belief in West Kingston is best described by the term magico-religious. Literary sources included the Bible, especially the Old Testament, and an American publication called the "Sixth and Seventh Book of Moses." But much of the ritual was derived from West African tradition. So likewise were the beliefs in active spirits, souls, and duppies and the preoccupation with dreams, visions, and possession. Considerable emphasis was placed on healing, and balm yards were visited by the sick who attributed their illness to an evil spirit conjured up by an obeahman in the pay of one of their enemies. These cults provided an outlet for the social and economic frustrations of the inhabitants of West Kingston and supplied the means whereby Negroes could exercise leadership roles.

The geographical compactness of the impoverished Negro population of Kingston is a misleading guide to its social cohesion. Dog-eat-dog typified most inter-personal relations in West Kingston, and it is doubtful whether the yards provided the basis for more than minimal cohesion. Religious organisations were divided into small groups, each coalescing around a local leader. The Negroes tended to withdraw from involvement in society, and the relation between black and white remained both symbiotic and apparently harmonious. For the most part the Negro accepted his humble role and the colour values of the whites.

COLOUREDS

The coloured inhabitants constituted just over 30 percent of the population of Kingston and formed the second largest racial group in the capital. They were well represented throughout the central part of the city, but mostly concentrated in East Kingston and the new suburbs south of Half Way Tree (fig. 29). Although they made up more than half of the population in some of the tenement areas in West and East Kingston, their proportions were relatively low in most of the slum areas near the Spanish Town Road and on the northern limits of the city. The heaviest concentrations were associated with areas of medium socio-economic status (fig. 26), and some lay within the zone to which large numbers of cross-town migrants from Kingston parish had been attracted. Many coloured people inhabited areas of low status and high densities of population, but percentages equivalent to the average for the city were found in several of the elite suburbs located to the north of Half Way Tree. Nevertheless, the social status and geographical location of the group was typically intermediate between the Negroes and whites. Coloured people tended to dissociate themselves from the slums and to penetrate the expensive white areas.

While the coloured population, in general, was of median status, many members belonged to the higher or to the lower social echelons. This threefold division is revealed by the employment data. A higher proportion of coloured males than of Negroes were self-employed or employers, while the proportion engaged in agriculture was lower. Of the typically urban occupations pursued by coloured men, general labouring was most important, followed by manufacturing and mechanical work, construction, clerical work, professional and public service, transport and communications, and personal service.

Coloured men had achieved much greater success than Negroes in obtaining white collar jobs in the civil service and the professions and in acquiring artisan and technical skills. Furthermore, they were more deeply involved in trade and finance than the

Negroes, though less so than the whites. The percentage of coloured women who were self-employed or employers was higher than for any other group. This was offset by the large number of women who were employed, and by the high proportion of wage earners who were domestic servants. However, there were not as many coloureds employed in domestic service as there were Negroes, and coloured women had shown considerable initiative in obtaining clerical and teaching posts.

On the basis of this analysis, it is possible to divide the coloured population into three groups: an upper class of professional and business men, a middle class of white collar workers and skilled artisans, and a lower class of manual workers and domestic servants. The relatively high unemployment rate reflected the size of the lower-class element, though there is evidence to suggest that white collar employment was in short supply during the early 1940s. The distribution of incomes substantiates this threefold classification. While more than 5 percent of wage earners received more than 200 shillings a week, 32 percent obtained less than 10 shillings. Twenty percent, however, earned between 40 and 100 shillings a week.

The diverse characteristics of the coloured population are revealed again when aspects of culture are examined. The incidence of illiteracy among the coloured people was less even than among the whites, and the rate was lower in the suburbs than in Kingston parish (table 13). More than 80 percent of the coloured inhabitants of Kingston parish had received only an elementary education, but secondary schooling, pre-professional, professional, and practical training were more widespread than among the Negroes (table 14). An outstanding feature was the high proportion of coloured people in St. Andrew who had received or were receiving secondary schooling (21.9 percent). Furthermore, the information on secondary education confirms the relatively high status of many of the coloured inhabitants in St. Andrew. Similar educational and social distinctions existed between the Negroes in the older and newer sections of the city, though among them it was much less marked.

Mating patterns and family structure synthesized the institutions practised by the Negroes and whites. More than 60 percent of the coloured population in the city were single, a proportion equivalent to that recorded for the Negroes (table 15). Marriage rates were higher than those for Negroes, but lower than for whites; common law unions were less prevalent than among Negroes, but more widespread than among whites. In addition, the educational distinction between inhabitants of the older parts of the city and the suburbs was repeated for mating practices. Marriage rates increased in the suburbs, and the incidence of concubinage declined. Similar, though less marked, trends occurred among the Negroes in Kingston.

Marriage, concubinage, and extra-residential mating therefore formed alternative practices among the coloured population; the nuclear family was by no means the norm. The complexity of the situation has been admirably summarised by Henriques.

> The brown and black middle class have a dual attitude towards concubinage and marriage. Behaviour is not affected by colour to any extent. Nor is economic position necessarily the determining factor. The two attitudes are: (a) a rigid conception of marriage, and (b) an indulgence in more or less open concubinage. ... Individuals in section (a) however much they may object to the behaviour of individuals in section (b) will not admonish them openly. Here is an example of class solidarity due to the general uneasiness of the social positions. The distinction between these sections is purely concerned with a Christian moral and religious outlook, there is no economic differentiation. They both unite in condemning black concubinage.[28]

Modally, the coloured population were members of the non-conformist churches. Some, however, were Anglicans, while others belonged to the various cults and sects. It was in this group therefore that racial status and cultural practice were perhaps most divergent. Most of the coloured people subscribed to cultural practices which, while partly derived from the traditions of the Negroes and whites, were distinct from them, and particularly so in the way in which the institutional ingredients were combined. Although this analysis indicates the limitations of colour or race in providing an explanation of the social structure, in general a brown skin was associated with median status. Henriques' study is replete with examples of the way in which a light skin improved a person's employment opportunities, of dark professional men "marrying light," and of black civil servants being excluded from private parties consisting of fair people.[29]

JEWS

The social and economic significance of Jewish inhabitants, who made up only 0.4 percent of the population of Kingston, was out of all proportion to their numbers. They formed a highly segregated element and were concentrated in areas surrounding Half Way Tree and in districts adjacent to the Alpha Institute on South Camp Road in East Kingston (fig. 30). Jews were almost completely absent from the low-ranking districts, and were well represented in areas of median status and in some of the elite suburbs. Although many Jews still occupied old family homes in East Kingston and some remained in Kingston Gardens, they, like the whites, were abandoning the older suburbs for new homes on the sparsely populated plain near Half Way Tree. In geographical terms, the Jews were dissociated from the Negroes, partly associated with the coloured population, and highly associated with the whites.

Among the Jews, males participated heavily in trade and in clerical and professional jobs. An outstanding feature was the high proportion employed in manufacturing and mechanical work; professional and public-service fields were less important than among the whites, however. Only a small proportion of the males worked as manual labourers, and the community as a whole was outstanding for its association with the wholesale and retail trade. Since managers and businessmen were excluded from the index of occupational

status (fig. 26), care must be taken not to attribute too lowly a rank to many of the areas inhabited by the Jews and some of the other minority groups. The unemancipated position of women in the Jewish community is indicated by low activity rates, and those who were employed were concentrated in white collar jobs.

The census contains no cross-tabulations defining the cultural characteristics of the Jewish population. As far as the census was concerned, Jews by racial origin were synonymous with Jews by religion. Those who had been converted to Christianity were classified as part of the white population. The followers of Judaism remained a semi-endogamous cell. Nevertheless, they had access to the same educational and economic institutions as the Christain whites, and the family forms and mating practices of the two groups were similar. By 1943 the distinctions between the Portuguese and German Jews, which had been marked during the nineteenth century, had disappeared, and the group as a whole was both cohesive and socially mobile.

SYRIAN AND SYRIAN-COLOURED POPULATION

While some tabulations for the 1943 census refer only to the Syrian population, others relate to the Syrians and Syrian-coloureds. It is therefore necessary to examine the groups together or separately as the data permit. The small Syrian community made up only 0.3 percent of the population of the city and was concentrated in central St. Andrew and in the eastern suburbs adjacent to Up Park Camp (fig. 31). With the exception of their location in the dry goods section in central Kingston, the distribution of Syrians closely resembled that of the Jews and, to a lesser extent, the whites. There were literally no enclaves of Syrians in the dilapidated slums; rather, they were confined to the new, sparsely populated suburbs which recorded a median or high socio-economic status.

The Syrian-coloured population numbered only 100 and accounted for 0.05 percent of the inhabitants of Kingston. They were located in isolated groupings scattered throughout East and West Kingston and the better suburbs near Half Way Tree (fig. 32). The highest concentration was recorded at Vineyard Town in East Kingston, adjacent to the district containing the highest proportion of Syrians. Together with the colored population, they were found in areas of all social ranks, but principally in those of median and lower status. The Syrian-coloureds therefore partook of the distributional characteristics of their racial progenitors. Products of extra-marital unions between Syrian shop-keepers and Negro or coloured women, their status was lower than that of the Syrians both on the grounds of pigmentation and of illegitimacy. Their social status and their links with the Syrian population depended largely on support from their Syrian fathers.

The Syrians and Syrian-coloureds, like the Jews, were essentially an urban group. They formed an important trading community, and most members were self-employed. By 1943 they had achieved a considerable amount of mobility, with increasing numbers employed in clerical and professional occupations. Nevertheless, the role of women remained a traditional one; few were employed, and most of those were engaged in family firms.

The relatively high status of the community as a whole was reflected in the paucity of domestic workers and the low rate of unemployment. Distribution of income provides the best guide to the status of the Syrians, however. Almost 18 percent of wage earners received more than 100 shillings a week, while only 2.4 percent earned less than 10 shillings. Unfortunately, there is no information about the income of self-employed workers or of Syrian-coloureds.

One of the outstanding features among the Syrian and Syrian-coloured population was the low rate of illiteracy in St. Andrew (1.6 percent) and the relatively high rate in Kingston (11.5 percent) (table 13). This social and spatial distinction reflected the influence of the Syrian-coloured population in Kingston parish, and the role of the older parts of the city as reception areas for immigrants,

many of whom could hardly speak or read English. Furthermore, the younger, better educated, and socially mobile Syrians were moving to the suburbs of St. Andrew. By 1943 almost 40 percent of the Syrians in Kingston had received or were receiving a secondary schooling; in St. Andrew the proportion was nearly 55 percent (table 14). The former proportion was lower than for the whites; the latter, higher. This provides a measure of the social mobility that was taking place among the group and the way in which it was expressed by migration to the suburbs. Persons with professional and pre-professional training were no more widespread than among the coloured population. However, the ability of the Syrians to purchase a secondary schooling for their children indicates the importance of trade as a channel for social mobility. By 1943, therefore, the Syrians were repeating the experience of the Jews after emancipation. Like the Jews, the Syrians possessed phenotypical characteristics that were highly valued in Kingston.

Marriage rates for the Syrians were only a little lower than for the whites in Kingston, but in St. Andrew the high proportion of young Syrians depressed the rate (table 15). Common-law unions were more frequent than among the whites though this difference may be attributed to the Syrian-coloureds. But if concubinage was rare and endogamy the norm, some extra-marital unions must have occurred to produce the Syrian-colored population.

In religion, the Syrians were either Roman Catholic or Anglican. They continued to form an endogamous socio-economic cell within the white population, though the stigma attached to the Syrian pedlars was rapidly being discarded. While the Syrian-coloureds were Creole by race, the Syrians were becoming Creole by culture and association.

CHINESE AND CHINESE-COLOURED POPULATION

The 3,350 Chinese, who made up 1.8 percent of the population, were widely distributed throughout the city, excepting only the Negro districts on the Spanish Town Road and the sparsely populated northern limits of the built up area (fig. 33). The largest concentration of Chinese was in the western part of the central business district on West Street, Princess Street, and Orange Street. This China Town acted as the nerve centre for group activities in the city, and many of the premises were occupied by wholesalers who served the Chinese shops, which had been established at Cross Roads and Half Way Tree or were scattered throughout the suburbs. The Chinese still monopolised the grocery trade, and their wide distribution was a faithful reflection of this activity. They are the only group whose distribution is explicable principally in economic terms, and their avoidance of the slums and rural fringe represented adjustments to market conditions. By 1943 some Chinese were moving out to median-status suburbs.

The Chinese-coloureds in Kingston numbered 2,428 and accounted for 1.3 percent of the city's inhabitants. A product of miscegenation, the group remained closely associated with the Chinese population (fig. 34). They were widely distributed throughout the city and, like the Chinese, achieved concentrations in East Kingston. But they were absent from the fashionable suburbs, and the highest proportion was located in China Town itself. They were well represented in areas of median status where the coloured population was numerous, and some were distributed through the densely populated slums of West Kingston where they mingled with the Negro inhabitants.

Among the minority groups the Chinese formed the largest trading community. The majority were self-employed, but even among wage earners trade was the outstanding employer. It was a well-established procedure for the Chinese to launch newcomers in business, and an initial period spent as a shop-assistant usually provided training for management and, ultimately, ownership of a grocery, laundry, restaurant, or bar. In addition to their concentration in trade, there is evidence of a movement into white collar jobs and into manufacturing. The proportions employed in professional

and public services, however, were lower even than among the Negroes. Chinese families were large, and most women were fully occupied at home; but some worked in groceries and especially in family-run businesses. Moreover, clerical work, personal service, manufacturing, and professional and public service were of some importance among women. The low proportion of men in general labouring and of women in personal service indicates that the Chinese had avoided the lowest socio-economic levels in the community.

There is evidence of the Chinese using trade and the independence it provided to obtain a foothold in white collar posts. Emulating the Jewish and Syrian entrepreneurs, they steered away from the civil service in the direction of better paid jobs in the private sector of the economy. Although unemployment was no more prominent among the Chinese than among the whites, information about the income of wage earners suggests that the group ranked socio-economically beneath the whites, Jews, and Syrians but above the coloureds and Negroes. Five percent earned more than 100 shillings a week, and 6.1 percent less than 10 shillings. The census contains no information about the Chinese-coloureds, but it is likely that they ranked either with the Chinese or the coloureds or, in some instances, with the lowest paid Negroes.

In education the Chinese and Chinese-coloureds were gradually overcoming the problems associated with their recent arrival and initially low status. The rate of illiteracy (12-13 percent) was higher than among the whites, Syrians, and coloureds, and in Kingston parish, higher even than among the Negroes (table 13). Here the rate was affected by the immigrant community in China Town. In St. Andrew illiteracy was fractionally lower. The Chinese and Chinese-coloureds were more poorly educated than the coloured population but better qualified than the Negroes. Although the proportions receiving practical, pre-professional and professional training were low, almost 10 percent in Kingston and 17 percent in St. Andrew were benefitting from secondary schooling (table 14). In this way the proceeds from trade were invested in education; the returns were measured in social mobility and in greater social acceptance.

The Chinese remained endogamous, the nuclear family providing the basis for a certain amount of cultural conservation. Fathers were authoritarians, arranging marriages and deciding on the occupations of their sons, daughters, and wives. The high proportion of Chinese who were single was a reflection of the youthful age structure of the population, since most families contained about six children.[30] Taking the age structure into account, marriage was almost as common as among the whites (table 15). Concubinage, however, was quite prevalent and especially so in St. Andrew. At first concubinage was a response to the shortage of Chinese women. By the end of the post-emancipation period it was noted that

the invariable Chinese pattern is dual. Nearly always the man marries a Chinese wife. Concubinage is practised at the same time. Concubines are drawn from the black and coloured lower class. There is no racial antipathy on either side. In fact black women frequently express their liking for Chinese as their "Sweet Man," or keeper. The Chinese are famous for the care they lavish on their concubines as opposed to the casual treatment often exhibited by the coloured islander.[31]

This explains both the size of the Chinese-coloured population, their partial acceptance among the Chinese, and their concentration in China Town.

In the realm of religion the Chinese rapidly became acculturated, the Anglicans and Roman Catholics, in particular, attracting large numbers of converts. Some of the older people, however, clung to Confucianism and Buddhism, and a temple was located in China Town.

Despite their associations with the Creole community, the Chinese remained basically a conservative, introspective and, to some extent, a strife-ridden group. Until 1916 gang fights were common. After 1920 the population increased, and a number of cultural and trading associations were established.[32] A Chinese sanitorium, an old folks' home,

a Freemason's Society, and a public school were founded in the 1920s, and the Chinese Benevolent Society, which dated back to the nineteenth century, was re-formed. In the 1930s a Bakers' Association and Chinese Athletic Club were established, and, in 1943 the Chinese Retailers' Association was started. A number of newspapers and magazines were published, and in time more and more were written in English.

Ironically, as factions disappeared, conflict developed between the Chinese-born and Jamaican-born generations. Fewer children were sent back to the mainland or to Hong Kong for education, and many of those who attended schools in Kingston adopted one of the various forms of Creole culture. Financial links with Hong Kong, which had been vital in the establishment of the trading community, became more tenuous. Furthermore, the restrictions on immigration were tightened between 1920 and 1940; soon afterwards the quota was cut to twenty persons a year, and Chinese residents were allowed to bring in only wives and children.[33]

Despite the loosening of the ties with China and the gradual acculturation of the younger generation, the Chinese were subject to discrimination, and occasionally to violence. In 1938 the unemployed in Kingston looted Chinese stores, and the elite described their business activities as "an octopus sapping the life of the island."[34] Antagonism to the Chinese, however, was based as much on racial as on economic grounds.

The rest of Jamaicans are beginning to look at the Chinese wall, and it is not a friendly look; it is a look that bodes ill, and a threat to the continuance of internal peace. If the Chinese keep piling up wealth and hate behind that wall, giving back nothing to the community they may find it expedient to go back "home" sooner than they hope.... They hate to see their women folk fraternize with anybody else, though they fraternize with the women of other groups.... They hate Negroes more than all ... though they have bred more half-Negro children than anyother group during the past fifty years.[35]

The Chinese in turn suffered from racial discrimination, and were frequently called by the derogatory terms "John" and "Chinaman." The Chinese-coloureds, likewise, were discriminated against by the Negroes who coined the term "Chinee Royal." While acculturation was slowly taking place, endogamy preserved the racial distinctiveness of the Chinese group.

EAST INDIAN AND EAST INDIAN-COLOURED POPULATION

The East Indians, who numbered 3,600 and made up almost 2 percent of the inhabitants of the capital, formed one of the largest of the minority groups. It was, however, the least important. The East Indians were largely confined to West Kingston, though a few resided in upper-class areas near Half Way Tree (fig. 35). Above all, they were clustered on the fringe of the built-up area in the north and west of the city. Even in West Kingston the main centres were not the densely populated tenements, but the low density slum at Back O'Wall and the newer settlement at Cockburn Pen to the west of the Hagley Park Road. These major concentrations were situated on land which was owned by members of the same racial group. The East Indians shared the low status of the Negroes, but the two groups formed separate entities, both geographically and socially.

The East Indian-coloureds constituted 0.7 percent of the inhabitants of the city. Like the Chinese-coloureds and Syrian-coloureds, they reflected the distributional and social characteristics of their Asian forbears and the coloured and Negro populations. The highest proportions of East Indian-coloureds occurred on the northern limit of the city and along the Spanish Town Road in West Kingston (fig. 36). In both areas high proportions of East Indians were recorded. Although the East Indian-coloureds were associated with districts of low status, few were enumerated in the worst areas such as Back O'Wall. Furthermore, there is evidence for their penetration into median- and high-status areas, particularly in East Kingston and

south of Half Way Tree, and for their occurrence in some of the tenement districts from which East Indians were notably absent.

The East Indians in Jamaica were primarily a rural labour force, and even in Kingston large proportions were engaged in agriculture. Market gardening was important in West Kingston. At Constant Spring, in the north, tobacco growing was a major occupation. The main alternative to agriculture was labouring. East Indians had failed even more conspicuously than the Negroes to obtain office jobs, though they were better represented than the Negroes in trade. This was due to the contribution of the Bombay merchants; it was they who resided in the upper-class districts near Half Way Tree. The two East Indian groups, the Bombays and the offspring of the indentured immigrants, remained quite distinct, socially, economically, and culturally.

A greater proportion of East Indian women were employed than was the case among the Syrian and Chinese immigrants. The largest group was engaged in agriculture followed by personal service, labouring, and trade, probably higgling (table 31). Many of the women in central St. Andrew were undoubtedly domestic servants but few worked as clerks. The low social status of the group as a whole is indicated by dependence on labouring and personal service.

Although the East Indians recorded a high rate of unemployment, which exceeded even that among the Negroes, their incomes were slightly higher. Fewer than 0.5 percent of wage earners received more than 100 shillings a week, but more than 50 percent earned above 10 shillings. In economic terms the East Indians ranked on par with or above the Negroes; in social terms they were subordinate to them. But some of the East Indian-coloureds achieved a higher status than either the majority of Negroes or East Indians and mingled with the coloured population in the suburbs.

The low socio-economic status of the East Indians is further revealed by data relating to education. Illiteracy rates in Kingston and St. Andrew were higher than for any other groups; figures of

31.8 and 46.3 percent were recorded in the two parishes respectively (table 13). Moreover, in Kingston, fewer than 5 percent benefitted from secondary schooling or from professional and pre-professional training (table 14). The proportion was lower in St. Andrew, but in both parishes post-elementary schooling was more widespread than among Negroes.

Although the caste system had broken down among East Indians, the emphasis on family and marriage remained strong. Marriage was much more common than among the Negroes, and only a little less frequent than among the whites, Chinese, and Syrians (table 15). In St. Andrew, the marriage rate was second only to that of the whites. The relatively high rate of concubinage was apparently at variance with the persistence of traditional values. At this date, however, customary marriages performed for Hindus and Muslims were not legally recognised[36] and were treated by the census as common-law unions. But concubinage, in a Creole sense, also occurred and was by no means confined to mixed unions. Generally, racial endogamy was emphasised, and large families were valued.

The erosion of caste was accompanied by the erosion of Hinduism.[37] Although 40 percent of Jamaican Hindus were located in the capital, no more than one quarter of the East Indians in Kingston were members of this religion. Muslim East Indians were either few in number or non-existent. But despite conversion to Christianity and the virtual disappearance of Hindi, certain Indian cultural traits were retained and grafted on to the new institutions. Even among Christians a katha, or prayer reading, usually accompanied by a dinner, was frequently held on the eve of weddings. Hindi kinship terms were still used, and roti remained an important dish. Furthermore, the term "Maharaj" was applied to members of the Brahmin varna, and Hindu priests were drawn from it.

East Indians formed a peripheral element in both a geographical and social sense. R. T. Smith found that "identification with the 'homeland' is minimal, and so there has been very little attempt, except in Kingston, to develop a pride and self-consciousness within the Indian group as a whole."[38] Even in the capital the East Indians tended to accept and play the role of coolie. Socially mobile men frequently made mixed marriages in preference to unions with poorly educated girls of their own race. Children of these unions were usually accepted among the East Indians in Kingston, though they were known to the Negroes by the derogatory term "Coolie Royal."

SOCIAL CHANGE

Despite the social and economic changes that occurred in Kingston during the post-emancipation period, the relationship between race and status remained close. But only the whites, Syrians, and Jews were unmistakably high ranking; the coloured, Negro, East Indian, Chinese, and mixed groups all appeared at various levels in the society and in a number of distinct locations in Kingston. The link between race and its symbol, colour, on the one hand, and social status on the other, was weaker than during slavery, and the process of "improving the colour" no longer conferred mobility of a socio-legal nature. Legal strictures were replaced by race, culture, and socio-economic status as the fundamental determinants of status, and the three variants of Creole culture, which had been established during slavery, were modified. Furthermore, the social status of certain members of the non-white groups changed, and even the Creole whites relinquished power in 1865 in favour of British trusteeship. Nevertheless, white domination was maintained. Within the three hierarchically arranged strata, social rank depended on colour and above all on culture and socio-economic status. Occupation, education, family, and religion were highly related, and the division of the coloured population into three socio-economic classes was undoubtedly an accurate guide to the three-fold cultural composition of the group.

Racial endogamy was maintained to a marked degree among the Jews, Syrians, Chinese, and East

Indians, and their social relations were primarily with members of their own group. The recent immigrants, in particular, remained as cellular entities exhibiting varying degrees of acculturation and assimilation to Creole society. In addition to their high social status, the Jews enjoyed considerable authority and power during the post-emancipation period, and as early as 1860 persons of Jewish name accounted for 11 of the 47 members of the House of Assembly.[39] They suffered relatively little loss of status after the introduction of Crown Colony government, unlike the coloured population whose progress was undoubtedly slowed down by the new constitutional arrangement. The Syrians and Chinese were fortunate to have arrived at a time when trading links with Britain were being loosened and opportunities for retailing in Kingston were improving. But all these groups possessed a phenotype that was more socially acceptable to the whites than that of the Negroes.

The low status of the Negroes, East Indians and, to a lesser extent, some of the coloureds is revealed in poverty, poor housing, and unemployment. Furthermore these groups were effectively excluded from the franchise. Before the end of slavery, unemployment in Kingston had affected the free coloured population and the lower class of whites. By the end of the post-emancipation period it was virtually confined to persons of low status. During slavery the provision of employment for the free-coloured and poor-white populations had been considered of no importance by the elite; after emancipation unemployment among the Negroes was attributed to idleness. Throughout slavery and the post-emancipation period, family connections and colour provided the passports to jobs. If employment was not available for people with influence it was created. But for those who were inferior in the eyes of the elite only low-grade jobs were found, and if these posts were rejected unemployment was the alternative. Two additional factors affected the incidence of unemployment: the reduction of the poor white population and the rapid growth of the Negro element, which, after 1838, was competing in a free labour market.

While a person's place of residence depended solely on financial considerations, these were largely defined by ascriptive factors such as family, colour, and education. Education was a purchasable commodity, and no attempt was made to ensure that secondary schooling was available to the poor. The laissez-faire social outlook of the whites discriminated against the Negro. Immigrants who were launched in business from footholds overseas were able to make their way upwards in the social scale. Generally speaking, social mobility was difficult to effect. Mobility within the strata depended on promotion at work or on "improving the colour."

Movement between the strata required acculturation, and the strata themselves remained as almost immutable categories. Friendships were circumscribed by factors such as colour, occupation, and income. Genotype was most important in the upper stratum and phenotype in the median. Dark people of median rank tried to improve their standing by associating with the lighter skinned, and brown men who married black women ran the risk of committing social suicide.

Despite the disappearance of tribal groups and the adoption of Creole English as the language of the lower stratum, social cohesion was only rarely attained among persons of low status. But when the disturbances broke out in 1938 the symbiotic relationship between the strata rapidly disappeared. Alexander Bustamante led the workers and the unemployed along the streets of Kingston and through the sugar estates, "and his offer was their demand, a better life here and now, in a country of which they formed the majority, but from whose society they had been actively excluded."[40] The Governor called in British troops and the disturbance quickly petered out. A West India Royal Commission was sent to the Caribbean, and ultimately made a series of recommendations, which became the points of departure for social and economic change. The People's National Party was formed by Norman Manley, a light-coloured barrister of considerable distinction. Its political philosophy was nationalist and socialist and it drew its support from the median stratum in Kingston. While the riots of 1938 provided the stimulus to change from within, they also created two organised forces, the People's National Party and the Bustamante Industrial Trade Union. These were to have an important impact on life in Kingston in the period of decolonization which began in 1944.

V: Social and Economic Change, 1944-1960

In 1944, in response to the riots of 1938 and to the agitation of the People's National Party for internal self-government, Britain allowed a general election to be held in Jamaica on the basis of univeral adult suffrage. Ministerial government was introduced and gradually extended after 1945. In 1953 the office of Chief Minister was created; in 1957 cabinet government was initiated; and in 1959 Jamaica became internally self-governing as a unit within the British West Indies Federation. The protracted period of decolonization was marked by the emergence of two major political parties, the People's National Party (PNP) and the Jamaica Labour Party (JLP). The latter was formed on the eve of the general election in 1944 as the political wing of the Bustamante Industrial Trade Union, and it polled 41.4 percent of the votes against the PNP's 23.5 percent. Power now was transferred to the median and lower social strata, and members of the upper echelon were forced to accommodate to the reallocation.

Bustamante, the charismatic leader of the JLP, developed no political programme but sought to preserve the very social order at which his movement was directed. A combination of Messiah and pragmatist, he remained uncommitted to any particular course of action, yet flexible enough to select from the PNP's radical socialist policy. Opportunities for rapid change were reduced further by the emergence of members of the middle stratum as leaders of the political parties and their trade union wings. The withdrawal of white colonial civil servants in the 1950s confirmed the transfer of political and bureaucratic power to the middle stratum, though local whites continued to form the commercial elite in Kingston. During the post-war period, therefore, the middle stratum, through its office holders, played an increasingly important role in defining goals for development.

In 1944 the PNP's nationalist policy had antagonised the upper stratum and failed to appeal to the lower ranks, who demanded more rather than less paternalism. The academic, socialist philosophy of the PNP failed to make much impact on the lower stratum. Moreover, the party's advocacy of nationalisation of the sugar industry and the public utilities alienated the elite together with many middle-ranking persons who otherwise sympathised with its nationalist ideals. Between 1944 and 1952 the upper stratum either voted for the JLP, abstained, or supported one of the minority parties. Many members of the median stratum who were unable to reconcile themselves to the PNP's socialist policy also abstained. In 1955, however, when power was more firmly invested in the local leadership, it became essential for the upper and middle strata to commit themselves to a political party.

The PNP had ousted its Marxist element in 1952, and by 1955 had espoused economic development and federation. This appealed to most members of the upper and median strata. Nevertheless, the success of the PNP at the 1955 election was primarily due to the large number of votes obtained through its trade union affiliate, the National Workers' Union, and through the calculated projection of Manley's charisma. Despite this political realignment, most of the poorest inhabitants continued to regard Bustamante as their redeemer. In addition an element in the elite, composed mostly of businessmen who were suspicious of the PNP's reforms, supported the JLP and used it as a bulwark against Manley's "socialism." The initial success of the PNP's programme resulted in its re-election in 1959.

During the course of the 1940s and 1950s the democratic system ensured that social and economic change gradually became political goals. Between 1955 and 1962 the PNP administration made an outstanding attempt to promote change by developing agriculture, tourism, and bauxite mining; by extending secondary education to a wider cross-section of school children; and by industrialisation. Structural change in Kingston hinged on the last two schemes in particular. In addition, a modest programme of slum clearance was embarked on, using funds provided by the British Government. Local leaders acknowledged that political action was required to modernise the community, to combat underdevelopment, and to expand wherever possible those schemes that had already been undertaken. It was realised that a policy of gradual social change would be difficult to promote without economic expansion and industrialisation, especially since the pace of population growth was accelerating.

POPULATION GROWTH

During the intercensal period 1943 to 1960 the population of Kingston increased by 86 percent to 379,600, while the population of Jamaica grew by 30 percent to 1,606,500 (fig. 8). Between 1943 and 1953, when a sample survey of population was undertaken, the number of inhabitants in the capital expanded from 202,900 to 289,200, giving an annual rate of growth of 3.7 percent. From 1953 to 1960, however, the rate rose to 3.9 percent, thus providing a clear measure of accleration. This acceleration was in part a function of the island-wide rise in natural increase from 15.3 per thousand in 1943 to 34.0 in 1960. The birth rate rose from 33.2 to 42.9 and the death rate was halved from 17.9 to 8.9. Between 1943 and 1960, 142,390 persons were born in Kingston—St. Andrew. Although many country women came to the capital for their confinement only to return to their home areas immediately afterwards, natural growth undoubtedly comprised the greater part of the total increase of 181,187.[1]

In addition to the natural increase, the population of Kingston experienced a net gain of 83,789 by internal migration, and a net loss of 44,904 caused by overseas migration, mostly emigration to Britain. The high level of emigration from Jamaica as a whole contributed to the relatively slow increase in the country's population, especially after 1953 (fig. 8). Nevertheless, internal movements were maintained at a high level. By 1960 almost one-quarter of Jamaica's population lived in Kingston, and the city's growth in that year almost equalled the population of Montego Bay (24,000), which had replaced Spanish Town as the second largest settlement in the island. Indeed, the role of internal migration expanded throughout the period, and in 1960, when the Department of Housing estimated that the population of the capital was increasing by about 20,000 persons per annum, half the growth was attributed to migration from the rural areas.

MIGRATION

Migration to Kingston resulted from real push factors and largely illusory pull factors. The most important push was population pressure, the rural symptoms of which were unemployment, land shortage, and declining soil fertility. Shortage of land was related to the pattern of land ownership as well as to population distribution and growth; for more than 45 percent of the island was still controlled by nine hundred individual proprietors or companies. Hoarding of land and shortage of land existed side by side, as they had since emancipation, the former ensuring the latter. As a result of this induced population pressure, few small farmers could purchase or rent a sufficient area on which to support themselves and their dependents without additional employment for wages. In many instances the problem was compounded by seasonal unemployment in the sugar industry. Moreover, the wages paid to casual agricultural labour were frequently so low as to be virtually unacceptable. In 1955, 62 percent of the males and 32 percent of the females in rural Jamaica were looking for work.[2] These figures provide an index of population pressure and a measure of the reservoir of potential migrants.

A further stimulus to migration was provided by the values and aspirations of boys and girls in rural Jamaica. Country children rejected the socially stigmatized agricultural pursuits of their parents, usually with their encouragement, and aspired to professional, white collar, or technical jobs, which were predominantly urban in location.[3] While the amenities and higher wages of the capital clearly operated as pull factors, Kingston appeared particularly attractive to migrants because it was believed that opportunities for non-manual jobs were greater there than in other parts of the island. Since newcomers who failed rarely returned to their home areas, the myth of the city of opportunity was maintained. Migration to the capital therefore became the geographical expression of an attempt on the part of the Negro to escape from the poverty and isolation of rural Jamaica; there was no aimless drift to the towns.

URBAN EXPANSION

Urban development was characterized by slow suburban growth and infilling between 1947 and 1952 and by rapid suburban expansion between 1952 and 1960 (fig. 14). Despite the quickening tempo of house-building during the latter period, it was only partly geared to the needs of the rapidly growing population (fig. 9). Some of the patches of recent housing in West Kingston indicated the progress of re-development schemes, but many apparently new dwellings represented the regeneration of squatter camps. By 1960 the suburbs were pressing against the foothills of the Blue Mountains, and opportunities for urban growth were largely restricted to the western part of the Liguanea Plain. At the end of the colonial period, therefore, the western section of the last of the concentric zones of urban development was being completed. In 1960 the first suburb beyond the Liguanea Plain was started at Harbour View, to the east of Long Mountain, on the delta laid down by the Hope River (pl. 1; fig. 2).

LAND USE AND HOUSING PROBLEMS

The land-use map for Kingston prepared by the Town Planning Department in 1952 (fig. 37) contains more information than the 1947 survey (fig. 24), and it is difficult to make detailed comparisons between them. But there is relatively little difference in the broad patterns they show. In 1952 the commercial area occupied the original town plan, and the wharves were still located at the bottom of the north-south streets. Commercial premises continued to penetrate the suburbs, and

the Half Way Tree Road (fig. 13) was a major thoroughfare along which change occurred. A large number of small shops were also concentrated on the Spanish Town Road. In this area, and along the Foreshore Road too, several factories had been located, though many industrial enterprises still occupied sites adjacent to the commercial area. Outstanding features were the high ratio of private to public open space (fig. 37)—there being a marked deficiency of parks in West Kingston—and the large amount of property owned by the government. This included the major institutions in the north and east of the city as well as the public offices on King Street and between the Parade and the Race Course. Furthermore, the government became increasingly involved in land-use problems, especially in areas of poor (third class) housing, predominantly in West Kingston.

Areas of poor housing were virtually coterminous with the slums that had been depicted in 1935 (fig. 25). Indeed, relatively little improvement in housing conditions in the capital had taken place between the 1943 census and the sample survey of 1953. The proportion of buildings with concrete walls increased from 20 to almost 50 percent, but corrugated iron remained the basic roofing material. Furthermore, 10 percent of households still depended on water from public stand-pipes, while more than 30 percent had access only to pit latrines. By 1953 no fewer than 68 percent of all households in the metropolitan area occupied accommodation of no more than one room. The housing problem, like unemployment, had become an established feature of the city's socio-economic system; both severely tested the power of the government to effect change.

Squatting persisted and even intensified after 1944, and 3,752 persons were enumerated in four camps in West Kingston in 1951. The four areas together represented "the worst example of slum life in the island."[4] The largest squatter settlements were at Trench Town (2,613), Dung Hill (285), and Kingston Pen (Back O'Wall) (844). The camp at Back O'Wall had been in existence at least since 1935. Only one of the 1,282 squatter households possessed a bath room, 75 percent had no sanitary convenience, and 83 percent were without a kitchen. The structures themselves were flimsy: more than a quarter were movable.

Household incomes averaged £2 a month, and separate rooms were frequently rented out to tenants to provide an additional source of money. Consequently, overcrowding was widespread in the squatter settlements, and many shacks housed three or more people. The most heavily populated camp, Trench Town, was on property belonging to Boy's Town. It had a density of 216 persons an acre. The property at Kingston Pen was privately owned, but the other two sites belonged to the government. This reflected the vigilance of private landlords and their determination to evict squatters. In contrast, the government adopted a passive but tolerant attitude, though in an attempt to deter migration to Kingston, the government refrained from improving facilities in the squatter camps.

As a result of the hurricane in 1951 a survey of housing conditions was undertaken in the middle-income areas of the capital[5] in which the annual income ranged between £300 and £800. Most of the households were located in areas of first- and second-class housing (fig. 37), and especially in East Kingston to the south of Up Park Camp and in central St. Andrew to the south of Half Way Tree. Seven thousand houses were visited, 4,800 in St. Andrew, and 2,200 in Kingston. Approximately 94 percent of the dwellings in middle-income areas were of one story. Of these, 60 percent had been damaged by the hurricane, but only 4 percent had originally been in poor condition.

Fewer than half the households owned their own homes, and there was a marked tendency for rented accommodations to be overcrowded. On average, houses contained 1.6 households, each with its own budget: 70 percent were occupied by one household and the remainder by two or more households. An index of overcrowding was computed based on the need for bedroom space. The standard which was established required that persons of the opposite sex should not share the same bedroom unless they were under ten years of age or were living together

as man and wife, and that no more than two people should occupy each bedroom (children under ten were counted as half a person). According to these criteria, 27 percent of the houses were overcrowded; the figures for Kingston were 41.6 percent and for St. Andrew 19.6 percent. Although overcrowded dwellings accounted for only just over a quarter of all the houses surveyed, they contained more than 40 percent of the population at an average density of 8.6 persons per house. Furthermore, most of the overcrowded premises were occupied by two or more households. There was a clear link between overcrowding and renting, and it was finally recommended that 53 percent of the overcrowded households—2,000 families—needed rehousing.

The persistence of slums in West Kingston, the extension of squatting, and the overcrowding in middle-income areas all represented symptoms of population pressure at various levels of living. Although these symptoms were affected either directly or indirectly by the rapid increase in the population, they were by no means equally serious. Together, however, they constituted one of the major urban problems during the period preceding independence.

GOVERNMENT TOWN PLANNING

The increasingly active role played by government in promoting change in Kingston was exemplified in the area of town planning. Although a Government Town Planner had been appointed in 1947, it was not until 1950 that a Planning Department was established in Kingston. The Town Planning Department was given no more than consultative powers, and the collection and mapping of information, with the exception of that relating to land use and population, was never undertaken. The change of government in 1955 had an impact, for the PNP stressed the necessity for planned development, a reflection of its socialist origins.

In 1958 the first Town and Country Planning Law came into operation enabling Provisional Development Orders to be placed on any area in the island. In the same year, the Government Town Planner was given the authority for interpreting the physical development aspects of Jamaica's first ten-year-plan, but this programme made no mention of either regional or town planning. Most of the subsequent work of the Planning Department was confined to the tourist area adjacent to Ocho Rios on the north coast. In Kingston planning activities were restricted to the siting of a link joining the northern suburbs to the Spanish Town Road—the Washington Boulevard (pl. 2; fig. 13)— and to the layout of government housing schemes. Through these sub-divisions, the government began to play an important role in developing land-use patterns. The initial intervention of the government, however, was not a spontaneous response to widespread need; just as the earthquake of 1692 had stimulated the planning of Kingston, the catalyst, in 1951, was provided by the hurricane.

HOUSING SCHEMES

The hurricane, like the earthquake and fire of 1907, created conditions that simply could not be ignored. In response, the British Government made available a grant of £1.24 million and a loan of £1.01 million toward the cost of repairing the damage in Jamaica. Between 1951 and 1959, the greater proportion of 2,700 houses built in urban areas by the Hurricane Housing Organization were located in Kingston. The scheme was initiated during the JLP administration, but it is generally agreed that the pace of construction was stepped up after 1955, when the PNP took office and realised that unless the grant was spent the funds would revert to the British Government.

Rehousing schemes were located on part of the site of the hurricane-destroyed squatter camp in Trench Town (fig. 38), at Long Mountain Pen and Norman Range in East Kingston, and at Tower Hill, Cockburn Pen, and Majesty Pen on the western periphery of the city (figs. 13, 38). With the exception of Trench Town and Cockburn Pen, these developments were located in open spaces and

involved the transfer of population from established slum areas. At Tower Hill and Cockburn Pen self-help methods were employed, and most of the buildings were constructed of wood, stone, and concrete. In other areas the houses were built to government specifications: at Trench Town large dwellings were provided for multiple accommodation. Apartments were located on the Spanish Town Road near Cockburn Pen, but most of the facilities in this scheme were provided on a shared basis, as they also were at Majesty Pen. Majesty Pen was one of the worst designed of the schemes. Households were allocated single rooms in buildings reminiscent of plantation barracks; kitchens had to be built in the yard by each household. Hurricane rehousing was sold at a variety of prices, but the government made a grant of 57 percent towards the cost, and the remainder was payable at the rate of 2 percent per annum over twenty years.

The Central Housing Authority embarked on a number of schemes which were also located on the flanks of Long Mountain and in West Kingston. Most of these were single-room dwellings that could be sub-divided into two rooms (pl. 10). In 1956 the Department of Housing was set up to co-ordinate the work of this agency and that of the Hurricane Housing Organization. By 1959 some 40,000 people had been housed in government schemes throughout Jamaica,[6] and more than a quarter of these were in hurricane rehousing. No detailed information is available for Kingston,[7] but it is clear that while many people had been rehoused, little headway had been made toward the removal of slum conditions. Furthermore, by the late 1950s the annual increase in the population of the capital was completely outstripping the efforts of the government to provide more houses.

A large proportion of the post-war suburbs was the work of private builders. After the PNP came to power in 1955 a number of middle-income housing schemes were begun on the periphery of the city, for which the government provided land at below market prices and also guaranteed the mortgages. The earliest middle-income scheme was at

Mona Heights on a 200 acre site that had originally been offered to the Federation of the British West Indies for its capital city. Seven hundred and twenty three-bedroom houses (pl. 5) were built at a price of £2,900 each. This undertaking was followed by slightly cheaper schemes at Pembroke Hall (pl. 2) and at Harbour View (pl. 1), the latter with more than 2,000 detached, single-storey units. The most expensive developments were at Trafalgar Park and at Shortwood, and in both instances the houses cost between £3,500 and £5,000. These schemes represented the first effort by the government to co-operate with private capital in the field of housing, and the earliest attempt to relieve overcrowding and to sponsor housing development among the middle-income group.

The PNP government derived its strongest backing from the coloured middle stratum in Kingston; no doubt it seemed logical to reward its supporters in this way. Housing policy reveals the importance of sectional interests in Kingston, and the close relationship between social structure, government action, and planning at this period. The development of Bluecastle, on the western edge of Mona Heights, as a civil-service housing scheme was a blatant example of rewards being given to a particular interest group. Nevertheless, the re-election of the PNP in 1959 when it took all but one of the seats in the capital, including the constituency in West Kingston, reflected its apparent success in the field of housing.

EDUCATION

The PNPs demand for equal opportunities in its manifesto of 1940 was essentially a call for peaceful revolution. This revolution could most easily and speedily be effected by the expansion of facilities for education and by ensuring availability to the population on the basis of merit rather than of wealth. In 1957 the government's educational policy was based on three fundamental principles:

(a) that every child should obtain a primary education—that is to say that buildings, teachers, equipment and services must be provided on a continuously expanding scale sufficient to provide universal primary education for all children between the ages of 7 and 11 inclusive.

(b) that the system should provide to the fullest extent that our finances will allow for further educational opportunities to those children who possess special ability in order that we may out of our own resources fill the needs of the community for trained people to take their place in industry, agriculture and farming, trade, commerce and the professions and provide for ourselves the special services which the country requires.

(c) that the educational opportunities provided by the Government should be open and available to all on the basis of genuine equality.[8]

Secondary education was considered important partly because of the shortage of economic skills and partly because it would provide an avenue for social mobility. The "National Plan" looked forward to "the progressive and steady increase in the numbers and sections of the community from which are drawn pupils receiving full-time education in Government and Secondary Schools, of Grammar School type, from the present figure of 10,000 to a total of 26,000 in ten years' time."[9] In 1957 a scheme was initiated under which 1,500 free places were awarded for entry to the Grant-Aided Secondary Schools. This award was made on the basis of the Common Entrance Examination, and by 1958 approximately a quarter of all the children in these schools were recipients of government grants. Furthermore, about 10 percent received an additional allowance to purchase books and to meet living expenses, and there is evidence that awards were being made to children from poor homes.[10]

Against this, however, must be set the knowledge that half the scholarships awarded between 1958 and 1960 were allocated to children from private schools and that the overwhelming majority of their parents could easily have afforded to pay for secondary education.[11] Although these children amounted to only a small proportion of the 11 to

13 age group, their social, educational, and cultural backgrounds gave them a marked advantage over their peers in a competitive examination.[12] The overcrowding of government primary schools formed an additional handicap for children from the lower stratum.[13] A factor of major social importance was the discrepancy in the subsidy provided to primary and secondary schools. In 1960 the government's allowance to secondary schools was £30 per child as against £2 in the primary schools.[14] This was interpreted in certain quarters as benefitting one section of the population at the expense of the largest group in the society. Furthermore, it demonstrated the extent to which the PNP had been captured by the middle stratum.

Nevertheless, great improvements in education clearly took place between 1943 and 1960, and these are illustrated by census data (tables 14, 16). Illiteracy rates were cut by almost a third in Kingston and by about a half in St. Andrew; in Jamaica as a whole the reduction was less. In all cases, literacy rates were higher among women than among men. The results in secondary education were even more striking, and especially so in the capital where persons with secondary schooling for the first time outnumbered the illiterate. The number of persons benefitting from a secondary education in Kingston and St. Andrew doubled, and in Jamaica as a whole more than doubled. By 1960 between 10 and 20 percent of the persons in the corporate area who were over 10 years of age had had, or were receiving, secondary schooling. However, these statistics do not necessarily indicate an improvement in the over-all quality of education; it seems that most children were ill fitted by the educational system for the jobs which were available in the community.[15] Furthermore, although the award of scholarships accelerated the rate of potential acculturation, especially between the lower and median strata, it did not disrupt social stratification. Indeed, the system of awards, like the middle income housing schemes, provided a means of social recruitment and involved virtually no restructuring of society.

INDUSTRIALISATION AND THE ROLE OF GOVERNMENT

Economic expansion, unequalled since the end of the eighteenth century, took place in Kingston during the 1940s. The shortage of consumer goods occasioned by the Second World War forced import substitution on a fairly large scale, and industries manufacturing the following articles were introduced or rapidly expanded: garments, hose, boots and shoes, tyre retreading and vulcanizing, perfumes, edible oils and fats, cornmeal, and stock feed. Established industries producing consumer goods for the home market also expanded, the increase in output being outstanding for concerns processing beverages and oil products. Moreover, exports of cigars, cigarettes, sugar, and rum increased rapidly between 1939 and 1946. But while the national income rose from £20 million in 1938 to £40 million in 1943, unemployment remained persistently high in Kingston, and the economy of the city continued to depend on the import-export trade.

After the war successive Jamaican governments laid considerable stress on the necessity for economic development. It was argued that, given the small size of the home market and dearth of natural resources, a high standard of living could be achieved only by exporting manufactured goods.[16] Furthermore, the terms of trade for manufactures were superior to those for agricultural products. Trade, therefore, was to remain the mainstay of the economy, but the basis was to be broadened to include manufactured goods.

Throwing the imperial policy of the eighteenth century into reverse, the government set out to encourage industrial development in Kingston. The legislation enacted to further this policy supplemented pre-war measures such as the Coconut Industry Aid Law (1931) and the Safeguarding of Local Industry Law (1935). The major statutes consisted of the Hotel Aid Law (1944), the Textile Industry Law (1944), the Cement Industry Law (1948), the Motion Picture Industry Law (1949), and the Manufacture of Buttons Law (1949). Tariffs which under the system of laissez-faire had been used only for raising revenue were increasingly employed for protection; and, in the case of the cement industry, a domestic monopoly was guaranteed. The year 1949 was crucial in this strategy since during it the Pioneer Industry Law was passed. This became "the fountain head of subsequent legislation in aid of industrial development in that it had a general application to industry and did not aim at the development of specific industries."[17] The Pioneer Industry Law was designed to encourage local entrepreneurs to engage in manufacturing for the domestic market and was modelled on techniques evolved in Puerto Rico. Income tax and import duty concessions were provided for a variety of industries which were not already established in the island on a substantial scale (table 17). These arrangements were particularly attractive to local firms and to the subsidiaries of foreign firms. But British and American companies were liable to be taxed on profits which were repatriated.

In 1952 the Industrial Development Corporation (IDC) was established in Kingston to "stimulate, facilitate and undertake the development of industry." Jamaican thinking about industrialisation was revealed in the first annual report of the corporation which disclosed that "its origins lay in the growing awareness of the very serious problem presented by the pressure of population on existing resources."[18] The government's objective was to provide employment for the increasing population and not specifically to produce more wealth; the emphasis was placed on social efficiency rather than on economic considerations. The IDC concentrated its attention on the capital. An industrial estate of 300 acres was established on reclaimed land at Three Miles in West Kingston and was provided with electricity and water. The IDC granted direct loans to provide working capital and supplied a variety of other services including market surveys and feasibility studies; in certain cases factory buildings were constructed for rental. However, only a limited number of local capitalists

were prepared to invest in manufacturing, and in 1956 two new incentive laws were prepared. These were designed to appeal particularly to investors from overseas.

The Industrial Incentives Law (1956) enabled concessions to be granted to any industry, old or new, provided the government was satisfied that it would benefit the country. Both economic and non-economic considerations were taken into account. Enterprises manufacturing approved consumer goods (table 18) were entitled to either 100 or 50 percent of the benefits of the law, the decision resting with the Governor-in-Council. This law provided for the same customs concessions as the Pioneer Industry Law, but established two alternative formulae for the operation of the tax holiday and depreciation. Dividends could be distributed tax free provided the recipient was living in Jamaica or in a country that did not apply double taxation. If tax would have to be paid in the investor's home country as a result of the Jamaican exemption, the concession was withheld and the tax collected locally.

The legislation embodied in the Export Industries Law (1956) was potentially the most attractive to foreign investors, and especially to established firms which already had an outlet for their products. Firms operating under this scheme were not allowed to sell in Jamaica; their initial imports of machinery, all imports of raw materials and fuel, and exports of finished products were exempt duty. Furthermore, they were allowed to choose between the tax reliefs offered by the other incentive laws. The proximity of Jamaica to the eastern United States, its position between the capital resources of North America and the markets of South America, its location in the sterling area, and its access to Commonwealth tariff preferences were thought to make Jamaica an ideal location for "free port" manufacturing. The two new incentive laws were more sophisticated than any legislation previously enacted and were symbolic of the PNPs determination to embark on national planning.

Between 1952 and 1960 the IDC was responsible for the establishment of 58 firms in Jamaica. Most were located in Kingston, and all received tax concessions; 22 operated under the Pioneer Industries Law, 17 under the Industrial Incentives Law, and 19 under the Export Industry Law. Although on average only six firms were attracted each year, the figure exceeded nine in 1957, 1958, and 1959. The acceleration was due principally to the Export Industry Law. This law influenced the nature of the industries that were attracted. The consumer goods approved by the government became more specialised, garments in particular making up the vast majority (table 19). Furthermore, all the firms operating under this law were of North American origin, the greater proportion being United States concerns. The high value-to-weight of the finished products enabled them to be flown to market, usually in the United States.

In an attempt to examine the significance to manufacturers of a variety of locational factors and to evaluate the importance of tax concessions, 58 firms operating under incentive legislation were sent a postal questionnaire in 1961. Fifteen firms replied, four Jamaican, eight United States, two Canadian, and one British. The response was biased—Jamaican concerns being under-represented and United States firms over-represented. Twenty-four operating factors were considered, and all were cited by firms as both advantages and disadvantages (fig. 39). The combined information for these firms has been assessed by calculating an advantage ratio for each factor, this being the number of firms citing each item as an advantage divided by the number citing it as a disadvantage. Any factor with a ratio of more than one may be interpreted as a net advantage in the view of the firms concerned.

The advantage ratios for each factor have been listed in order of significance. When all the scores are combined, the advantages of Jamaica as an industrial location outweighed the disadvantages (combined advantage ratio 1.89). The outstanding factor according to these firms was the availability of tax exemption, followed by low wage rates, the attitude of the community, and the efficiency of machinery and equipment. The principal disadvan-

tages were the shortage of skills (though most firms employed unskilled workers), the high cost of electric power and transport, the absence of raw materials, and the unreliability of the labour force; namely the traditional obstacles to industrialisation which the incentive laws and the foreign entrepreneurs were supposed to overcome. A similar survey carried out by Taylor[19] among United States firms in Puerto Rico showed almost identical results, the overall advantage ratio being slightly higher (1.96). The comparison can, however, be misleading. The period of tax exemption in Puerto Rico was longer than in Jamaica, and double taxation did not apply to United States firms. Furthermore, the fact that the number of new factories in Jamaica in the late 1950s barely equalled one-tenth of those in Puerto Rico indicates the marginal nature of these successes when viewed in a Caribbean context. Nevertheless, there was some comfort in the thought that Jamaica was still at the beginning of its programme.

Although the attempt by the government to stimulate industrialisation made only a small inroad in the non-industrial structure of the economy of Kingston, it should be judged above all by its impact on employment. Most of the factories sponsored by the IDC were in Kingston, and these firms employed 3,451 persons in 1960 and created approximately 450 jobs each year. Assuming, as the IDC did, a multiplier effect of two, the total number of jobs created in all sectors of the economy cannot have exceeded 900 a year. Over a period of ten years fewer than 10,000 jobs had been created in this way. This figure was almost equalled by the number of migrants who were arriving in the capital each year during the late 1950s. Since firms associated with the IDC provided 3,400 new jobs out of the 9,000 added in all factories in Kingston between 1949 and 1960, or more than half the factory employment created since 1952, the conclusion reached by W. D. Voelker is particularly significant: "Assuming Jamaican I.D.C. plant employment grows as rapidly as in Puerto Rico, there will be about 40,000 more people employed in Jamaica in ten years—but in Jamaica about 400,000 more people will have been born."[20] The basic problem stemmed from the fact that manufacturing relied increasingly on automation and was capital, rather than labour, intensive; the average cost of creating each new factory job was estimated at £2,000.[21] Furthermore, in the long term the availability of cheap labour was probably more critical for foreign-owned businesses than the incentive laws as such. But competition between the two unions, the Bustamante Industrial Trade Union and the National Workers Union, was liable to push wages higher and higher and eradicate this attraction.

The manufacture of garments was the most successful of the footloose industries in Kingston. Skilled seamstresses were plentiful, as they had been since emancipation, and wages were only a fraction of those existing in New York where the trade unions were well established. But employment for men was in short supply, both in this and in other industries. By 1960 two-thirds of the employees in factories established by the IDC were women. There was therefore no sign that manufacturing, even with government help, would be able to create sufficient new jobs in the future to eradicate unemployment, and establish a stable basis for the development of the higher standard of living to which the poorest elements in the population were increasingly aspiring.

DEVELOPMENT AND EMIGRATION-COLONY AND CAPITAL

Although the pace of change accelerated during the post-war period, it is difficult to capture the optimism of the years between 1955 and 1960. At the end of 1959 the *Jamaica Times* reported "industry is booming, spearheaded by the activities of the Jamaica I.D.C.," and the only daily paper, the *Gleaner*, concluded that "industry made great strides; trade and commerce multiplied; housing development and other construction were such as the island had never seen before. Tourism prospered."[22] But neither source revealed the part played by a massive hire-purchase boom in inflating the economy. This reached dangerous proportions and encouraged wide-scale indebtedness among the middle stratum.

Between 1954 and 1960 the sale of electricity to industry doubled to 50 million kilowatt hours, and by 1960 it was widely believed that the economy had reached the "take-off" level. Per capita national income at current prices rose from £32.5 in 1943 to £128 in 1960, while the Gross Domestic Product increased from £70 million in 1950 to £230 million in 1960. This rate of growth was exceeded by only two other countries, Puerto Rico and Japan. The major contributors to the G.D.P. in 1960 were wholesale and retail distribution (£39.5 million), agriculture, forestry and fishing (£29.6 million), and miscellaneous services (£29.6 million), followed by a new group of activities: manufacturing (£29.4 million), construction and installation (£26.1 million), and mining (£21.5 million).[23]

Between 1950 and 1960 the total number of long and short stay tourists visiting the north coast trebled from 74,800 to 226,900. In Kingston, however, economic development depended principally on trade, manufacturing, construction, and government service. Trade, of course, embraced the import and export of commodities, and it is noteworthy that the value of overseas transactions increased about eightfold between 1938 and 1956.

Although progress was made, certain fundamental problems remained. The contribution of agriculture to the G.D.P. increased very slowly, from £24.0 million in 1954 to £29.6 million in 1960, despite the government's farm development programme. Land settlement schemes and land authorities were initiated, but no comprehensive system of land reform was undertaken. These conditions directly affected the rural population, encouraged migration and therefore impinged on the housing and employment problems in Kingston. Furthermore, incomes remained generally low and unequally distributed. While 92 percent of the classified labour force earned less than £300 a year in 1959, 20 percent of the remainder received more than £1,000.[24]

Given these economic structures, the outstanding examples of social mobility occurred through politics. After 1944 the majority of elected politicians were brown or black. By 1951 the lower chamber was "more representative of the colour characteristics of Jamaica than any other high status group."[25] Even so, the darker elements were under-represented, if one's sole criterion was proportionality, and this was still true in 1960. A marked change also took place in the racial composition of the civil service. Brown and black civil servants replaced white expatriates as permanent secretaries and other high-ranking officials. The bureaucracy was expanded and provided a major avenue of advancement for educated Negroes. An element of self-congratulation crept into public references to race. In 1961 Norman Manley, the premier, described the British West Indies, and Jamaica in particular, as "made up of people drawn from all over the world, predominantly Negro or of mixed blood, but also with large numbers of others, and nowhere in the world has more progress been made in developing a non-racial society in which also colour is not psychologically significant."[26] But by this time Negro racist organizations in Kingston were becoming increasingly belligerent.

Perhaps the most paradoxical feature of the period was the large volume of emigration to Britain. Despite the high rate of economic growth, the number of migrants annually from Jamaica increased from 2,000 to 39,000 between 1953 and 1961. More than two-thirds of the migrants were inhabitants of the rural areas, and their departure was associated with the slow rate of economic growth in the agricultural sector. However, variations in the rate of migration were determined more by demands for labour in Britain than by fluctuations in economic conditions in Jamaica.[27] Throughout the island there was a permanent demand for outlets, as there had been during the second half of the nineteenth century. By 1960 it was clear that despite the efforts of successive governments to promote social and economic change, structural realities provided major obstacles to innovation. The problem was especially acute in Kingston where natural increase was being constantly augmented by in-migration. Government planning and co-operation between the public and private sectors in the fields of housing, industry, and education formed a marked contrast with the unplanned growth of the population. Undoubtedly the main safety valve for population pressure was provided by emigration to Britain, though this was a personal rather than a government-inspired solution. Emigration was no panacea, but it was vitally important in Kingston, where it was responsible for siphoning off potential cityward migrants and for actually removing more than 45,000 people from the capital between 1943 and 1960.

VI: Urbanisation in Kingston on the Eve of Independence

In 1960 Kingston was the capital of a colony on the eve of independence. However, it was not generally anticipated that Kingston would ever become the capital of an independent state. Jamaica was a member of the West Indies Federation which had been formed in 1958 after eleven years of negotiation between the islands and the British Government. The date of independence had been fixed for 1962, and plans were being made to build a capital at Chaguaramas, Trinidad. There was every likelihood, therefore, that while Kingston's pre-eminent position among the towns of Jamaica would not be affected, its functions would be downgraded and certain members of the bureaucracy lost to the federal capital.

Although Kingston had a population of 379,600 and contained more than 70 percent of the Jamaicans who were living in settlements with more than 1,000 residents, no attempt had been made to demarcate a city boundary or to create an organization capable of administering the urban and suburban sections of Kingston as defined by the 1960 census. The Kingston and St. Andrew Corporation was still responsible for administration within the urban, suburban, and rural areas of its jurisdiction, and certain offices of local government were maintained at Half Way Tree. But the corporation was responsible only for fire, roads, public health, and poor relief, and the pressing social and economic problems of the capital were left to the central government.

LAND USE

The first detailed survey carried out in Kingston by the Town Planning Department was the mapping of land use at the scale of 1:1,250. A generalized version of that map provides an introduction to the spatial structure of the capital in 1960 (fig. 40). Retail shops were located in several areas, the largest and most prosperous of which were situated in the central business district, especially to the south and west of the Parade (Victoria Park). Within this area high-class shopping was confined to King Street and in particular to the section between the parish church and Barry Street (pl. 6). The west side of King Street generated a higher volume of pedestrian traffic, and probably of customers too. It was on the shady side of the thoroughfare and shielded from the afternoon sun. The poorest element in the population rarely frequented this area, except as beggars and car-watchers, though a change in clientele took place during the late 1950s when a Woolworth's was opened. The great majority of stores, however, were owned by Syrians, Bombay businessmen and, to a lesser extent, Chinese.

The area to the south and west of the Parade was concerned almost exclusively with the sale of dry goods and here the majority of the shops belonged to Syrian traders. Further south, on Princess Street, Barry Street, and Orange Street most of the premises were owned by Chinese retailers. Developed around the grocery trade, this China Town also contained modern supermarkets, laundries, restaurants and bars. But it would be incorrect, even at this date, to suggest that wholesaling and retailing were completely divorced. Both aspects of trade were maintained side by side by some Chinese grocery firms on West Street. Furthermore, on Harbour Street manufacturers' agents both wholesaled and retailed articles supplied by British and North American firms. Most of these concerns were owned by Jewish businessmen or were limited liability companies formed either by local capitalists or by groups with trading interests throughout the West Indies.

The commercial area acted as the focus for the city's car and bus flows but parking spaces were inadequate to cope with the traffic. Furthermore, the main roads leading to the northern suburbs were incapable of carrying peak-hour traffic efficiently. Between 1949 and 1960 the number of cars in Kingston increased from 7,900 to 19,500, and in 1948 buses replaced trams as the medium of public transport.

Subsidiary shopping centres were located at Cross Roads and Half Way Tree. Each had a branch of the largest chain of supermarkets and the former, a Woolworth's store. Smaller centres containing groceries, barbers' shops, and pharmacies were situated at Matilda's Corner, Mary Brown's Corner, Four Roads, and Papine (pl. 11).

Retailing premises were also distributed along the ribbon developments which followed the main lines of communication. The Slipe Road, Old Hope Road, Half Way Tree Road, Maxfield Road, and, above all, the Spanish Town Road carried clear traces of this type of development. At the junction between West Queen Street and the Spanish Town Road (pl. 12) the Syrian dry-goods shops gave way to the stalls of pots and pans, groceries, restaurants, bars, and food shops of West Kingston. Further west, along the Spanish Town Road, the ferroconcrete of the central business district was replaced by wooden and concrete sheds. These sheds housed vendors eking out a living from sales of cheap food, clothing, and alcohol. In addition, groceries and bars were located on street-corner sites throughout the densely populated tenements (pl. 13).

In the western section of the capital shops encountered competition from street vendors (pl. 12) and market sellers. Higgling was concentrated at the Coronation Market in West Kingston, but fruit was also sold by women on most street corners. Street higglers were liable to be "moved on" by the police, but the risk was more than offset by the dues charged in the city's markets. Conditions of extreme poverty in West Kingston gave rise to an illegal market situated on the Spanish Town Road slightly beyond Three Miles. A wide variety of vegetables and ground provisions was on sale, though there was no market supervisor and no control over hygiene. The market specialised in charcoal and supplied fuel for the cooking pots of West Kingston.

Two further aspects of retailing deserve attention. A market still stood at the foot of King Street on the site originally occupied by the Negro market. Now called the Victoria Market, it specialised in the sale of local handicrafts to passengers from North American tour ships which visited the island in spring and autumn. Owing to the size of the city, the congestion of traffic in the downtown area,

and the wealth of the suburban inhabitants, a centrifugal movement occurred within the retailing sector of the capital's economy. Commercial premises rapidly invaded the Half Way Tree Road, one of the busiest arteries. In an attempt to control this process, the Town Planning Department undertook a road line study in the area. More important still, a group of businessmen launched a new commercial centre immediately to the north of the Half Way Tree Road on the site of the former Knutsford Park Race Course at New Kingston (figs. 13, 16). Although the lots were rapidly surveyed and bought, no building had taken place by 1961 (fig. 40). It was widely rumoured that the scheme was simply an exercise in land speculation, and that the purchasers could neither afford not to buy the land as an insurance against the decline of the central business district nor afford to develop it unless they transferred their trade to the new site. Simultaneously Tropical Plaza was developed by a local businessman on a more modest site adjacent to the Constant Spring Road to the north of Half Way Tree. A number of speciality shops, a supermarket, a pharmacy, and several offices, almost all air-conditioned, were laid out on three sides of a large car park. The plaza's clientele was drawn from the northern suburbs, where most residents owned a car.

Kingston possessed a professional quarter composed of insurance agents, real estate agents, solicitors, barristers, doctors, and dentists which was located on Duke Street to the east of the main shopping centre. It provided adequate parking facilities for clients yet was close to the law courts and public transport facilities on King Street. A similar clustering was also found at Cross Roads. Banks fell into a category of their own, since they provided private services in conspicuous locations. The largest banks were Canadian- or British-owned and were situated on King Street and at Half Way Tree. Near the latter, a Canadian bank provided drive-in facilities.

In 1960 Kingston was still the largest port in Jamaica, handling 40 percent of the island's exports of sugar, 90 percent of its trade in general cargo—

especially the imports of consumer goods and brand-name foods—and almost all its imports of refined petroleum. Land devoted to wholesaling was largely confined to the area between Harbour Street and the "finger" piers. Ships calling at the port rarely exceeded 6,000 tons, and facilities for handling, storing, and transporting goods remained antiquated. Improvements were confined to the building of warehouses for certain export crops such as coffee and cocoa. These warehouses, located on the Marcus Garvey Drive in West Kingston, within easy access of the cramped port, were operated by government statutory boards. The proximity of the wharves to the central business district, the use of donkey carts for haulage, the narrowness of the streets, and the frequency of intersections added to the congestion of the commercial area.

Measured quantitatively, the contribution of industry to land use in Kingston was still small. As in 1952 (fig. 37), factories remained scattered throughout the southern and western sections of the grid, though the majority were confined to small sites on the fringe of the central business district. Some concerns were located in St. Andrew, especially on cheap land adjoining the Sandy Gully. The major modern concentration was in West Kingston. Concerns financed by local capital were situated on the Spanish Town Road at Three Miles, having removed from premises in central Kingston. The Industrial Development Corporation's industrial estate mainly provided sites for firms established by foreign investors. This was an efficient location for industry, since West Kingston had relatively easy access to the port via the Marcus Garvey Drive.

The growing influence of the government on the pattern of industrial and residential land use has already been discussed. In addition, the government made a direct impact through its public buildings, utilities, institutions, and parks. The earliest purpose-built government offices in the capital were erected on King Street after the earthquake and fire of 1907; these were still used in 1960. With the expansion of government functions during the post-war period, new offices were opened in the area to the northeast of the commercial area. Here the large mansions of the late Victorian period provided suitable accommodation (pl. 3). By 1960 both East Race Course and South Race Course were occupied by government departments (pl. 14), all with easy access to the new House of Representatives (pl. 15) which had been built adjacent to Headquarters House in the northern part of the grid. Executive branches of both the local and the national governments were also located at Cross Roads and Half Way Tree. There was a marked tendency for government offices that were not frequented by the public to be built inland away from expensive and congested sites near the city centre. Dilapidated offices were being replaced by modern structures, and in some instances a concentration and rationalization of functions occurred.

Public control over water supply and broadcasting contrasted with Canadian ownership of telephones and electricity. These utilities clustered like beads along the thoroughfares linking the downtown area with Cross Roads and Half Way Tree. Schools and hospitals, the penitentiary, mental hospital, Up Park Camp, King's House, and the campus of the University College of the West Indies (fig. 13) were largely confined to the eastern section of the city. However, there was a gradation from the prison and mental hospital in southeast Kingston to King's House and the university in the northeast, with Up Park Camp placed strategically in between.

In contrast with the large areas occupied by these institutions and by Up Park Camp in particular, there was a marked shortage of public open space throughout the rest of the city. Parks were confined to the Parade (Victoria Park), the Race Course (George VI Memorial Park), and the Hope Botanical Gardens. The last occupied part of the former sugar plantation of Hope Estate, while the University College, slightly to the east, contained the ruined aqueduct, sugar factory, and much of the land which had once belonged to the Mona Estate. Recreation was therefore confined largely to facilities supplied by churches, theatres, cinemas, and sports and social clubs—the private sector. Some of these were located in the eastern half of the eighteenth-century grid, but most were situated on or near Windward Road, Slipe Road, and Half Way Tree Road as well as at Cross Roads and Half Way Tree, since proximity to main lines of communication and to a suburban clientele were crucial locational factors.

Cinemas represented the most popular form of entertainment; the newest, air-conditioned buildings were at Cross-Roads. A drive-in cinema had been constructed on Washington Boulevard in the suburbs of northern St. Andrew. But West Kingston was particularly lacking in recreation centres, though the area had several churches, cinemas, and branches of the Y.M.C.A. and Y.W.C.A. The tenement districts were well supplied with bars. Night life was confined to Cross Roads and Half Way Tree, while the "red light" area was located in East Kingston, especially in districts adjacent to Harbour Street and the Windward Road.

The distribution of sports' grounds followed a similar pattern, with West Kingston once more revealed as underprivileged. It was particularly unfortunate, therefore, that although attempts had been made to persuade the government to build the new National Stadium at Tinson Pen to the south of the Spanish Town Road, a site adjoining Up Park Camp in East Kingston was preferred. Despite the growing influence of the government over decisions affecting land use, a large proportion of the open space on the periphery of the built-up area, especially in the west and northwest, was privately owned. Encouraged by the government's proposal to control Sandy Gully, speculators had already subdivided much of the neighbouring land (pl. 2).

The Town Planning Department divided residential properties into three categories: good, medium, and poor (fig. 40). Good housing was located in the northern and eastern suburbs. In these areas four-fifths of the households occupied dwellings constructed of durable materials such as reinforced concrete, brick, or stone (fig. 41).[1] Poor housing was concentrated in the yards and tenements on the north side of the Spanish Town Road in West Kingston and also occurred in isolated clusters adjacent to the gully courses in the northern suburbs and in restricted areas in central and East Kingston (pl. 16).[2] In most of these districts fewer than 50 percent of the households occupied dwellings of concrete, brick, or stone, and a correspondingly high proportion inhabited small wooden buildings or simply shacks (fig. 42). Housing of medium quality occupied an intermediate geographical position between the two extremes.

There was therefore a tendency for the quality of buildings to be related to their age, and for residential land use to be associated with patterns of urban growth (fig. 14). In the east, however, much of the older housing was described as medium quality, while in the west the recent government housing schemes ranked either as medium or poor. The magnitude of the housing problem was revealed in 1960 when it was estimated that 120,000 people, or one-third of the city's inhabitants, were living in dilapidated accommodation, the greater proportion being concentrated in West Kingston.

DISTRIBUTION AND DENSITY OF POPULATION

By mapping data published for the 830 enumeration districts into which Kingston was divided for the census of 1960, it has been possible to depict areas of distinctive population distribution and density (fig. 43). Population density decreased from south to north and from west to east, the highest densities being associated with the tenements and yards in West Kingston. To a marked degree the population distribution coincided with land-use patterns. The central business district and port area recorded densities of fewer than 40 persons per acre. On its periphery, however, densities rose to between 100 and 400 persons per acre. The largest concentration and highest density was associated with the single story tenements of West Kingston (pl. 17). In these areas buildings had been constructed one behind the other until almost the entire plot was covered. Densities ranging from 2 and 320 persons an acre and decreasing towards the outskirts characterised the zone on the fringes of this tract. More than 29 persons per acre were recorded in the shack yards and government housing schemes in West Kingston, and only in the north did they fall much below 10 persons per acre.

Low densities prevailed throughout the northern suburbs, though isolated population concentrations occurred on the banks of the storm-water gullies which dissected the Liguanea Plain (pl. 7). These outliers formed pockets in the areas of relatively dispersed population and corresponded with the outliers of poor housing (fig. 40). However, in only one area did the density exceed 90 persons per acre.

The distribution of population in 1960 was similar to that recorded in 1943 (fig. 18). Densities were markedly higher in 1960, though the central business district recorded a decline.[3] But the increases were by no means uniform, and the southeastern and western sections accounted for a remarkably high proportion of the intercensal growth. The western tenements and yards, in particular, increased rapidly in population, but expansion also occurred along the Spanish Town Road and many of the victims of the 1951 hurricane were relocated at Tower Hill and Cockburn Pen. These changes were accompanied by the rapid growth of the population in the central and northern suburbs. By 1960 only 14 percent of the population of St. Andrew was described as rural (fig. 8).

LAND VALUES

In 1961 the property owned by the government, was widely dispersed, and only in West Kingston did the government possess tracts large enough to enable it to influence development. Nevertheless, the government acquired potential power over future land use through the system of Provisional Development Orders and it proposed eventually to introduce a new system of rating and taxation based on unimproved values. These values repre-

sented "the sum that a plot might be expected to realize at the time of valuation if offered for sale and if no improvements had been made."[4] Under this system dilapidated premises which were situated within areas of high value would be subject to the same levy as new buildings. It was hoped that this method of valuation would stimulate development in the decaying parts of the city and in those areas where speculation was rife. In addition, it would increase the government's revenue, since rateable values in Kingston had not been revised since 1937 unless property had changed hands. This had discouraged mobility and had been an important factor influencing the persistence of retailing patterns, especially among the Chinese and Syrians.

A preliminary map of unimproved land values has been prepared using data provided by the Land Valuation Commission (fig. 44). This map is based on property sales in Kingston in 1960 and 1961 and complements and summarises many of the patterns of land use and population which have already been analysed. Unimproved values exceeded 30 shillings a square foot throughout both the central business district and the area occupied by wharves and warehouses. Highest values reaching 200 shillings a square foot were recorded on the western, shaded side of King Street, while the intersection with the peak value (slightly more than 200 shillings) was formed by King Street and Barry Street. Moving outwards from the central business district, values decreased in a series of almost concentric bands and throughout most of the suburbs ranged between 0.61 and 1.62 shillings a square foot.

Values exceeding 30 shillings a square foot were recorded along the Slipe Road and at Cross Roads, Half Way Tree, and the embryonic New Kingston. Furthermore, high values occurred in the newest of the high-ranking suburbs at Barbican in northeastern St. Andrew. The eighteenth century grid in its entirety was valued at more than 11.5 shillings a square foot, but values dropped more rapidly to the west of the central business district than to the east. Indeed, relatively high values obtained throughout East Kingston. The whole of the foreshore in West Kingston was quite valuable and so were many of the oldest, most densely populated tenement areas on the fringe of the central business district. The lowest values ranging between 0.23 and 0.61 shillings a square foot were confined to an enclave located at Mona Heights, where the government had provided land cheaply for the middle-income housing scheme, and to a larger belt including the yards and government housing schemes of West Kingston. Great discrepancies between land value and land use occurred in the area of the tenements and on the foreshore in West Kingston. Even more outstanding was the polarisation between parts of West Kingston and central and northern St. Andrew with regard to land values, residential land use, and population density. Throughout central and northern St. Andrew (pls. 18, 19, 20), population densities dropped below 10 persons an acre (fig. 43), and land values ranged between 0.61 and 4.31 shillings a square foot. These properties were, of course, large, expensive, and in good condition (fig. 40).

EMPLOYMENT AND UNEMPLOYMENT

Despite the economic changes which had taken place, the pattern of employment in Kingston in 1960 (table 20) remained basically similar to that in 1943 (table 9). Furthermore, the employment structure of the city still differed markedly from the national pattern. This was explained by the low proportion of the urban labour force which was employed in agriculture and by the correspondingly high proportion which was engaged in manufacturing, personal service, construction, and public service. Public service describes the occupation of most of the people who had been placed in the category "other" by the census. In most capital cities it might be expected that approximately two-fifths of the labour force would be employed in public service and more than 10 percent in the construction industry. But the low proportion involved in manufacturing (24 percent) and, in par-

ticular, the high proportion still engaged in personal service (21 percent) indicate a continuing weakness in the employment structure of the city. Moreover, the census figures showing that 38,700 persons were employed in manufacturing gave an inflated picture of factory employment. Manufacturing concerns with ten or more workers employed only 17,000 people in Kingston in 1960.[5] Probably no more than 10 percent of the classified labour force worked in factories, even when account is taken of enterprises established through the Industrial Development Corporation. Over half the people described by the census as employed in manufacturing were undoubtedly seamstresses, carpenters, and other self-employed workers.

There was also a marked difference between Kingston and Jamaica as a whole with regard to the distribution of employees in the various occupational groupings (table 20). In only one grouping—manual and service—did the proportion of the island's labour force (61.3 percent) exceed that of the capital city (40.6 percent). In professional, supervisory, clerical and sales, craft and technical occupations, and non-professional occupations that required special training, the proportions recorded for Kingston were much higher than for the island as a whole. Although a relatively high proportion of the urban labour force was employed in the clerical, technical, and professional occupations to which rural Jamaicans and, furthermore, most Kingstonians aspired, over 40 percent was engaged in manual and service occupations.

The problem of economic development was compounded by the rapid growth of population; as a result of natural increase and in-migration, the annual increment to the labour force approached 10,000 persons. The task of finding additional employment on this scale was made almost impossible by the large numbers in Kingston who were already out of work. According to material published by the 1960 census, 18.4 percent of the city's potential labour force of 179,000 was either voluntarily or involuntarily unemployed.[6] Part-time employment also was widespread in Kingston, and 30 percent of the classified labour force of 169,000 received employment for less than five days during the week preceding the census. Over 10,000 people in Kingston were looking for their first job, and they accounted for almost one-third of the total number of unemployed; approximately 70 percent of this group was under 21 years of age,[7] and unemployment was chronic among school-leavers. These conditions were primarily the result of secular and not of seasonal, frictional, technological, or cyclical unemployment; they had existed in Kingston for almost thirty years and were associated with "an economy in equilibrium so that there is always a reservoir of involuntarily unemployed."[8] Unemployment which had been originally cyclical or associated with trade cycles had been transformed during the 1940s and 1950s into a permanent feature of the socio-economic structure of the city.

Unemployment in Kingston increased from 15.5 percent of the potential labour force in 1946, to 18.4 percent in 1960. In the latter year the figure for the island as a whole was 12.6 percent. The population of Jamaica was slowly concentrating in the capital, and so was unemployment. By 1960 more than half the unemployed Jamaicans were residing in the corporate area.[9] Opportunities for work failed completely to meet the expectations of rural migrants, and it is significant that 36 percent of the males and 51 percent of the females who were looking for their first job in 1960 had been born in the rural parishes of the island. Manufacturing could not absorb the rapid growth of the population, and no system of social security existed to cushion the effects of unemployment. In these circumstances the personal-service industry was important as an employer of domestic servants, gardeners, yard-boys, and odd-job men but at wages barely above subsistence rates.

Using full-time unemployment as the first criterion, it can be seen that conditions of population pressure had persisted in Kingston throughout the period 1944 to 1960; at the latter date 33,000 members of the potential labour force were affected. Since the potential labour force made up almost 50 percent of the population of the city, the total number of workers and dependents who were directly affected by unemployment may be estimated as at least 60,000.

Two maps have been prepared showing the distribution of involuntary full-time unemployment (fig. 45) and part-time unemployment (fig. 46) among the population aged over fourteen. The former, which defines the areas experiencing "hard core" unemployment, corresponds with the general pattern of population density (fig. 43). However, the relationship is only partial; for although the tenements of East and West Kingston record high population densities, they did not suffer conspicuously from full-time unemployment. The highest incidence, which surpassed 39 percent, occurred at Tower Hill, a government housing scheme on the western extremity of the city, where the population density was decidedly lower. The highest rates of unemployment in West Kingston ranged between 20 and 30 percent. These were confined to areas peripheral to the tenements and, in particular, to some of the shack yards which lay adjacent to the Spanish Town Road. Rates of unemployment were generally low throughout the suburbs, but some increase was recorded in the pockets of denser population which followed the Barbican Road.

A closer association with high densities of population is shown in the map of part-time unemployment. Although the highest rate of more than 57 percent was once more recorded at Tower Hill and two distinct zones of unemployment are in evidence in the central and northern suburbs, the yards and tenements suffered quite noticeably from part-time unemployment. In these areas the rates rose from 16 to 41 percent. A map showing the distribution of persons seeking their first job has also been prepared (fig. 47). On it distribution corresponded closely with the areas of full-time unemployment.

OVERCROWDING

The overcrowding of dwellings in Kingston was one of the clearest indices of the persistence and growth of population pressure. Following standard procedure, the Town Planning Department defined as overcrowded dwellings in which there were more than two persons per habitable room or more than eight people to each hygienic water closet. Applying these criteria to data supplied by the 1960 sanitary survey and by the 1960 census, areas were demarcated in which overcrowding existed (fig. 48). The sections which were badly affected were confined to the single-story tenements and yards of West Kingston and, in lesser degree, to central and East Kingston. In contrast, the northern suburbs enjoyed better conditions, with the notable exceptions of the pockets of dense population on the banks of the storm-water gullies. Although overcrowding was widely associated with poor housing (fig. 40), especially in West Kingston, its incidence is more logically explained by the distribution and density of population (fig. 43). Some overcrowding was experienced wherever densities exceeded ten persons per acre, and severe overcrowding occurred wherever densities surpassed 100 persons per acre. However, while there is a cartographic relationship between high densities of population and overcrowding, some areas which recorded low densities of population also suffered from this condition. This occurred because most areas in West Kingston lay beyond the zone served by the public sewerage system (fig. 49; table 21). The absence or inadequacy of facilities, such as cess pits, in certain of the sparsely populated parts was simultaneously a product and an index of population pressure.

A further contributor to the problem of overcrowding must be taken into account, namely, house tenure (table 22). By far the greater proportion of housing was rented in the form of tenements, rooms and flats (table 23; fig. 50), and in the yard districts of West Kingston shacks had been constructed on rented lots. Throughout the sections of the city built before 1920, fewer than one-third of the dwellings were owned by their occupiers, and only in the central and northern suburbs did the percentage exceed 50. As at previous periods, there was a marked tendency for overcrowding to be associated with letting, and for the availability of rented accommodations to encourage overcrowding. Furthermore, suburbs in which rented accom-

modations were relatively scarce tended to record low densities of population, and where fewer than half the households were living in rented dwellings overcrowding was slight or non-existent.

While overcrowding was associated with various types of unemployment and with tenancy, much of the rented accommodation in West Kingston and inner East Kingston was dilapidated, and some lacked sewerage facilities. Conditions in these areas were exacerbated by inadequate water supply. Throughout the greater part of the city, including the tenements, more than 75 percent of the households received public supplies of piped water in their dwellings (fig. 51). But the proportion dropped to below 25 percent in some of the densely populated sections of West Kingston and in the overcrowded "pockets" in St. Andrew. Yards were served by public water supplies on a communal basis; in many instances groups of yards shared a stand-pipe. The availability of water for irrigating the lawns and gardens of the northern suburbs emphasized the deprivation of some of the overcrowded sections of the city.

Between 1943 and 1960 the percentage of households in the corporate area relying on pit latrines had decreased from 54 to 39, while the proportion inhabiting dwellings constructed of concrete had increased from 13 to 53 percent.[10] Nevertheless, by 1960 more than half the households in the capital still occupied no more than one room, and approximately one-third of the inhabitants were living in substandard accommodation.

The combination of poor housing and overcrowding created slums in West Kingston and part of inner East Kingston which were virtually coterminous with the derelict areas recognized in 1935 (fig. 25). Although some rehousing had been effected in these areas, in general they were characterised by population increase and social stagnation; the high rates of secular unemployment exemplify this condition. By 1960, therefore, the distinction between the slums and the better areas was as marked as, if not more marked than, it had been in 1943; gross population densities at the two dates support this contention.

In 1960 the Central Planning Unit of the government of Jamaica estimated that 80,000 people were living in overcrowded accommodation in Kingston. Most were in West Kingston or inner East Kingston, and many were confined to areas which suffered from unemployment. According to the census, half the household heads who were looking for work were tenement dwellers. The number of persons directly affected by both unemployment and overcrowding was remarkably similar and suggests that these phenomena were closely connected.

ADAPTATIONS TO POVERTY AND OVERCROWDING

In West Kingston population pressure affected even the most elementary human requirements, outstanding among which were housing, work, and food. The solution to these basic needs was found within the context of a sub-culture that had been developed for decades among persons living at the subsistence level. This sub-culture is suitably described by the Jamaican terms "cotching" and "scuffling."

Between 1946 and 1959 only 40,000 people were housed in government schemes in the whole of Jamaica. Permanently unemployed persons who were unable to obtain subsidised, government housing had either to "cotch" (to put up for the night as best they could) or to become squatters. In 1961 the police estimated 20,000 squatters, a figure far greater than that recorded in the previous year's census (table 22).[11] The squatter camps were located on the fringe of the tenement area in West Kingston (pl. 21) and on the outskirts of the built-up area of the city (fig. 52), and usually occupied land owned by the government. The camps on the outskirts of the city had developed during the period of rapid population growth which took place after 1953. Moonlight City on the foreshore in West Kingston, for example, was set up during 1959, its adult population doubling from 54 to 106 between July, 1960 and July, 1961. The oldest squatter settlements were at Trench Town (pl. 21) and Back

O'Wall on the fringe of the tenements; with interruptions squatters had been living in the latter area since the 1930s. In both areas squatting had rapidly regenerated after the 1951 hurricane, and in Trench Town squatters had quickly captured government-owned land which had been cleared and prepared for rehousing. Population densities were much higher in the older camps (fig. 43). Furthermore, large, almost impregnable, stockades had been raised around each parcel of captured land in Trench Town (pl. 22), whereas low fences sufficed as property boundaries in Moonlight City (pl. 23). The stockades in Trench Town were a reflection of competition for land which, in turn, was affected by the density of the population. The morphology of some of the older squatter camps closely resembled that of the more decrepit rent yards of West Kingston.

It was doubtful in Jamaican law whether the property at Back O'Wall remained in the legal possession of its original owner. Private owners forfeited their land to squatters after six years of continuous residence provided the land was fenced; otherwise the period was twelve years. Crown land, however, was relinquished only after 60 years of squatting, and this probably explains the greater tolerance shown by government. Disputes over privately owned land were by no means rare. One of the best-known squatter camps in Trench Town was situated on land belonging to a school called Boy's Town. The squatters claimed that the land was theirs, and most household heads were recorded in the census as owners (fig. 50).

Even in the older camps, population densities rarely exceeded 150 persons per acre; these were lower than the figures recorded in the adjacent areas. However, the concentration of population within the squatter camps was out of all proportion to the facilities which were available. Dwellings consisted of one-room huts constructed from packing cases, fish barrels (fig. 42; pl. 24), cardboard (pl. 23), and polythene. In an attempt to deter squatters the government had refused to supply public amenities, and pit latrines—though illegal—had been dug and water was collected from stand-pipes or stolen from fire hydrants (compare fig. 51). Although these conditions were later remedied (pl. 25), approximately 1,000 people shared one stand-pipe in the Boy's Town squatter camp at the beginning of 1961. In certain respects, however, the squatters enjoyed better conditions than the inhabitants of the tenements; they rarely slept more than three people to a room and paid no rent for their accommodation. But tenancy was not unknown in some of these camps, for once squatters had captured a piece of land and built a high stockade around it, they frequently charged a ground rent to anyone who wanted to build on *their* land.

Squatting was a way of life as well as an expression of extreme overcrowding. The social stigma attached to the inhabitants of the squatter camps and poorer tenements and yards made it extremely difficult for people from these areas to find employment; less than 10 percent of the factory workers on the Industrial Estate in West Kingston lived in that part of the city. Many squatters were lapsed literates or illiterate, malnourished, and lacking in personal discipline; and most were regarded by businessmen as unemployable. The problem was compounded by the tendency of many people to describe themselves as skilled workers when they were semi-skilled or unskilled. Furthermore, some refused employment which, they felt, undervalued their ability.

However, while the existence of full-time unemployment tended to encourage squatting, squatting gave rise to a form of unemployment which was not strictly speaking unemployment at all. The adult population of the squatter camps abandoned the search for paid employment, at least temporarily,[12] and relied on "scuffling," or scraping a living from petty manufacturing (pl. 26), pimping and prostitution, begging, stealing, and selling scrap salvaged from the corporation dump, or "dungle," on the foreshore in West Kingston. People involved in these activities were, technically speaking, self-employed, but most regarded themselves as unemployed and so did society at large. It is highly probable, therefore, that most who scuffled for a living were classed by the census as unemployed.

Scuffling provided an important alternative to paid employment, especially in the areas in which the incidence of full-time or secular unemployment was high. The availability of this alternative, and partly illegal system prevented wages from being depressed so that conditions of full and socially acceptable employment could develop. However, while the incidence of unemployment did not necessarily imply idleness, the existence of scuffling provided a socio-economic index of extreme population pressure and overcrowding.

The essence of the sub-culture of cotching and scuffling was summarised by the phrase "living on the dungle." During the 1930s people had literally done so. Even in 1960 one major squatter camp was situated on the seaward edge of the dump in West Kingston, while some of the poorest inhabitants cotched in the wrecked car bodies which littered its surface. Furthermore, since most of the squatter settlements lay within easy reach of the dungle, it continued to act as a major source of saleable goods and building materials and of food discarded by groceries, supermarkets, restaurants, and private households. Droves of squatters awaited the arrival of the garbage carts and, as they disgorged their contents, competed for them with the John Crows (pl. 27). In this way the participants of the sub-culture maintained a parasitic relationship with the more prosperous inhabitants of the city.

In one form or another social diseases affected most of the overcrowded sections of the city, and the squatter camps suffered no more conspicuously in this respect than the tenements and yards. As a result of improvements in public health since the 1930s, the major social diseases were confined to tuberculosis and typhoid, the former being associated with the overcrowding of rooms, and the latter with inadequate sewage disposal and the contamination of food and drinking water. A map has been drawn showing the distribution of notified cases of tuberculosis occurring between 1 December 1959 and 30 November 1960, and of notified cases of typhoid recorded between 1950 and 1960 (fig. 53).

Both these diseases were closely associated with the overcrowded sections of Kingston, and their incidence was particularly high in the west of the city. There was a tendency for tuberculosis to be associated with the yards and tenements and for typhoid to be linked to the squatter settlements.

SOCIO-ECONOMIC STATUS

An index of socio-economic status has been prepared and mapped for Kingston in 1960 (fig. 54). This provides another guide to the spatial arrangement of the social structure of the city and, by implication, contains a certain amount of information on employment. The index was compiled in the following way. The occupations listed in table 20 were placed into three major socio-economic categories—professional and supervisory; clerical, sales, non-professional with special training, craft and technical; manual and service—and the percentage of the working population in each group was calculated for each enumeration district. The percentages in group one, two, and three were multiplied by the values 1, 2, and 3 respectively, and the result for each enumeration district was summed to give an index with limits set theoretically at 100 and 300. In Kingston the index scores actually ranged between 175 and 300. The greater the proportion of professional and supervisory occupations in an area, the higher its status, and the lower its index score.

It is possible to obtain similar scores in areas recording unlike combinations of occupations. Enumeration districts with a large percentage of clerical workers and few servants are indistinguishable from others in which the relatively high proportion of professionals is offset by the presence of servants. But this is not a major problem, and a map showing the distribution of wage earners receiving more than £1,000 per annum (fig. 55) confirms the general pattern of socio-economic status in the city.

The map of socio-economic status reveals impor-tant thresholds which were depicted by the status scores 273.24 and 233.10. Areas of high, medium, and low status were confined to the ranges 175.00-233.10, 233.11-273.24 and 273.25-300.00, respectively. Generally speaking, socio-economic status in Kingston decreased from east to west and from north to south. Areas of low status embraced the lanes in the central business district and the southern flanks of Long Mountain, together with all of West Kingston. High socio-economic status was confined to certain sections of East Kingston, to China Town in central Kingston, and above all to the area to the north of Cross Roads. In almost all these districts more than 10 percent of the wage earners received more than £1,000 per annum.

Neighbourhoods of median status lay in the geographically intermediate zone between these highly polarized social areas and effectively immunized the high-ranking suburbs from the slums. In few of these median status areas did any of the wage earners receive incomes of more than £1,000 per annum. In the central and northern suburbs, median status and high incomes were recorded together, and it may safely be assumed that these were areas of high socio-economic status.

The major cleavage in socio-economic rank clearly occurred where the status score 273.24 was recorded. This cleavage was represented by a line dividing the low status areas of West Kingston and parts of central and East Kingston from the median and high status areas to the north and east. But outliers crossed this divide. For example, high scores were recorded in China Town in central Kingston, while low status typified the pockets of denser population in northern St. Andrew. Nevertheless, the line was a fundamental factor in the geography of Kingston, and its existence provided a spatial expression of a highly stratified social structure. Relationships across this line, where they occurred, were confined to economic activites and were summarised by the roles of owner-tenant, employer-employee, or, more generally, superordinate-subordinate. Similar relationships also occurred between employers and domestic servants within the high ranking areas.

The dividing line acted as a reference to which other patterns were related and together with the boundary between areas of high and median status provided a framework for the social geography of the city. The inverse cartographic relationship between areas of high, medium, and low socio-economic status, and similar intensities of unemployment, overcrowding, and population pressure indicate a relationship between low status, unemployment, high densities, poor housing, and disease which was causal rather than coincidental.

Some overcrowding, however, was recorded in areas of median status (fig. 48), though conditions had improved greatly since 1953. This improvement was due partly to the provision of middle-income housing schemes and partly to changes in the criteria for defining overcrowding. Some part-time unemployment also affected the suburbs in central St. Andrew, and here unemployment was usually described by the euphemisms "resting" and "on holiday." In contrast, areas of the highest status almost completely escaped these conditions.

MIGRATION

In 1960 approximately half the inhabitants of the capital had been born elsewhere in the island (fig. 56).[13] Recent migrants were scattered throughout the suburbs, though a degree of concentration in the tenements and yards of West Kingston and the housing estates of the far west appears. The educational level of migrants was better than the national standard, and many of the newcomers to the high status suburbs had probably received a secondary education,[14] though some were undoubtedly domestic servants who lived with the family for whom they worked. Furthermore, the map incorporates migrants who had moved from Kingston parish to new housing schemes, as at Mona Heights in St. Andrew. Most of the rural migrants were driven, through economic circumstances, into the low status, overcrowded sections of the city where they augmented population densities and population pressure. Such were the densities that recent migrants rarely were more than one-sixth of the population (fig. 58); only in the newer housing schemes and the sparsely populated suburbs did newcomers constitute more than one-quarter of the inhabitants.

The proportion of the population which had been born in the city was lower in certain parts of central and northern St. Andrew than in many areas in West and East Kingston (fig. 59). Over the years the high-ranking suburbs had received large numbers of the Creole elite and expatriate British as well as a constant stream of female domestic servants. These were the only districts (fig. 60) in which the sex ratio fell much below the city's average of 820. This ratio had risen since 1943 (775) due to the predominance of males in the migratory flow to Kingston and to the acceleration in the rate of natural increase in the city; consequently by 1960 the age and sex structure of Kingston was more pyramid-like in shape (figs. 9, 57). Two other features deserve attention. The central business district contained relatively few local-born and only a small number of recent migrants. China Town, for example housed a large number of immigrants of long standing. Conversely, the areas on the urban-rural fringe were increasingly occupied by newcomers, thus reflecting the expansion of the suburbs.

Although recent migrants were closely associated with the overcrowded yards and tenements, more than 50 percent of the population in many of these districts had been born in the corporate area (fig. 59). Few of the squatter camps, with the possible exception of those in Trench Town, were even minor reception areas (fig. 56). There is no sign that the migrants formed a distinct group with special difficulties of their own: their problems were an integral part of the syndrome of poverty which characterised West Kingston.

But while they were absorbed into the densely populated tracts, their presence diluted the amount of housing and work which was available. The migrants gravitated to those areas in which unemployment was the norm and swelled the ranks of those who were still seeking their first job. Simpson has admirably summarised the relationship between migration, housing, and employment:

> Every day young people from the country districts arrive in the Kingston-St. Andrew Metropolitan area, and many of them gravitate to West Kingston. ... Some men come with the hope of finding work in Kingston; others come on trucks bringing produce to market and decide to stay in the capital. Fewer girls than men migrate to the city, but a number arrive daily on the trucks and buses from the country. They come to work as domestics, and some of them obtain a job within a week or so. Others become prostitutes or "scuffle" for a living. Many of the incoming men, finding little or no employment, soon fall into the practice of "living around," i.e. of gambling and stealing. Newcomers try to find a relative with whom they can stay, or a friend, or a stranger who is sympathetic. If they find work, they pay rent; they provide their own food, usually by buying bread, cakes, fish, etc. at the tiny shops which dot West Kingston. If they have no money, relatives or friends, they have to "live hard" (get their bread in some other way).[15]

MOBILITY

Although most migrants to Kingston remained in the city, it would be incorrect to imply that no return movement to the rural areas took place. There was also a considerable amount of mobility in Kingston, both within and between certain social areas. The journey to work and shopping trips were major causes of daily population movement. But even here certain social distinctions existed in the mode of transport employed. While the inhabitants of the high ranking suburbs travelled by car, the poorer inhabitants relied on the public bus service or walked.

A guide to the magnitude of residential mobility in Kingston appears in the work of M. G. Smith. He observed that "the minimum annual rate of residential mobility among this urban lower class is . . . equal to 40 per cent of the total number of households."[16] Rates of mobility varied from one part of the city to the other; in West, central, and

East Kingston the minimum annual rates were 50, 36, and 28 percent, respectively.[17]

In an attempt to extend the coverage, both socially and spatially, ten enumeration districts with a total population of 5,000 have been selected for analysis here (fig. 61). The district called Inner West Kingston was located in the single-story tenement area, which was added to the city during the nineteenth century, while Denham Town, slightly farther to the west, was redeveloped by the government during the late 1930s. Richmond Park, Upper Deanery Road, and Hopefield Avenue were all established as suburbs between the two World Wars, and Barbican, the most northerly of the selected districts, was started during the 1950s. Rennock Lodge, on the flank of Long Mountain, dates from the same period but is a government housing scheme. The three remaining districts were all drawn from West Kingston. Majesty Pen was built by the government during the early 1950s, while Boy's Town and Moonlight City were squatter camps.

A comparison was made of the electoral rolls for July, 1960, and July, 1961, in an attempt to measure the annual rate of residential turnover, or mobility, in each district. Several problems were encountered. The information was confined to persons aged over twenty-one years, and this provided no guide to the number of dependents who were likely to be affected. It is impossible on the basis of the evidence to distinguish between mobility and mortality. Furthermore, the rates of turnover were minimal, and people could pass undetected through each district during the interval between checkpoints. Consequently, where turnover was highest, under-enumeration of mobile persons is most likely.

The number of persons who were resident in each district in 1960 but absent in 1961 has been expressed as a percentage of the population recorded on the electoral roll in 1960 (table 24). The socioeconomic scores for Barbican and Rennock Lodge are questionable. Barbican recorded a population density and mobility rate similar to those for Hopefield Avenue, but fieldwork also suggested that Barbican was a high status area. Conversely, the status score for Rennock Lodge seems too high, given a population density of 67 persons per acre and its position as a government housing scheme.

By transferring Barbican to its correct position at the top of the social scale, four fairly distinct zones of mobility can be seen. Rates were moderate at Hopefield Avenue and Barbican, high at Richmond Park, Upper Deanery Road, and Rennock Lodge, and very high in the tenements of Inner West Kingston; the lowest rates were recorded in the two squatter camps at Moonlight City and Boy's Town (4 and 5 percent respectively). Furthermore, the rates of mobility which were measured at Inner West Kingston (41 percent) and Rennock Lodge (28 percent) were comparable to those recorded by M. G. Smith in West and East Kingston (50 percent and 28 percent), though he was using a rather different yardstick.

Any attempt to explain these patterns must be tentative. It seems likely that much of the mobility in areas of high socio-economic status was due to the arrival and departure of domestic servants. This also affected the middle-ranking areas, where there was a large amount of house renting with tenants moving to other districts and especially to the middle-income housing schemes. The densely populated tenements of Inner West Kingston received new migrants to the capital; high rates of mobility were related to this influx, to the breakdown of domestic units, and to the avoidance of rent arrears. Rates of mobility were lower at Denham Town and Majesty Pen largely because they were government schemes. Moonlight City and Boy's Town clearly represented the bottom of the social scale; the low rates of mobility indicate that there was little or no escape from the squatter camps once they had been reached.

To develop a broader understanding of population movements in Kingston, information was collected on mobility between a number of residential districts. Two new housing estates at Mona Heights and at Harbour View (on the delta of the Hope River) were selected, and details were obtained

about the former residence of their occupants. The two investment companies which had financed the schemes agreed to supply the previous address of 10 percent of the mortgagees who made up almost all of the householders. The cost of purchasing a house at Harbour View was slightly more than £2,000 and at Mona Heights about £2,900. Mortgagees had paid at least 10 percent of the purchase price and possessed an annual income of about £800 in the case of Harbour View and £900 to £1,000 in the case of Mona Heights. In both these middle-income housing schemes, however, groups of individuals had been allowed to combine their salaries to reach the prescribed levels.

Although persons at Mona Heights (fig. 62) tended to have inhabited slightly higher ranking areas than those at Harbour View (fig. 63), both maps depict similar source areas in the median status districts of the city. These source areas ran southeastward from Eastwood Park to Bournemouth Gardens, via Half Way Tree and Cross Roads and included three of the ten selected enumeration districts: Richmond Park, Upper Deanery Road, and Rennock Lodge (fig. 61), all of which had recorded fairly high rates of turnover (table 24). Furthermore, this zone of outward mobility coincided with the middle-income areas which had been described as overcrowded in 1953 and comprised most of those districts which were still moderately overcrowded in 1960 (figs. 43, 48).

The schemes at Mona Heights and Harbour View clearly offered a considerable opportunity for persons in the middle-income group to purchase a house. However, some renting occurred at Mona Heights as a result of speculators entering the market. An outstanding feature was the failure of both schemes to siphon off any of the inhabitants of the slums. People from these areas were financially incapable of such a move. Migrants to the schemes moved from similar social areas, and it is highly probable that an identical pattern typified most cross-town movements of population.

It is possible to distinguish between several patterns of mobility in Kingston. Movement to the two largest middle-income housing schemes and to most of the other new suburbs, too, was restricted to persons inhabiting at least median-ranking areas. Many servants also penetrated these suburbs, but their status was essentially a dependent one. Mobility was highest in the tenements, but most of this was directed to similar areas, and few of the inhabitants moved to the suburbs. In 1961, for example, it was discovered that 43 percent of the households in one tenement area in West Kingston had changed their address during the previous year without leaving the neighbourhood.[18] Finally, the squatter camps acted as the settling basins for the most impoverished element in the population and together with the worst housing schemes, as at Majesty Pen, formed slums of despair rather than slums of hope from which new migrants might have ascended the social scale. These patterns indicate the rigid nature of the social stratification and its faithful reflection in spatial terms.

It is also possible to make a tentative distinction between cityward migration, internal migration within Kingston, and emigration, both with regard to the groups and to the areas involved. The migration of landless country people from the rural areas was directed to the tenements and yards of West Kingston, which were characterised by high rates of residential mobility. Few migrants penetrated the source areas for the new housing schemes, and few settled immediately in the squatter camps. It is clear that the government's policy of not supplying basic amenities in the squatter settlements provided no deterrent to migrants.

The slum dwellers were scarcely more able to afford to emigrate to Britain than to enter the suburbs. Emigration involved artisans, sugar-factory workers, tractor drivers, members of the land-owning peasantry, and their dependents.[19] Many of the migrants from Kingston were drawn from the ranks of privileged unionised labour and from some of the relatively higher ranking low-status areas. Emigration, like the move to the suburbs, involved the more prosperous inhabitants who had greater ability, if less necessity, to move. But the disillusionment and frustration experienced by young in-migrants who failed to find employment in Kingston constituted a major social problem; many lived under even worse conditions than those they had experienced in the rural areas.

VII: The Social Structure of Kingston on the Eve of Independence

Polarisation of socio-economic groups and strong contrasts in material conditions characterised Kingston in 1960. How did racial and cultural factors affect or reflect the socio-economic stratification? Had racial segregation increased or declined since 1943? How were cultural differences expressed spatially? In this chapter an attempt is made to answer these questions and to consider the spatial aspects of voting behaviour and political protest on the eve of independence.

FAMILY

Throughout slavery and the post-emancipation period, many aspects of the family had remained unchanged; illegitimacy continued to account for more than 60 percent of all live births. In 1960 more than 60 percent of household heads in the tenements were females; between 25 and 60 percent of household heads in parts of East Kingston and in some of the squatter camps, housing estates and yards in West Kingston were also females. Only in the northern suburbs did the rate fall below 25 percent (fig. 64).

Within West Kingston wide fluctuations in female headship were recorded without corresponding variations in socio-economic status (fig. 54) or in the sex ratio (fig. 60). The incidence of household headship among females of low status was largely dependent on patterns of mating. Wherever female headship was widespread (pl. 30), so was extra-residential mating; where female headship was comparatively rare, as in the northern suburbs, consensual cohabitation or marriage predominated. However, since extra-residential mating depended on visiting, various neighbourhoods recording different patterns of household headship were linked together by this practice.

The incidence of the common-law union has been mapped for women aged over fourteen (fig. 65); none of these women had ever been married. Consensual cohabitation was widespread in West Kingston, where it involved at least 20 percent of the female population. A distinction must be made

between East Kingston and the median ranking areas to the south-east of Half Way Tree which recorded high proportions of female heads but relatively few common-law unions and the more northerly suburbs in St. Andrew where female headship and consensual cohabitation were rare. This information is amplified by the map showing the distribution of women aged over fourteen who had never married but were mothers (fig. 66). Only in parts of East, central and, above all, West Kingston did more than one-fifth of the unmarried women acknowledge motherhood. Of equal importance was the paucity of mothers of illegitimate children in East Kingston and to the south of the Half Way Tree Road, despite the high proportion of female heads in these districts. The northern suburbs possessed few female heads, few common law unions and few mothers of illegitimate children.

It appears that female headship carried different implications in each of the three major districts— West Kingston, the northern suburbs, and East Kingston together with the area to the south of the Half Way Tree Road. The family structure of the northern suburbs, in particular, differed markedly from that of West Kingston. Marriage, legitimacy, and male headship were the norm. To test these relationships, a map has been prepared showing the distribution of females aged over fourteen who were legally married, cohabiting, and mothers (fig. 67). Taking the figure of 24.8 percent as the major division between areas in which a significant proportion of the women were or were not legally married, cohabiting, and mothers, it was found that this dichotomy was expressed spatially. North and east of a line running southeast from Eastwood Park Gardens and Collins Green to Bournemouth Gardens, marriage, cohabitation, and parenthood were the norm. In inner East, central, and West Kingston, parenthood frequently occurred without cohabitation and usually without marriage.

Marriage in West Kingston involved middle-aged partners and had little to do with the process of procreation; it therefore had a different status, function, and implication from the same institution in the northern suburbs. Conditions in the zone lying between these two areas were essentially heterogeneous. To the south of the Half Way Tree Road and also in East Kingston marriage, cohabitation, and parenthood were widespread but so too was the incidence of female headship. These areas contained an amalgam of some of the practices common to both West Kingston and the north-east suburbs.

It is possible, therefore, to construct a typology of mating and family patterns in Kingston. The high-ranking suburbs in the north contained nuclear, biological families of husband, wife, and children. Marriage, mating, and parenthood succeeded one another in that order. The household head was male; the family and household usually coincided, and these areas contained "more divorcees than. bastards."[1] In West, central, and parts of inner East Kingston illegitimacy, concubinage, and extra-residential mating were the norm. Marriage occurred in later life, "very often after the birth of grandchildren," and there was "no equation between family, household and mating relation even as a social ideal."[2] In these areas, therefore, there were three alternative mating forms: the extra-residential relationship, consensual cohabitation, and marriage.

> None has an exclusive place within a series, nor within the individual life cycle. Despite a tendency for adults to begin their mating career extra-residentially and to complete it with marriage, there is ample evidence that many begin by marrying and later resume extra-residential or consensual mating as "single persons." Consensual cohabitation will be singularly unstable in these conditions, since marriage establishes no permanent union, and since other alternative mating forms are always open to both partners. Under these conditions the definition and fulfilment of parental roles by persons of either sex becomes uncertain, and accordingly many women despatch the offspring of these unions, past and present, to rural kinsfolk.[3]

Male heads of households rarely accommodated their own children, though they usually housed the children, and frequently the kin, of their resident mates. Half-siblings were common in households in West Kingston. Furthermore, where extra-residential mating was widespread, many adults formed single-persons households, while others chose to live with siblings rather than with mates.

In East Kingston and the area immediately to the south of the Half Way Tree Road the forms of mating and family which obtained in the other two areas frequently occurred together. Men lived with their legal wives and lawful issue, but some maintained mistresses who were heads of their own households. Part of East Kingston formed the "red-light" section of the city. The absence of concubinage and denial of illegitimate offspring characterised both these median status districts. However, in reality, both districts contained two distinct mating patterns. At one pole was found "a creolized version of Victorian marriage"[4] and at the other a sophisticated form of extra-residential mating.[5] It was in this middle section of the population that "men's legal and illegitimate issue"[6] were most sharply distinguished.

RELIGION

The sample data from the census have been tabulated into four basic religious groups: denominational Christians, Roman Catholics, "other" Christians, and non-Christians. The denominational Christians were composed of the adherents of the Anglican, Methodist, Moravian, Presbyterian, Baptist, and Congregational churches (table 25)—the respectable spectrum of organised Christianity in Jamaica. Most of these were located in the eastern, central and northeastern sections of the city (fig. 68) where they accounted for between 25 percent and 75 percent of the population. However, the percentage in central and West Kingston and on the fringe of the built-up area rarely exceeded 37 and only in exceptional cases surpassed 50.

The Roman Catholics, who comprise just under one-quarter of Kingston's population and represent an urban enclave within a predominantly Protestant country, were widely distributed throughout the city. They tended to be under-represented in West Kingston (fig. 69), and to be concentrated in those parts of East Kingston and central St. Andrew where the proportion of denominational Christians was also high. However, Roman Catholics were numerous in the north of the city where denominational Christians formed only a small minority of the population.

The group which has been termed "other" Christian covers a variety of sects and cults ranging from the various branches of the Church of God down to Revival Zion and Pocomania. They comprised more than 50 percent of the population in parts of East Kingston, upper St. Andrew, and throughout West Kingston (fig. 70; pl. 32). The suburban areas recorded lower proportions. Denominational Christians and Roman Catholics therefore tended to be isolated from the sectarians and cultists.

Non-Christians made up only a fraction of the population and were of marginal importance. Composed of Confucians, Buddhists, and above all, Hindus, they were widely scattered throughout West Kingston (fig. 71). The first two religions were associated with the Chinese, and it was significant that more than 10 percent of the inhabitants of China Town was classified as non-Christian. But the highest proportion of non-Christians was associated with the East Indian enclave at Cockburn Pen, where almost a quarter of the population were Hindu. Although the location of non-Christians was by no means identical with the distribution of "other" Christians, it was largely subsumed by it.

The inhabitants of the high ranking suburbs practised orthodox Christianity, though this was replaced in certain areas by agnosticism. Beneath the lower limit of the denominational groups was found a number of rapidly growing American sects such as the Church of God (table 25). Fundamentalist views also tended to typify all the non-conformist denominations. In contrast with the orthodox churches, the Afro-Christian cults stressed continuous revelation, prophecy in tongues, interpretation of omens and dreams, and the manipulation of the dead. In areas suffering from deprivation in so many spheres of life, they provided an emotional outlet, a form of recreation, and an opportunity for low-status inhabitants to exercise leadership roles.[7]

The revivalists regarded the Hope River as the Jordan and, following Bedward, baptised their converts in its depleted stream. One of the outstanding features of West Kingston, and Back O'Wall in particular, were the towering prayer flags which fluttered over the balm yards, which were frequented by the sick who attributed their illness to obeah and, ultimately, to the malevolence of neighbours. In this way religion in West Kingston competed with orthodox Christianity, agnosticism, and the government's medical services.

EDUCATION

Considerable differences in both formal and informal education were recorded in Kingston (table 16). In an attempt to analyse these differences and the areas characterised by them, census information on education was grouped into three categories, consisting of persons who had had or were receiving secondary schooling and the remainder who were subdivided according to whether their formal training had lasted for fewer than six years or between six and eight years. Since the analysis included all persons aged ten and above, the results depended to some extent on the age of the respondents and their current progress in the school system.

North of Cross Roads and, in particular, northeast of the Half Way Tree Road, more than half the population aged ten and over had received, or were receiving, a secondary school education (fig. 72). In the highly prestigious area bounded by the Hope, Old Hope, Constant Spring, and Half Way Tree Roads, the proportion rose to two-thirds, despite the presence of a large number of servants. South of Collins Green, however, the percentage dropped precipitiously to below 10, and throughout most of West Kingston and parts of East Kingston failed to reach 3. Nevertheless, isolated sections in the tenements of central and East Kingston recorded moderate percentages. In the far east of the city almost half the population were benefiting from a secondary education, and here conditions were similar to those existing at Collins Green.

The map showing the distribution of persons spending between 6 and 8 years in non-secondary schools (fig. 73) is partly a mirror image of the previous one. The percentage fell below 30 in the northern suburbs, except where the low-status enclaves were located and was low also in parts of East Kingston and the most depressed sections of West Kingston. Throughout the southern parts of the city proportions in excess of 50 percent were widespread. The effect of the mirror image is completed by the map showing the distribution of persons spending fewer than six years in non-secondary schools (fig. 74). They were heavily concentrated in West Kingston, where they accounted for more than 50 percent in some areas. Such large proportions were rarely attained in either East Kingston or the central and northern suburbs. Once more a social and cultural cleavage is noticeable between West Kingston and the northeastern suburbs, the former recording a large number of people with non-secondary schooling, the latter a high percentage with secondary training. In East Kingston and to the south of the Half Way Tree Road moderate proportions fell into each category.

These highly polarised patterns are reinforced by the distribution of educational institutions receiving government aid in 1960. These comprised teacher-training colleges, the best secondary schools, senior schools, primary schools, and infant schools. There were only three teacher-training colleges in Kingston, one at Shortwood in upper St. Andrew and the others near Cross Roads. Secondary schools, likewise, were confined to the northern, eastern, and central parts of the suburbs; none was in West Kingston. Conversely, senior schools catering to children between the ages of 11 and 15 were heavily concentrated in the southern half of the city and especially in West Kingston. These were non-secondary schools, and their pupils

took the Jamaica School Certificate rather than the General Certificate of Education. Primary schools for children aged 7 to 11 were insufficient in number and frequently overcrowded.

Infant education was virtually neglected, and the Alpha Institute maintained the only recognised school of its kind in Kingston. The secondary schools, teacher-training colleges, and the University College of the West Indies, too, were all situated in positions which emphasized rather than blurred the cultural dichotomy between West Kingston and the northern suburbs. Even so, children in West Kingston undoubtedly had greater access to all three types of institutions than ever before (fig. 72).

The secondary school system has been admirably described in a report from the Jamaican Ministry of Education.

> The boys and girls received a good training in character and morals, a recognition of the value of *esprit de corps* and team work, and a good grounding in academic subjects. For two generations at least the professions and the upper ranks of commerce and industry have been recruited from these schools. ... The schools have been open to the charge that the content of the curriculum was too English and that their pupils learned nothing about their native country. The product of the secondary school, it is said, is ignorant of Jamaica's problems and indifferent to the poverty of the masses. Although the Island is ultimately dependent upon its agriculture, the secondary school boy or girl is usually completely uninformed on any aspect of this predominant industry. ... In recent years the schools have endeavoured to meet these criticisms.[8]

The education imparted in the non-secondary schools was totally different. Learning was by rote and the discipline often harsh. Work of a creative or imaginative nature was largely neglected and in some instances discouraged. Relatively few teachers in these schools had been trained for their work.

The education received by the lower-class child

was "really a formal teaching of reading, writing and arithmetic, a little hygiene and much Biblical knowledge."[9] Primary education was hampered by absenteeism among children and by the failure of parents to appreciate that regular attendance was essential to the gradual accumulation of knowledge.[10] Illiteracy and lapsed literacy were by no means uncommon among the products of the non-secondary schools (fig. 75; table 26). Rates were still relatively high in West Kingston despite the overall reduction in illiteracy between 1943 and 1960. But in China Town facility in a Chinese dialect existed as an alternative to English as did Hindi at Cockburn Pen. Furthermore, informal training in folk culture was important throughout West Kingston.[11]

The education system both reflected and reinforced the social structure. Secondary schooling was essentially elitist, while the non-secondary system was associated with a subordinate culture; within that culture education contributed to the proliferation of disorganised personalities[12] and to the growing disequilibrium between aspirations and job opportunities. The median stratum had access to both the secondary and non-secondary schools, and in the latter achieved good attendance rates and comparatively high levels of attainment.

Linguistic patterns, also, coincided with these social and ecological divisions.

It has been found that middle and "upper class"natives do not know the meaning of 30 percent of the words current in the Anglicized folk dialect. It would also be surprising if those Jamaicans who habitually speak this folk dialect should know more than 70 percent of the words commonly used by those who do not. Bilingualism in such societies in a characteristic of cultural hybridism, and such hybrid cultural adjustment is most typical of the intermediate section. Thus while the small top section speaks and understands English, but not dialect, and while the large bottom section only speaks and understands dialect fully, the intermediate section tends to employ either linguistic form according to the occasion.[13]

SOCIAL AND CULTURAL PARAMETERS

An attempt has been made to measure statistically the interrelationship between certain facets of education, family, and religion. It is, of course, difficult and perhaps dangerous to reduce a complex institutional system to a single index, but the procedure is essential to quantification. Inspection of the maps suggests that the percentage of females aged fourteen and over who had never married but were in common-law unions and the percentage of the population who were members of non-denominational churches[14] were critical aspects of family structure and religion. Furthermore, the percentage of the population aged ten and over who had received or were receiving secondary schooling was selected as a significant indicator of educational and cultural achievement.

The statistical analysis encountered three procedural problems. The calculation of correlation coefficients for these three variables would have been time consuming had observations for all 830 enumeration districts been employed. Therefore, the enumeration districts were numbered from one to 830, and a sample of 100 was selected using a table of random numbers. The second problem stemmed from the fact that the data for all three variables were highly skewed and could not be normalised. It was impossible to calculate product moment correlation coefficients or to embark on an analysis using multiple correlation and regression, since both methods require data to be normally distributed. A non-parametric method—the Kendall rank correlation—had to be used. While ranking the data prior to computation, the order was arranged from low scores to high.

The highest coefficient linking any two of these three variables was -.47 recorded between secondary education and common-law union (table 27). For this coefficient the null hypothesis can be rejected at the level of significance .00003, and it may safely be assumed that these two variables are associated in the population from which the sample was drawn. With varying degrees of confidence, all of them high, a similar conclusion can be reached for the other coefficients examined. The second highest value of r also involved secondary education, this time relating it to non-denominational Christians. In this instance r was -.30. The lowest coefficient was recorded between common-law marriage and non-denominational Christians. This coefficient was .14, and the level of significance was lower.

Since different methods of correlation yield different coefficients for the same pairs of variables, it is difficult to know whether an r value of -.47 can be described as high. In this study, however, it seems clear that correlations between the selected aspects of education, family, and religion are fairly strong. Secondary schooling was negatively correlated with common-law unions and with the Afro-Christian cults and sects, while consensual cohabitation was rather weakly but positively correlated with the non-denominational groups. By far the most important relationship existed between common-law unions and secondary education. Family influence was critical for social and educational advancement, since fee-paying was still important at the secondary schools.

A close link between culture and socio-economic status has already been proposed. Taking simply the relationship between secondary education and socio-economic status,[15] this seems proven. The coefficient of correlation for these variables was .48, the highest recorded in the entire analysis. Although it is difficult to distinguish between cause and effect, it seems almost certain that education continued to be more a measure of ascription than achievement; the correlation between education and family tends to support this view (table 27).

The analysis confirms the existence of three cultural groupings and their hierarchic arrangement in the social scale. Furthermore, the various values of r indicate the degree of correlation between facets of the institutions which define these cultural groupings. By mapping together the indices of family, religion, and education, areas which evince varying degrees of cultural homogeneity can

be demarcated. The end product provides a social and ecological guide to the cultural complexity of the city (fig. 76).

Taking the hundred sample enumeration districts which were used in the correlation analysis, the average percentage for non-denominational Christians was 46.9, for common-law unions 19.7, and for secondary education 14.2. When the first two averages are rounded to 50 and 20 percent, it is apparent that they correspond closely with critical divisions on their respective maps. Using the evidence of the correlation coefficients it was decided to make education the principal component and family the secondary one. The average value for secondary education (14.2 percent) was abandoned as a boundary mark in favour of two others, at 50 percent and 10 percent using evidence from figure 69. Areas were grouped into those where the percentage of the population with secondary education exceeded 50, ranged between 50 and 10, or fell below 10 (fig. 76). Within these three divisions, areas were grouped on the basis of percentages higher or lower than the critical values established for the indices of family and religion. By classifying areas on these bases, twelve types of cultural zones could have been distinguished; in reality, their number was confined to ten. These ten zones have been combined to produce three sets of cultural combinations (fig. 76).

The lower cultural group (III), with its core in West Kingston, was spatially divorced from persons of high cultural status, most of whom were in central and northern St. Andrew (I). This group contained only two cultural complexes, as compared with four in each of the others. Between the upper and lower groups, and differentially acculturated to each, the median element (II) occupied a shatter belt, culturally, socially, and geographically. Although it was more closely related to the upper group than to the lower, its family structure and patterns of mating were distinct.

The map evidence reveals an urban community split into three cultural divisions which were hierarchically arranged. Furthermore, except on the northern fringe of the city, where the accuracy of the index of socio-economic status has already been questioned, the correspondence between socio-economic rank and cultural status was extremely close (figs. 54, 76). Each social stratum was culturally distinct from the others, though the banding on the map (fig. 76) suggests a continuum rather than a water-tight division of cultural practices.

Within each of these cultural-geographical systems other cultural practices were represented. Servants in St. Andrew, for example, were cultural aliens in the areas in which they worked. Their presence confused the ecological situation and helped to minimise the coefficients of correlation. Even when these factors are taken into account, the cultural situation was extremely complex and especially so in areas of median status.

RACIAL DISTRIBUTIONS

In the analysis of data for 1943, culture was approached through race; in this chapter the two are divorced analytically but compared later both ecologically and systematically. Furthermore, by mapping racial distributions for 1960 it is possible to make a direct comparison with conditions in 1943 and to examine the spatial and social implications of these patterns.

In 1960 the white minority (table 28) was called European by the census. The Europeans were heavily concentrated in central, northeastern and northern St. Andrew (fig. 77; table 29) and comprised more than 20 percent of the population in several areas. Europeans were almost completely absent from West Kingston and were found only in pockets in East Kingston. Between 1943 and 1960 the white population of Kingston, St. Andrew, and Jamaica declined (figs. 10, 11, 12), despite an increase in the expatriate business community. In Kingston two trends were noteworthy (figs. 77, 27); large numbers withdrew from the central business district, East Kingston, and from the area to the south of the Half Way Tree Road, and moved to the northeastern suburbs. Simultaneously, some of the white enclaves were diluted by the arrival of non-white residents. In over-all terms segregation increased, and the major concentrations of Europeans were if anything greater in 1960 than they had been in 1943; to some extent, however, this apparent polarisation may have been due partly to the increase in the number of enumeration districts.

Although many Jews had converted to Christianity before 1943, becoming either Anglican or Catholic, a number retained their original faith and supported the synagogue on Duke Street. By 1960 probably the greater part of the inhabitants of Jewish origin had merged with the white or European population from whom they were distinguishable only by their Portuguese or German names. Most of the Jews resided within or close to the segment formed by the Hope, Old Hope, and Half Way Tree Roads, and in certain areas they comprised more than 20 percent of the population (fig. 78). Smaller groupings, composed of several families, were found in northern and central St. Andrew and in East and West Kingston. The group was highly segregated, dissociated from the slums, and virtually synonymous with the European population.

Population movements among the Jews repeated those recorded by the Europeans (figs. 78, 30). Between 1943 and 1960 the Jews in the corporate area declined from 723 to 522. They withdrew from the older residential districts located in East Kingston and near Half Way Tree in favour of the newer, more attractive, and prestigious areas in central and northern St. Andrew.

In the 1960 census the Negro population, described as African, made up 73 percent of the population of the capital (table 28). The African inhabitants of Kingston were concentrated most heavily in those areas from which the European population was absent (fig. 79). As in 1943 these two racial groups were spatially polarised. Throughout large sections of central, West, and East Kingston, more than 85 percent of the population were African; the yards and government housing estates of West Kingston and some of the tenements, too, were virtually Negro ghettoes (pls.

30 and 31). Although the proportion of Africans in the population dropped in central St. Andrew, it rarely fell below 25 percent. Moreover, it was high wherever the proportion of Europeans was low and moderately high even in some areas in which the whites were well represented.

The Negro, or African, population of Kingston and particularly of St. Andrew continued to grow quite rapidly between 1943 and 1960 (figs. 10, 11). Increased segregation in West Kingston was partly offset by the penetration of the central and eastern suburbs. Whether they were house occupiers or servants is not clear, but large numbers undoubtedly belonged to the former category. In contrast, the contribution of the Africans to the population on the northern fringe of the city declined as light-coloured migrants moved out to the newest suburbs.

The coloured population of mixed white and Negro ancestry were termed Afro-European by the census. They comprised less than 14 percent of the population (table 28), for enumerators were asked to distinguish between them and the "other races" in which mixtures of Syrian, Chinese, East Indian, and Jewish origin had been added to the Afro-European amalgam. The Afro-European group is particularly elusive, for many of its members undoubtedly attempted to pass as white or to qualify for the nebulous category of "others." Afro-Europeans were widely distributed throughout the city and recorded no massive concentration comparable to that of the Negroes in West Kingston (fig. 80). Rarely did they account for more than 50 percent of the population, and proportions this high were confined to parts of East and West Kingston, to areas adjacent to Half Way Tree and Cross Roads, and to the socially important sector lying between the Half Way Tree, Hope, and Old Hope Roads. Afro-Europeans still were found at all levels of society, but it is noteworthy that while they were absent from the government schemes, they made up more than one-third of the inhabitants in the middle income housing at Mona Heights.

The "other" races accounted for about 5 percent of the city's population (table 28). Their distribution repeated the pattern of the Afro-Europeans and was distinguished from it only by being more clear-cut or geographically segregated (fig. 81). They were numerous in East Kingston and in central and northern St. Andrew, and in certain districts accounted for more than a quarter of the inhabitants: together with the Europeans and the Afro-Europeans they were markedly under-represented in West Kingston. However, as a group they were lighter skinned and occupied a higher social status than the Afro-Europeans.

If the Afro-Europeans and "other" races are considered together, their distribution may be compared with that of the coloured population in 1943 (fig. 29). At both dates the patterns were similar, with East Kingston and central St. Andrew near Half Way Tree the areas of major concentration. Although some increases were recorded in West Kingston, the coloured population had withdrawn slightly from Kingston parish and had penetrated many of the white residential areas (figs. 10, 11). For the most part, however, this coloured population was still essentially a median group located both genealogically, socially, and geographically between the whites and Negroes.

The Syrians, constituting less than 0.3 percent of the population, were the smallest of the minority groups in Kingston (table 28). Throughout the greater part of the city there were no Syrian residents (fig. 82). Together with the Europeans and Jews they were concentrated in central and northern St. Andrew and almost completely absent from West Kingston (table 29). Their highest proportions were on the periphery of Up Park Camp, in Barbican, and on the northern fringe of the built-up area. To the south of the Half Way Tree Road their distribution was sporadic, though one small concentration was recorded. During the intercensal period the Syrians had withdrawn from Kingston parish, and their numbers in St. Andrew had increased fairly rapidly. Simultaneously, the Syrian population in East Kingston declined (fig. 31), and many inhabitants left the areas near Half Way Tree for the newest of the northern suburbs.

Fewer than 2 percent of the population were Chinese (table 28), though they accounted for more than 40 percent of the population in China Town, at Cross Roads, and near Constant Spring and were located in enclaves in East Kingston and northern St. Andrew (fig. 83). They were widely scattered in West Kingston, but nowhere accounted for more than 20 percent of the population. Between 1943 and 1960 the Chinese population of Kingston parish declined, while that of St. Andrew increased rapidly. Many Chinese migrated to the residential suburbs and made substantial contributions to the population of the newest developments. Nevertheless, their departure from the city centre was less rapid and complete than for the other minority groups, and their contribution to the population of China Town actually increased (figs. 33, 83). The pattern of Chinese population was less dependent on economic as opposed to social factors than it had been in 1943.

The Chinese-coloured population, called Afro-Chinese in the census, was almost as large as the Chinese population, (table 28; figs. 10, 11). They were widely scattered throughout the southern and northwestern sections of the city, but rarely accounted for more than 20 percent of the inhabitants in any one enumeration district (fig. 84). Highest concentrations were recorded in East and West Kingston and west-central St. Andrew. Between 1943 (fig. 34) and 1960 they withdrew from China Town in favour of locations in East and West Kingston and the central suburbs. By 1960 they were more closely associated, spatially, with the Afro-European and "other" races than with the Chinese population, though links between them still existed. It is significant that the Chinese coloureds were among the three groups to record population increases in Kingston parish (fig. 10).

By 1960 the East Indian population of the capital was fractionally smaller than the European group (table 28; figs. 10, 11). They were concentrated on the fringe of the city, especially in West Kingston, northern St. Andrew, and eastern St. Andrew (fig. 85). In all these areas they accounted for less than 10 percent of the population. The highest concen-

tration was in the hurricane rehousing scheme at Cockburn Pen. Small cells of East Indians were distributed throughout East and West Kingston and near Half Way Tree, but few were living in the most prestigious suburbs. Between 1943 and 1960 the East Indian population of Kingston parish declined, while that of St. Andrew increased. Comparison between the maps at these dates reveals several other changes (figs. 85, 35). The former concentration in Back O'Wall had been broken up by the resettlement schemes which followed the 1951 hurricane. East Indians were drawn off to Cockburn Pen, where a large enclave already existed, or to August Town. The proportion of East Indians living in East Kingston and in the area south of the Half Way Tree Road increased, but the East Indians remained essentially a peripheral group whose pursuits were still, in part, agricultural.

The East Indian-coloured population was termed Afro-East Indian in the census. By 1960 they were slightly more numerous than the pure East Indians (table 28; figs. 10, 11). Together with the Afro-Europeans they were widely distributed (fig. 86) and showed a marked tendency towards moderate concentration in parts of East and West Kingston and in central and northern St. Andrew. In location they closely resembled the Chinese-coloured population and, to a lesser extent, the East Indians. Only rarely did they account for more than one-fifth of the population in any enumeration district. The Afro-East Indian population increased rapidly between 1943 and 1960, and expansion was recorded even in Kingston parish. Much of this growth was probably due to miscegenation. During the same period the major concentration of Afro-East Indians shifted from the periphery of the city (fig. 36) towards the middle-class suburbs.

RACE AND STATUS

The distributions of these various racial groups form patterns which can be interpreted socially (fig. 54). Probably the most outstanding feature was the polarisation of Europeans and Africans, which was expressed in both social and geographical dimensions: the European element was confined to the high-ranking suburbs, while the Africans were heavily concentrated in the slums of West Kingston. By 1960 Negro civil servants and professionals were fairly well represented in the suburbs of East Kingston and St. Andrew. The Afro-Europeans and "other races" were located genealogically, socially, and geographically between the poles occupied by the Negroes and whites, but on the basis of residence they merged territorially and socially with both. Syrians and Jews repeated the pattern established for Europeans from whom they were racially and geographically indistinguishable. Together with the Europeans they occupied areas inhabited by Negroes but were markedly absent from the Negro ghetto in West Kingston. The distribution of Chinese, unlike that of the other racial groups, was still partly influenced by commercial as distinct from social or socio-economic factors. Even in West Kingston most of the Chinese living there owned groceries or bars. Nevertheless, they tended to repeat the pattern of residence recorded by the coloureds and whites, and their movement into the high-ranking suburbs was possibly an expression of social mobility. The East Indians, in contrast, remained closely linked with the Negro population and shared their low status and their association with West Kingston. But, like the Negroes, they too had started to move into central St. Andrew. Both the Afro-Chinese and Afro-East Indians were aligned more closely with the coloured population than with the Chinese or East Indians from whom they were partly derived. This pattern differed from that recorded for 1943, when they stood both geographically and socially between the Chinese and East Indian population on the one hand and the coloured on the other.

Despite the withdrawal of the white groups from East Kingston and from the zone to the south of the Half Way Tree Road between 1943 and 1960, neither area suffered a great loss in socio-economic status. The sequence of invasion and succession, involving Africans, Chinese, Afro-Europeans, Afro-

Chinese and Afro-East Indians, was a measure of the upward mobility of certain members of these groups and of the slight downward mobility of the districts. Meanwhile, the white population from these areas moved on to the expanding fringe and created the newest elite suburbs with their spacious gardens, swimming pools, and neo-classical or modern architecture (pls. 19, 20). In the far west of the city the pattern of urban growth was the responsibility of the government, and this became a district composed predominantly of East Indians and Negroes. Private enterprise was joined by public housing in the last of the concentric zones of urban growth: both areas contrasted with the squatter camps, which were literally Negro-made.

By 1960 the minority groups were more heavily concentrated in Kingston than ever before (table 30), but Africans were still predominantly rural in location. The minority groups, and especially the Jews, Syrians, and Europeans, were highly segregated in Kingston, but this was largely the result of voluntary decisions. With few exceptions the Negroes were unable to obtain property in the suburbs. Discrimination was enforced financially; property developers usually stipulated the minimum price for houses built on their sub-divisions.

To test statistically the relationship between socio-economic status, education, and race, the various racial groups were placed into one of three hierarchically ranked categories. The highest category comprised Europeans (including Jews) and Syrians, the median one Afro-Europeans, Chinese, Afro-Chinese, Afro-East Indians, and other races, and the lowest Africans and East Indians. These general groupings seem justified on the basis of fieldwork, the cartographic evidence, and the information included in table 31. The percentage of the population falling into each of these categories was calculated for the 100 sample enumeration districts. The top category was multiplied by 1, the median by 2, and the lowest by 3, and the results summed to give an index whose value ranged, theoretically, from 100 to 300. The Kendall rank correlation coefficient for socio-economic status and race (as measured by these indices) was lower than that recorded between race and secondary education (r = .23). A light skin colour contributed positively to high socio-economic status, and hence to employment, and slightly more strongly to secondary education.

It appears that socio-economic status was determined more by secondary education than by race (table 27). To test this, a Kendall partial rank correlation coefficient was calculated. This measures the correlation between socio-economic status and education with the influence of race on both the other variables taken into account. When the influence of race was partialled out, the value of r was .476. Since this value is almost identical with that recorded between socio-economic status and secondary education (.48), it may be concluded that the relation between these two variables (as measured by these scales) was virtually independent of the influence of race. However, educational standards were only just becoming a measure of achievement by 1960, and ascriptive factors such as race, religion, and family remained important in defining social patterns and social status. Furthermore, race and colour were important outward symbols of the social situation.

PATTERNS OF ASSOCIATION

During fieldwork membership lists were collected for six of the best-known clubs. The only important ones for which information was not available were the Jamaica Club and the Constant Spring Golf Club. A 1:3 sample was taken from the list of members of each club, and using the telephone directory and the 1960 edition of the *Jamaica Who's Who,* maps were prepared showing the place of residence of members who were living in Kingston. Four of these clubs were, in theory, open to all members of the public, while two, by their very names, were restricted to a particular minority group. The first four were sports and social clubs. Liguanea provided facilities for golf, swimming, and indoor games. It had several sports teams which

competed with other clubs. St. Andrew was essentially a tennis club, while the Royal Jamaica Yacht Club and Kingston Cricket Club were primarily concerned with sailing and cricket. The Yacht Club's competitions were mainly internal, but Kingston Cricket Club participated in regular public features. All four clubs were either in central St. Andrew or in East Kingston. None was situated to the south or west of the Half Way Tree Road.

Members of the Liguanea Club (fig. 87) were concentrated in the segment bounded by the Half Way Tree, Constant Spring, and Old Hope Roads. The club was located off the Half Way Tree Road, and most members lived to the north-east of it. Members were drawn principally from the upper social stratum (fig. 76) or, to a lesser extent, from the median stratum. No members resided in either East, central, or West Kingston. There was a close cartographic relationship between the distribution of the membership and the location of Europeans (fig. 77) and, to a much lesser extent, of Syrians and other races. Afro-Europeans, East Indians, and Africans recorded relatively low proportions in the districts from which the membership was drawn (figs. 79, 80, 85). The close alignment between the map of members and the distribution of Europeans was causal and not coincidental; half the club's committee contained persons with Jewish names.

St. Andrew Club was situated at Cross Roads, and the distribution of its members closely resembled that recorded for Liguanea Club. Although two members were drawn from the downtown area, one coming from the former elite district of Kingston Gardens, most lived in the northeastern suburbs. Furthermore, they possessed cultural backgrounds and racial characteristics similar to the members of the Liguanea Club and inhabited areas of equally high socio-economic status (fig. 54). No members resided in either East or West Kingston. The distribution of members of the Royal Jamaica Yacht Club and Kingston Cricket Club repeated these patterns, though each had a few members who lived in East Kingston. All four clubs were run by people of high social status, and in many instances members belonged to two or more of these clubs. But the influence of the Jews in Liguanea was not repeated.

These four maps indicate patterns of association both within and between clubs. Furthermore, they provide an independent check on the distribution of high ranking members of society, and the location of areas of high social status. Outstanding was the paucity of club members in East and West Kingston. On these grounds East Kingston was sharply distinguished from the area to the south of the Half Way Tree Road with which it shared many cultural and socio-economic features. West Kingston was confirmed as an area of low status, its inhabitants participating in different forms of recreation.

Within the membership of these four clubs should be found the capital's elite, by which is meant "persons occupying the 'command posts' in government, business, religion, education, law, medicine."[16] Most of the elite were listed in the 1960 edition of *Who's Who,* where criteria for inclusion were "special prominence in creditable lines of achievement, as agreed by consensus, or substantiated by actual work accomplished; [and] those arbitrarily included on account of official positions."[17] Examining the 1:3 sample, it was found that St. Andrew, Liguanea, and the Royal Jamaica Yacht Club had 67 percent, 66 percent, and 64 percent of their membership, respectively, listed in *Who's Who.* For Kingston Cricket Club the proportion was slightly lower, 59 percent. The cricket club was widely known as the "brown man's club," and its members described Liguanea as "the Jew's Club." Certainly a white skin was a great advantage for applicants for membership to Liguanea. Both elite and non-elite members were found in each of these clubs, though elites were dominant both numerically and as office-holders. Patterns of association probably crossed the elite-non-elite boundary more frequently than they crossed the boundary between the upper and median strata. At this level of society colour was clearly still important. Most members of Liguanea Club, for example, were white, while members of the Kingston Cricket Club were high ranking but light coloured.

If this analysis is correct, Negroes and Afro-Europeans of high status should be poorly represented in these clubs, with the possible exception of Kingston Cricket Club. Persons satisfying both these criteria were found in the civil service, and data were collected for the 39 permanent secretaries and principal assistant secretaries—the leading civil servants—in the Jamaica ministries. Twenty-two were Anglicans, thirty-three had been educated at local secondary schools and one, an expatriate, in Britain. Only ten of these thirty-nine civil servants belonged to any of these clubs; nine to the Kingston Cricket Club, and one, the son of a planter, to St. Andrew. None were members of Liguanea or the Royal Jamaica Yacht Club. Another seven, however, belonged to the Melbourne Club, reputedly the civil servant's club, and one to Kensington, both located in East Kingston. This information supports the views that Kingston Cricket Club was a "brown man's club," that Negroes of high status rarely penetrated these clubs, and that race and colour were important factors affecting inter-personal relations in the upper stratum. Virtually all the civil servants examined earned more than £1,900 per annum. Since the entrance fee to St. Andrew, for example, was only £8.8.0., it is unlikely that these patterns of club membership were due entirely to financial factors. It seems safe to conclude that "social status and membership in social and recreational clubs are based upon the delicate nuances of shade on the one hand and family background coupled with economic success on the other."[18]

Information for clubs established by some of the minority groups supports these interpretations. The Chinese, for example, were conspicuously absent from membership of the four clubs which have been considered. As early as 1937 they had formed the Chinese Athletic Club on the Molynes Road to the west of Half Way Tree (fig. 88). In 1960 members were widely scattered throughout the city and faithfully reflected the distribution of the Chinese population (fig. 83). Members were drawn from China Town and from the median- and high-ranking suburbs. Some, too, were residents of East and West Kingston. Many of the older Chinese were not associated with the club. They either withdrew into the isolation of their homes and businesses or participated in other, more traditional activities, such as the Chinese Masonic Society. The younger Chinese resented their inability to obtain admittance to the Kingston Cricket Club. But the Chinese Athletic Club was regarded as isolationist and potentially racist by some groups of sportsmen.

Club Alaif, the recreational centre for Syrians, was located on the western edge of Vineyard Town (fig. 88). The situation here was totally different. Its activities were declining as members lost their sense of identity with Syrian origins and penetrated the highest echelons and the clubs of the elite. Nevertheless, quite large numbers of Syrians (fig. 82) retained membership in the club, usually on a family basis.

The East Indian population, like the African, played only a marginal role in the members' clubs, and their exclusion was highly significant. Although they had formed Club India in a house on the Old Hope Road, the membership was confined to just over 30 persons, all of whom gave as their address premises in downtown Kingston. It is noteworthy that the majority were Bombay businessmen or professionals, and that as a group they were socially divorced from the majority of East Indians of indentured origin.

Modally, the white elite were members of the Liguanea, St. Andrew, and Royal Jamaica Yacht Clubs. In these clubs they mixed with some of the other members of the upper stratum and possibly with a few people of median status. The upper stratum was divided into at least two main groups on the basis of colour, with Kingston Cricket Club forming the focus of association for the non-white element. Coloured people of Negro phenotype were admitted to the latter, but many joined the less prestigious clubs and in particular those associated with their place of work. Members of the median stratum frequented lesser known members' or proprietory clubs. The latter were numerous in central and East Kingston and in the area adjacent to the Maxfield Road on the northern limit of West Kingston. Some of the Chinese, Syrians, and Bombays

organised their own recreation, but the poorest East Indians and the Negroes, in particular, were rarely club members. West Kingstonians used waste ground for cricket, and games of dominoes flourished wherever there was shade. Patterns of clubbing suggest that few members of any of the social strata habitually associated with groups other than their own.

CULTURE, RACE, AND OCCUPATION

In Kingston in 1960 an individual's social status was determined by culture, socio-economic status, and race. Of these three elements, culture and socio-economic status were the most important and most closely related. Furthermore, they were mutually reinforcing. These conditions were not new. In 1943, for example, the coloured population had been divided into three socio-economic classes which were synonymous with the three social strata. The concordance between socio-economic status and culture presents a major methodological problem; either may be taken as a proxy for social status. The dichotomy between economic and cultural variables is in many ways false, for economic distinctions have developed out of the cultural differences which characterize the strata and vice versa. Each stratum represented a separate cultural world with its own distinctive system of family structure, religion, and education or, in the case of the median stratum, its own distinctive combination and synthesis of institutions. The concordance between socio-economic and cultural areas in Kingston entrenched the differences between, and the hierarchic ranking of, the strata; within these strata both colour and class distinctions were important. The information on club membership, for example, suggests that the upper stratum was divided into elite and non-elite groups and that colour affected patterns of association.

The upper social stratum in Kingston was composed of Europeans, Syrians, and Jews with a small accretion of coloureds, Chinese, and Negroes—the Europeans being divided into Creoles and expatriates. In contrast with the situation in 1943 the Europeans were involved in industry and commerce as opposed to government and administration. Members of this group inhabited the high ranking suburbs of central and northern St. Andrew and dominated the commercial, professional, and industrial life of the city (table 31). Stripped of their political power, they still exercised considerable influence over social and economic development through their monopoly of essential skills. Furthermore, they were well represented in the Legislative Council. In a community perennially beset with the problems of unemployment, they controlled appointments and promotions throughout much of the private sector of the economy. One Jamaican observer has noted that "there are 'English' or white people who are English or white enough to want to help out people who look like themselves when it comes to the matter of a job."[19] Generally speaking, members of all racial groups within this stratum mixed freely on public occasions, but the more private the function the more selective its racial composition. The entry of Negroes into the home of most whites was taboo unless they were domestic servants. Furthermore, Europeans normally married within their own racial group and sometimes brought out brides from Britain.

Persons of Jewish origin formed a minor enclave within the European population. They inclined towards endogamy and based their commercial and professional enterprises on family and community ties. But they adhered to the cultural and economic values of the upper stratum and played prominent roles within it.

Syrians still monopolized the dry goods trade, though they were well represented in commerce, the professions, and the hotel business and were among the few industrialists in the city. The cohesion of the Syrian group was declining as increased numbers penetrated the elite and joined the European clubs. However, the Syrians, also, emphasised family ties and endogamy, though brides were rarely sought from the Middle East. The Syrians and Jews possessed three advantages which were denied to the other minority groups: they were phenotypically white, free from the taint of unfree labour, and culturally identified with the elite. Their social mobility depended on financial success rather than on acculturation.

The middle-ranking social stratum in Kingston was composed of Afro-Europeans, Afro-Chinese, Afro-East Indians, "other" races, Chinese, and Negroes. This was the most heterogeneous of the strata and contained both persons born into it and recruits from the lower ranks of the population. In this section, therefore, shade of skin colour was probably most critical and sub-group cohesion least. The core element was composed of Afro-Europeans and "other" races (table 31). According to Nettleford, they "indulge in a strange love-hate relationship with the whites of both local and expatriate vintage who threaten their claim to the inheritance from Britain. They regard themselves as the true heirs to the governing class."[20] Members of this stratum were firmly established in East Kingston and in the area to the south of the Half Way Tree Road; from both club membership and religion it seems that the latter area was more closely aligned with the upper echelon, and the former with the lower stratum. It is perhaps significant that districts chosen from the areas occupied by this group of people recorded some of the highest rates of residential mobility (table 24).

People of median social status occupied a wide range of occupations but were usually employed in subordinate, white-collar posts in private offices and the civil service. Secretarial jobs throughout the private sector were virtually monopolised by fair-skinned girls of median status (table 31). The civil service provided a major avenue of advancement for Negroes who, by 1960, accounted for 70 percent of government employees in the capital. The expansion of the bureaucracy during the 1950s contributed to the changing racial composition of the stratum. Located geographically and socially between the slums and the high-ranking suburbs, the median stratum suffered from moderate degrees of unemployment and overcrowding of accommodation, and it was for this group of people that the middle-income housing schemes were devised.

The Chinese were closely identified with the median stratum. Through the Chinese Retailers' Association, they controlled the grocery trade and were well represented in commerce, real estate, and industry, both as employers and employees (table 31). Chinese girls worked as clerks in the banks and as typists in other private enterprises. Although the Chinese could purchase admittance to secondary schools and the university, they had been less successful than the Syrians in achieving social mobility. This was due to their large numbers, to the suspicion with which the other groups regarded them, and to the ambivalence with which they viewed their future in Jamaica. Although Nettleford claims that "the bond among the Chinese of Jamaica may be said to be a racial Chinese one and not a sophisticated Jamaican one,"[21] this description applies particularly to the older generation. Despite the severance of links with mainland China as a result of the Second World War and the Communist Revolution, some contact with Hong Kong was maintained. For the older Chinese, Kingston offered an excellent opportunity for trade but was never regarded as home. The increasing number of Jamaican-born Chinese, however, slowly developed a different orientation. Most grew up as Catholics and were educated in Kingston for white-collar jobs. And if the younger generation were in any sense emotionally committed to China, it was to the regime of Mao Tse-tung rather than to that of Chiang Kai-shek. The conflict between the generations was most sharply defined in economic terms. Chinese boys, and girls in particular, wanted to work in offices and banks, not in family groceries. In 1961, therefore, Chinese immigrants were still being sponsored by businessmen, as the sex ratio indicates (table 29). Chinese brides, were sought from overseas, with the intention that they should help their husbands in the grocery trade.

The younger generation continued to withdraw from this patriarchal system and to adopt the values and culture of the brown Creoles. However, they encountered both parental opposition and the hostility of the other groups. The members of the upper stratum still associated them with salt-fish shops, while the Negroes objected that the Chinese employed only Chinese helpers. Furthermore, there was a tendency for the Negroes and Afro-Europeans to denigrate the industry and thrift of the "Coolies."

While the older Chinese therefore formed a cultural cell whose activities were concentrated on their traditional associations—the Benevolent Society, Masonic Lodge, Public School, and Hospital—the younger generation, who were acculturated to the median stratum, formed an endogamous enclave whose recreation focussed principally on the Chinese Athletic Club. Although this group was to some extent ethnocentric, it objected strongly to discrimination on the part of other groups and clubs. Young adults and adolescents, in particular, mixed with their peers of different races. Furthermore, many Chinese maintained "outside" children born to Negro or coloured women. The Chinese-coloured population grew rapidly between 1943 and 1960, and Afro-Chinese girls were widely appreciated as the beauties of the island.

The lower stratum was composed of Negroes with small accretions of East Indians, Afro-Europeans, Afro-Chinese, Afro-East Indians and "other races" (table 31). This group was heavily concentrated in West Kingston and more closely associated than any of the others with the syndrome of poverty. The internal composition of the stratum was differentiated in terms of colour and class, though colour was less important than in the median stratum. Most men worked as labourers or artisans, while women were employed as seamstresses and domestic servants. Three ranks could be distinguished: unionised labour, non-unionised workers, and the unemployed. Among the last group, the sub-culture of squatting, "scuffling", and "living on the dungle" was widespread. However, the entire stratum experienced high densities of population, overcrowding, and disease and was constantly being augmented by the arrival of country folk. Poverty and low status were highly correlated, and the cults and sects provided a means whereby the indigent adjusted to their impoverishment. Although colour was probably less critical for social status within this group than within any of the others, most persons of low status tended to labour under a sense of inferiority.

Most of the East Indians in Kingston belonged to the lower stratum (table 31). The core of this enclave was comprised of 700 Hindus, most of whom were reputedly endogamous. However, the Hindu Samaj had a regular membership of no more than 40 persons, and many of these also belonged to the East India Progressive Society. Activities centred on Varma Hall in West Kingston and a school at Cockburn Pen where Hindi was taught twice a week to some 20 to 30 children. The Hindu Samaj organized communal prayers and household *kathas*. The kathas were performed by a Sanath-anist pundit, a Brahmin who had been born in India. He was one of the few licensed priests of Indian origin living in Jamaica. The pundits were of high caste and Hindi was spoken at kathas, but Indian culture had largely been eroded: many East Indians had joined the cults and sects prevalent among the lower stratum. A small Moslem Sunday School was also maintained in Cockburn Pen, but the impetus had come from a group of Trinidadian students who were studying at the university at Mona. Rivalry between Hindus and Moslems was slight, and the principal division in the East Indian community was still between Bombays and the descendants of indentured labourers.

Religious observance among the Bombays took the form of family services. The Bombays occupied a cultural cell within the median stratum, while the Afro-East Indians ranked socially with the Afro-Europeans. Despite the emphasis on endo-gamy among East Indians, the rapid growth of the Afro-East Indian population testifies to the extent of inter-racial mating.

In Kingston in 1960 the three social strata were similar in institutional content to those described during slavery. They formed relatively closed systems or, more accurately, immutable categories. For although some individuals may have associated with strata to which they did not belong culturally, patterns of culture and association seem to have

been highly consistent. Mobility between the strata depended on acculturation, and this was extremely difficult to effect. Scholarships to secondary schools were few and hard to obtain, and many of the children in the lower stratum were brought up by grandparents and older people whose concepts and outlook were derived from the Victorian period. Acculturation was mainly achieved through education, hence its significance as recorded by the coefficients of correlation (table 27). Before the late 1950s, acculturation was confined mainly to the minority groups or to those of mixed racial ancestry who, through either economic success or family links, were able to secure a secondary schooling.

The racial composition of all strata became more diverse as a result, but the relationships among status, colour, culture, and economic position in 1960 were basically the same as they had been in 1943. Only the white group was indisputably high ranking. Acculturation depended on economic advancement, but this was possible only for those who received patronage from the whites—especially their illegitimate offspring—or for those who were launched in trade with financial assistance from overseas. The Negroes' almost complete failure to obtain help of this kind goes some way to explain their paucity in commerce, which in turn, accounts for their lack of mobility (tables 31, 32). The importance of the government's educational policy in the late 1950s is patently obvious. It attempted to reverse the economic-educational cycle by making secondary schooling the key to economic advancement. And if the lower stratum interpreted the scholarship system as patronage, this accorded well with the view that "government must provide."

Each social stratum contained a number of endogamous racial or cultural cells which were only partially assimilated or acculturated. The situation was probably even more complex in 1960 than it had been in 1943; the discordance within strata among status, culture, and race was reflected in some of the low ecological correlations recorded in table 27. Mobility within strata was by no means easy to effect. Job promotion and marrying light were important in the two higher strata, and patronage was essential. Mobile Negroes usually made their way upwards through the relatively impersonal ranks of the teaching profession and the civil service. Even in the lower stratum a sharp distinction was maintained between unionised and nonunionised labour, and upward mobility was difficult to effect.

The three strata were hierarchically arranged so that status was inversely related to population size: the largest stratum was socially and culturally subordinate. In Kingston the most pronounced boundary divided the median and lower strata. Within strata, the races, colours, cultural cells, and sub-cultures provided targets for mutual and conflicting hostilities. Furthermore, in the lower stratum, the poverty of West Kingston bred a particularly vicious form of dog-eat-dog mentality so that antagonisms—often expressed in the form of obeah—were mostly internalized. Nevertheless, by 1960 Jamaican society was in a state of crisis. In Kingston a Negro racist organisation had developed, and the community was split into opposing camps over Jamaica's continued membership in the West Indies Federation. Examination of these factions reveals in greater depth the nature of social relationships and group attitudes on the eve of independence.

THE CULT OF RAS TAFARI

Socio-cultural and socio-economic structures in Kingston combined to produce a rigidly stratified and geographically polarised urban community. These conditions were clearly expressed in material culture and symbolically summarised by race and colour. It was not surprising, therefore, that a protest movement should have developed in Kingston, or that it should have couched its appeal in racial as well as in cultural terms. The cult of Ras Tafari denounced and repudiated Jamaican society, establishing an entirely different set of values which may be summarised by the term "negritude."

The Ras Tafari movement was confined almost entirely to Kingston, though a small group was also located at Montego Bay. Census information was collected from the Ras Tafari brethren in 1960 but never published, because during the enumeration period conflict developed between the movement and the police in Kingston, and many of the cultists refused to co-operate. Consequently, while it has been possible to map the distribution of the Ras Tafari using data from the sample, their proportional representation is grossly underestimated. Despite these problems, the sample provides an accurate guide to their location in the capital (fig. 89). The movement was confined to two major zones, on the fringe of the tenements and on the periphery of the city; the heaviest concentrations were recorded on the foreshore in West Kingston, at Back O'Wall and in Trench Town. The cult was confined to the lower social stratum (fig. 76), to the predominantly Negro districts of West Kingston (fig. 79), and above all to the squatter camps (fig. 52; pl. 32). But, while the movement was an integral part of the syndrome of poverty, its protest was directed as much against the social system as against inequality in material conditions.

The origins of the cult, like those of the social system itself, were rooted in the past. The first preachers of the divinity of Ras Tafari, later known as Haile Selassie, Emperor of Ethiopia, were Leonard Howell, Joseph Hibbert, and Archibald Dunkley, all of whom had begun their mission work in Jamaica during the early 1930s.[22] But the field had been prepared by Marcus Garvey, who had proclaimed "Africa for the Africans at home and abroad," and "one god, one aim, one destiny." In the United States where he was for a time highly successful, Garvey had advocated black nationalism and the return of Negroes to the promised land of Africa. He met with little success in his native Jamaica, and his relationship with the founders of the Ras Tafari movement remains obscure, though Garvey was soon revered by the cultists as a major prophet sent to "cut and clear." Despite the occasional imprisonment of its leadership, the movement slowly developed in West Kingston. The West India Royal Commission referred to it in 1938, and in 1943 the census schedules for Trench Town listed several Ras Tafarians. Little more was heard of the movement, though Simpson estimated that twelve groups were in Kingston in 1953 each with a membership of between 20 and 150.[23] In 1954 the police raided a camp which had been established by Howell at Pinnacle, to the northeast of Spanish Town. Stores of ganja, or marijuana (a "sacred weed" to many of the brethren), were impounded, and the cultists were dispersed, a large number coming to Kingston. During the late 1950s the movement gathered impetus in the capital, where some of its development was channelled into branches of the Ethiopia World Federation Incorporated, which had been established by Emperor Haile Selassie in 1937. Malcontents were recruited from the slums, and the cult competed with the Christian sects for the diminishing membership of Revival Zion. This change was of the utmost social and political importance. Whereas the Afro-Christian cults had stressed sublimation, the Ras Tafari rejected the social and political system and demanded radical and immediate change.

By 1960 the movement was powerful in West Kingston. In that year it was claimed that "if the declared Ras Tafari brethren in Kingston are estimated at between ten and fifteen thousand, the undeclared but closely integrated sympathizers may be equal in number, and the sum of these two may be somewhat less than the numbers of people in Kingston who might take the side of the Ras Tafari brethren if circumstances seemed favourable."[24] Potential supporters were therefore approximately equal in number to those who in 1960 were suffering from unemployment and overcrowding. The protest movement was spearheaded by the squatters but supported throughout the slums. Awareness of the discrepancy between economic growth on the national scale and stagnation in West Kingston, sharpened by rising expectations, had contributed to disaffection within the lower stratum. Furthermore, the high incidence of population pressure in the Negro areas of West Kingston and its low incidence wherever lighter-skinned people were located had brought a large number of Negroes to the point where a racist interpretation

of their poverty seemed logical. The movement, therefore, consisted of two groups: a hard core for whom it represented a valid alternative religion and a new socio-cultural complex, and a larger group for whom it provided a vehicle for protest against socio-economic conditions. The first element was heterogeneous, made up of artisans, people who scuffled for a living, ganja smokers, revolutionaries, mystics, criminals, and pacifists.

The most obvious source of division and dispute among the Ras Tafari focussed on the treatment of the hair. The brethren fell into three categories: the locksmen, whose hair was matted and plaited and never cut; the beardmen, who wore moustaches and beards but did not plait their hair; and the baldhead, or "clean-faced," men who were distinguishable from the ordinary Negro only by the yellow, green, and red pompom or scarf. Clean-faced men were mostly employed. The locksmen regarded themselves "as the most elect and purest adherents of the doctrine, the persons who have suffered most for their religion and race, and the vanguard, the Ethiopian warriors."[25]

Lacking an organised priesthood, the brethren professed widely divergent beliefs. But three tenets were common to all the Ras Tafari. The poor people, the black people, were Africans; Haile Selassie, King of Kings, Lord of Lords, and the conquering Lion of Judah, was God; and the redemption of the black children of Israel would be attained only by breaking the yoke of the white Babylonian captivity and by repatriation to Africa. Moreover, most brethren embraced the out-group belief that the ways of the white man are evil, especially for the black.

Reversing the white bias of the society, the Ras Tafari embarked on their own brand of ethnocentrism. God was black and so was Christ; the Negroes were the true children of Israel, who had been carried into captivity as a result of their transgressions and were held in Jamaica under the oppressive yoke of the white and brown Babylonians. Black men, it was claimed, were slaves and suffered even more severely now than during the eighteenth century because they were now mentally chained. Some of the views came surpsingly close to those held by the African slaves during the eighteenth century. The Ras Tafari, however, imagined that their repatriation would occur during their life time and not after death. This sense of immediacy added to the tension in Kingston, for it was widely believed that Marcus Garvey had prophesied that 1960, or the 1960s, was the time for redemption.

While the Afro-Christian cults and the sects had stressed emotional escapism, the Ras Tafari demanded emigration or quite literally the opportunity to reject Jamaica. Repatriation to Africa was both stimulated by, and contrasted with, emigration to Britain. Jamaican emigrants to Britain envisaged a period of temporary settlement, while the Ras Tafari were going "home" forever. Neither group was prepared for the country to which they intended migrating, though emigrants to Britain were usually informed about employment conditions by friends or relations. However, the Ras Tafari were quite ignorant of their homeland; theirs was a pseudo-Africa in which West Africa and Ethiopia were mentally transposed. The final distinction between these two migrations—one actual, the other potential—resided in the fact that the Ras Tafari could not pay their passage to Africa. But the mystical element in the cult envisaged some form of divine translation to the promised land.

During the period 1958 to 1961 the objective of certain elements within the movement changed considerably. It became increasingly clear that the government was not prepared to finance repatriation. Some of the brethren adopted the slogan "repatriation or revolution." At the same time, criminality got a foothold within the movement, and it became stronger numerically and more belligerent. In March, 1958, Prince Edward C. Edwards held a convention of Ras Tafari brethren at Kingston Pen adjoining Back O'Wall. Thereafter criminality and violence increased steadily in the movement and the moderate wing, represented by groups such as Local 37 on Salt Lane, lost control. In 1959 a fight took place between the Ras Tafari

and the police at the Coronation Market, and in the same year a man calling himself the Reverend Claudius Henry promised his flock that he would lead them back to Africa. The police eventually raided his headquarters and found a variety of weapons, dynamite, and two letters addressed to Fidel Castro asking for support in capturing Jamaica. Soon after Henry's arrest, his son arrived in Kingston from the United States, with the aim of seizing the government and freeing his father. Retreating to the hills with a small band of followers he attempted to launch a guerilla campaign. A few days later he was captured, but not before two British soldiers and three Ras Tafari had been killed. Although only a small section of the Ras Tafari movement had been associated with the Henrys, the bloodshed attracted attention to the movement. "Whereas it had previously been an object of amused scorn, it was now regarded for the first time as a serious threat to the island's security."[26]

Soon after the Henry affair several Ras Tafari leaders invited representatives of the University College of the West Indies to study their movement. Smith, Augier, and Nettleford reported that

the great majority of Ras Tafari brethren are peaceful citizens who do not believe in violence. We have no evidence that the Ras Tafarians as a group are being manipulated by non-Ras Tafarians with violent beliefs, such as communists. Ras Tafarian doctrine is radical in the broad sense that it is against the oppression of the black race, much of which derives from the existing economic structure. But it has no links with Marxism either of analysis or of prognosis. . . . For Jamaican leftists, the violent part of the Ras Tafarian spectrum is a gift. Capitalist, bourgeois and proletariat can be directly translated into white, brown and black. Revolution becomes Redemption with Repatriation as the issue provoking bloodshed.[27]

The three university lecturers made a number of recommendations, outstanding among which are the following.

The Government of Jamaica should send a mission to African countries to arrange for immigration of Jamaicans. Representatives of Ras Tafari brethren should be included in the mission.

The general public should recognize that the great majority of Ras Tafari brethren are peaceful citizens, willing to do an honest day's work.

The Ethiopian Orthodox Coptic Church should be invited to establish a branch in West Kingston.[28]

Finally, they emphasised that rehousing and slum clearance were essential for an improvement in social relations.

This report dealt a bitter blow to the members of the upper and median strata, whose members had developed a stereotype which reduced the Ras Tafari to the level of sub-humans. An almost complete breakdown of social relations occurred between the two superordinate strata and the lower class, and West Kingston was studiously avoided by the inhabitants of the better suburbs. Even the police were reluctant to enter the heavily barricaded squatter camps. The upper strata refused to concede that the expanding economy had completely by-passed a large section of the population, and in their eyes West Kingstonians, in general, and Ras Tafarians, in particular, were unemployed because they were idle. Consequently, while the locksmen tended to regard themselves as above employment, they were treated as unemployable by society at large. But most brethren were Ras Tafarians because they were unemployed, not unemployed because they were Ras Tafarians.

The upper strata argued that Jamaica was a free society and that no one was compelled to live in squatter settlements; their disregard for the appalling conditions in the slums followed logically from this premise. Ras Tafari was depicted as a lunatic fringe, requiring either brainwashing or internment; they could go to Africa, but not on public money. The Ras Tafari developed equally stereotyped opinions. The upper strata were in league with the British imperialists, and Negro civil servants and white-collar workers were their

stooges. They vilified the brown population in particular, describing them as mulattoes, quadroons, and spittoons. Indeed, the full force of their hatred was directed verbally at this section and its political leader Norman Manley. One group of Ras Tafari used to punctuate their meetings with the cry "Manley is Pharaoh! Pharaoh let my people go!" A favourite Biblical parody ran: "He layeth me down to sleep on hard benches; he leadeth me by the still factories."

By 1960 the view of the squatters had crystallized into a demand for "freedom here where we have struggled without reward for so long—then repatriation." During 1961 the social and political situation was particularly tense and nowhere more so than in Kingston. The Ras Tafari had become a critical element; social and racial attitudes were highly polarised, and a referendum was to be held to decide whether Jamaica should remain in the West Indies Federation. In the midst of this crisis the government embarked on two expedients relating to emigration and housing.

An Unofficial Mission to Africa was despatched by the government in the spring of 1961 to investigate the possibilities for repatriation. It visited Ethiopia and a number of countries in West Africa. The mission was composed of interested parties and produced a highly optimistic report. They claimed to have found "in all territories a ready acceptance of the principle of 'repatriation of Africans living abroad, to the ancestral land' ..."[29] Furthermore, they reminded Premier Norman Manley that "since the Mission was not empowered to enter into commitments with these African States, their governments declared their readiness to enter into discussions with your government so as to deal with the mechanics of future migrations."[30]

The social tension which had been almost unbearable for months was immediately released: there was widespread interest in emigration to Africa among the non-Ras Tafari in the lower stratum who were determined to escape from the city's slums. The report dealt a further blow to the upper strata, whose members seemed incapable of understanding that repatriation provided an ideal short-term solution to population pressure and discontent in Kingston, and might possibly save landless migrants from contamination by the city's slums. Furthermore, they failed to appreciate that the report would undermine the influence of the rapidly growing group of leftists in the Ras Tafari cult who appeared to revere Karl Marx as devoutly as Haile Selassie. These leftists were far more interested in revolution than in either repatriation or Marxism and by 1961 had established tenuous links with Castro's Cuba.

In the same year also the government decided to tackle the problem of overcrowding in Kingston. It decided to ignore the problem of the tenements and the yards and to concentrate on the squatter camps at Trench Town and Back O'Wall. This project enabled the government to develop two of the most derelict pieces of property in the city without having to pay a high price for the land and by rebuilding within the area to be demolished to prohibit the regeneration of squatter camps. This scheme was devised to demonstrate the concern of government for the social improvement of the slum areas and to remove one of the bases for agitation by the Ras Tafari.

Unfortunately, the process of amelioration which preceded redevelopment was hindered by lack of co-operation among various agencies of government. Responsibility for development in Kingston was invested in the Kingston and St. Andrew Corporation, the Central Planning Unit, the Department of Housing, and the Town Planning Department. Consequently, when it was decided that additional stand-pipes were needed in the Boy's Town squatter settlement, responsibility for implementation was passed to and fro until the Water Commission, a department of the Kingston and St. Andrew Corporation, finally undertook the work (pl. 25). During the four-month waiting period much potential good-will was lost. This dilatoriness revealed the reluctance of many civil servants to act quickly for the benefit of an outcaste group and expressed the hostility shown by most members of the two upper strata to plans for redevelopment in West Kingston.

Before the rehousing scheme could be implemented, the squatters had to be convinced that the intentions of the government were genuine, and that they would not be made homeless by the redevelopment. Contacts of a charitable nature between the superodinate and subordinate strata were fairly unusual, though certain voluntary organisations maintained services such as soup kitchens, play centres, and a Boy's Town in West Kingston (fig. 90). Reinforcing the alienation of the squatters, particularly in the Back O'Wall area, was the Marxist element in the Ras Tafari cult. The Marxists were determined to maintain a situation which caused so much dissatisfaction with the government, engendered hatred towards the white and coloured populations, and thereby guaranteed considerable support for their activities in West Kingston. During 1961, however, the climate of opinion in the slums gradually altered. The favourable report of the Mission to Africa, together with the charitable activities of religious groups working from the Ebenezer Church adjacent to Back O'Wall, eventually undermined the Marxists' control of this area and removed the opposition to change. Urban redevelopment started in the middle of 1961 and aimed, during the first phase, to produce 294 houses at a cost of £280,000, almost half of which was contributed by the United States Government.[31]

While amelioration was taking place, and partly as a result of it, the core element in the Ras Tafari movement polarised and split. The religious brethren placed their hopes in repatriation, while the Marxists became increasingly committed to revolution. The Marxists were hampered by their failure to capture the religious element and by the tenuous nature of their link with other members of the lower social stratum. Recent events had strengthened the position of the religious brethren who remained suspicious of the wolf in sheep's clothing, as they termed the Marxists. Furthermore, despite their verbal violence towards the upper strata, the non-Ras Tafari members of the lower ranks still suffered from a sense of inferiority. Cohesion within this group could only be achieved by outside provocation—for example, by massive police action in West Kingston. In a crisis such as this, the Marxists might have established their leadership. But, although they eulogised the Mau Mau movement in Kenya and talked admiringly of Dessaline's butchery of the whites in revolutionary Haiti, the Marxists feared that an attempted coup would result in swift military intervention by the British.

Soon after the middle of 1961, therefore, the Marxists attempted to draw the Ras Tafari movement into the fold of a new political party, the People's Political Party, which had been launched by Millard Johnson and several black, middle-class supporters from their headquarters on the Spanish Town Road. Johnson had recently visited West Africa, and by resurrecting the name of Garvey's party, appearing in African robes, showing films of Africa, and making a direct appeal to race attempted to establish a foothold in the lower social stratum. It rapidly transpired that the PPP was virtually a front for the People's Freedom Movement (PFM), a Communist party organised by Richard Hart. The majority of the Ras Tafari brethren remained suspicious of these manoeuvres, the more so since Johnson had denied the divinity of Ras Tafari. Furthermore, the prospects of amelioration and repatriation seemed to have improved.

POLITICAL PATTERNS AND THE REFERENDUM OF 1961

By the late 1950s two major and by no means dissimilar parties, the PNP and the JLP dominated the political scene in Jamaica. Each was backed by a trade union movement drawing its support from the upper sections of the lower social stratum. However, the trade union movement provided only part of their following and in Kingston the PNP and JLP shared the loyalties of all three social strata.

The percentage of the vote cast in favour of the PNP at the 1959 election has been mapped for each polling district, these being identical to the enumeration districts used in the 1960 census. The city was divided into eight constituencies, the eastern and western extremities being incorporated into rural seats. Omitting the latter from consideration, all but one of the urban constituencies returned PNP candidates in 1959. The results for the individual polling districts, however, revealed quite distinctive patterns of political affiliation. The strength of the PNP (fig. 91) lay in East Kingston and in the area to the south of the Half Way Tree Road; both districts were dominated by the median stratum. Equally, the JLP controlled West Kingston from Trench Town to the housing estates, all of them districts inhabited by the lower ranks of the population. The JLP also took more than half the votes in the segment between the Half Way Tree, Old Hope, and Constant Spring Roads—the area occupied by the elite. This reflected the influence of domestic servants, traditionally JLP supporters, and the persistence of conservative values among some members of the upper stratum.

An interesting result was recorded in the constituency of Kingston Western. This seat was marginal and changed hands as a result of the election. Political gerrymandering was commonplace in this constituency, and more votes were recorded in Back O'Wall than should legally have been cast. The part played by the Ras Tafari movement in this area is by no means clear, though it was claimed that agents of the PNP had promised them repatriation to Africa if they voted for the party and it was returned to power. On the other hand, it seemed likely that most of the support for the PNP in this constituency came from the better tenement districts.

The referendum held in September, 1961, to decide Jamaica's membership in the West Indies Federation reflected the crisis which existed in Kingston on the eve of independence and provides a clear picture of the society in action. Ostensibly, the major problems created by federating the British West Indies had, by the late 1950s, been reduced to a number of politico-economic issues. Outstanding among these were the questions of proportional representation, tariffs, trade, and income tax, location of the capital city, and mobility of labour. By the middle of 1961 the points at issue had almost all been resolved in the interest of the largest islands, Jamaica and Trinidad. Within Jamaica, however, two opposing camps had been formed, one supporting and the other contesting Jamaica's continued membership in the Federation. Nominally, attitudes to federation were split along party lines, the PNP being pro-federation, the JLP against it. Premier Manley, unable to confirm Jamaica's continuing membership, submitted the decision to a referendum. The result was crucial, since the West Indies were due to become independent in 1962.

While the referendum apparently resolved itself into a competition between the West Indian nationalism of the two higher strata and the parochialism of the lower, in Kingston social and racial issues were predominant. In view of the failure of the government to cut the high rates of overcrowding and unemployment in the slum areas, the development of the Ras Tafari movement, and the dissociation of the lower stratum from the political ideals of the superordinate groups, the result of the referendum in Kingston was never in doubt. One of the leaders of the Ras Tafari was certainly expressing a view widely held in West Kingston when he claimed "federation is a millstone round my neck." The Ras Tafari, PPP, and the PFM all recognized that federation could be an extremely conservative and legalistic form of government, capable of maintaining the status quo and, furthermore, powerful enough to subdue internal revolts once the British army had withdrawn. They stigmatised the federation as another form of imperialism devised by the British Colonial Office with the approval of local leaders. For the median and upper strata, however, federation provided a guarantee against the dangers of radical change. Indeed, one near-white civil servant confided, "I want federation and I do not care how much it costs me. We need federal troops to keep West Kingston in its place." In an attempt to secure the status quo, a small anti-federation element in the elite began to

advocate a link with the United States. A similar proposition had been made on the eve of emancipation, and the similarity of objectives at both dates is instructive.

In September, 1961, the people of Jamaica rejected federation by a small majority. A map showing the results in Kingston (fig. 92) locates and summarises the opinions, hopes, and fears of the city's inhabitants. The pro-federal strongholds were situated in East Kingston and the area to the south of the Half Way Tree Road, both median stratum districts. However, considerable support for federation was also enlisted throughout the areas occupied by the upper echelon. In these districts a swing of at least 10 percent had been recorded in Manley's favour since 1959 (fig. 91). This was partly due to changes in population, but above all to a rapprochement achieved between the upper and median strata in the face of widespread disaffection in West Kingston. In the slums the lower stratum either abstained or registered an equally massive rejection of federation.

The result of the referendum jolted the superordinate groups out of their perennial complacency into a state of panic. Private conversations revealed widespread fear that Jamaica was about to repeat Haiti's disastrous history—an opinion that had also been current in the 1820s and again in 1865. However, the result of the referendum led to a reduction of tension in Kingston, and members of the lower stratum began to re-identify with Jamaican society. Simultaneously, the latent centrifugality in the PPP-PFM alliance came into operation. Interpreting the result as a vote of no confidence in the government the JLP immediately agitated for a general election to be held prior to independence. This they won, the PPP failing to gain a seat. In the capital the marginal constituency of Kingston Western was returned to the JLP, their candidate being a sociologist and businessman of Syrian origin.

In 1962, therefore, Kingston was the capital of a colony that was moving rapidly towards independence on the schedule prepared originally for the West Indies Federation. The referendum was lost,

the PNP defeated, and the country led by Bustamante, a conservative, pro-colonial politician who
had never been an advocate of independence. The
PPP was broken, the PFM routed, and the two-
party system confirmed; the Marxist Ras Tafarians
were discredited and the brethren were left to
dream of their return to Africa. However, while
the lower stratum rejoiced that is was to be free,
there existed the possibility that in independence
a greater degree of symbiosis might be achieved
between the social strata.

VIII: Neocolonialism and Colonialism

Independence has imposed no hiatus on the processes that were taking place in Kingston at the end of the colonial period. Since 1962 property developments have provided a veneer of modernization, but they have not been accompanied by radical social and economic change. Population growth has continued to outstrip employment and housing, though West Kingston has been subject to more effective political control and manipulation by the established political parties. Moreover, the Ras Tafari have been replaced as the leading critics of the social, political, and economic systems by intellectuals of the black power movement.

LAND-USE CHANGES

During the past decade significant changes have been effected in the pattern of commercial land use.[1] Although additional office buildings have been constructed in the city centre, a rival concentration has emerged at New Kingston, to the north of the Half Way Tree Road. In the retailing sector outstanding features have been the growth of suburban shopping plazas and the relative decline of the central business district. The centrifugal forces in the retailing system have occurred in direct response to increases in population and to the enlargement of the residential area. By the early 1960s it was clear that the economic activities of the downtown area were in jeopardy and that an engineering scheme was needed to enable the city to expand beyond the confines of the mountain-girt Liguanea Plain. It rapidly transpired that a number of development projects might go a long way toward solving these problems.

The proximity of the port to the central business district added greatly to the congestion of the commercial area, and in the port itself the handling of cargo was slow and hampered by the system of finger piers. With the demand for alongside berths and with the possibilities for containerization in mind, a Foreshore Development Corporation was set up by local capitalists to construct Newport West (fig. 93). The area to be developed lay next

to the Marcus Garvey Drive and the industrial estate and was covered by garbage dumps, marsh, and squatter camps. Population densities were low, and the squatters were quickly driven out by the police.

By 1966 most of the wharf owners in the old port had established berths at Newport West, and the waterfront adjacent to the city centre was ready for development. The government was in an ideal position to achieve this; it owned a substantial proportion of the property, was able to purchase or acquire the remainder, and could initiate the rezoning of the entire area. Newport East (fig. 93) had been reclaimed by this time and was in government hands; it was possible to offer it to the lumber trade in exchange for their property in the old port. To plan and carry out the development project the government set up the Kingston Waterfront Redevelopment Company under the chairmanship of a director of the corporation responsible for the creation of Newport West. The government in cooperation with the United Kingdom Ministry of Overseas Development invited the British firm of Shankland, Cox and Associates to produce a plan for the area. They have subsequently zoned it for shops, offices, hotels, apartments, car parks, public open space, and cultural activities. A hoverport to connect the city centre with the Palisadoes International Airport and a berth for visiting cruise ships are also included. Pedestrians will be separated from vehicles, open space will be created within relatively easy access of the slums of West Kingston, and the appearance of the waterfront will be greatly enhanced. The developments are in private hands. The first stage of the programme was carried out by a British firm of property developers and was finished during 1973.

Initially, after independence it was thought that urban growth would be difficult to accommodate, for the Liguanea Plain now has relatively little land available for subdivision. No legally defined fence inhibits expansion, but the mountains provide an effective barrier. Even in the west, where the Liguanea Plain grades into the Plain of St. Catherine and facilitates the growth of the city across the Rio Cobre in the direction of Spanish Town, Caymanas sugar estate forms an effective green belt separating Kingston from its potential satellite. Furthermore, soon after independence the government decided that the good land at Caymanas should be retained for agricultural use.

In the light of these factors the town planning department decided that Kingston should expand southwestwards around Hunt's Bay. The process was divided into a series of stages, the first focussing on the area near Dawkins Pond, the later ones extending southwards into the Hellshire Hills (fig. 93). There were two major attractions in this scheme; the entire area south of the Rio Cobre is poor-quality agricultural land and the Hellshire Hills are owned by the government. The major problem with this strategy was to devise a method for linking the new settlement to Kingston. Although the Sandy Gully Scheme was complete, the Rio Cobre was still liable to flash floods which severed the route along the north side of Hunt's Bay. A solution was put forward and engineered by the Portmore Land Development Corporation, a private body closely related to the Foreshore Development Corporation. In 1969 they linked the area near Dawkins Pond to Newport West by means of a causeway and bridge and the new town of Portmore is being created, with civic, recreational, residential, industrial, commercial and resort areas. The town planning department has been involved with the developers in preparing an outline plan for the settlement. It is hoped to build 30,000 houses over a ten-year period and to make a major contribution to Kingston's housing needs.

These schemes are not without their problems. The waterfront developments have eliminated fishing communities as well as squatters camps. Furthermore, the causeway and bridge may create a scour at the Rio Cobre's outlet into the harbour, which will disrupt the siltation basin in Hunt's Bay and adversely affect the ship channel through Kingston Harbour. The positive effects of the city centre development may be muted. The population of the city centre has declined further since 1960, and it may prove difficult to enliven the social life of the area. It is doubtful whether members of the upper and median strata will find the apartments of the redeveloped area more attractive and secure than the suburbs in the north of the Liguanea Plain.

The government hopes that the redevelopment of the waterfront will stimulate spontaneous renewal throughout the central business district; but there are two inhibiting factors. The growth of suburban shopping plazas has already siphoned off much of the clientele of upper and median status. Furthermore, urban property will probably not be refurbished until the land-tax system is revised. As the city centre increasingly caters to the lower stratum, the commercial future of the redevelopment may depend heavily on tourism and visiting cruise ships. Some critics see the redevelopment as a gimmick to attract the tourist and also attack the government for allowing a private company to initiate a new town at Portmore—essential though this may be from the point of view of population growth.

POPULATION PROBLEMS

Preliminary tabulation of the 1970 census shows that quite rapid population increases have remained characteristic of the city, though the rate of growth has decelerated during the last decade. Kingston parish, together with St. Andrew, recorded 550,000 inhabitants in 1970, the increase over the preceding ten years being slightly more than 3 percent a year. This decline in growth may be due to errors in enumeration in 1970. Nevertheless, statistics for the island as a whole suggest several reasons why the growth rate decelerated during the 1960s. Between 1960 and 1969 the Jamaican rate of natural increase fell from 33.2 to 26.1 per 1000; the birth rate dropped from 42.0 to 33.3 per 1000; and more than 20,000 people emigrated annually in 1967, 1968, and 1969, the majority going to the United States.[2] This heavy outflow was comparable to the movement to Britain which was largely brought to an end by the Commonwealth Immigrants Act of 1962. The cumulative influence of emigration over the last two decades has probably been more effective in reducing the national birth-rate than the government's family planning pro-gramme which was started in 1966. The recent impact of emigration on the capital cannot yet be evaluated, though outward movement has un-doubtedly been a factor invalidating Roberts' pro-jection of 612,000 to 634,000 inhabitants for the corporate area in 1970.[3] Nevertheless, the city has had to absorb about 130,000 people between 1960 and 1970, and this has exacerbated the labour and housing problems.

It is impossible to follow changes in the rate and incidence of unemployment since 1960. Neither the Government Employment Bureau nor the Depart-ment of Statistics have collected data of this kind, and the results of the 1970 census are not yet available. It is likely that Kingston has experienced worsening employment conditions during the past decade. An Unemployed Workers' Association was formed in the early 1960s to protest the few jobs created by the building of the Esso oil refinery in West Kingston. Official attempts to provide new employment have continued along orthodox paths but have enjoyed little success. In no year since independence has the Industrial Development Corporation been able to supply as many as a thousand new jobs.[4]

To provide adequate accommodation for King-ston's 130,000 new inhabitants at a density of four persons per house (a ratio used by the town plan-ners), about 32,500 new houses would have been required between 1960 and 1970. Even if this rate of building had been achieved, it would have made no impression on the pre-existing problem of over-crowding. The year 1965 was quite the best for house-building, but fewer than 2,500 new units were constructed under the various government and private schemes.[5] In most years the output of all types of government-financed housing barely ex-ceeded 1000 units. Furthermore, the majority of the new houses were provided by twenty-six mort-gage insurance schemes which, like those at Mona Heights and Harbour View, drew their residents

from the more densely populated middle status areas rather than from the tenements and yards. New housing for the poor has been negligible, and rehousing has made scarcely any impression on the problem of overcrowding. The emphasis on middle-income schemes is not difficult to explain; the government has found it easier to underwrite the loans of other agencies than to supply the funds required for low-income housing. Kingston's poor are quite unable to make reliable repayments for long-term loans.

Data from the Sanitary Survey of Kingston and St. Andrew show that the concentration of popula-tion in the slum areas has substantially increased.[6] Between 1960 and 1967 almost 50 percent of the city's total population growth was absorbed by the tenements, yards, and government housing schemes adjacent to the Spanish Town Road. This zone with dilapidated housing increased in popula-tion from 120,000 to 164,000, and the greater part of this expansion must have been housed in accom-modation that was either overcrowded to start with or rapidly became so. As the population has in-creased, new single-story buildings have been crammed into the area and the existing property has been subdivided. In contrast, the situation in the central and northern suburbs has improved over time; the indices of persons per room and persons per water closet were low in 1960 and lower still in 1967; and since the late 1960s infilling with luxury apartments and town houses has occurred along several of the main roads in St. Andrew. Kingston has experienced, from the demographic viewpoint, a variant of the process by which "the rich get richer and the poor poorer"; between 1960 and 1967 the sewerage system was extended north-ward into the sparsely populated suburbs and not westward into the slums of West Kingston.

It is impossible to measure change in the squatter population since 1960, though it is clear that squat-ting has not grown on anything like the same scale as in some South American cities. But despite the efforts of the government, squatting has certainly not been eradicated. The Boy's Town camp was cleared in 1962 and Back O'Wall razed in 1966-67—

in both instances to make way for urban renewal. A number of smaller camps adjacent to the foreshore in West Kingston were obliterated during the construction of the oil refinery and the development of Newport West. Elsewhere the squatter settlements have persisted or expanded; at Moonlight City squatters returned after 1968. Three years earlier the inhabitants had been paid small cash sums by a local businessman to leave the area, freeing it for development.

The government's policy is not to rehouse squatters, and the occupants of the camps that were destroyed have either sought accommodation in the tenements and yards, where they inflated the population densities, or squatted in other areas in West Kingston. A rash of huts soon appeared along the flanks of the lower part of the Sandy Gully, and squatters gradually colonized the subdivision at Riverton City, at the western extremity of the Spanish Town Road. This development had been laid out by speculators in about 1960 but had remained unoccupied. The squatters captured its scrub-covered parcels and established an illegal "site and service" scheme.

Two urban renewal projects were carried out between 1962 and 1968. Both are in West Kingston on the sites of the former squatter camps at Trench Town and Back O'Wall (Tivoli Gardens). About 450 units were eventually planned for Trench Town and 800 for Tivoli Gardens.[7] They were not intended for the inhabitants of the original squatter camps,[8] despite verbal promises to the squatters by officials who visited them. By the mid-1960s many of the shacks in Trench Town had been replaced by single-and multi-story housing, and a similar process has subsequently taken place at Tivoli Gardens. These schemes were conceived by the PNP during its last year in office, and implemented by the JLP which formed the government in 1962.

During the 1960s discontent among West Kingstonians has been controlled and manipulated by the two political parties. The provision of homes and jobs has become a major political exercise carried out for the supporters of the victorious party. Paradoxically, the struggle in West Kingston has not been for structural change but to secure power for one's party and, via the party, access to resources that are in chronically short supply. Prior to the 1967 election, mobs representing both parties took to the streets in the two constituencies where the renewal schemes were located. As both constituencies were held by the JLP, the object of the PNPs supporters was to intimidate their opponents, drive out the voters, and capture the seats at the poll. But the police and army intervened, a state of emergency was declared in West Kingston, and the JLP retained both constituencies.

SOCIAL PROTEST AND SOCIAL CONTROL

After 1962 the JLP administration did not disrupt the alliance between the upper and median strata; indeed the leadership of the party reflected this alignment. Initially, after independence, an improvement took place in social relations, and West Kingstonians began to express mild optimism about the future. The sense of "being free," the election of a new government, the skilful use of patronage, the initiation of schemes for urban renewal, and the promise of economic development produced a relatively calm period which contrasted with the years immediately preceding independence. The militant Ras Tafari lost much of its appeal, nothing came of repatriation to Africa, and many cultists were either drawn into the newly established chapter of the Ethiopian Orthodox Church or were scattered in the diaspora which followed the drive against the squatter camps.[9]

But as the decade progressed and it became clear that no major changes were going to be effected, the poorest element in the population once more became disillusioned. In 1965 street riots were aimed at the Chinese and other business groups, but the 1967 election confirmed the JLP in power and ensured the continuation of its policy. In 1968, however, a new protest movement emerged in

Kingston, based on the campus of the University of the West Indies at Mona. In that year Walter Rodney, a Guyanese who lectured on African history at the university, was barred from re-entering Jamaica after attending a congress of black writers in Montreal. University students protested against his exclusion and rioting took place in the city centre.

The movement, which gathered momentum in late 1968, derived its inspiration from three sources: it looked back to Marcus Garvey and the Ras Tafari; it employed the verbal techniques of black-power advocates in the United States; and it deployed many of the arguments for radical change which had been developed by members of the New World Group. This organization had been founded in Guyana in the early 1960s, and an affiliate had soon been established in Kingston, where its members were closely associated with the university. They expressed and published opinions highly critical of Jamaica's "neo-colonialist" government, of the organization of the bauxite, sugar, and banana industries, and of the role played by foreign-owned banks and insurance companies. Rodney's importance stems partly from his catalytic influence on the events of 1968, but more especially from his use of the concept of black power.

According to Rodney, black power has three objectives: "the break with imperialism which is historically white racist; the assumption of power by the black masses . . . ; and the cultural reconstruction of the society in the image of the blacks."[10] The movement contends that political power is now invested in "a white, brown and black petty-bourgeoisie who are culturally the creations of white capitalist society and who therefore support the white imperialist system because they gain personally and because they have been brainwashed into aiding the oppression of black people."[11] Public meetings have been exhorted to reject "the assumption that white Europeans have a monopoly of beauty and that black is the incarnation of ugliness," and told to "assert that black is beautiful."[12]

But black power leaders have explained that their movement does not necessarily exclude mulattoes, Chinese, East Indians, or whites—provided they support its objectives. Black power has become the banner for protesters in Kingston because the two-party system has debased the language of socialism, because political ideology is largely incomprehensible to the lower stratum, and because a link had to be found between the Negro intellectuals in the movement and the poor whom they hoped to lead. During slavery racism was employed by the whites to maintain the status quo; recently it has been used—so far without much success—to invoke solidarity among the lower stratum and to challenge the established order.

The political parties have responded in ways designed to contain, isolate, and undermine the movement. Since the leadership of the JLP and PNP is predominantly black, both parties have argued that black power is already a reality. Politicians have readily accepted the notion of black dignity. The JLP government named Marcus Garvey a national hero, invited Emperor Haile Selassie to Jamaica, and erected statues to "folk" leaders in its attempt to express solidarity with the lower stratum. But the published works of Malcolm X, Elijah Mohammed, and Stokely Carmichael were banned, and black-power leaders in Kingston were dubbed "misguided socialists." Nevertheless, public opinion gradually became critical of foreign capital, and the government eventually announced plans for local participation in foreign-owned banks in Kingston. The election of the PNP to office early in 1972 has provided the country with a more radical leadership, and the list of banned books has been repealed.

SUMMING-UP

This study of Kingston contains two basic themes. The first has been concerned with the analysis of the city's socio-economic characteristics and demographic growth, and the second has focussed on social structure and social change. The preceding pages have raised a number of problems of interpretation.

SPATIAL STRUCTURE

Most social scientists specializing in studies on cities use as frames of reference, either explicity or implicitly, the spatial models developed by Burgess and Hoyt. Burgess, in a seminal paper written in the mid 1920s,[13] argued that the city was organized in a series of concentric zones at the heart of which lay the central business district. Moving away from the centre, Burgess's ideal city consisted of an area in transition devoted to poor quality residences and to wholesaling and light manufacturing; three separate zones of low, medium, and high class residences; and beyond the built-up area, a peripheral district occupied by commuters. Although the commuter zone hardly exists in Kingston and it is difficult to distinguish a zone in transition, land use patterns in the capital partly follow the guidelines of Burgess' scheme.

Nevertheless, there is a tendency for some land-use patterns to form wedges either bounded by or following major lines of communication. The westward expansion of the slums along the Spanish Town Road and the concentration of elite homes in the zone bounded by the Old Hope and Constant Spring Roads are reminiscent of the land-use model developed by Hoyt in the late 1930s.[14] Hoyt claimed that the city was organised in sectors, and that once established these sectors expanded away from the city centre along lines of rapid communication as urban growth took place. The expansion of housing along the Windward Road in East Kingston and the development of a small industrial sector in the west reflect, on the microscale, the influence of communications on the spatial growth and organization of the capital.

From the point of view of the social geographer, the great advantage of Burgess's model lies in its systematisation of social patterns. According to Burgess, social status increased with distance from the city centre, and this generally applies in Kingston. Major discrepancies are the peripheral location of many of the squatter camps and public housing schemes. Burgess, like Hoyt, saw the spatial structure of the city as essentially an expression of market forces. In the commercial area of Kingston, patterns of land use reflect the ability of various enterprises to purchase or rent sites. Residential patterns express the degree of choice which members of various socio-economic groups can exercise in their selection of accommodation; and choice is conditioned by land values and transportation costs. But government housing in Kingston is located not by the recipients but by the town planners. Furthermore, squatters neither purchase nor rent their dwellings: their sole requirement is the availability of open land, and this alone influences their distribution.

During the last decade work carried out in developing countries has prompted students to re-examine and modify the models of urban land use devised by American social scientists. The universal application of Burgess' scheme in particular has been questioned by Sjoberg. He describes three main aspects of land use which, he argues, distinguish the preindustrial city from the industrial town postulated, implicitly, by Burgess. These features are: (1) the pre-eminence of the central area over the periphery, particularly as portrayed in the distribution of social classes; (2) certain finer spatial differences according to ethnic, occupation, and family ties; (3) the low functional differentiation in other land use patterns.[15]

Omitting the second of Sjoberg's points, which is adequately covered by Burgess' original work,[16] the other generalizations throw light on changes which took place in the spatial structure of Kingston, especially during the eighteenth and nineteenth centuries. Prior to 1750 the merchant elite were located near the harbour, while Negro huts were situated on or close to the edge of the built-up area. By 1800, however, the social gradient was being reversed as the white elite established permanent residences in pens on the Liguanea Plain. Since the beginning of the nineteenth century, social distributions have followed closely Burgess' model, and this has been due primarily to the introduction of modern European values and technology, including transport.

Lack of specialisation in land use was a further hallmark of Kingston during slavery and the early part of the post-emancipation period. The focal point of the city was formed not by a central business district but by the Parade, on or near to which were located the town's religious and public buildings. Harbour Street and the adjacent warehouses formed an incipient central business district. Retailing was in the hands of wholesalers, and there was virtually no specialization by commodity. Merchant houses adjoined the Negro market, and the social and economic atmosphere of this commercial area was similar to that of the bazaar. Relatively little distinction was made between workplace and residence, and houses were used as homes, workshops, or places in which public business or private transactions were conducted. While the concentration of public buildings on the Parade represented one of the most specialised forms of land use, the Parade was employed for hangings, military displays, and recreational purposes. During the nineteenth century, however, Kingston increasingly diverged from the pre-industrial model. Land use specialisation increased as the central business district developed, banks were established, the retail trade was opened up, and the suburbs expanded. The focus of the city shifted away from the Parade towards Harbour Street and King Street. The movement towards modernisation was greatly influenced by the influx of British skills and values after 1865. Public systems of transport, electricity, sewerage, and water supply were introduced or expanded, and this had a profound effect on the patterns of urban growth and morphology.

Careful examination of the spatial models developed by Burgess and Sjoberg suggests that they can be reconciled, and that "the proper conclusion that should be drawn from ecological analysis is that ecological patterns of industrial, preindustrial and 'developing' cities are determined by the same set of variables."[17] But as the values of these variables differ from society to society and from time to time within the same society, so the spatial patterns differ too. The distribution of squatters in Kingston partly conforms to Sjoberg's scheme; in a negative way, it is also explicable by Burgess' model.

One of the outstanding features in Kingston is the close correspondence between spatial and social structure. This is partly due to the size of the city, to the simplicity of the topography, and to the sharp contrast between "haves" and "have-nots." According to the 1960 census, the city was divided into a number of clear-cut socio-economic spaces; and, since there were correlations between occupation and education, family, religion, and colour, the distribution of cultural and racial groups tended to follow socio-economic patterns. Most of the socio-cultural areas of the city are separated from one another by sharp lines on the map, and these are usually traceable in the field by examining land-use changes. The transition from the slums to the area of medium quality housing on the northern edge of West Kingston, for example, is made in a matter of a few yards. Furthermore, there has been relatively little change in socio-economic patterns through time. Some of the pens on the lower Liguanea Plain have been incorporated into zones of middle- and lower-class housing, but few areas outside the eighteenth-century grid have had a succession of different socio-economic groups passing through them.

Three factors are highly important: elite districts were established on the upper part of the Liguanea Plain almost two hundred years ago and together with the areas of median status provided a barrier to the northward expansion of the slums; persons of low status have been crammed, at ever increasing densities, into the most dilapidated sections of the city; and the radial expansion of social areas has been the norm since 1920. Furthermore, the social valuation placed on the various parts of the Liguanea Plain has changed little through time. Despite land reclamation, West Kingston has remained the residence of the poorest inhabitants, while the upper Liguanea Plain has been given over to the elite. These valuations are partly responsible for the emergence of both concentric zones and sectors in the residential patterns of the capital. It is hardly surprising that throughout the present century persons of median status have lived either on the east side of the city or occupied the buffer zones between the upper and lower strata.

Little is known about the way in which members of the various strata perceive the urban environment or make their way around in the city.[18] Nevertheless, there is evidence that the higher strata prefer paths which avoid West Kingston and now rarely frequent the city centre. Urban growth and spatial separation undoubtedly have enhanced social separation and nurtured the formation of group stereotypes. The physical growth of the city has had a further consequence. The squatter camp at Moonlight City on the foreshore in West Kingston and the elite homes in the Red Hills are visible one from the other. The contrast in material conditions between these two areas acts as a constant reminder to the squatters of their deprivation and provides a stimulus to their anti-white attitudes.

OVERCROWDING

Kingston provides a classic example of an overcrowded metropolis. Population pressure is increasing because population growth is self-generating while the economy is not. Migration to the city is completely unrelated to the opportunities for employment,[19] and unemployment is widespread and secular in nature. The overcrowding of accommodation affects more than one-fifth of the city's inhabitants, and squatting, cotching, and scuffling represent long-established and illegal adaptations to perpetual poverty. How valid are the criteria of overcrowding? It may be argued that the index used to define the overcrowding of accommodation, namely a density of more than two persons per room or more than eight persons to each hygienic water closet, is setting too high a standard of living for the inhabitants of Kingston. Nevertheless, these are the criteria used by government agencies in Jamaica; in a practical sense they provide the basis on which political decisions affecting urban renewal have been taken. In all probability they fall below the level of expectations of indigent Kingstonians.

The second index of overcrowding—unemployment—is difficult to handle. Although the statistics have been drawn from official sources and enable increases in unemployment (and overcrowding in the broadest sense) to be measured through time, there is every reason to be cautious; for unemployment frequently masks illegal self-employment. But however carefully these statistics are interpreted, they lead to the inescapable conclusion that Kingston cannot absorb the rapidly growing population and cannot provide jobs which the inhabitants consider desirable. By West Indian standards the pressures on housing and employment in parts of Kingston occur at a very low level of living, but at one involving malnutrition rather than starvation.

Faced with this massive problem, successive Jamaican governments have adopted the view that economic development would provide a cure for unemployment and eventually bring about social change. But as there seems to be no verification of this process, it is perhaps worthwhile looking at alternative strategies which might have been adopted. Unemployment might have been tackled by a programme of public employment, as it was for a short time in the early 1950s; squatting and overcrowding could have been eliminated by government rehousing. Both policies would have required government intervention and the diversion of considerable development funds. Consequently, even if the symptoms of unemployment and overcrowding had been removed, the cost would have been detectable on the financial balance sheet. An alternative and cheaper policy might have involved the recognition of the squatter camps, provision of basic amenities, and granting of title to land. Where government assistance has been forthcoming, many squatter settlements in Latin America have been up-graded by their occupants on a self-help basis and gradually incorporated into the fabric and social life of the towns.[20]

Prior to independence no attempt was made to turn to the other side of the population/resource ratio and to introduce family planning. This failure was due to a combination of factors. These include the difficulty of dealing with persons of low social status among whom illegitimacy is the norm and to whom most forms of planning are anathema, pressure from the Roman Catholic minority in Kingston, fear that birth control could be regarded as an infringement of personal liberty, and knowledge that public discussion of family limitation would be greeted by a spate of wall slogans in West Kingston claiming that "birth-control is aimed at wiping out the black man." Only since 1966 has it been possible to create a bi-partisan policy on family planning.

Historically, the main safety valve for population pressure in both Kingston and Jamaica has been emigration. Major outflows occurred in 1850 and at the turn of the century, in both instances reducing or almost removing unemployment. But emigration to Britain between 1953 and 1960 and to North America since 1967 has failed to reduce unemployment in Kingston. Furthermore, while internal migration has carried some of the worst symptoms of population pressure to the city, emigration has resulted in the loss of some of the city's best qualified workers. One point is clear; throughout the entire period since emancipation population surplus in Kingston has been expressed either in terms of emigration or overcrowding or both. Ideas about the growth of the capital now tend to be divided along urban/rural lines. Agricultural experts insist that the towns, and especially the capital, will have to absorb the surplus rural population, increased, perhaps, through mechanization in the sugar industry, while urban planners hope that rural migration can be slowed down.

RACE, CULTURE, AND STATUS

The social structure of Kingston is made up of three hierarchically organised strata which can be described as essentially white, brown, and black. Each is separated from the others by sharp breaks on the socio-economic scale, and within each grade fairly distinct cultural practices are maintained. How fundamental are the differences between these cultures? All Kingstonians speak English, though a Creole variant incorporating a number of Twi loan-words of West African origin is widespread among Negroes of low status.[21] Strong family ties are recognised by the entire population, but among the lower stratum kin are used for the placement of children but rarely as the basis for economic co-operation. Furthermore, the matrifocal family and high rates of illegitimacy are peculiar to this group. While Christianity is the only major religion, the lower stratum is closely involved in non-denominational sects or Afro-Christian cults. It is a paradox that the social element which displays African survivals remains essentially unaware of them, yet has been vitally interested in the pseudo-Africa conjured up by the Ras Tafari.

The cultural differences between the upper and middle strata are relatively slight and depend on nuances of family form and religious belief. M. G. Smith has described these strata as cultural sections and argued that the moral axioms and value system of any one section are not those of another. "Materialism provides the formative principle or reference point in the value system of the upper section, while social status dominates the value system of the intermediate section, and values of immediate physical gratification are central among the third section, spiritual as well as secular values reflecting these principles."[22] Although the social strata in Kingston are not so sharply distinguished culturally as, say, the Chinese and Malays in Malaya, the great virtue of the pluralist point of view is that it stresses that there are "divisions in Jamaican society which are different in degree and in kind from those which separate the classes of English or North American society."[23]

The relevance of the plural model becomes clearer when the discussion is placed in an historical context. In Kingston the initial social contact was between African slaves and white masters. As the Africans became creolized, various aspects of tribal culture were lost. But despite the erosive influence of slavery, the Negroes retained certain generalised versions of West African culture and some survivals derived principally from the Ashanti. During the eighteenth century a coloured group of median status slowly emerged as a result of island-wide miscegenation. In Kingston they remained an intermediate element distinguished from the whites by their colour and status, and by their acceptance of certain cultural practices derived from the lower stratum.

The three cultural traditions were ranked hierarchically. This is still so, and social mobility between the strata depends on acculturation. However, it would be misleading to imply that the content of these cultural strata has remained unchanged since emancipation. Even during slavery various modifications took place,[24] and by the end of the period the missions, and in some instances the established church, were acculturating the Negro slave. But the process of culture change was incomplete. The decline in missionary work after 1865 bequeathed to the twentieth century an Afro-Christian tradition overlaid by a veneer of Victorian values. The whites, too, became more Victorian in their behaviour as the nineteenth century progressed, and this process was greatly enhanced by the arrival of expatriate officials after 1865. These two traditions, the Afro-Christian and the British, provide the basis for cultural pluralism: the middle stratum embraces elements of both, but disrupts neither.

The middle and lower strata have been caught in a state of arrested acculturation. Internally they have changed, but less through direct contact with one another than through the infusion of ideas and values brought from outside by agents from Britain, and, more recently, from North America. Since the end of the Second World War both the median and lower strata have been involved in the spiral of rising expectations; but each visualises the material prospects for its future through its own cultural lenses.

It may be argued that much of the behaviour of the lower stratum in Kingston is consistent with what Oscar Lewis calls "the culture of poverty."[25] Many of the social and cultural characteristics of the poorest element in the city are similar to those attributed by Lewis to the slum dwellers of Mexico City,[26] and San Juan, Puerto Rico.[27] Although both these cities have had rather different social histories from Kingston, this comparison draws attention to the influence of status on culture or, more precisely, on acculturation. Before emancipation the culture of the free coloureds was largely conditioned by their intermediate legal status. Much of the present-day behaviour of the lower stratum, likewise, is explicable in terms of current socio-economic problems and needs. Structural situations both prevent acculturation and validate the inherited culture pattern. For the individual of low status, acculturation is even more difficult to achieve than these remarks suggest. Discussing the problem of mobility between the lower and median strata, Madeline Kerr concludes that "this is difficult, probably impossible, to effect without extreme tension. ... In the middle class he has to adopt another family system with a different ideology. He has to be married, own certain prestige goods, belong to a respected church, and in general have a very different view of general relations."[28]

Leaving aside the question of social mobility, the beliefs and values of persons of lower status inhibit their participation in the modern sector. Fundamentalist belief in the Bible has been identified as a major conservative influence.[29] For Kingstonians of low status the Bible verifies balmyard miracles and visions, prophecies and healings, and supplies authority for the existence of duppies. As Kerr indicates, preoccupation with the supernatural "in itself need not be pathological, but it takes a destructive form when people holding these beliefs try to compete in the modern world."[30] Furthermore, within the lower stratum, tensions are created by the inability of the population to live up to the pseudo-Victorian standards of morality, family organization, and behaviour set by the missionaries during the nineteenth century.

The fact that people are trying to adjust to a pattern which in itself is an economic impossibility; the fact that children are brought up to adjust to a family situation in which the mother is basically the most important person yet the father has to be respected as if he were; the fact that a coloured man knows that he will have more difficulties than his white neighbour in reaching posts of responsibility; the fact that whiteness is identified with "good" and desirable, and black with "bad" and undesirable; the fact that the majority of people know that is is unlikely that they will spend their lives at anything more than subsistence level; all these cause the most far-reaching psychological reactions.[31]

Outstanding among these are the Negro's tendency to blame others for his own misfortunes, and his dependence on outside help, often from the government.

Race and colour carry important implications, both psychological and symbolic, though they are less critical as formative principles of the social stratification in Kingston than either socio-economic status or culture. Despite their partial acculturation to Creole society, racial distinctiveness is important for the recent immigrant groups. Colour, however, remains of the greatest significance among the middle stratum, and here nuance of shade is a vital social arbiter. Colour also distinguishes between the commercial and political elites, but at the lower level of the hierarchy it is of little significance in interpersonal relations. The lower stratum is separated from its superordinates by social and geographical distance, and Negroes of low status are unable to distinguish between white minority groups such as Syrians and Jews. Despite the divisive forces operating in the lower stratum, there is a growing awareness among its members of the need to establish a corporate identity, and it is at this level of tentative group activity that the rejection of the white bias is particularly important.

NATURE OF SOCIAL CHANGE

Throughout the city's history the upper stratum has been preoccupied with maintaining the status quo. But relations between the strata have changed. Emancipation was the major turning point, and it was imposed by the mother country. After emancipation authority was derived not from the white upper stratum but from the enfranchised male population. Nevertheless, political power was retained by the upper stratum and shared with the median. To prevent electoral power passing into the hands of the lower ranks, the upper and median strata transferred authority to the British Crown in 1865. By this manoeuvre the influence of the upper echelon was maintained. Relations between the strata returned to a situation reminiscent of the period of slavery, though status was no longer legally defined, and British arbitration could, theoretically, be invoked.

The coloured middle stratum soon regretted the support it had given to the introduction of Crown Colony government after the Morant Bay Rebellion. Its members suffered social and political demotion and, in Kingston, were phased out of the civil service. During the latter part of the nineteenth century the coercive form of the judicial system gradually took shape. The law was, of course, highly sectional in content. An attempt was made to stamp out the funeral wakes of the Negro by imposing fines, and in 1898 obeah was made punishable by flogging.[32]

The post-emancipation period was brought to an end by the riots of 1938. After 1944 authority was increasingly vested in the electorate, and the lower stratum in particular. But political power was transferred to the median stratum, especially after 1953. During the PNP administration lasting from 1955 to the eve of independence, the link between the two upper strata was reforged. Together they promoted economic development, multi-racialism, and federation. Under this political system, power would have been shared with similar social elements in the other British West Indian islands, and the federation called upon to arbitrate in internal disputes between the strata. In Jamaica this would have secured the status quo from which both the upper and median strata benefitted so enormously and would have permitted the appropriation of political power, re-creating the situation which had existed between 1832 and 1865. Furthermore, the federation would undoubtedly have supplied an external guarantee for the established order comparable to that enjoyed during the period of Crown

Colony government. But while the conservative revision of 1865 succeeded, that of 1961 failed. Nevertheless, the coalition between the median and upper strata has persisted through the first decade of independence.

Only those changes which were not crucial to the social order have been implemented. The reluctance with which the upper stratum conceded full civil rights to the Jews, free Negroes, and coloured people at the close of the period of slavery contrasts with their extreme opposition to emancipation. When a scholarship system was introduced during the late 1950s to support entry to the secondary schools, it recruited children from the lower stratum and beheaded its potential leadership. It is significant that no major national leader has emerged from this section of the population. Of even greater importance was the failure of the PNP to maintain and to win support for the socialist policy it professed in the early 1940s. This policy was the closest either party got to changing the hierarchic structure of the social system in Kingston and Jamaica during the colonial period. The opposition encountered from the whites, and the failure of the intellectual element within the middle stratum to establish a sense of identity with the Negro lower class, emphasize the problem of implementing a programme of rational and thorough-going change. This helps to explain the problems and policies of the black power movement since 1968. The fate of the workers' movement led by Bustamante in 1938 is also instructive. Two factors were critical; the rioters lacked organization, and they were confronted by the forces of the colonial power. Bustamante emerged as a charismatic leader whose aim it was not to overturn society but to perpetuate his movement and the social order to which his followers were hostile.

The social system has depended for its maintenance on the superior cohesion and power of the small superordinate group and its ability to secure assistance from the middle stratum. Negroes have been subject to the legal violence of the statute book, and in periods of crisis naked force has been deployed on the streets of Kingston. Under these conditions, members of the lower stratum have had three courses of action open to them; withdrawal, resignation, or revolt. If resignation has been most commonly adopted, the pattern of withdrawal has certainly become well established. Slaves ran away, and some of the Africans committed suicide in their attempt to return to their homeland. After emancipation many of the ex-slaves withdrew into the interior to become peasants; in more recent times the indigent in Kingston have become squatters. At the end of the colonial period the cult of Ras Tafari represented the most extreme form of withdrawal from Kingston's society, advocating a variety of apartheid which actually involved physical segregation through emigration. Nevertheless, withdrawal has frequently been transformed into revolt. In Kingston slaves had their plans for insurrection, like the Ras Tafari in 1961, and even made attempts to overthrow their masters. In both cases the protest was expressed through magico-religious or religious channels. Black power may lack this deep emotional appeal.

Social changes in Kingston have been phased with the changes that occurred throughout Jamaican society; hence the vital importance in this study of the years 1834, 1865, 1938 to 1944, and 1961-1962. Political decisions made from 1865 through 1962 affected Kingston's status and role as capital, while there was a close association between emancipation and the abandonment of mercantilism for free trade, and between the granting of adult suffrage and the espousal of economic development. These political changes were either imposed or authorised by the British Government, but all were preceded by protests made by members of the lower stratum, if not in Kingston then in the rural areas. The referendum of 1961 contained the only major peaceful protest, and in Kingston the result faithfully reflected the spatial organisation of the social system. Since independence of the city's hierarchic social structure has become even more clearly expressed spatially as the upper and median strata have pressed northwards into the foothills or spilled over into new peripheral developments, either way increasing their distance from the growing slums.

The coalition between the median and upper strata has been firmly established; the median stratum fills the principal political and bureaucratic roles, while the upper stratum operates behind the scenes and controls the economy. These strata remain in command of the situation, running the two-party system and the trade unions, manipulating the land, labour, and housing markets, and controlling the regulatory arms of government—the police and the defence forces. Jamaica's motto for independence "Out of Many One People" is scarcely closer to realization than it was ten years ago, and Kingston is still beset by the unresolved problems of the colonial period.

Tables

TABLE 1

Growth and Racial Composition of the Population of Kingston, 1700–1861*

Year	White	Coloured	Negro	Total
1700				5,000[a]
1762		1,093[b]		
1774	5,000[c]	1,200[c]	5,000[c]	11,200
1788	6,539[d]	3,280[d]	16,659[d]	26,478
1790	8,000[e]	1,500[e]	14,000[e]	23,500
1807	8,500[f]	3,500[f]	18,000[f]	30,000
1812	10,000[g]	2,500[g] (free coloured)	18,000 (slaves)	33,000[g]
		2,500[g] (free Negroes)		
1817			18,000[h]	
1828				35,000[i]
1832			12,531[j] (slaves)	
1861				27,400[k]

* The terms "Negro" and "coloured" are probably interchangeable with "slaves" and "free non-white" respectively. Many writers are not clear on this point, however

[a] This calculation is based on the difference between the population of Port Royal in 1668 (8,000) and the number listed on the death roll at the end of 1692 (3,000).

[b] Both free Negroes and people of colour, calculated from the certificates of freedom (see W. J. GARDNER, *History of Jamaica*, 1872, 173).

[c] E. Long, *History of Jamaica*, 1774, Vol. III, 103. Clearly, the figures are under estimates. See Bryan Edwards, *The History, Civil and Commercial, of the British Colonies in the West Indies*, 1793, Vol. 1. 922.

[d] EDWARDS, *op.cit.*, Vol. 1., 261–2.

[e] W. BECKFORD, *A Descriptive Account of the Island of Jamaica*, Vol. 1., XXXI.

[f] R. RENNY, *An History of Jamaica*, 1807, 103.

[g] *Jamaica Almanack*, 1832, 27.

[h] GARDNER, *op.cit.*, 254.

[i] G. W. ROBERTS, *The Population of Jamaica*, 1957, 51.

[j] *Returns of Registration of Slaves*, 1832.

[k] *Census of Jamaica*, 1861.

TABLE 2

Sex Ratios for Kingston, St. Andrew and Jamaica, 1861–1943

(Males per 1,000 females)

Year	Kingston	St. Andrew	Jamaica
1861	671	934	938
1871	680	987	954
1881	704	973	950
1891	708	939	917
1911	723	891	916
1921	721	826	881
1943	775	774	937

Source: Censuses of Jamaica.

TABLE 3

Racial Composition of the Population of Kingston
(In percentages)

Year	Black	Brown	White	East Indian	Chinese	Syrian	Total
% of Kingston's population							
1788[a]	63.0	12.4	24.6	—	—	—	100.0
1881[a]	49.7	36.4	13.0	0.5	0.2	—	100.0
1943[b]	60.2	30.7	2.8[c]	2.6[d]	3.1[e]	0.3	100.0
% of racial group resident in Kingston							
1788[a]	6.7	32.8	21.8	—	—	—	9.0
1881[a]	4.3	12.8	34.6	1.9	85.0	—	7.6
1943[b]	15.6	30.2	60.4	20.4[d]	50.3[e]	61.7	19.3

Sources: B. EDWARDS, *The History, Civil and Commercial, of the British Colonies in the West Indies*. Vol. 1, 1793, 922; Censuses of Jamaica for 1881 and 1943.

[a] Kingston parish

[b] Kingston and suburban St. Andrew

[c] includes Jews

[d] includes East Indian Coloureds

[e] includes Chinese Coloureds

TABLE 4

DISTRIBUTION OF OCCUPATIONS, 1881 AND 1921
(In percentages)

Occupation	1881			1921		
	Jamaica	Kingston	St. Andrew	Jamaica	Kingston	St. Andrew
Professional	0.8	3.5	2.1	1.3	4.8	3.9
Domestic	2.6	8.6	1.5	6.1	14.9	8.9
Commercial	1.3	5.6	0.8	2.4	10.7	4.9
Agricultural	35.9	6.2	25.9	33.3	0.8	21.8
Industrial	8.3	24.4	4.8	8.6	26.0	10.6
Indefinite and non-productive..	51.4	51.5	65.0	48.3	43.1	49.8
Total population	580,804	38,566	34,982	858,118	62,707	54,598

Sources: Censuses of Jamaica for 1881 and 1921.

TABLE 5

RELIGIOUS GROUPS IN KINGSTON, ST. ANDREW,
AND JAMAICA IN 1881
(In percentages)

Religious group	Kingston	St. Andrew	Jamaica
Episcopalian (Anglican) ..	25.91	22.06	19.76
Presbyterian	4.08	0.72	3.66
Wesleyan Methodist	23.54	14.22	9.55
Baptist	7.88	16.83	13.95
Congregationalist	0.90	0.35	0.91
Moravian	0.10	0.05	2.77
Roman Catholic	17.26	4.26	1.89
Jewish	2.83	0.22	0.43
Pagan	0.16	0.37	0.76
Other Christian sects	17.60	42.39	45.06
Total	38,566	34,982	580,804

Source: Census of Jamaica, 1881.

TABLE 6

CONDITION OF DWELLINGS, 1943

Location	Total dwellings	Condition					
		Good		Fair		Bad	
		Number	%	Number	%	Number	%
Jamaica	322,609	54,418	16.86	119,704	37.08	147.046	45.60
Kingston	34,789	7,795	22.41	17,668	50.80	9,275	26.70
St. Andrew	35,993	10,634	29.60	14,079	39.14	11,206	31.16

Source: Census of Jamaica, 1943.

TABLE 7

CONSTRUCTION OF DWELLINGS, 1943
(In percentages)

	Jamaica	Kingston	St. Andrew
Type of dwelling			
Barracks	2.6	0.0	0.3
Single family one storey ..	85.0	62.0	80.1
Single family two storeys .	1.8	6.0	2.0
Duplex	0.1	0.0	0.2
Tenement	8.2	28.5	15.1
Other and not specified...	2.2	3.3	2.1
Outside walls			
Wood	49.29	57.60	63.00
Concrete	3.90	16.99	10.09
Brick	1.89	10.71	1.29
Wattle	18.63	0.15	10.50
Nogging	4.11	11.56	10.04
Spanish wall	14.60	0.83	1.13
Thatch	2.30	—	0.14
Mortar	4.81	1.04	3.88
Other and not specified ..	0.54	0.11	0.44
Roof			
Wood	27.21	19.81	14.82
Galvanized iron	46.45	77.99	76.10
Thatch	24.51	—	6.72
Tile	0.29	0.08	1.09
Other and not specified ..	1.28	0.21	1.33

TABLE 7

	Jamaica	Kingston	St. Andrew
Floor			
Wood	89.59	99.36	94.70
Concrete	1.27	0.23	0.41
Earth	8.58	0.27	4.52
Other and not specified ..	0.44	0.14	0.55

Source: Census of Jamaica, 1943.

TABLE 8

KITCHEN AND TOILET FACILITIES, 1943
(In percentages)

	Jamaica	Kingston	St. Andrew
Kitchen facilities			
In dwelling	3.2	8.1	13.2
Outside dwelling	83.6	84.7	72.5
None	13.2	7.2	14.4
Toilet facilities			
Water closet	10.9	65.0	25.4
Pit latrine	69.7	34.4	73.2
Bucket	0.8	0.5	0.1
None	18.5	0.1	1.2

Source: Census of Jamaica, 1943.

TABLE 9

EMPLOYMENT BY INDUSTRY IN KINGSTON AND ST. ANDREW, 1943

	Kingston				St. Andrew			
	Males		Females		Males		Females	
Industry	No.	%	No.	%	No.	%	No.	%
Agriculture	521	1.82	38	0.15	7,577	22.85	1,476	1.75
Quarrying	8	0.03	3	0.01	74	0.22	62	0.24
Fishing and forestry	500	1.74	0	—	286	0.87	1	—
Electricity, gas and water...........	314	1.09	11	0.04	466	1.41	46	0.18
Manufacture and mechanic	6,919	24.10	778	2.72	5,656	17.10	863	3.33
Construction	5,514	19.20	151	0.59	5,515	16.67	200	0.77
Transport and communication	4,044	14.06	71	0.28	2,097	8.97	68	0.26
Trade	4,227	14.69	4,995	17.39	3,754	11.33	4,613	17.80
Finance, insurance, and real estate ...	148	0.52	76	0.28	283	0.86	149	0.58
Public services	4,623	16.10	5,014	17.45	4,100	12.39	3,438	13.27
Domestic service	534	1.86	9,513	33.01	2,052	6.19	11,148	43.09
Odd jobs	1,419	4.94	203	0.79	1,939	5.85	278	1.07
Total	28,771	100.00	25,791	100.00	33,095	100.00	25,906	100.00

Source: Census of Jamaica, 1943.

TABLE 10

INCIDENCE OF SPECIFIED DISEASES IN THE POPULATION
SURVEYED IN THE SLUM AREAS OF KINGSTON BETWEEN
1933 AND 1935.
(In percentages)

Area	Tuberculosis	Dysentery	Enteric fever
Trench Pen	3.78	0.27	1.08
New Town, Hannah's Pen,			
Victoria Town	1.20	0.10	0.63
Admiral Pen	0.43	0.29	0.14
Kingston Pen and Back O'Wall	0.30	0.20	0
Spanish Town Road	2.91	0.76	0.76
Lower Smith Village	2.28	0.28	0.57
Smith Village	17.49	3.51	7.75
Fletcher's Land	1.02	0.43	1.36
Rae Town	1.73	1.04	0.35
Price Lane	1.87	0	3.27
Hannah Town	1.48	0.23	1.17

Source: *Memorandum dealing with the Development of Trench Pen Township . . .* , Central Housing Advisory Board, Kingston, 1936, Appendix (Part A), 2.

TABLE 11

RACIAL COMPOSITION OF KINGSTON AND
SUBURBAN ST. ANDREW AND JAMAICA, 1943

	Kingston–Suburban St. Andrew[a]		Jamaica	
Race	No.	%	No.	%
Black	113,570	60.17	965,960	78.10
Coloured	58,027	30.74	216,348	17.50
White	4,627	2.45	13,809	1.12
Chinese	3,350	1.77	6,886	0.60
Chinese Coloured . . .	2,428	1.29	5,508	0.45
East Indian	3,634	1.93	21,393	1.70
East Indian Coloured	1,249	0.66	5,114	0.40
Syrian	495	0.26	834	0.06
Syrian Coloured	100	0.05	171	—
Jews	723	0.38	1,259	0.10
Others	250	0.14	848	0.08
Total	188,764	100.00	1,237,063	100.00

Source: *Census of Jamaica, 1943.*
a Excluding Port Royal and institutions

TABLE 12

SEX RATIO IN KINGSTON, ST. ANDREW, AND JAMAICA, 1943

Race		Kingston	St. Andrew	Jamaica
Black	Male	29,454	39,471	472,348
	Female	36,758	45,903	493,612
	Ratio	802	860	957
Coloured	Male	14,381	12,314	28,272
	Female	21,370	17,338	118,076
	Ratio	605	710	832
White	Male	844	2,830	6,288
	Female	846	3,804	7,521
	Ratio	992	744	836
Chinese & Chinese	Male	2,353	1,111	6,922
Coloured	Female	1,801	974	5,472
	Ratio	1,305	1,142	1,265
East Indian &	Male	895	1,701	13,405
East Indian	Female	1,008	1,813	13,102
Coloured	Ratio	888	939	1,023
Jewish	Male	203	324	625
	Female	163	372	634
	Ratio	1,231	871	986

Source: *Census of Jamaica, 1943.*

TABLE 13

ILLITERACY AMONG THE POPULATION AGED OVER SEVEN, 1943
(In percentages)

Race	Jamaica	Kingston	St. Andrew
All Races	25.55	8.35	15.42
Black	28.16	10.11	15.11
Coloured	13.82	3.96	3.46
White	3.62	4.76	3.64
Chinese and			
Chinese Coloured	13.93	12.70	12.38
East Indian and			
East Indian Coloured . . .	48.60	31.82	46.25
Syrian and Syrian Coloured.	5.70	11.50	1.55

Source: *Census of Jamaica, 1943.*

TABLE 14

Education of the Population Aged over Seven, 1943

(In percentages)

Level of education	Black	Coloured	White	Chinese and Chinese Coloured	East Indian and East Indian Coloured	Syrian and Syrian Coloured	All Races
Jamaica	100	100	100	100	100	100	100
Elementary	70.49	71.10	34.97	73.70	49.10	46.10	70.49
Practical training	0.47	2.18	3.62	2.71	0.70	4.91	0.86
Secondary education	0.64	7.08	44.60	9.30	1.44	41.59	2.63
Pre-professional	0.25	1.07	4.91	0.33	0.13	1.05	0.43
Professional	0.04	0.32	8.29	0.11	0.06	0.82	0.20
Illiterate	28.16	13.82	3.62	13.93	48.60	5.70	25.55
Kingston	100	100	100	100	100	100	100
Elementary	85.90	80.90	37.62	73.51	62.30	48.60	82.97
Practical training	1.44	4.12	4.29	3.42	1.64	4.35	2.44
Secondary education	2.40	10.17	42.80	9.95	4.28	37.68	5.95
Pre-professional	0.33	7.49	5.06	0.34	0.25	0.73	0.55
Professional	0.07	0.17	5.42	0.60	0.13	0	0.20
Illiterate	10.11	3.96	4.76	12.70	31.82	11.50	8.35
St. Andrew	100	100	100	100	100	100	100
Elementary	82.09	66.68	33.30	66.20	47.98	35.32	74.10
Practical training	1.19	5.28	5.96	3.95	1.77	5.41	2.36
Secondary education	1.44	21.85	48.99	16.63	3.43	54.60	9.32
Pre-professional	0.32	1.64	2.53	0.52	0.35	1.80	0.92
Professional	0.07	0.94	9.01	0.39	0.18	1.29	0.78
Illiterate	15.11	3.46	3.64	12.38	46.25	1.15	12.42

Source: Census of Jamaica, 1943.

TABLE 15

CONJUGAL CONDITION, 1943
(In percentages)

Conjugal Condition	All races	Black	Coloured	White	Chinese and Chinese Coloured	East Indian and East Indian Coloured	Syrian and Syrian Coloured
Jamaica							
Total population	1,237,063	965,960	216,348	13,809	12,394	26,507	1,005
0–14 years	36.55	36.99	34.41	20.22	44.69	51.89	36.14
Single	67.20	69.10	67.65	49.00	70.01	60.48	64.88
Married	17.11	15.52	20.82	42.51	23.93	26.98	30.42
Common law	11.56	12.65	7.80	0.89	4.86	9.85	1.59
Widowed	2.91	2.69	3.55	6.96	0.39	3.92	2.81
Divorced	0.08	0.05	1.31	0.57	0.02	0.17	0.30
Kingston							
Total population	110,083	66,212	35,751	1,790	4,154	1,903	153
0–14 years	25.12	23.34	26.36	14.81	43.37	34.48	27.46
Single	65.47	65.65	66.25	54.10	65.40	57.19	60.80
Married	16.92	14.04	19.28	35.39	35.79	28.05	33.34
Common law	14.31	17.49	9.60	1.85	5.37	9.78	1.96
Widowed	3.13	2.72	2.65	8.10	1.16	4.78	3.92
Divorced	0.12	0.09	0.17	0.56	0.07	0.11	—
St. Andrew							
Total population	128,146	85,374	29,652	6,633	2,085	3,514	467
0–14 years	29.88	30.82	27.48	20.25	48.18	37.73	38.14
Single	63.60	65.30	63.50	46.76	67.90	55.65	67.46
Married	21.76	17.86	25.82	45.15	26.20	31.98	29.32
Common law	9.42	13.44	5.79	0.36	4.17	8.40	0.22
Widowed	3.79	2.96	4.40	0.71	1.63	3.90	2.57
Divorced	0.16	0.06	0.29	0.65	—	0.11	0.44

Source: Census of Jamaica, 1943.

TABLE 16

STANDARD OF EDUCATION ATTAINED BY POPULATION AGED 15 YEARS AND OVER, 1960

Secondary education	Kingston		St. Andrew		Jamaica	
	No.	%	No.	%	No.	%
Males						
Nil	1,381	3.9	5,410	6.6	83,811	19.0
Under 2 years non-secondary	102	0.3	426	0.5	3,737	0.8
2–3 years non-secondary	978	2.7	3,943	4.8	32,968	7.5
4–5 years non-secondary	5,378	15.0	14,184	17.4	95,526	20.9
6–8 years non-secondary	22,664	63.3	41,141	50.6	191,993	43.5
Jamaica local 2d and 3d year.........	908	2.5	1,547	1.9	6,194	1.4
No secondary school certificate	2,960	8.3	6,883	8.5	15,075	3.4
With secondary school certificate.....	1,314	3.7	6,315	7.8	12,114	2.7
Degree	133	0.4	1,499	1.8	2,406	0.5
Total	35,818	100.0	81,348	100.0	440,823	100.0
Females						
Nil	1,607	3.3	5,573	5.2	68,804	13.6
Under 2 years non-secondary	184	0.4	493	0.5	3,528	0.7
2–3 year non-secondary	1,426	3.0	4,771	4.5	32,323	6.4
4–5 years non-secondary	7,824	16.2	18,978	17.8	106,224	20.9
6–8 years non-secondary	30,304	62.8	55,980	52.6	248,451	49.0
Jamaica local 2d and 3d year	1,380	2.9	2,646	2.5	10,795	2.1
No secondary school certificate	3,986	8.3	10,111	9.5	21,417	4.2
With secondary school certificate.....	1,513	3.1	7,237	6.8	14,051	2.8
Degree	37	0.1	575	0.5	890	0.2
Total	48,261	100.0	106,364	100.0	506,483	100.0

Source: Census of Jamaica, 1960.

TABLE 17

PRODUCTS APPROVED UNDER THE PIONEER INDUSTRIES LAW
1949–1959

*Byprocrete building units
    Product
Gypsum products
Cocoa processing and manufacturing
*Laundry blue
Tool handles
Salt
Carbon dioxide gas
*Limestone
Wirebound box shooks, packages, and sanitary spoons
Jelly crystals, dessert and pudding powders, baking mix with
    icing mix
*Paper
*Anhydrous alcohol
Metal containers
Plastic products
Pre-stressed and post-stressed concrete products
*Assembly of radio receiving sets, fluorescent lamps, and trans-
    formers for electrical equipment
Ice cream cones
*Handblocking on fabrics
Peanut and cashew products
*Boards from celluslistic materials
*Fish meal and fish manure
Canning of special grade pineapples
Acid filled batteries (accumulators)
Paint, varnish and enamel
Plywood and veneers
Drinking straws
Acetylene
Holloware
Dry ice (i.e., solid carbon dioxide)
*Bleached coir fibre for spinning and weaving and coir bristle
    fibre
*Corrugated paper and cardboard
Heavy purpose containers from paper, cardboard or other
    paper products
Gramophone records
Distilled gin
*Printing of textiles by silk screen and other methods
*Grass drying machines
Grass drying
*Papier mache articles
Slide fasteners (zippers) from aluminum and brass
*Galvanising of iron and steel

TABLE 17

Product
Dehydration of fruits and vegetables and the manufacture of fruit and vegetable pulps
Paper products
*Steel castings
Sanitary napkins (pads)
Sodium carbonate
*Chrome-plating of materials and articles made from metal
Splitting and punching of mica
Mastic asphalt

* Not being manufactured in 1961.

TABLE 18

PRODUCTS APPROVED UNDER THE INDUSTRIAL INCENTIVES LAW
1956–1959

Product	Product
Foam rubber	*Paper
*Light packaging	Banana chips
Brake linings	Pharmaceuticals
Holloware	*Powdered Molasses
Crown corks	Lighting equipment
Plastic products	*Matches
Metal windows and doors	*Radio receiving sets
Nails, fence, staples, and tacks	*Soluble coffee
*Barbed wire and wire fences	Bags of transparent cellulose film
*Rubber compounds	*Motor vehicles
Juke boxes	*Rubberised coir pads
Aluminium furniture	Billiard tables
*Ceramic products[a]	Dental cream
*Steel wool	*Sulphuric acid
*Glass and glass products[a]	*Aluminium truck and bus bodies
Aluminium extrusions	
Metal awnings and sun-shades	*Quilted products
*Plasmophalt	*Straight pins and safety pins
*Baker's yeast	Dining tables and chairs
*Aluminium shingles	*Locks
*Brushes	Metal furniture
Banana products	*Self-contained room air-conditioners
*Finished textile fabrics	*Organic fertilizers
*Paper clips and wire hooks	*Waxed paper

* Not being manufactured in 1961.
[a] Production to begin shortly (1961).

TABLE 19

PRODUCTS APPROVED UNDER THE EXPORT INDUSTRY LAW
1956–1959

Product	Product
Knitted goods	Work trousers
Leather buttons	Typewriters and cases[a]
Mica films and blocks	°Mosaic and glazed tiles
Ladies undergarments	Baseballs and softballs
°Waterproof pants for babies	°Parquet tiles
°Elastic yarn	Baseball gloves and mitts
Indoor footwear	°Costume jewellery and buttons
Leatherwear and novelties, handbags, and hand luggage	°Citric acid
°Insignias and novelties	Textile printing rollers
°Embroidered articles	°Radio receiving sets
Scientific and industrial models	Banana powder
Metal buttons	Frozen fruit and vegetable products[a]
°Beaded vamps	°Optical contact lenses
°Raffia ornaments	Dresses, skirts, dusters and robes
Shirts and pyjamas	°Sporting equipment
°Soft footwear	°Repair kits
°Artificial flowers	°Printed cloth
Frozen coconut[a]	Ladies' underwear[a]
Woven woollen products and blankets	°Yarn
	°Sectional poles
°Outerwear, jackets and coats	Yarn and cloth from jute fibre[a]

° Not being manufactured in 1961.
[a] Production to begin shortly (1961).

TABLE 20

EMPLOYMENT BY INDUSTRY, AND BY OCCUPATION FOR
KINGSTON AND JAMAICA, 1960

	Kingston[a]		Jamaica
	Number	%	%
Industry			
Agriculture	2,039	1.20	37.80
Manufacturing	38,680	23.88	14.76
Construction	19,872	11.74	8.20
Personal service	36,324	21.46	14.51
Other	72,299	41.66	24.62
Occupation			
Professional	1,491	0.88	0.37
Supervisory	8,217	4.86	3.96
Clerical and sales	34,667	20.50	11.38
Craft and technical	48,693	28.80	20.83
Non-professional with special training	3,321	1.96	0.86
Manual and service	68,547	40.56	61.25
Other	4,267	2.52	1.29

Source: Census of Jamaica, 1960.
[a] Kingston Parish and suburban St. Andrew.

TABLE 21

PRIVATE DWELLINGS CLASSIFIED BY KIND OF TOILET FACILITIES, 1960

Location	Private dwellings		Pit latrine		Water closet		Other		No facility	
	No.	%	No.	%	No.	%	No.	%	No.	%
Jamaica	401,771	100.0	293,583	73.1	80,028	19.9	3,896	1.0	2,474	6.0
Kingston	36,662	100.0	5,274	14.5	30,900	84.2	12	0.1	476	1.2
St. Andrew	77,049	100.0	39,151	50.8	37,357	48.5	192	0.2	349	0.5

Source: Census of Jamaica, 1960.

TABLE 22

PRIVATE DWELLINGS CLASSIFIED BY KIND OF OCCUPANCY, 1960

Location	Owner occupier		Tenant		No rent		Squatter		All households	
	No.	%	No.	%	No.	%	No.	%	No.	%
Kingston	5,181	14.0	30,086	82.0	780	2.0	615	2.0	36,662	100.0
St. Andrew	27,241	35.4	45,332	58.8	2,169	2.8	2,306	2.9	77,049	100.0
Jamaica	221,351	55.1	151,840	37.8	23,892	5.9	4,688	1.2	401,771	100.0

Source: Census of Jamaica, 1960.

TABLE 23

TYPE OF DWELLINGS, 1960

Type of dwelling	Jamaica		Kingston		St. Andrew	
	No.	%	No.	%	No.	%
Private	401,771	100.0	36,662	100.0	77,049	100.0
House	261,973	65.2	7,694	21.0	37,418	48.5
Rooms or flat.	54,210	13.5	7,220	19.7	16,440	21.1
Out room ...	6,093	1.5	1,117	3.0	1,569	2.1
Tenement ...	65,073	16.2	19,142	52.2	20,269	26.3
Barracks	6,232	1.6	56	0.2	20	—
Part of commercial building ..	8,190	2.0	1,433	3.9	1,333	1.7

Source: Census of Jamaica, 1960.

TABLE 24

SOCIO-ECONOMIC STATUS, RESIDENTIAL MOBILITY, AND POPULATION DENSITY IN KINGSTON, 1960

Enumeration district[a]	Socio-economic status score	Population density per acre	Annual adult mobility %
Hopefield Avenue	189	6	19
Richmond Park	211	21	28
Upper Deanery Road.......	243	25	31
Rennock Lodge	243	67	28
Barbican	251	8	19
Denham Town.............	280	208	16
Inner West Kingston........	292	179	41
Majesty Pen[b]	300	15	14
Moonlight City	300	15	4
Boy's Town	300	68	5

[a] Enumeration districts and polling districts in Kingston were identical in 1960.

[b] Majesty Pen and Moonlight City occupied the same enumeration district; they were, however, distinguishable on the electoral rolls.

TABLE 25

Religious Classification, 1960

Religion	Kingston		St. Andrew		Jamaica	
	No.	%	No.	%	No.	%
Adventist	4,444	3.6	12,270	4.1	78,360	4.9
Anglican	34,156	27.7	71,868	24.3	317,643	19.7
Baptist	14,902	12.1	39,848	13.5	306,037	19.0
Brethren and Plymouth Brethren	1,424	1.2	4,397	1.5	14,555	0.9
Christian Science	83	0.1	158	0.1	341	0.0
Church of God	8,867	7.2	31,806	10.7	191,231	11.8
Congregational	1,408	1.1	3,389	1.1	22,440	1.4
Friends	87	0.1	224	0.1	3,977	0.2
Hindu	34	0.0	773	0.3	1,181	0.1
Jewish	27	0.0	495	0.2	600	0.0
Methodist	9,703	7.9	21,828	7.4	108,858	6.8
Moravian	2,554	2.1	4,958	1.7	52,467	3.3
Pentecostal	955	0.8	1,672	0.6	14,739	0.9
Pocomania	47	0.0	83	0.0	811	0.1
Presbyterian	4,565	3.7	8,891	3.0	82,698	5.1
Roman Catholic	26,410	21.4	53,964	18.2	115,791	7.2
Salvation Army	986	0.8	1,102	0.4	10,416	0.6
Other religion	662	0.5	1,693	0.6	14,876	0.9
No religion	805	0.7	23,457	7.9	183,738	11.4
Not stated	3,949	3.2	13,137	4.4	89,555	5.6
Total	123,403	100.0	296,013	100.0	1,609,814	100.0

Source: Census of Jamaica, 1960.

TABLE 26

Illiteracy among the Population Aged Ten Years and Over, 1960

Literacy	Kingston		St. Andrew		Jamaica	
	No.	%	No.	%	No.	%
Males						
Read and write	38,840	196.0	86,910	92.7	427,027	80.9
Read only	183	0.4	845	0.9	5,600	1.1
Illiterate	1,443	3.6	5,977	6.4	94,936	18.0
Population aged 10 years and over	40,466	100.0	93,732	100.0	527,563	100.0
Females						
Read and write	51,618	96.4	113,303	94.3	514,155	86.6
Read only	272	0.5	959	0.8	5,641	1.0
Illiterate	1,643	3.1	5,842	4.9	73,868	12.4
Population aged 10 years and over	53,533	100.0	120,104	100.0	593,664	100.0

Source: Census of Jamaica, 1960.

TABLE 27

KENDALL RANK CORRELATION COEFFICIENTS FOR
SELECTED VARIABLES

Variable	Variable	r	p
Socio-economic status	Secondary schooling.	.48	<.00003
Socio-economic status	Race	.21	.0009
Secondary schooling	Race	.23	<.0003
Secondary schooling	Non-denominational Christians	−.30	<.00003
Secondary schooling	Common-law union .	−.47	<.00003
Common-law union	Non-denominational Christians	.14	.0143

TABLE 28

RACIAL COMPOSITION, 1960
(In percentages)

Race	Kingston	St. Andrew	Jamaica
African	73.4	73.2	76.8
European	0.4	2.2	0.8
East Indian	0.6	2.0	1.7
Chinese	1.9	1.4	0.6
Syrian	0.1	0.3	0.1
Afro–European	14.2	12.9	14.6
Afro–East Indian	2.4	1.8	1.7
Afro–Chinese	1.7	1.2	0.6
Other	5.3	5.0	3.1
Total	123,403	296,013	1,609,814

Source: Census of Jamaica, 1960.

TABLE 30

CONCENTRATION OF RACIAL GROUPS, 1960

Race	Kingston– St. Andrew	Jamaica	% in Kingston– St. Andrew
African	307,387	1,236,706	24.8
European	6,940	12,428	55.8
East Indian	6,679	27,912	23.9
Chinese	6,667	10,267	64.9
Syrian	907	1,354	66.9
Afro–European	55,752	235,494	23.6
Afro–East Indian	8,208	26,354	31.1
Afro–Chinese	5,635	9,672	58.2
Others	21,241	49,627	42.8
Total	419,416	1,609,814	26.4

Source: Census of Jamaica, 1960.

TABLE 29

MALE AND FEMALE POPULATIONS AND SEX RATIOS FOR THE RACIAL GROUPS, 1960

Race	Kingston			St. Andrew			Jamaica		
	M	F	Sex ratio	M	F	Sex ratio	M	F	Sex ratio
African	40,738	49,898	816	99,378	117,373	846	598,691	638,015	938
European	267	286	933	3,002	3,385	886	5,751	6,677	861
East Indian	308	446	690	2,907	3,018	963	13,886	14,026	990
Chinese	1,358	1,000	1,358	2,246	2,063	1,088	5,693	4,574	1,244
Syrian	40	51	784	427	389	1,097	707	647	1,092
Afro–European ...	7,140	10,326	691	16,420	21,866	750	109,086	126,408	862
Afro–East Indian..	1,256	1,707	735	2,264	2,981	759	12,040	14,314	841
Afro–Chinese	953	1,139	836	1,666	1,877	889	4,631	5,041	918
Other	2,855	3,635	785	6,543	8,208	797	22,954	26,673	860
Total	54,915	68,488	801	134,853	161,160	836	773,439	836,375	924

Source: Census of Jamaica, 1960.

TABLE 31

LABOUR FORCE AGED 14 YEARS AND OVER, 1960

Main occupation	Total		African		European		East Indian and Afro–East Indian		Chinese and Afro–Chinese		Afro–European		Others	
	No.	%	No.	%	No.	%	No.	%	No.	%	No.	%	No.	%
Kingston, males	29,412	100.0	22,178	100.0	167	100.0	755	100.0	1,137	100.0	3,852	100.0	1,323	100.0
Professional and supervisory	1,620	5.5	898	4.0	71	42.5	51	6.8	232	20.4	270	7.0	98	7.4
Clerical and sales.........	4,986	17.0	3,114	14.0	35	21.0	164	21.7	571	50.2	763	19.8	339	25.6
Craftsmen and technical ...	12,817	43.6	10,083	45.5	29	17.4	323	42.8	176	15.5	1,661	43.1	545	41.2
Professional services	375	1.3	265	1.2	4	2.4	12	1.6	9	0.8	61	1.6	24	1.8
Manual and service	9,156	31.1	7,472	33.7	28	16.8	187	24.8	139	12.2	1,033	26.8	297	22.5
Not specified or ill defined..	458	1.6	346	1.6	0	0.0	18	2.4	10	0.9	64	1.7	20	1.5
St. Andrew, males	70,224	100.0	52,241	100.0	1,912	100.0	2,297	100.0	1,968	100.0	8,602	100.0	3,204	100.0
Professional and supervisory	6,860	9.8	2,645	5.1	1,192	62.3	246	10.7	533	27.0	1,534	7.8	710	22.2
Clerical and sales.........	10,761	15.3	6,017	11.5	334	17.4	448	2.0	1,025	52.0	2,212	25.7	725	22.6
Craftsmen and technical ...	25,478	36.3	20,833	39.9	165	9.0	715	3.1	258	13.1	2,705	31.5	802	25.0
Professional services	776	1.1	462	0.9	46	2.0	27	0.1	19	0.9	179	2.1	43	1.3
Manual and service	25,525	36.3	21,655	41.4	167	9.1	823	36.0	121	6.1	1,877	21.8	882	27.5
Not specified or ill defined..	824	1.2	629	1.2	8	0.0	38	0.2	12	0.6	95	1.1	42	1.3
Kingston, females	26,278	100.0	19,639	100.0	112	100.0	707	100.0	719	100.0	3,832	100.0	1,219	100.0
Professional and supervisory	482	1.8	298	1.5	14	12.5	15	2.1	33	4.6	91	2.4	31	2.5
Clerical and sales	5,876	22.4	3,834	19.5	41	36.6	209	29.6	482	67.0	962	25.1	348	28.5
Craftsmen and technical ...	4,634	17.7	3,487	17.8	9	8.0	122	17.3	64	8.9	738	19.3	214	17.6
Professional services	725	2.8	467	2.4	5	4.4	29	4.1	9	1.3	164	4.3	51	4.2
Manual and service	13,350	50.9	10,668	54.3	41	36.6	307	43.4	121	16.8	1,685	43.9	528	43.3
Not specified or ill defined..	1,161	4.4	885	4.5	2	1.8	25	3.5	10	1.4	192	5.0	47	3.9
St. Andrew, females	58,707	100.0	43,773	100.0	941	100.0	1,597	100.0	1,358	100.0	8,349	100.0	2,689	100.0
Professional and supervisory	1,553	2.6	691	1.6	188	20.0	48	3.0	87	5.4	395	4.7	144	5.4
Clerical and sales	14,450	24.6	8,156	18.6	482	51.2	675	42.3	1,024	64.1	3,129	37.5	984	36.6
Craftsmen and technical ...	9,080	15.5	7,135	16.3	25	2.7	221	13.8	72	4.5	1,232	14.8	395	14.7
Professional services	1,513	2.6	913	2.1	39	4.1	41	2.6	37	2.3	304	3.6	179	6.7
Manual and service........	30,152	51.3	25,369	57.9	200	21.3	529	33.1	124	7.8	3,012	36.0	918	34.1
Not specified or ill defined..	1,951	3.3	1,509	3.4	7	0.7	83	5.2	14	0.9	277	3.3	69	2.6

Source: Census of Jamaica, 1960.

TABLE 32

WAGE EARNERS BELONGING TO THE VARIOUS RACIAL GROUPS, CLASSIFIED BY INCOME, 1960

Wage earners	Total	African	European	East Indian	Chinese	Syrian	Afro–European	Afro–East Indian	Afro–Chinese	Others
Kingston, males	23,003	17,532	108	119	347	14	3,030	457	329	1,067
Nil	138	116	0	0	0	0	9	2	1	10
Under £50	1,644	1,351	0	9	7	0	174	30	11	62
£50–99	2,913	2,404	6	13	10	11	299	37	35	108
£100–199	5,988	4,878	7	34	40	1	664	96	63	202
£200–499	8,982	6,627	49	42	186	7	1,259	199	155	460
£500–999	1,760	973	27	15	85	4	388	62	48	158
£1,000–1,999	187	83	11	1	9	0	56	9	3	15
£2,000 and over ..	13	4	1	0	2	0	4	1	0	1
Not stated	1,381	1,096	7	5	8	1	179	21	13	51
Kingston, females	18,064	13,414	70	97	196	8	2,693	396	254	936
Nil	234	194	1	2	1	1	20	2	3	10
Under £50	3,247	2,676	1	11	5	0	367	53	20	114
£50–99	5,462	4,359	4	15	14	0	705	82	39	244
£100–199	4,351	3,183	11	30	40	2	676	116	68	225
£200–499	3,093	1,859	33	23	106	3	634	107	87	241
£500–999	526	248	12	6	27	2	138	18	24	51
£1,000–1,999	9	1	5	0	0	0	3	0	0	0
£2,000 and over ..	0	0	0	0	0	0	0	0	0	0
Not stated	1,142	894	3	10	3	0	150	18	13	51
St. Andrew, males....	52,045	38,451	1,566	934	687	120	6,858	767	535	2,127
Nil	601	525	1	13	1	0	52	1	0	8
Under £50	4,352	3,680	8	64	12	0	328	49	24	187
£50–99	7,845	6,695	11	147	17	2	635	83	29	226
£100–199	13,360	11,223	37	283	61	5	1,197	161	84	309
£200–499	14,685	10,868	120	276	246	20	2,152	268	237	498
£500–999	5,026	2,480	286	70	211	48	1,262	116	107	443
£1,000–1,999	2,721	745	654	25	84	30	822	47	33	281
£2,000 and over ..	765	109	380	7	19	9	170	5	3	63
Not stated	2,690	2,126	69	49	36	6	237	37	18	112
St. Andrew, females ..	41,679	30,303	779	369	526	64	6,395	708	512	2,023
Nil	850	754	1	9	0	1	55	4	3	23
Under £50	6,801	5,784	5	36	5	0	638	71	20	242
£50–99	12,701	10,907	20	68	16	2	1,129	131	34	403
£100–199	7,895	6,247	28	77	49	1	1,035	124	76	258
£200–499	7,183	3,861	255	112	272	27	1,937	207	236	576
£500–999	3,778	1,259	370	33	162	27	1,278	111	128	410
£1,000–1,999	266	65	62	1	5	4	86	7	5	31
£2,000 and over ..	22	3	9	9	0	0	6	1	0	2
Not stated	2,174	1,723	29	33	16	2	231	52	10	78

Source: Census of Jamaica, 1960.

Figures

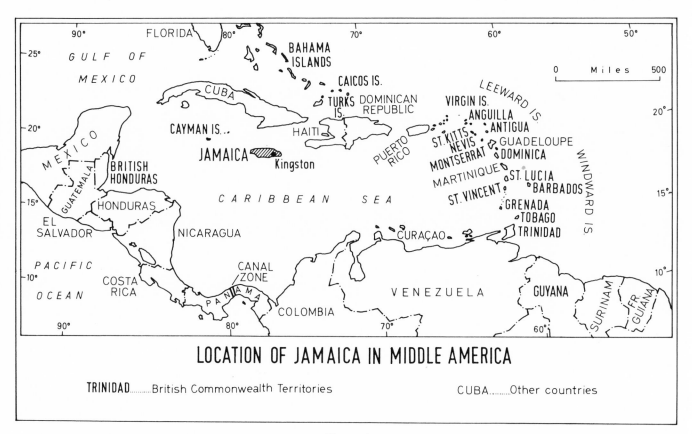

Figure 1.

RELIEF AND DRAINAGE OF THE KINGSTON AREA

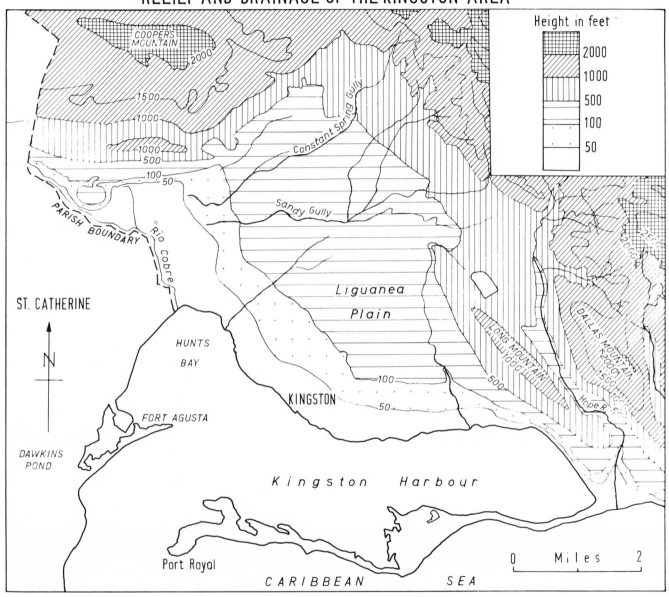

Figure 2.

LITHOLOGY OF THE KINGSTON AREA

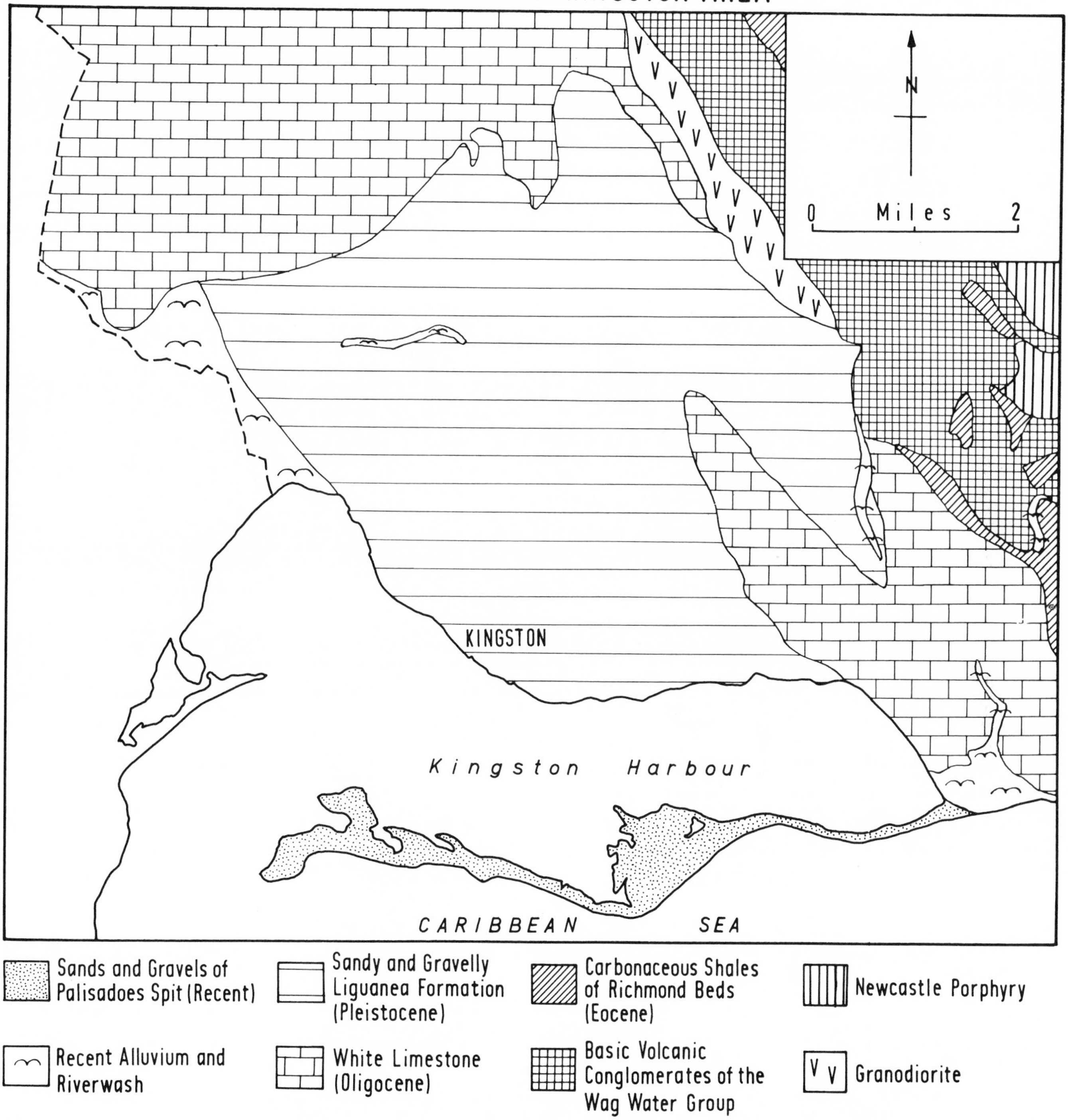

N

0 Miles 2

KINGSTON

Kingston   Harbour

CARIBBEAN   SEA

Sands and Gravels of
Palisadoes Spit (Recent)

Recent Alluvium and
Riverwash

Sandy and Gravelly
Liguanea Formation
(Pleistocene)

White Limestone
(Oligocene)

Carbonaceous Shales
of Richmond Beds
(Eocene)

Basic Volcanic
Conglomerates of the
Wag Water Group

Newcastle Porphyry

Granodiorite

Figure 3.

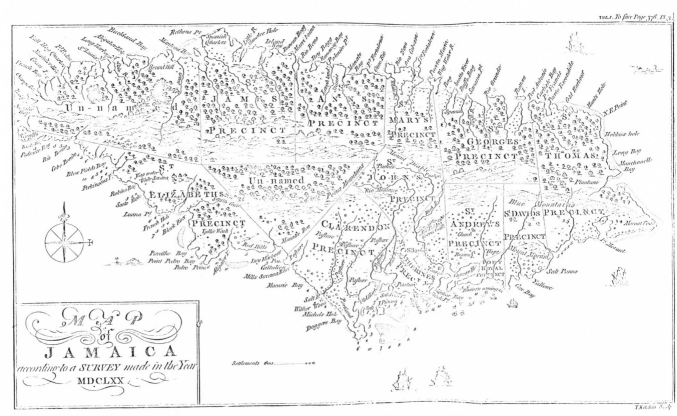

Figure 4. From E. Long, History of Jamaica, 1774, vol. 1.

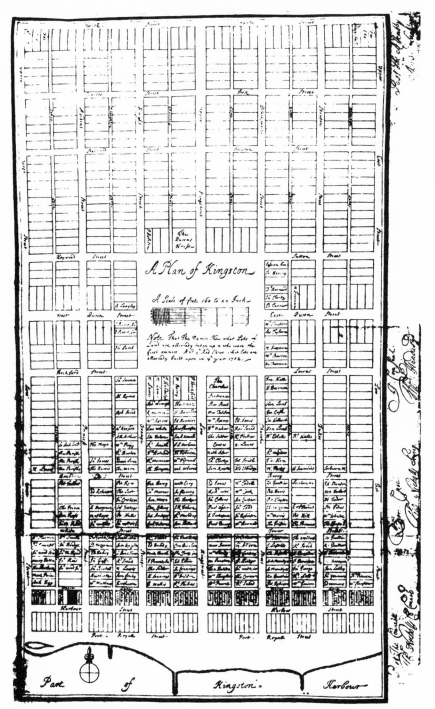

Figure 5. Made by Christian Lilly; copy was photographed from the original at the Institute of Jamaica.

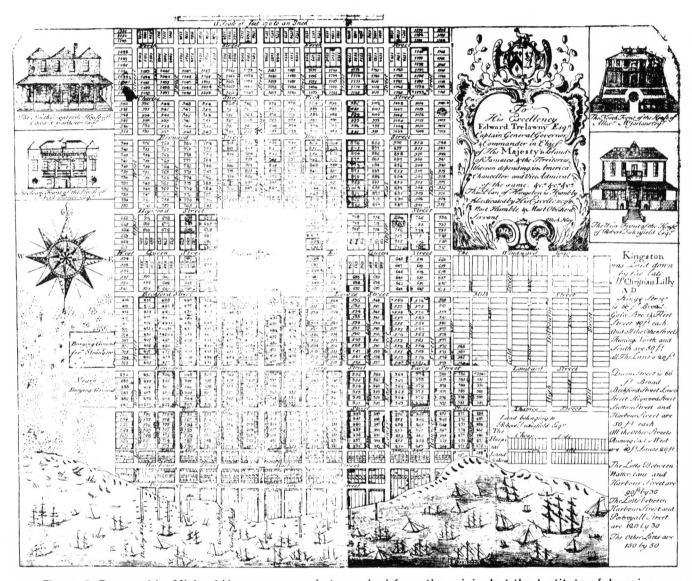

Figure 6. Prepared by Michael Hay; copy was photographed from the original at the Institute of Jamaica.

Figure 7. Made by Richard Jones and first appeared in P. Brown, **The Civil History of Jamaica**, 1756; copy taken from E. Long, **History of Jamaica**, 1774, vol. 1.

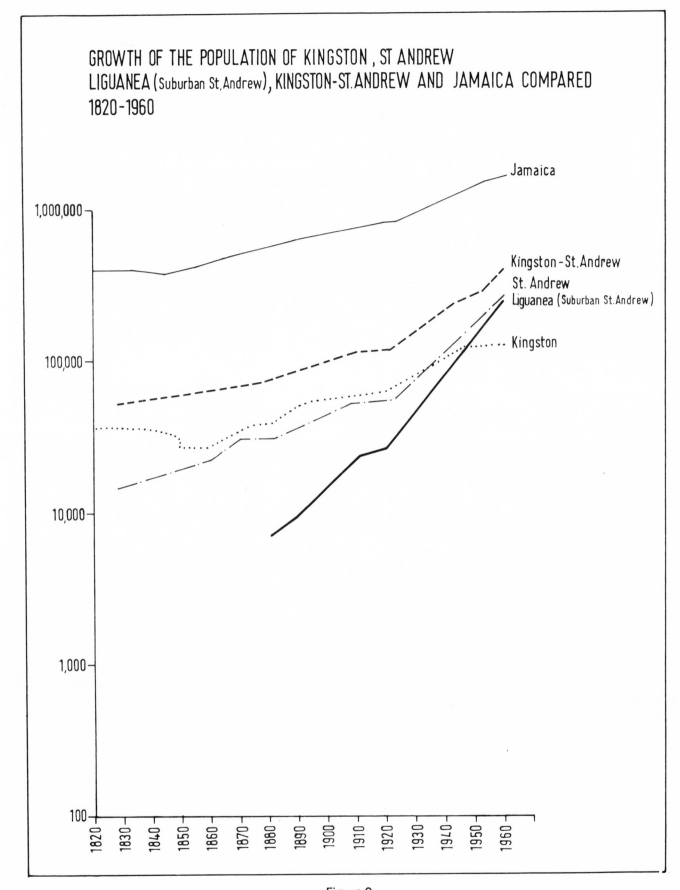

GROWTH OF THE POPULATION OF KINGSTON , ST ANDREW
LIGUANEA (Suburban St.Andrew), KINGSTON-ST.ANDREW AND JAMAICA COMPARED
1820-1960

Figure 9.

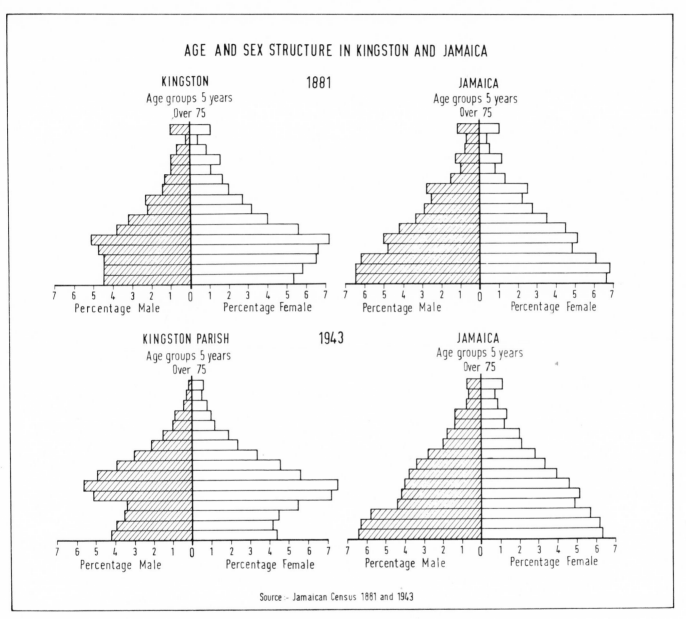

Figure 8.

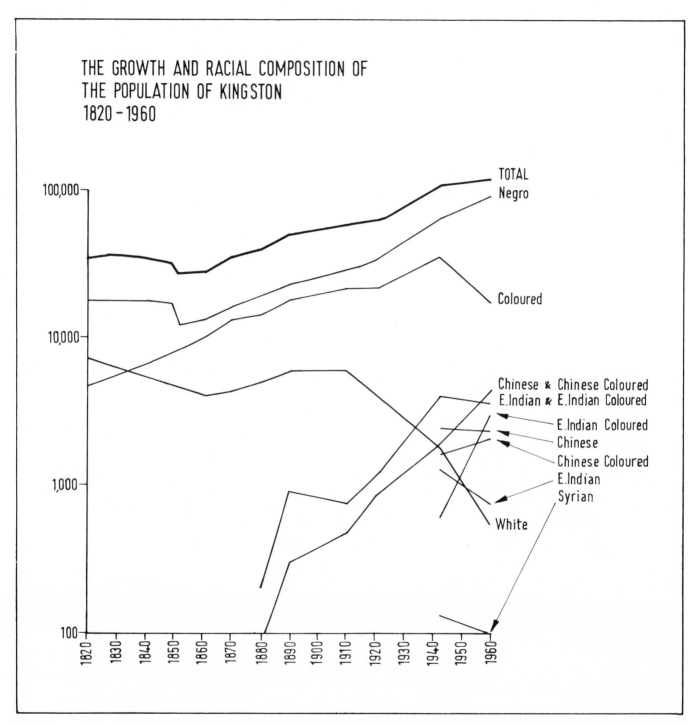

Figure 10.

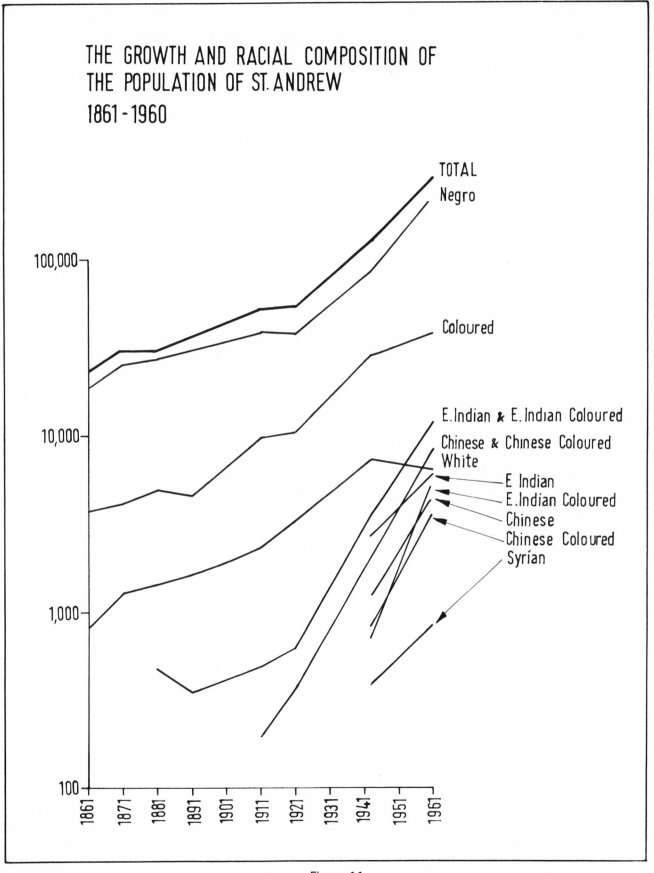

Figure 11.

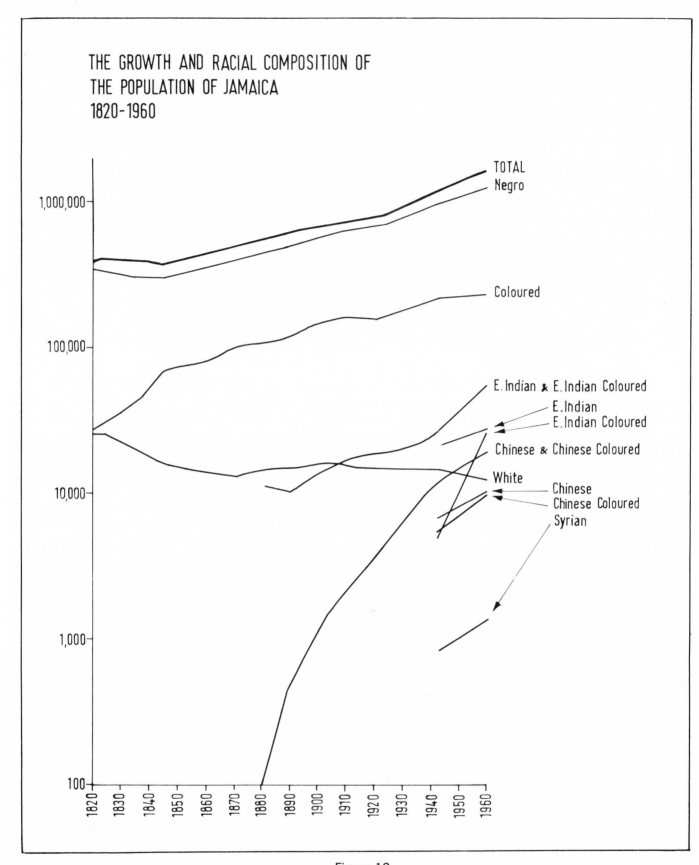

THE GROWTH AND RACIAL COMPOSITION OF
THE POPULATION OF JAMAICA
1820-1960

Figure 12.

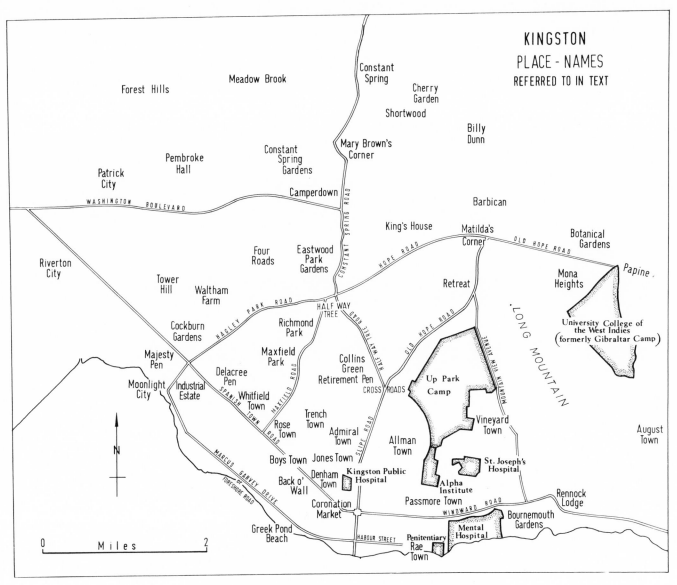

Figure 13. Kingston place-names referred to in text.

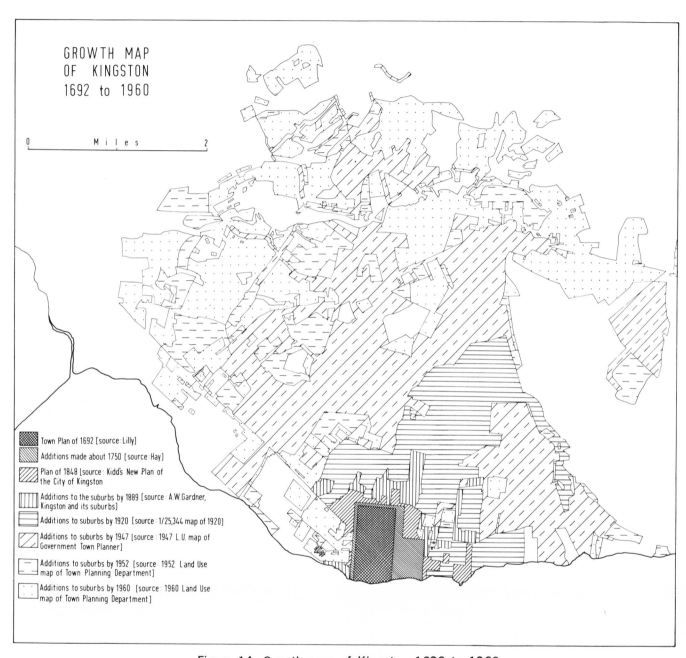

GROWTH MAP
OF KINGSTON
1692 to 1960

0   Miles   2

Town Plan of 1692 [source: Lilly]

Additions made about 1750 [source: Hay]

Plan of 1848 [source: Kidd's New Plan of the City of Kingston

Additions to the suburbs by 1889 [source: A.W.Gardner, Kingston and its suburbs]

Additions to suburbs by 1920 [source: 1/25,344 map of 1920]

Additions to suburbs by 1947 [source: 1947 L.U. map of Government Town Planner]

Additions to suburbs by 1952 [source: 1952 Land Use map of Town Planning Department]

Additions to suburbs by 1960 [source: 1960 Land Use map of Town Planning Department]

Figure 14. Growth map of Kingston 1692 to 1960.

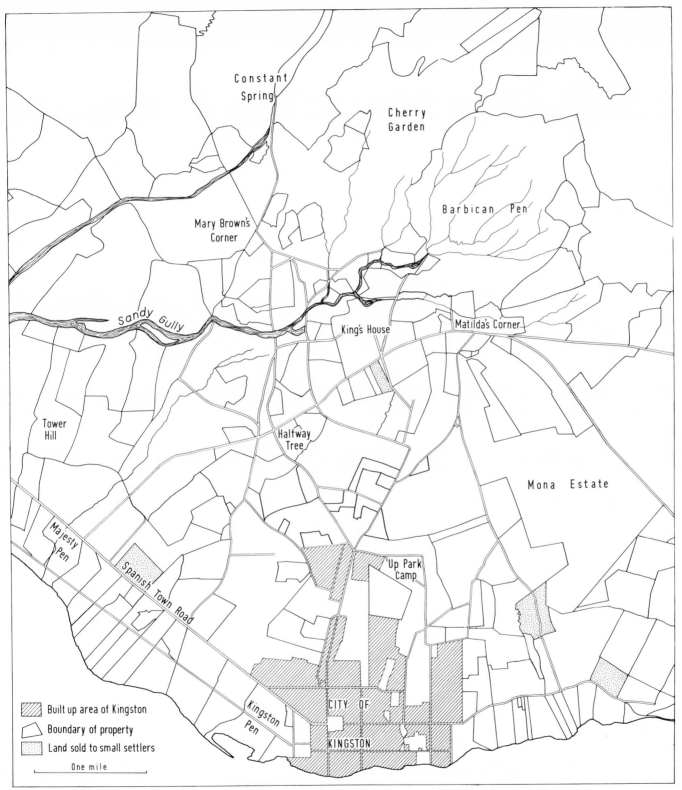

Figure 15. Pens and other properties on the Liguanea Plain in 1872.

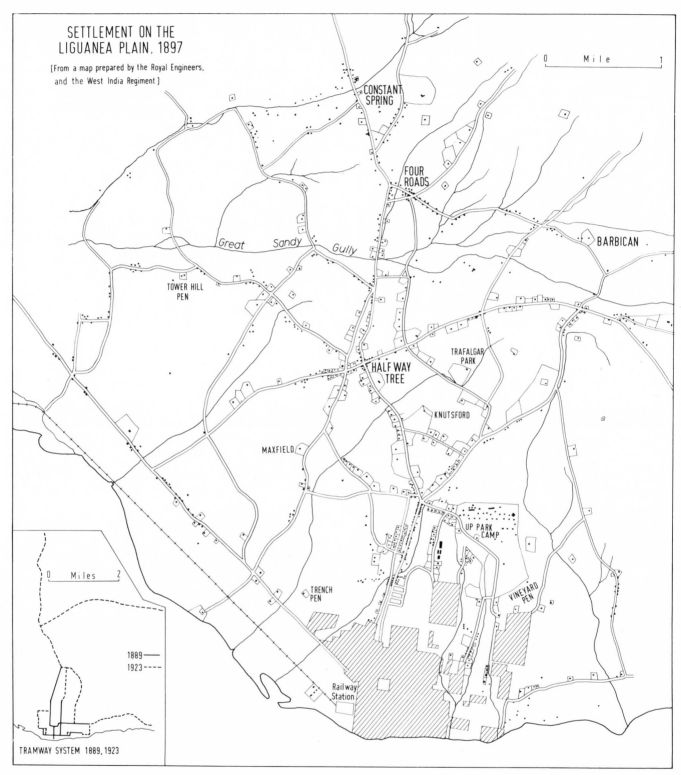

Figure 16. Settlement on the Liguanea Plain, 1897 (from a map prepared by the Royal Engineers and the West India Regiment).

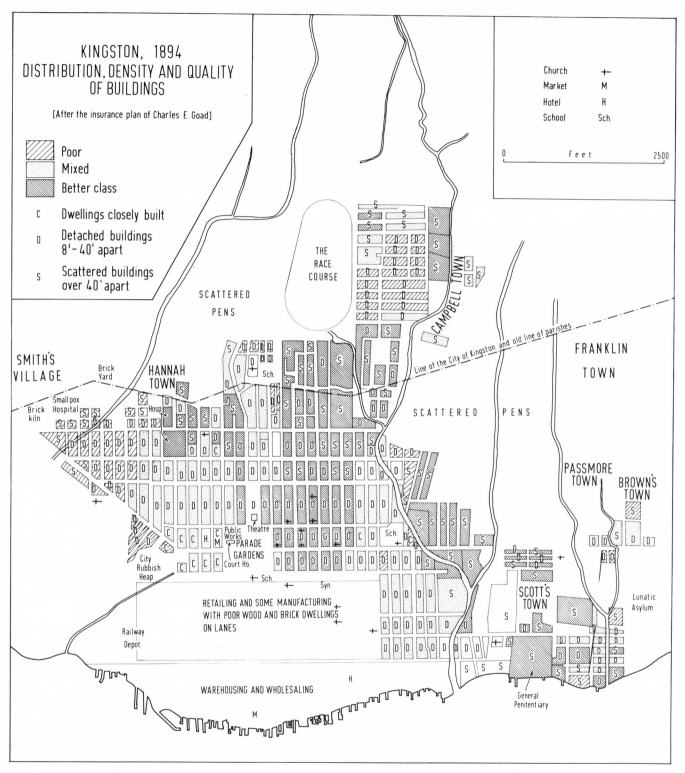

Figure 17. Kingston, 1894: Distribution, density and quality of buildings (after the insurance plan of Charles E. Goad).

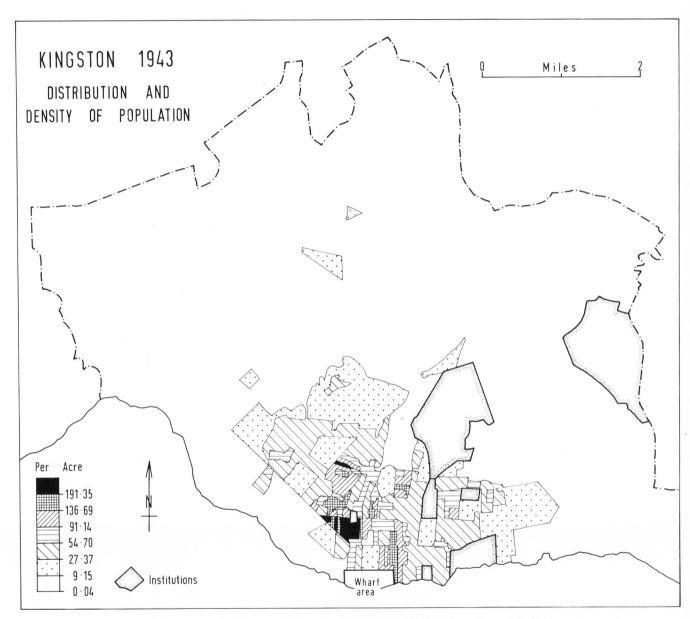

Figure 18. Kingston, 1943: Distribution and density of population.

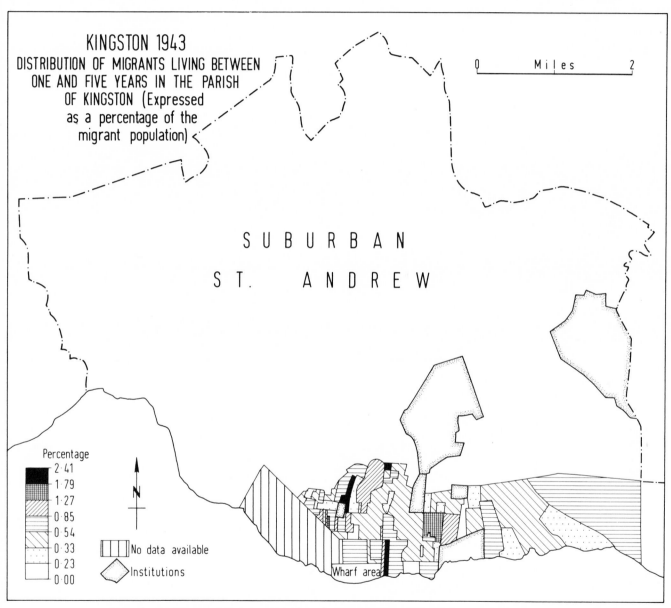

Figure 19. Kingston, 1943: Distribution of migrants living between one and five years in the Parish of Kingston (expressed as a percentage of the migrant population).

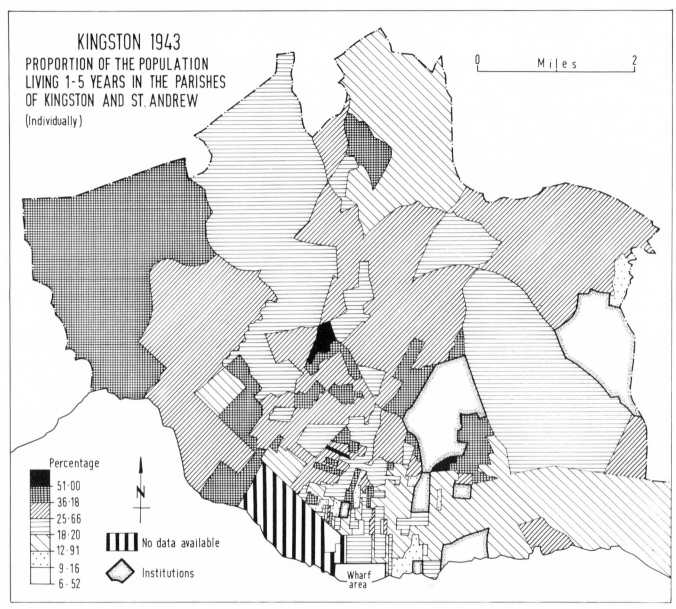

Figure 20. Kingston, 1943: Proportion of the population living one to five years in the parishes of Kingston and St. Andrew (individually).

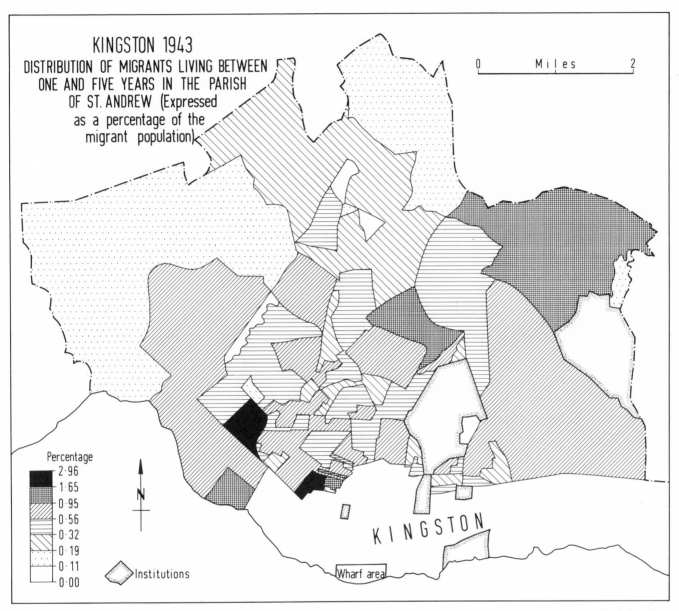

KINGSTON 1943
DISTRIBUTION OF MIGRANTS LIVING BETWEEN
ONE AND FIVE YEARS IN THE PARISH
OF ST. ANDREW (Expressed
as a percentage of the
migrant population)

Percentage

2·96
1·65
0·95
0·56
0·32
0·19
0·11
0·00

Institutions

KINGSTON

Wharf area

Figure 21. Kingston, 1943: Distribution of migrants living between one and five years in the Parish of St. Andrew (expressed as a percentage of the migrant population).

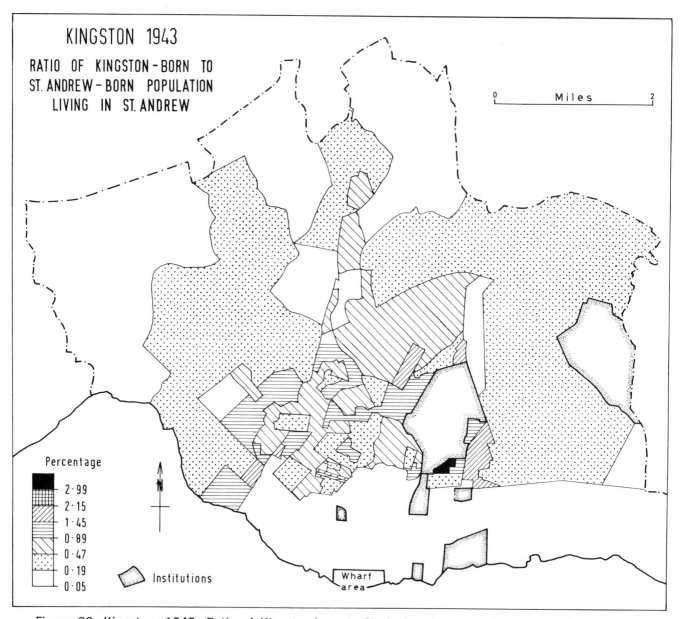

Figure 22. Kingston, 1943: Ratio of Kingston-born to St. Andrew-born population living in St. Andrew.

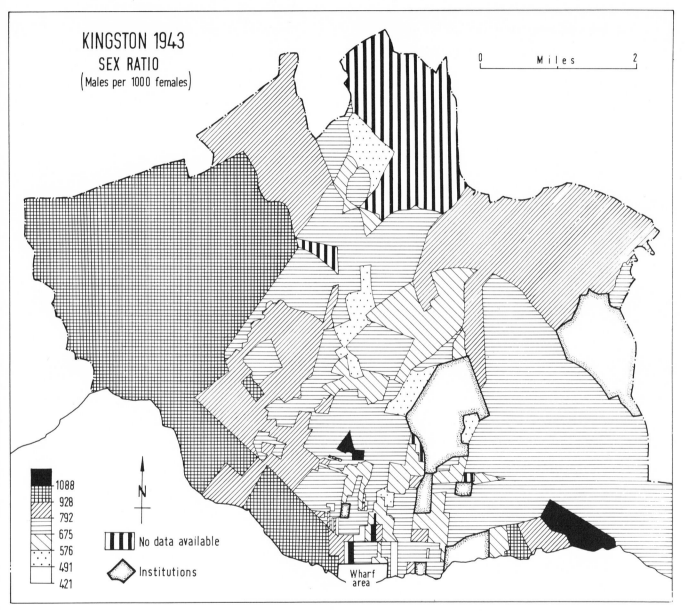

KINGSTON 1943
SEX RATIO
(Males per 1000 females)

0   Miles   2

1088
928
792
675
576
491
421

N

No data available

Institutions

Wharf
area

Figure 23. Kingston, 1943: Sex ratio (males per 1,000 females).

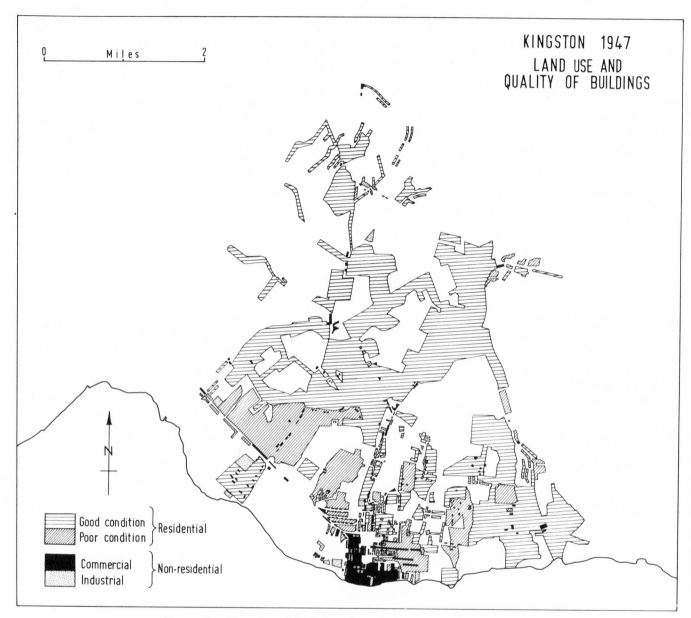

Figure 24. Kingston, 1947: Land use and quality of buildings.

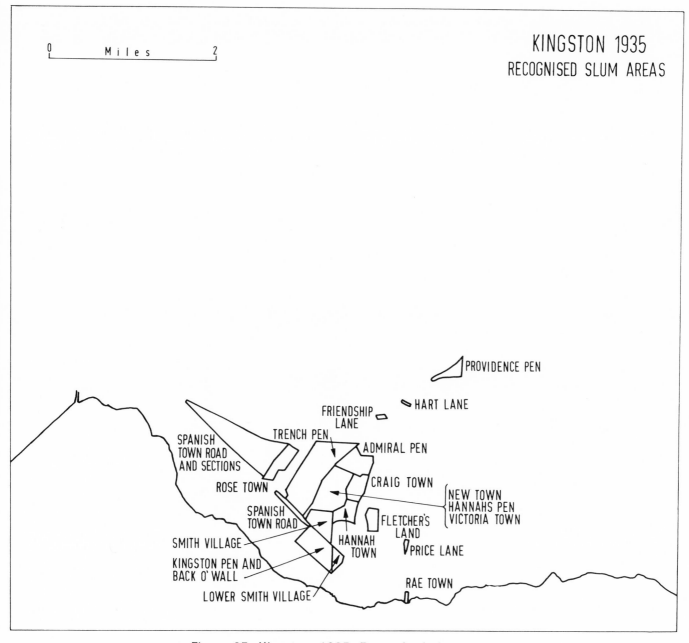

Figure 25. Kingston, 1935: Recognized slum areas.

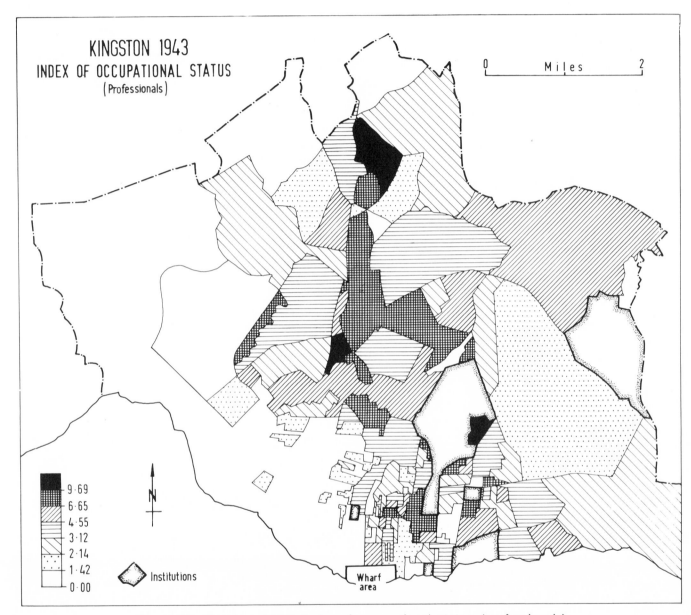

Figure 26. Kingston, 1943: Index of occupational status (professionals).

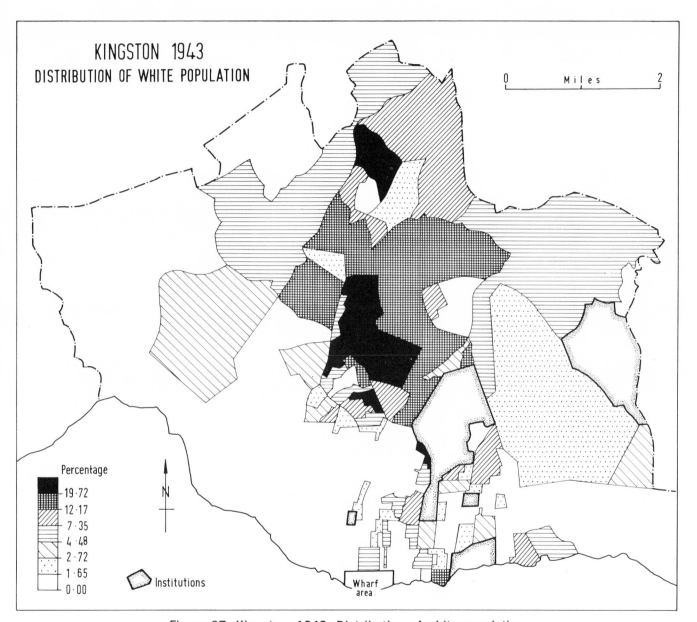

Figure 27. Kingston, 1943: Distribution of white population.

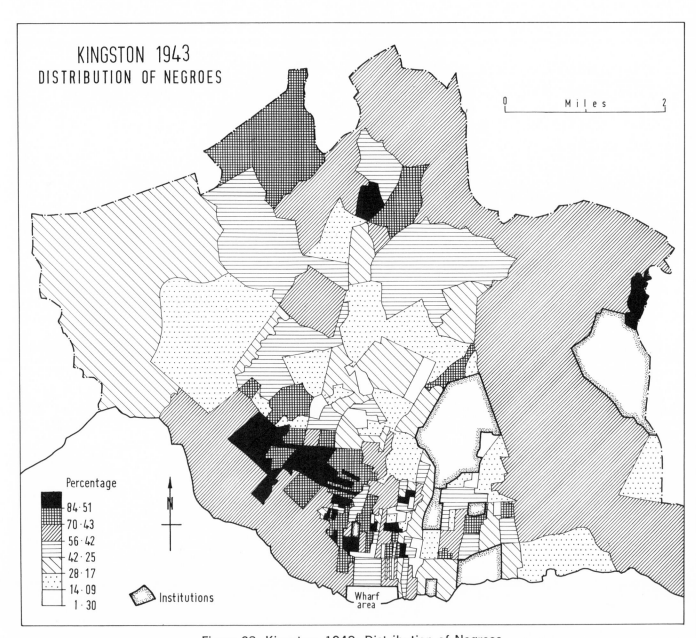

Figure 28. Kingston, 1943: Distribution of Negroes.

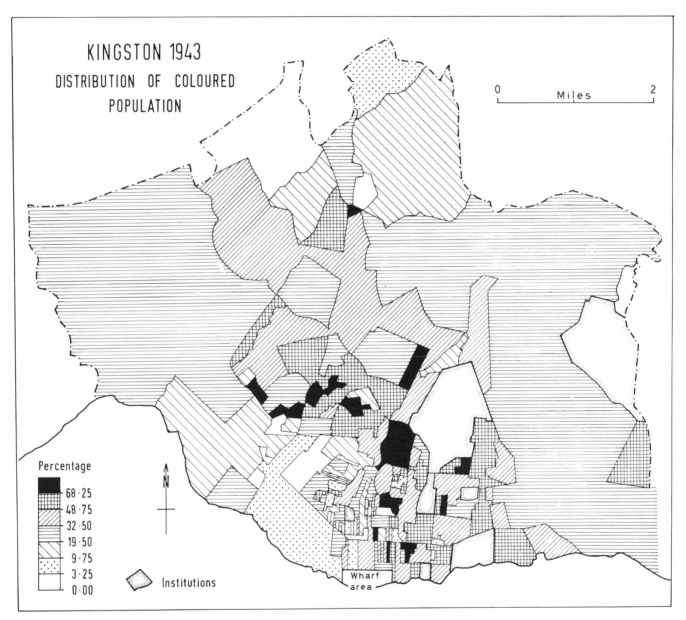

Figure 29. Kingston, 1943: Distribution of coloured population.

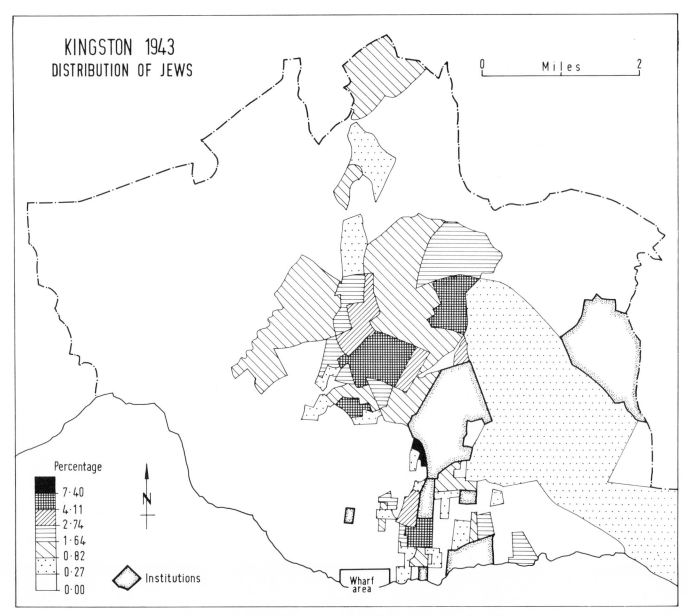

Figure 30. Kingston, 1943: Distribution of Jews (race).

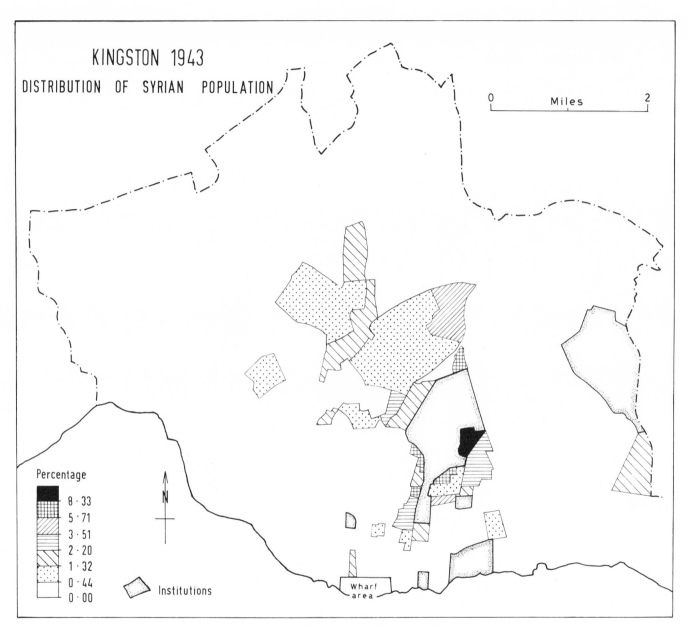

Figure 31. Kingston, 1943: Distribution of Syrian population.

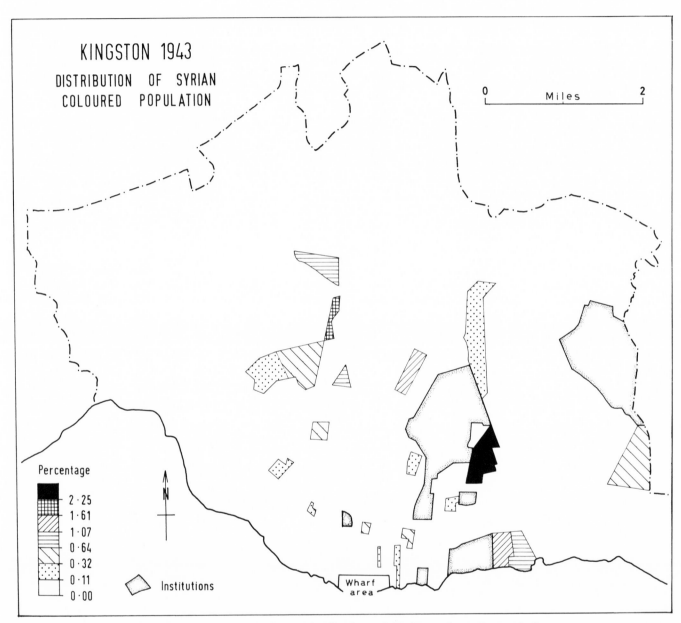

Figure 32. Kingston, 1943: Distribution of Syrian-coloured population.

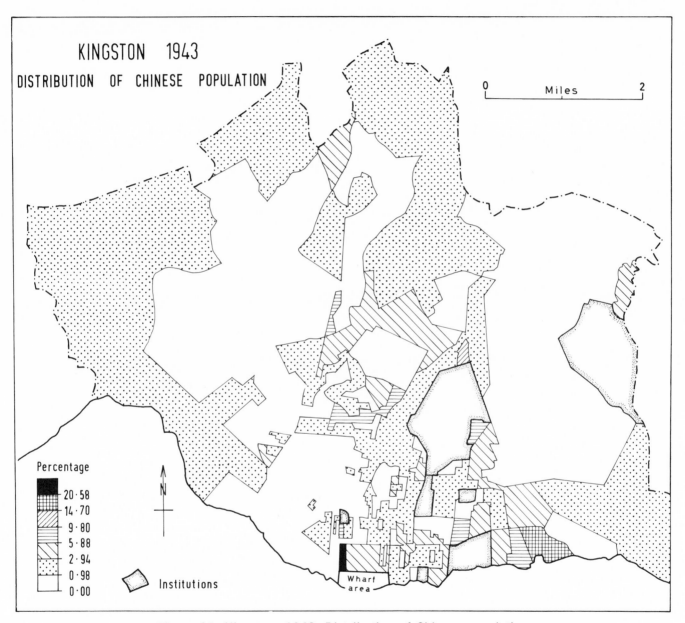

Figure 33. Kingston, 1943: Distribution of Chinese population.

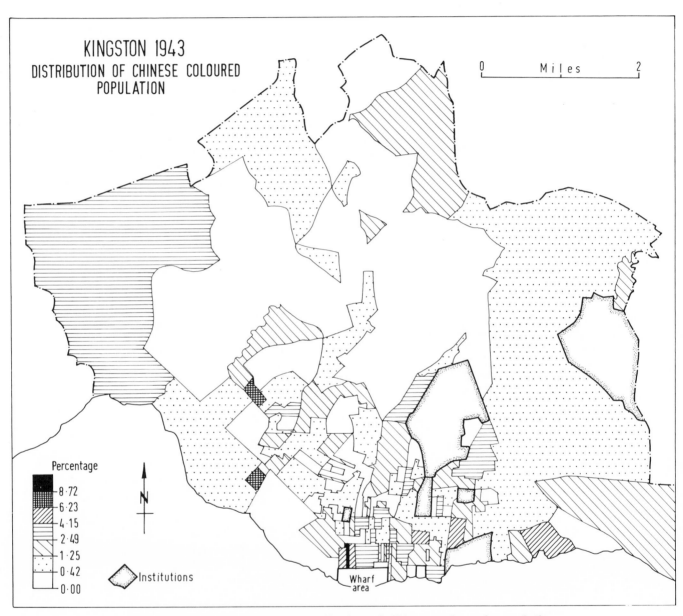

Figure 34. Kingston, 1943: Distribution of Chinese-coloured population.

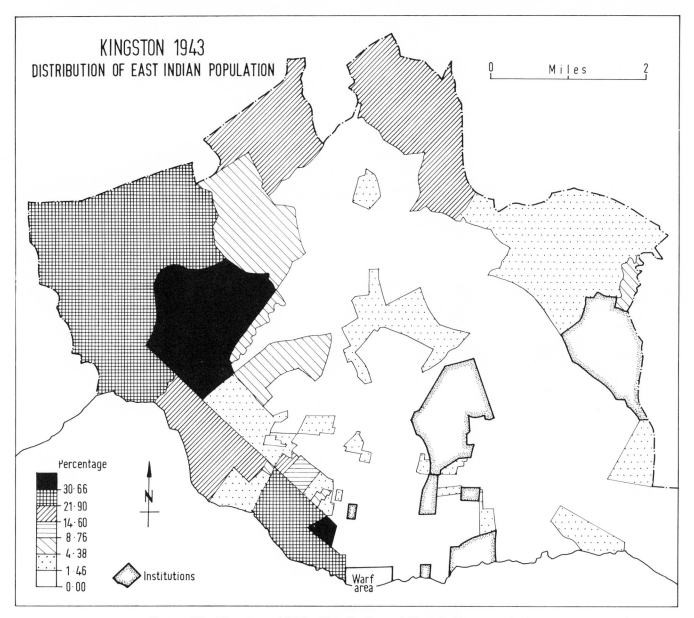

Figure 35. Kingston, 1943: Distribution of East Indian population.

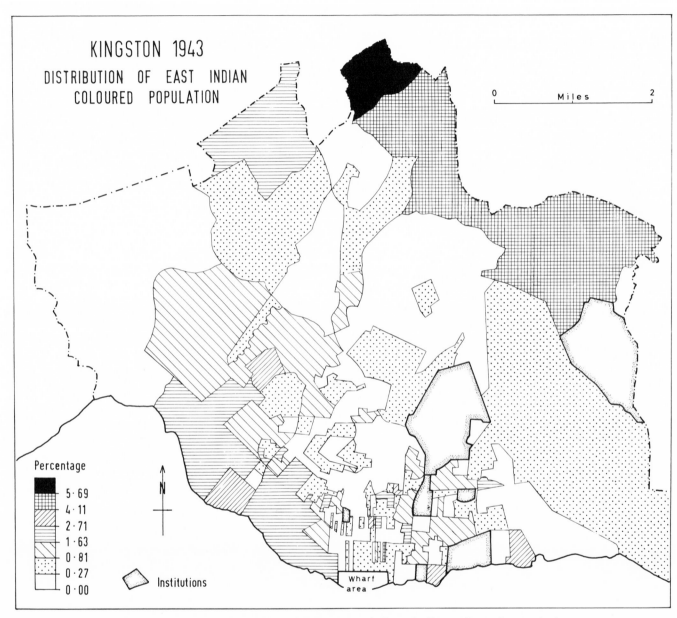

Figure 36. Kingston, 1943: Distribution of East Indian-coloured population.

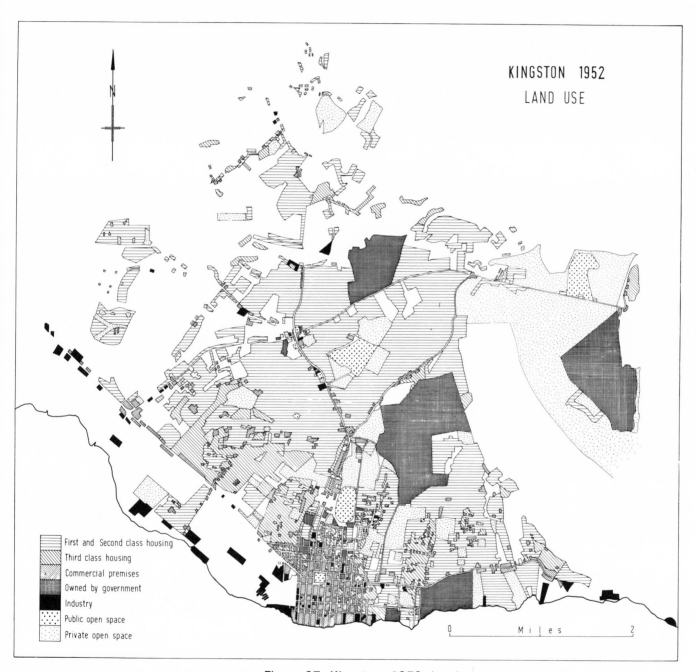

Figure 37. Kingston, 1952: Land use.

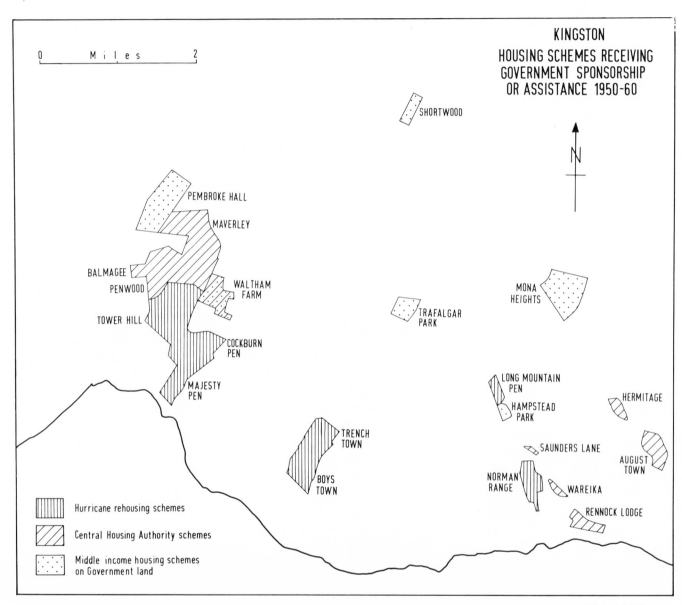

Figure 38. Kingston housing schemes receiving government sponsorship or assistance, 1950–1960.

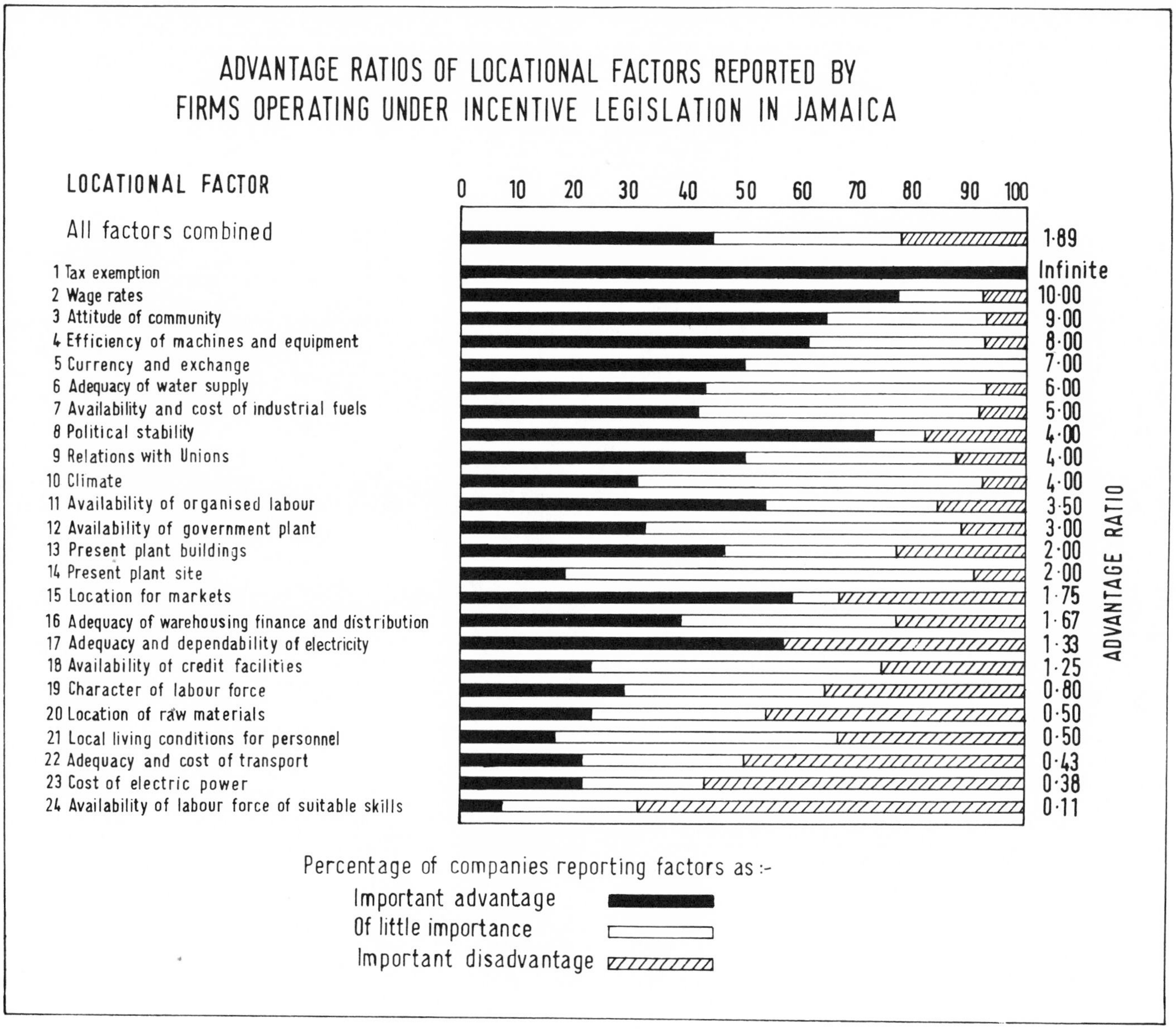

ADVANTAGE RATIOS OF LOCATIONAL FACTORS REPORTED BY FIRMS OPERATING UNDER INCENTIVE LEGISLATION IN JAMAICA

LOCATIONAL FACTOR

	Advantage Ratio
All factors combined	1·89
1 Tax exemption	Infinite
2 Wage rates	10·00
3 Attitude of community	9·00
4 Efficiency of machines and equipment	8·00
5 Currency and exchange	7·00
6 Adequacy of water supply	6·00
7 Availability and cost of industrial fuels	5·00
8 Political stability	4·00
9 Relations with Unions	4·00
10 Climate	4·00
11 Availability of organised labour	3·50
12 Availability of government plant	3·00
13 Present plant buildings	2·00
14 Present plant site	2·00
15 Location for markets	1·75
16 Adequacy of warehousing finance and distribution	1·67
17 Adequacy and dependability of electricity	1·33
18 Availability of credit facilities	1·25
19 Character of labour force	0·80
20 Location of raw materials	0·50
21 Local living conditions for personnel	0·50
22 Adequacy and cost of transport	0·43
23 Cost of electric power	0·38
24 Availability of labour force of suitable skills	0·11

Percentage of companies reporting factors as :-

Important advantage

Of little importance

Important disadvantage

Figure 39. Advantage ratios of locational factors reported by firms operating under incentive legislation in Jamaica.

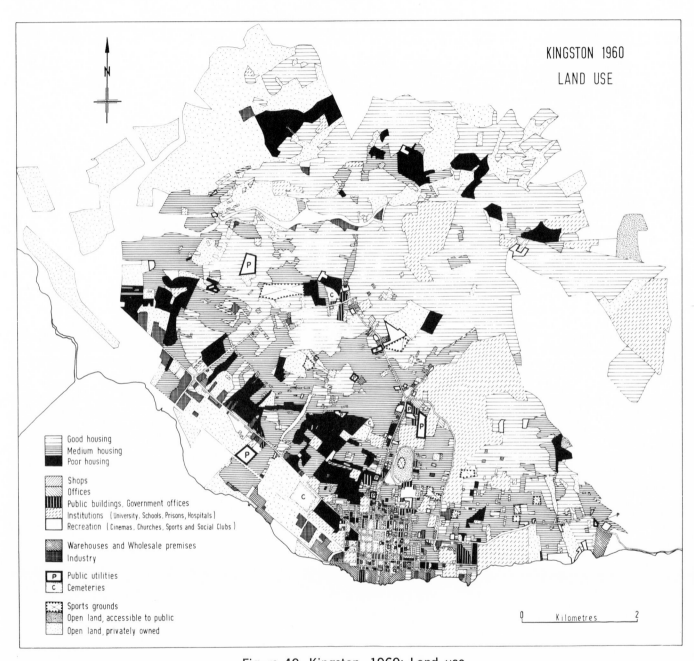

KINGSTON 1960

LAND USE

Good housing
Medium housing
Poor housing

Shops
Offices
Public buildings, Government offices
Institutions (University, Schools, Prisons, Hospitals)
Recreation (Cinemas, Churches, Sports and Social Clubs)

Warehouses and Wholesale premises
Industry

P Public utilities
C Cemeteries

Sports grounds
Open land, accessible to public
Open land, privately owned

0   Kilometres   2

Figure 40. Kingston, 1960: Land use.

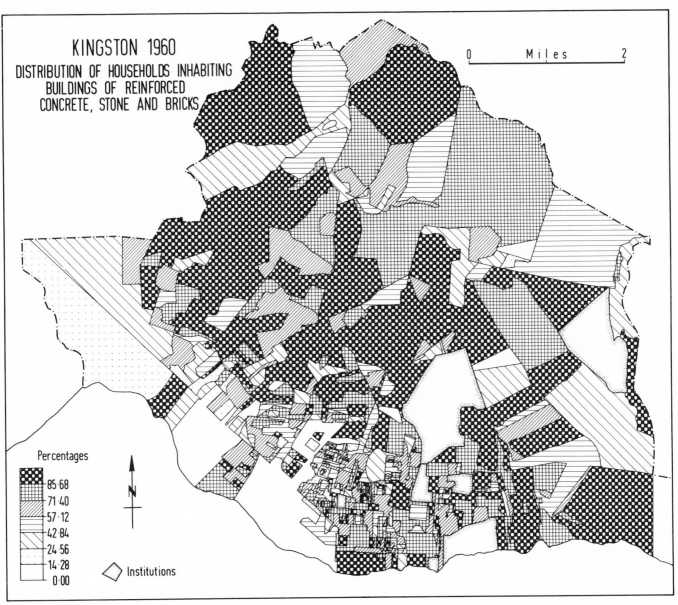

Figure 41. Kingston, 1960: Distribution of households inhabiting buildings of reinforced concrete, stone, and bricks.

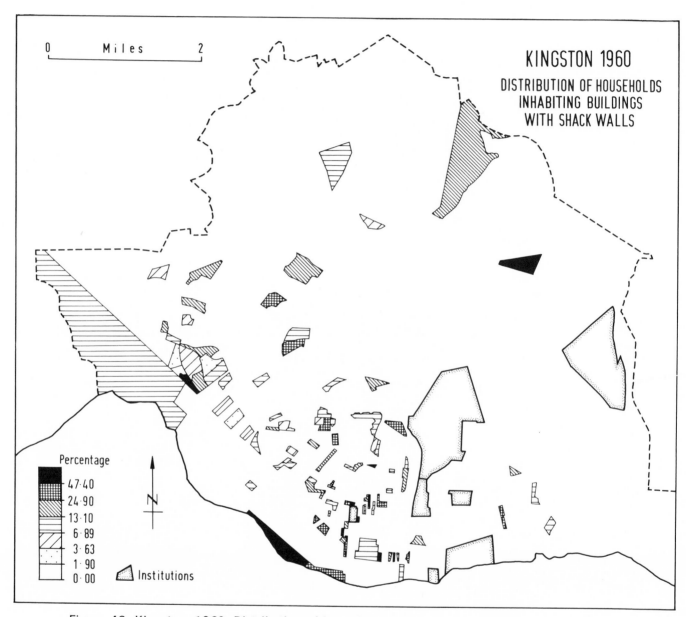

Figure 42. Kingston, 1960: Distribution of households inhabiting buildings with shack walls.

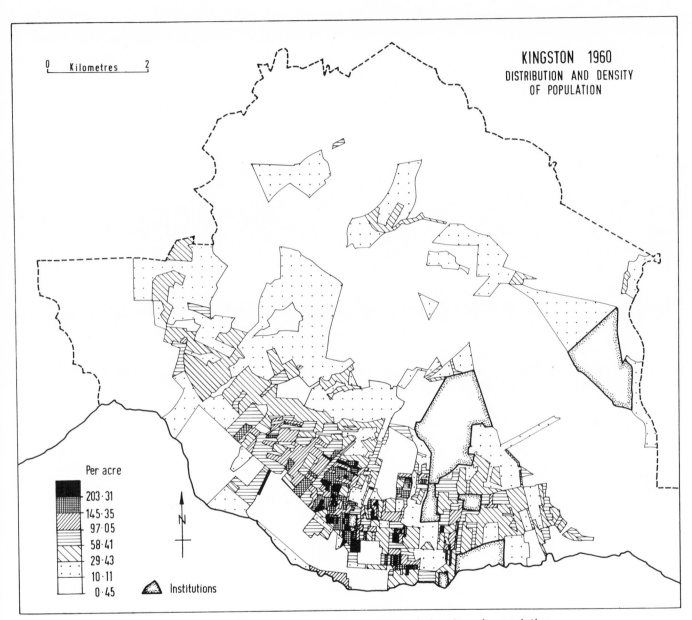

Figure 43. Kingston, 1960: Distribution and density of population.

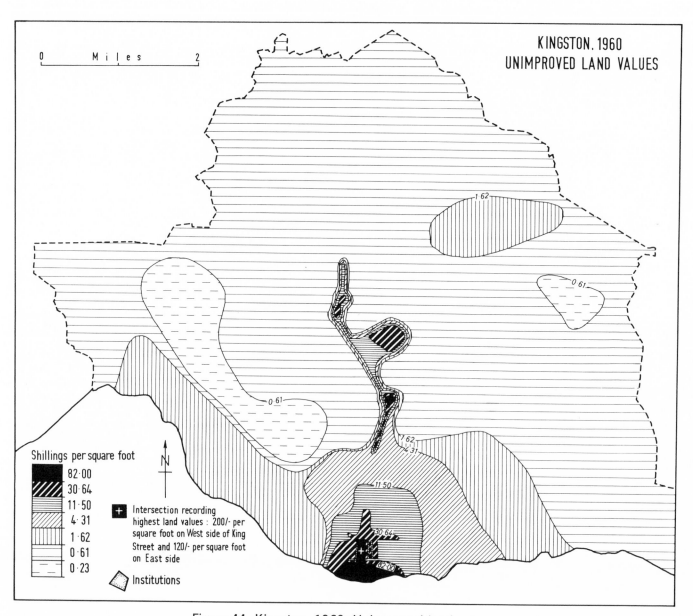

Figure 44. Kingston, 1960: Unimproved land values.

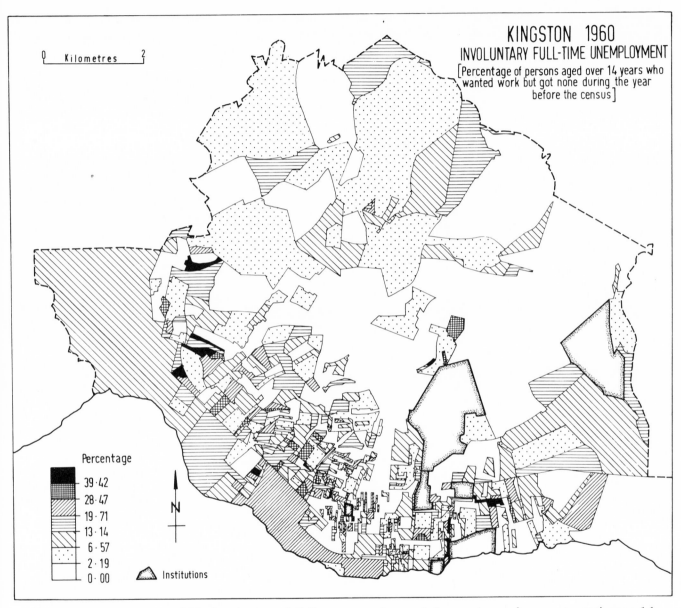

Figure 45. Kingston, 1960: Involuntary full-time unemployment (percentage of persons aged over 14 years who wanted work but got none during the year before the census).

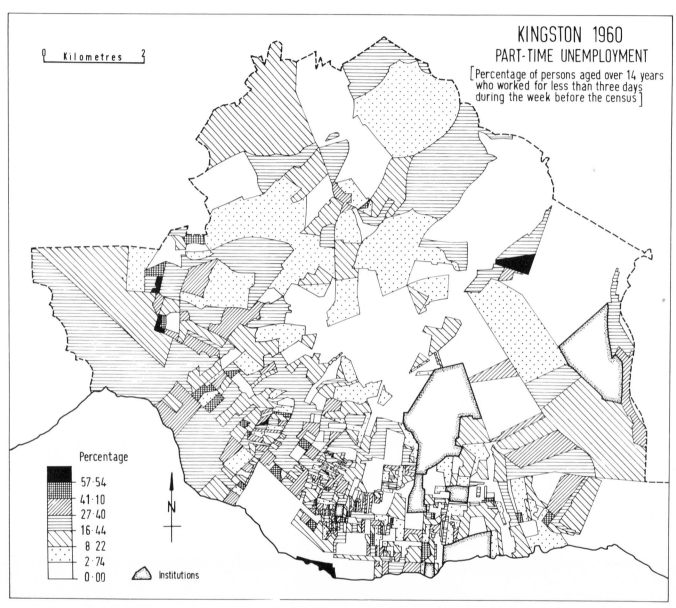

Figure 46. Kingston, 1960: Part-time unemployment (percentage of persons aged over 14 years who worked for less than three days during the week before the census).

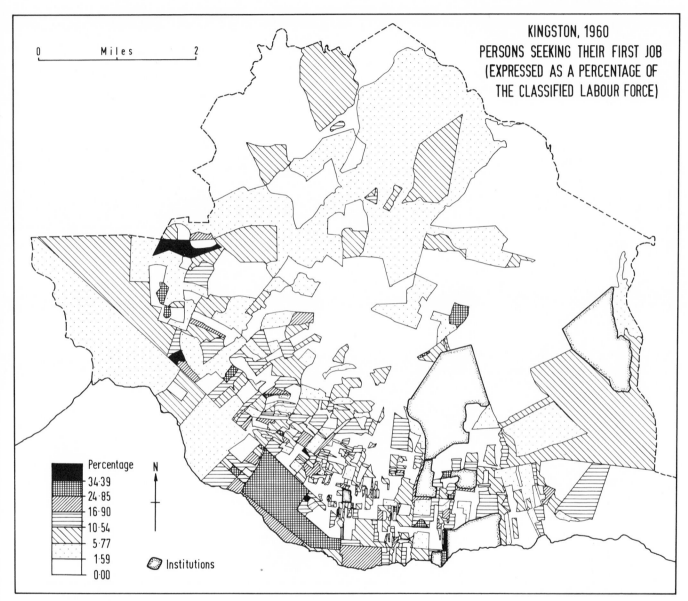

Figure 47. Kingston, 1960: Persons seeking their first job (expressed as a percentage of the classified labour force).

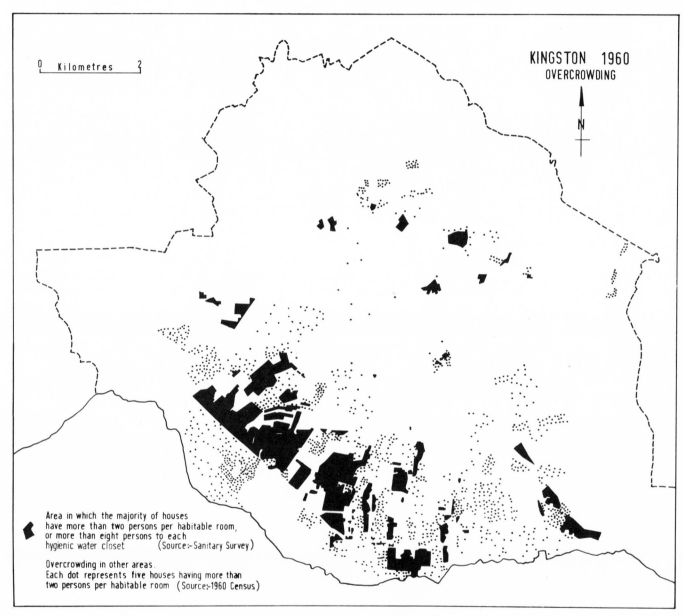

Figure 48. Kingston, 1960: Overcrowding.

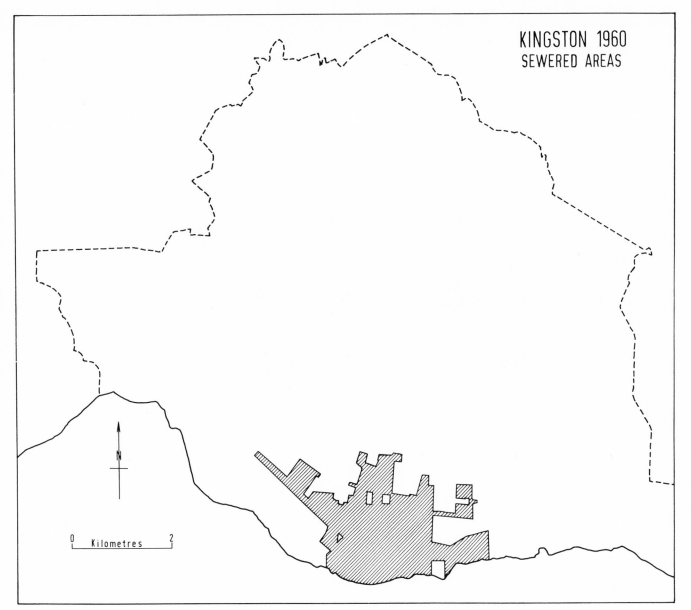

KINGSTON 1960
SEWERED AREAS

0 Kilometres 2

Figure 49. Kingston, 1960: Sewered areas.

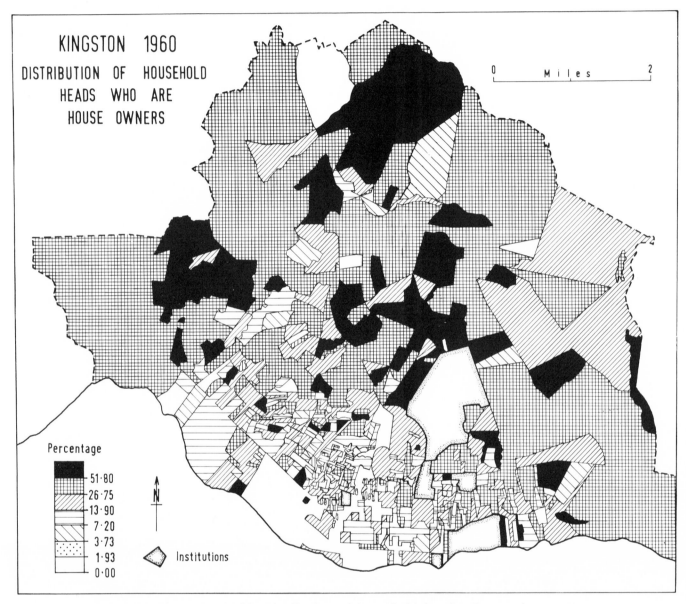

Figure 50. Kingston, 1960: Distribution of household heads who are house owners.

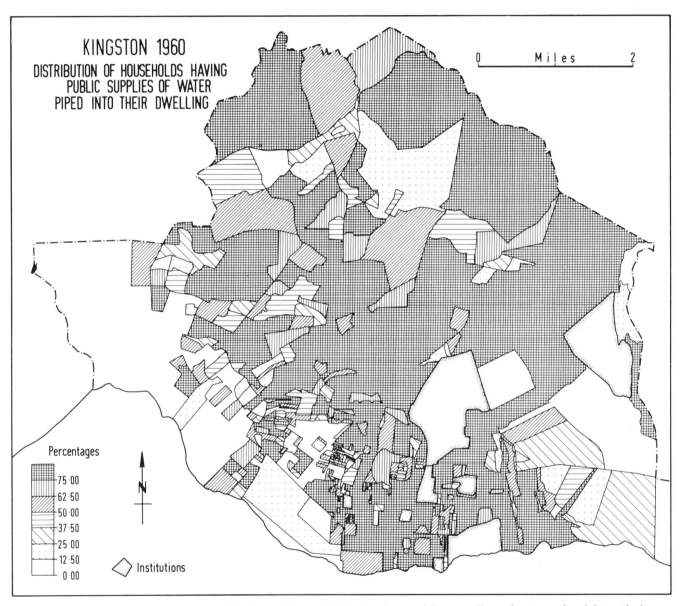

Figure 51. Kingston, 1960: Distribution of households having public supplies of water piped into their dwelling.

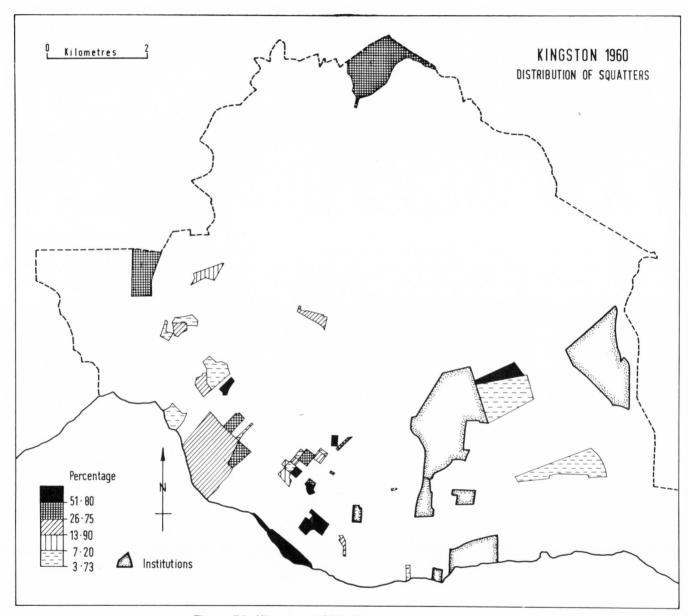

Figure 52. Kingston, 1960: Distribution of squatters.

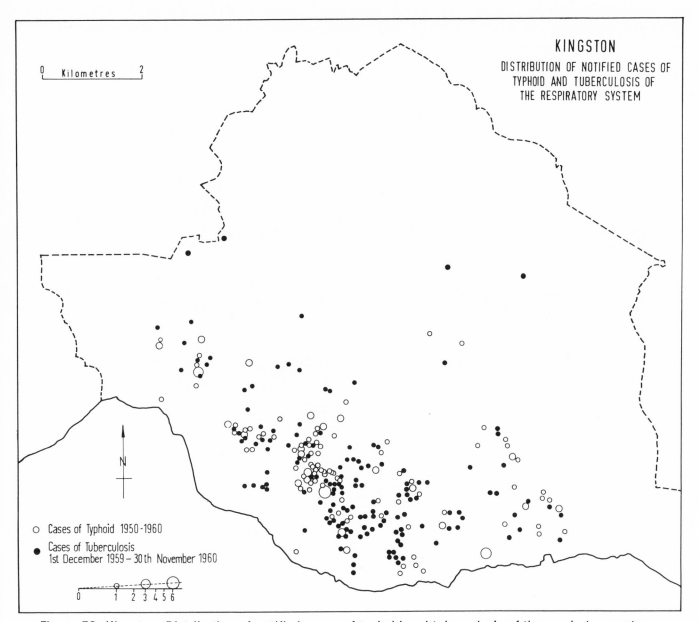

Figure 53. Kingston: Distribution of notified cases of typhoid and tuberculosis of the respiratory system.

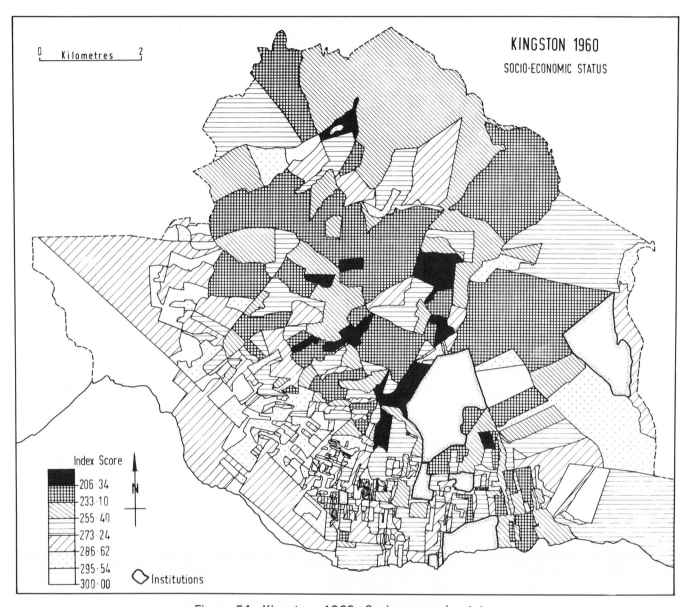

Figure 54. Kingston, 1960: Socio-economic status.

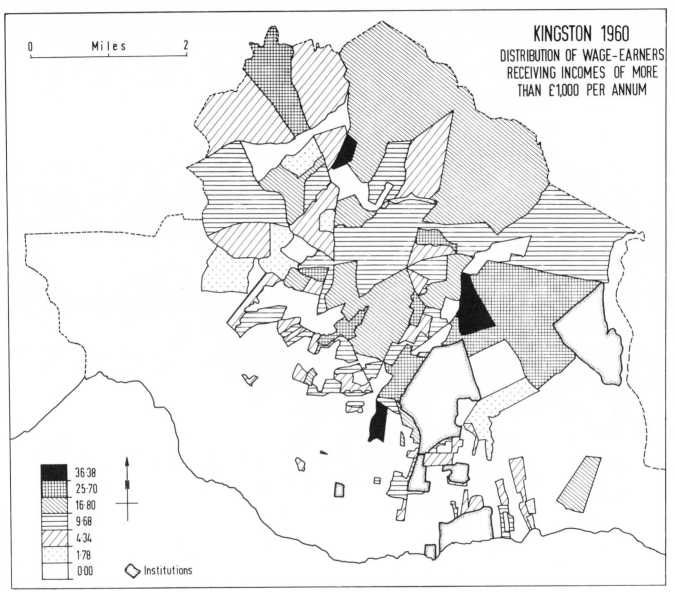

KINGSTON 1960
DISTRIBUTION OF WAGE-EARNERS
RECEIVING INCOMES OF MORE
THAN £1,000 PER ANNUM

0   Miles   2

36·38
25·70
16·80
9·68
4·34
1·78
0·00

◇ Institutions

Figure 55. Kingston, 1960: Distribution of wage-earners receiving incomes of more than £1,000 per annum.

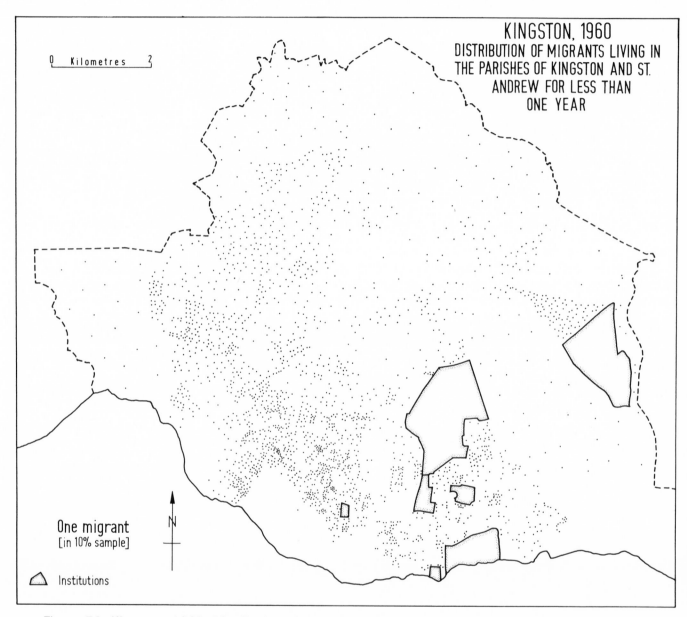

Figure 56. Kingston, 1960: Distribution of migrants living in the parishes of Kingston and St. Andrew for less than one year.

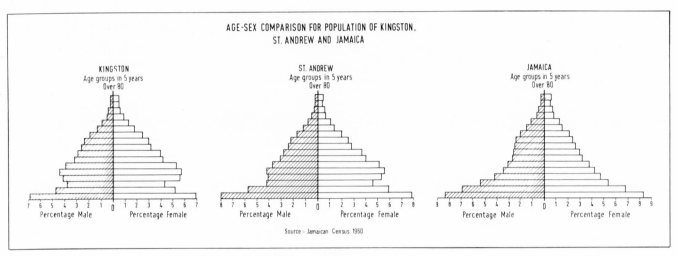

Figure 57. Age-sex comparison for population of Kingston, St. Andrew, and Jamaica.

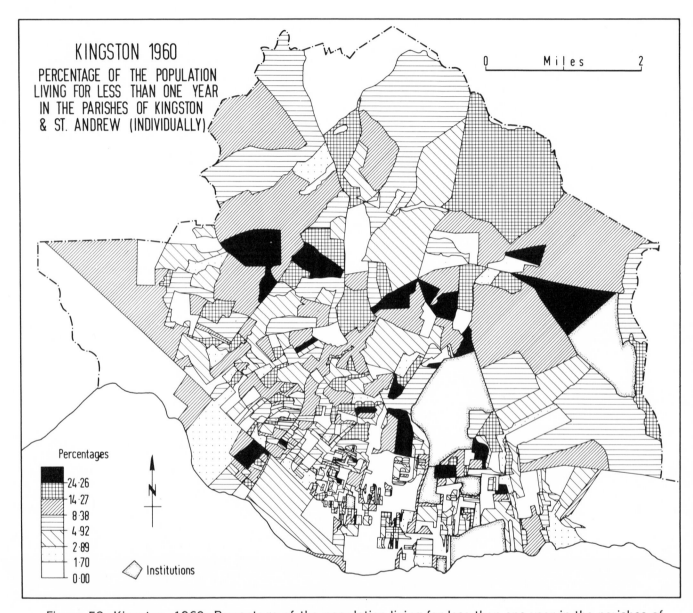

KINGSTON 1960

PERCENTAGE OF THE POPULATION
LIVING FOR LESS THAN ONE YEAR
IN THE PARISHES OF KINGSTON
& ST. ANDREW (INDIVIDUALLY)

0   Miles   2

Percentages

24·26
14·27
8·38
4·92
2·89
1·70
0·00

Institutions

Figure 58. Kingston, 1960: Percentage of the population living for less than one year in the parishes of Kingston and St. Andrew (individually).

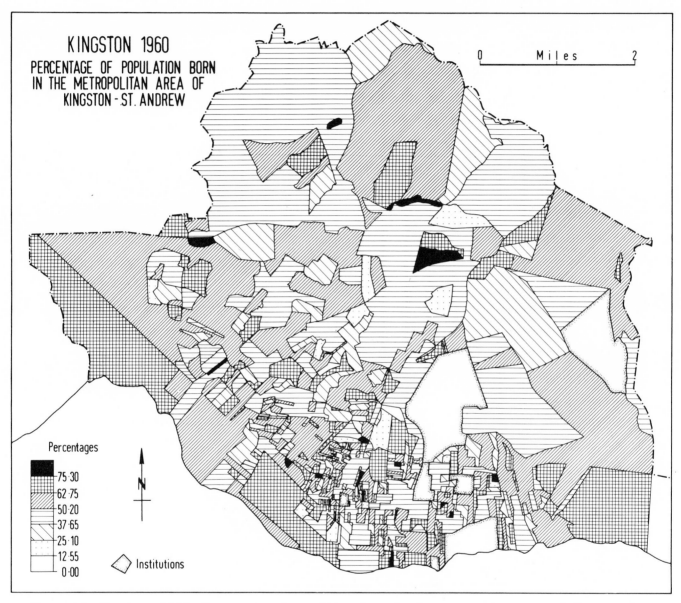

Figure 59. Kingston, 1960: Percentage of population born in the metropolitan area of Kingston–St. Andrew.

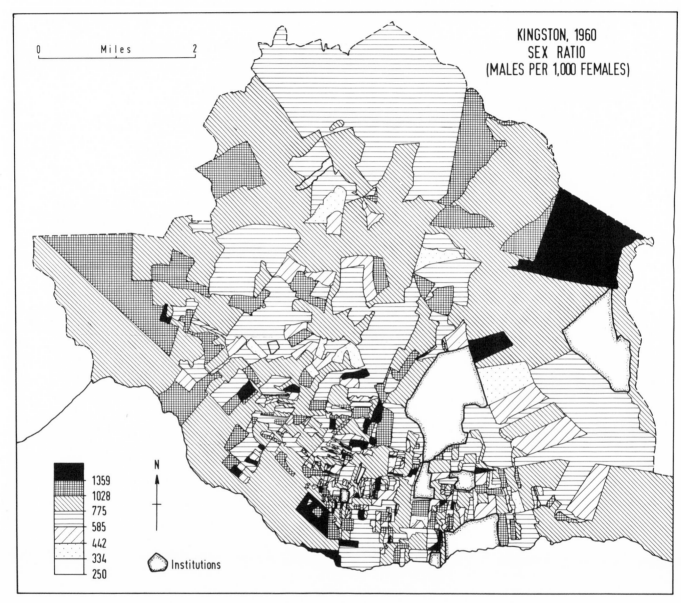

Figure 60. Kingston, 1960: Sex ratio (males per 1,000 females).

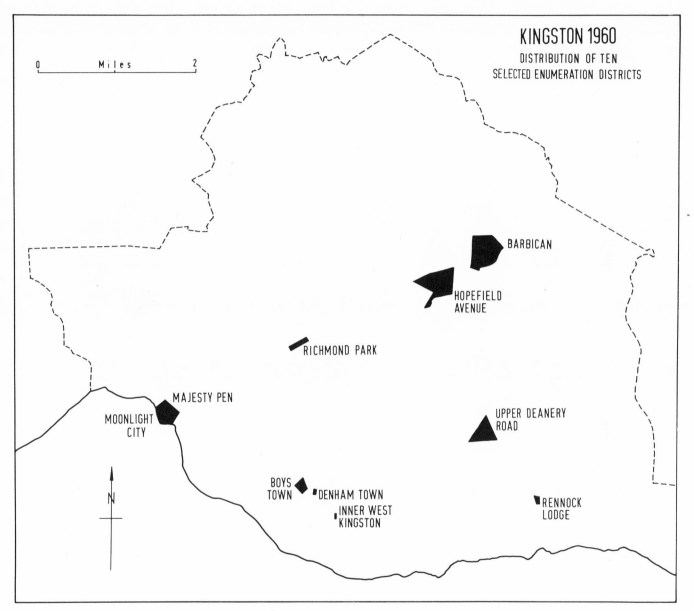

Figure 61. Kingston, 1960: Distribution of ten selected enumeration districts.

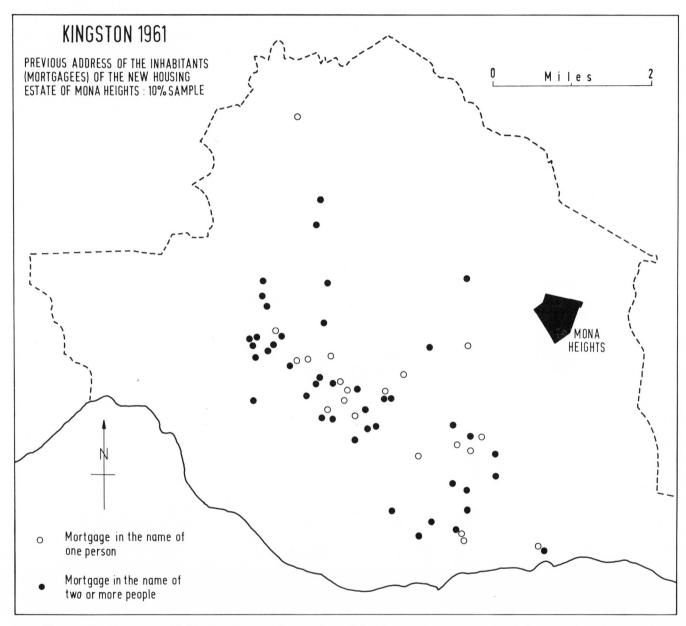

Figure 62. Kingston, 1961: Previous address of the inhabitants (mortgagees) of the new housing estate of Mona Heights: 10% sample.

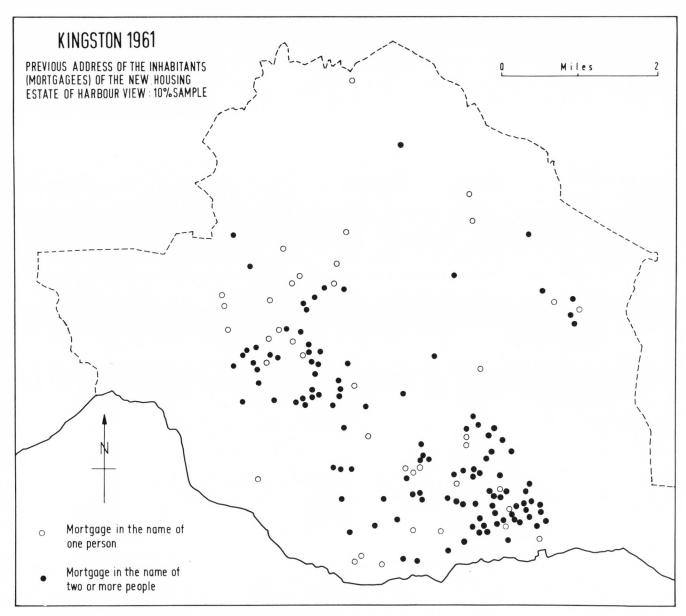

KINGSTON 1961

PREVIOUS ADDRESS OF THE INHABITANTS
(MORTGAGEES) OF THE NEW HOUSING
ESTATE OF HARBOUR VIEW : 10% SAMPLE

0   Miles   2

○   Mortgage in the name of
      one person

●   Mortgage in the name of
      two or more people

Figure 63. Kingston, 1961: Previous address of the inhabitants (mortgagees) of the new housing estate of Harbour View: 10% sample.

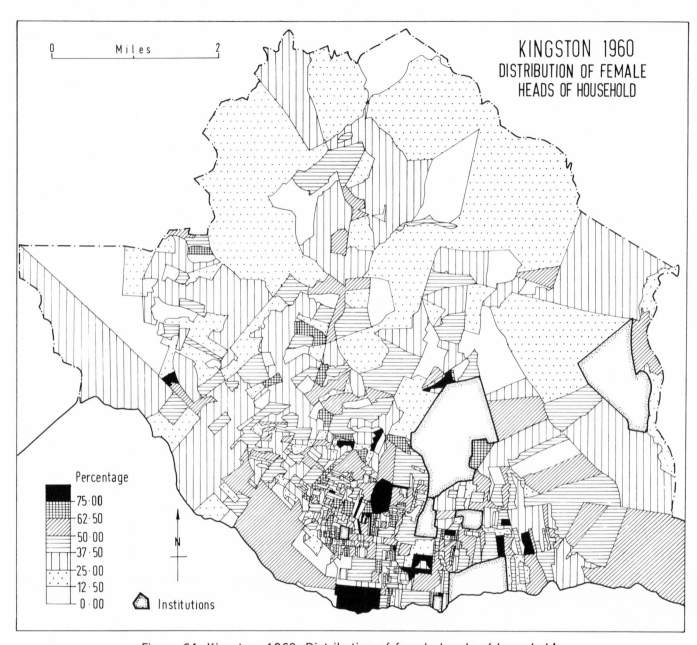

Figure 64. Kingston, 1960: Distribution of female heads of household.

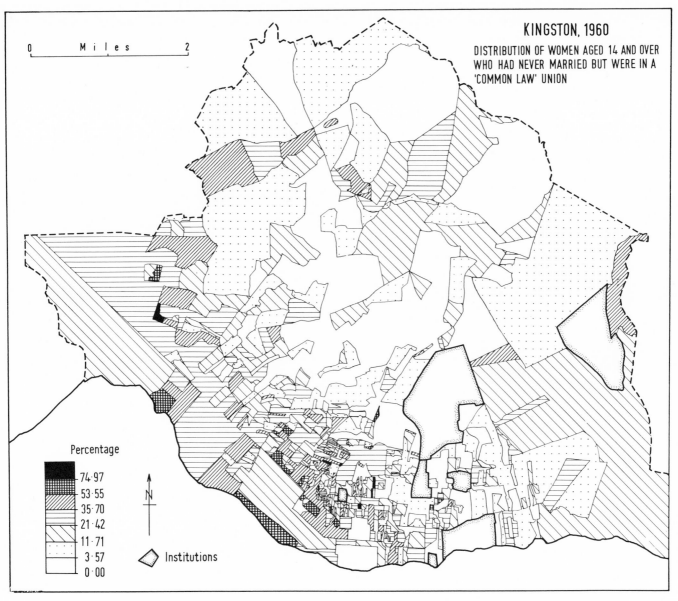

Figure 65. Kingston, 1960: Distribution of women aged 14 and over who had never married but were in common law unions.

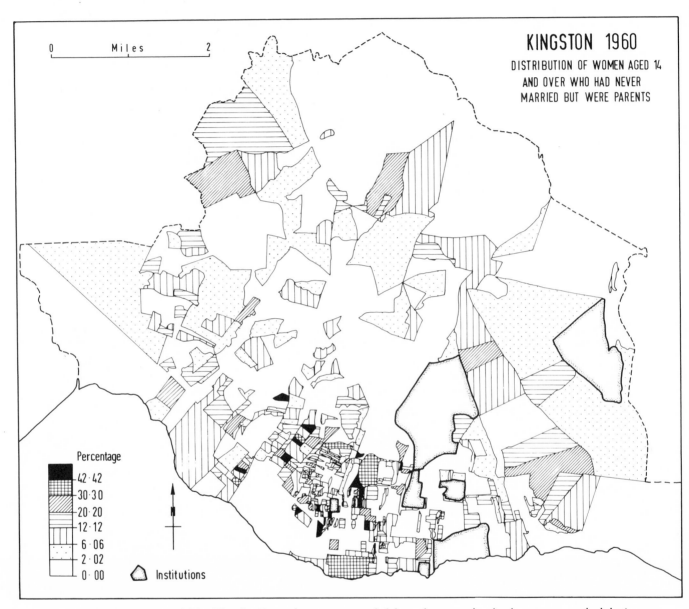

Figure 66. Kingston, 1960: Distribution of women aged 14 and over who had never married but were parents.

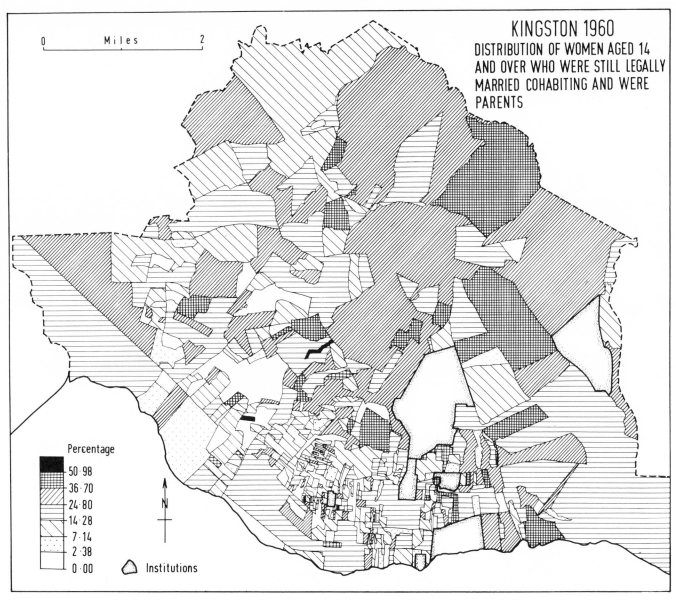

Figure 67. Kingston, 1960: Distribution of women aged 14 and over who were still legally married, cohabiting, and were parents.

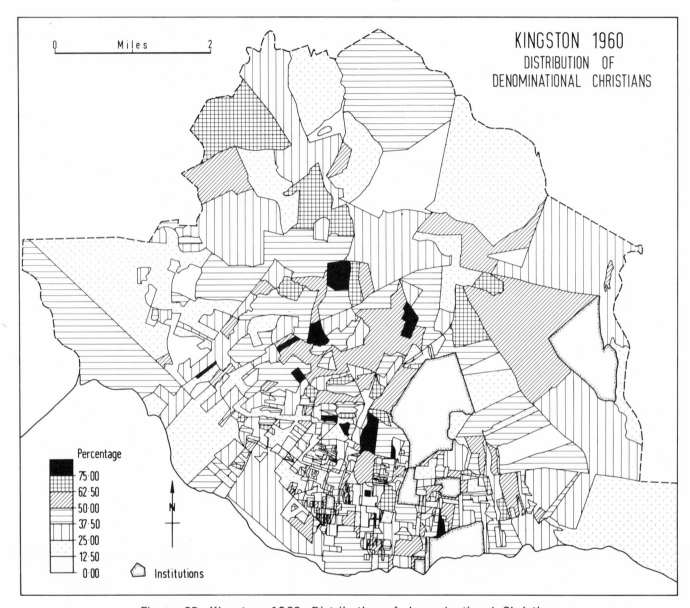

Figure 68. Kingston, 1960: Distribution of denominational Christians.

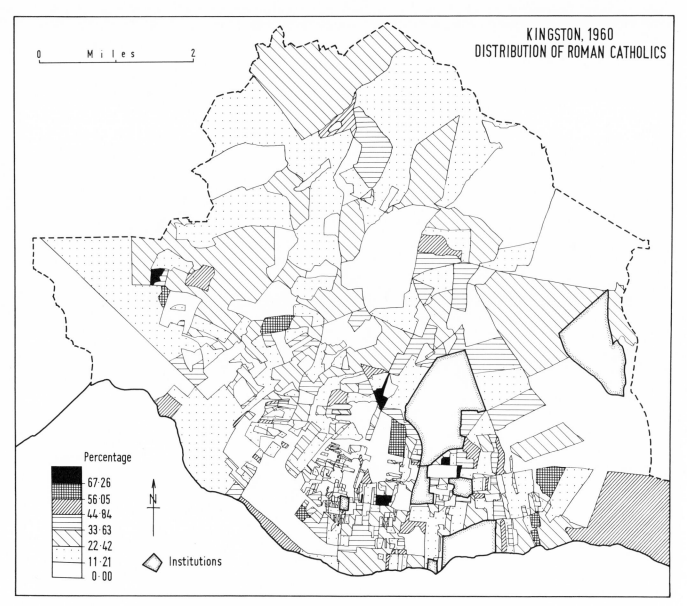

KINGSTON, 1960
DISTRIBUTION OF ROMAN CATHOLICS

Percentage

67·26
56·05
44·84
33·63
22·42
11·21
0·00

Institutions

Figure 69. Kingston, 1960: Distribution of Roman Catholics.

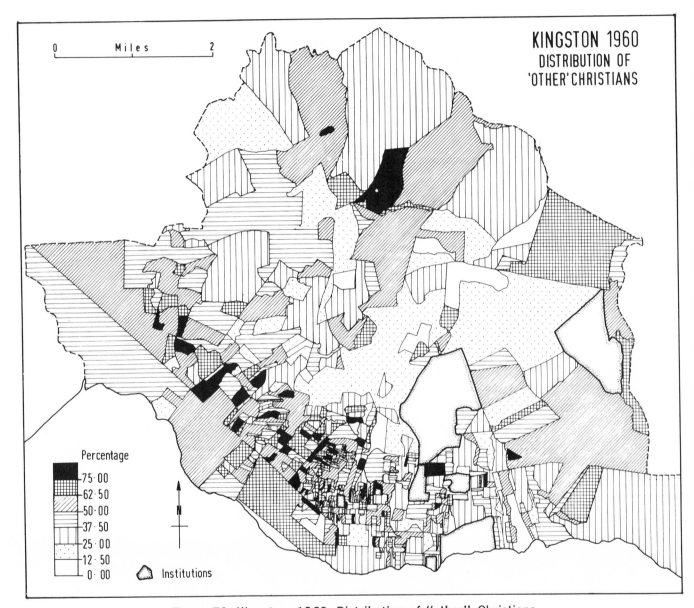

Figure 70. Kingston, 1960: Distribution of "other" Christians.

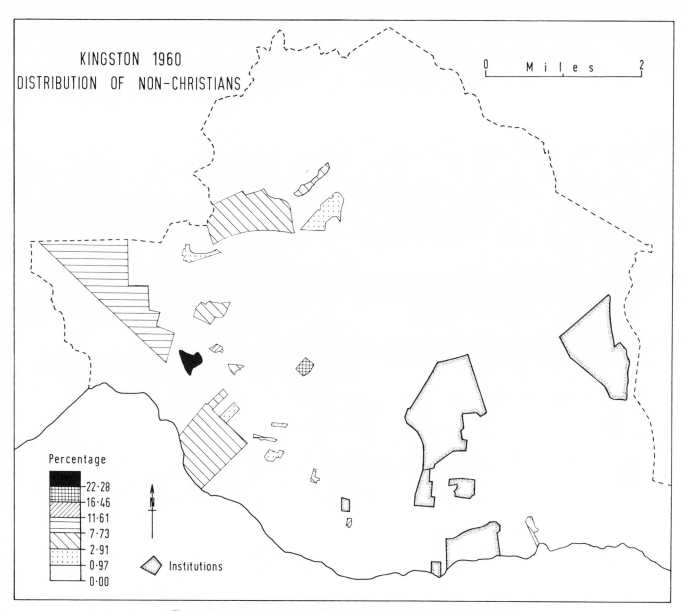

KINGSTON 1960
DISTRIBUTION OF NON-CHRISTIANS

0 Miles 2

Percentage

22·28
16·46
11·61
7·73
2·91
0·97
0·00

N

Institutions

Figure 71. Kingston, 1960: Distribution of non-Christians.

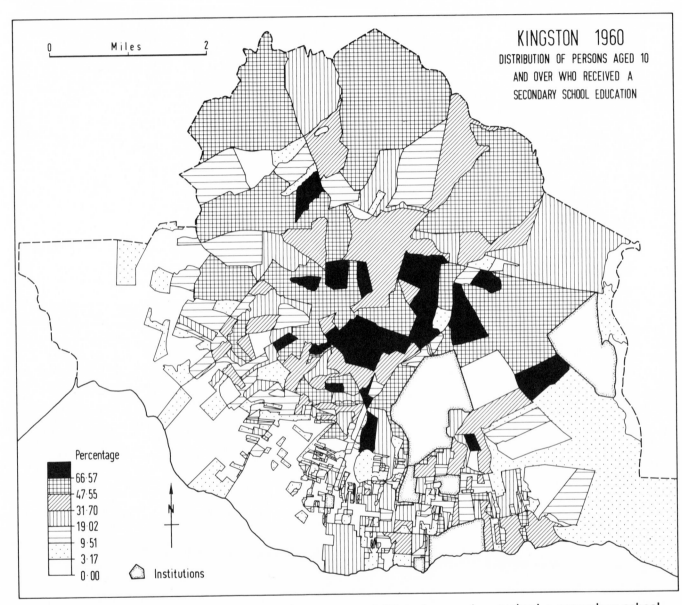

Figure 72. Kingston, 1960: Distribution of persons aged 10 and over who received a secondary school education.

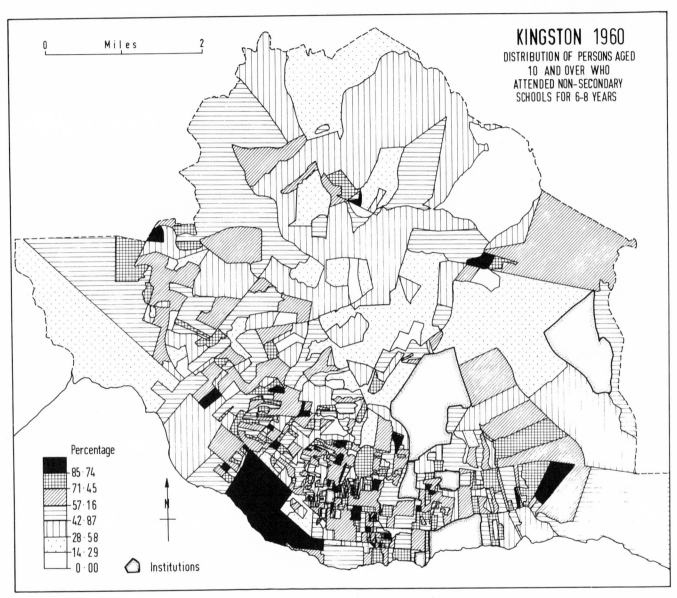

Figure 73. Kingston, 1960: Distribution of persons aged 10 and over who attended non-secondary schools for 6 to 8 years.

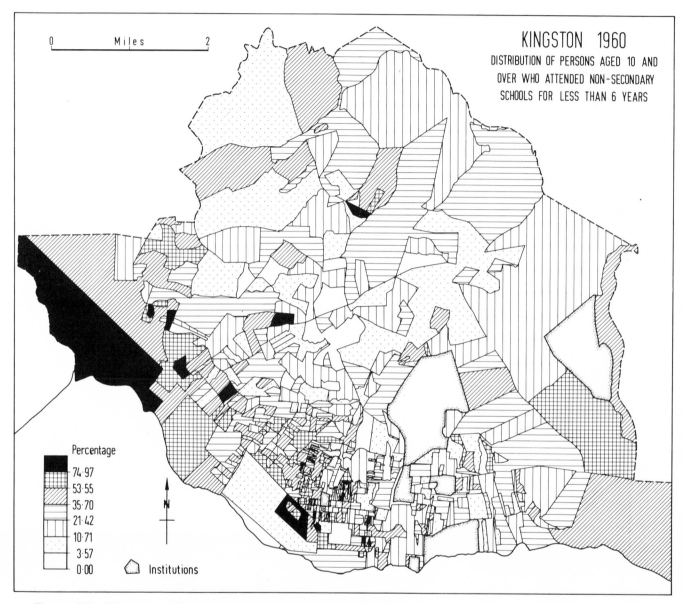

Figure 74. Kingston, 1960: Distribution of persons aged 10 and over who attended non-secondary schools for less than 6 years.

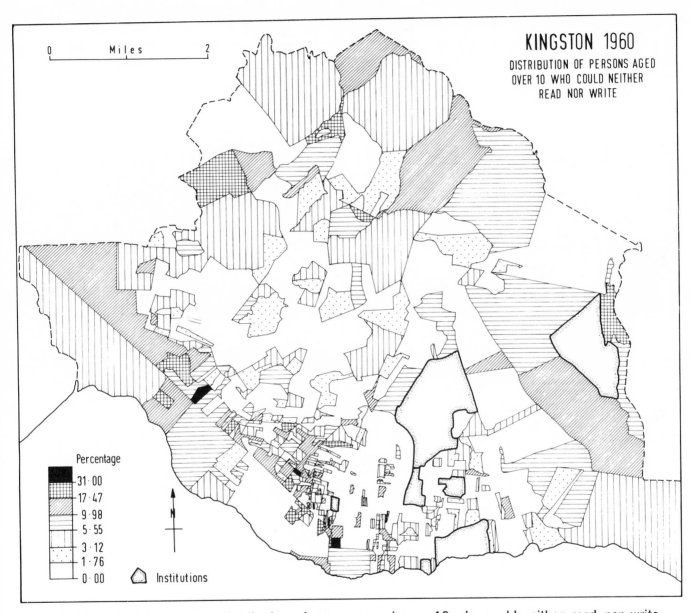

Figure 75. Kingston, 1960: Distribution of persons aged over 10 who could neither read nor write.

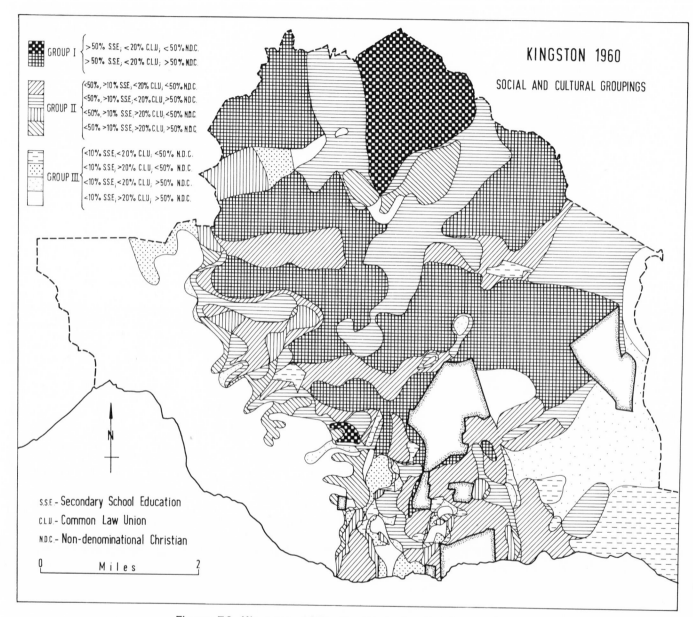

Figure 76. Kingston, 1961: Social and cultural groupings.

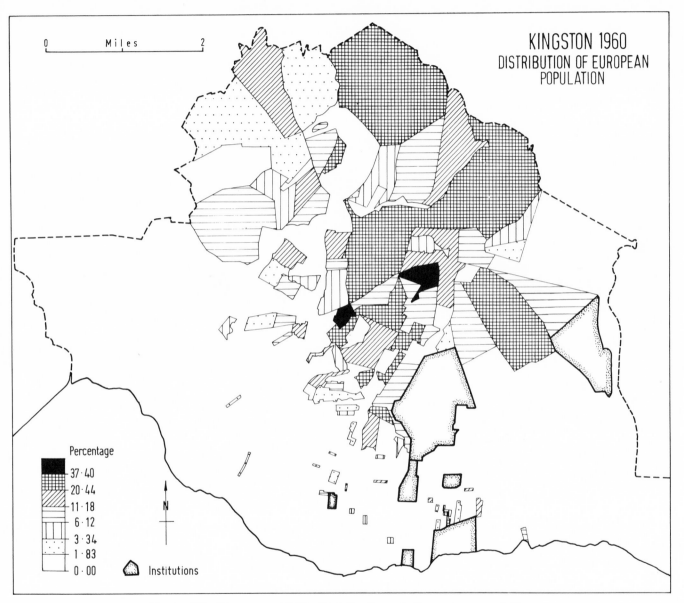

Figure 77. Kingston, 1960: Distribution of European population.

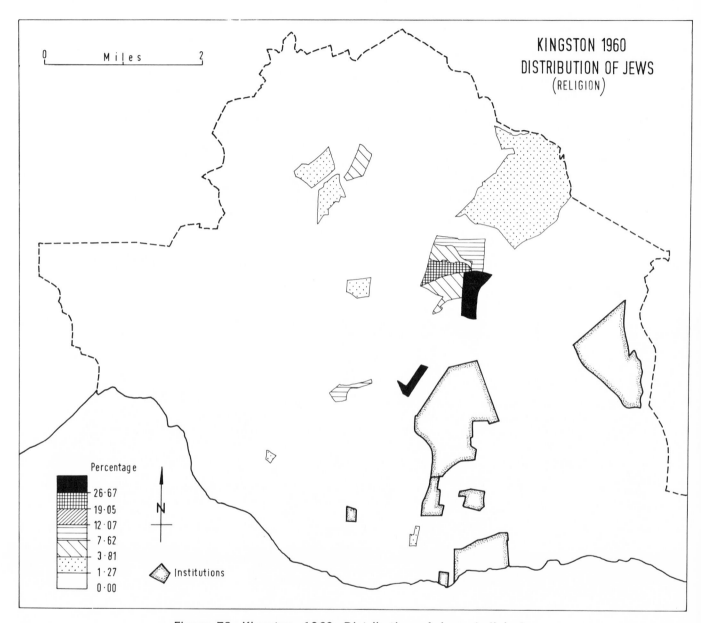

Figure 78. Kingston, 1960: Distribution of Jews (religion).

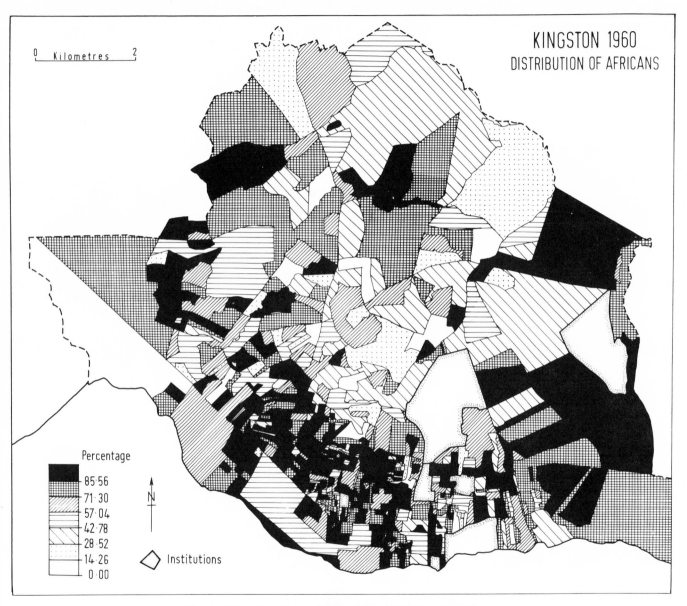

Figure 79. Kingston, 1960: Distribution of Africans.

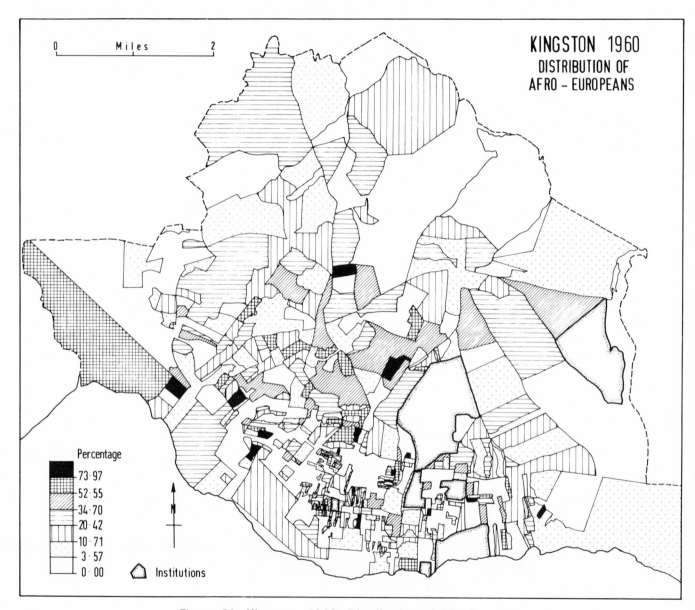

Figure 80. Kingston, 1960: Distribution of Afro-Europeans.

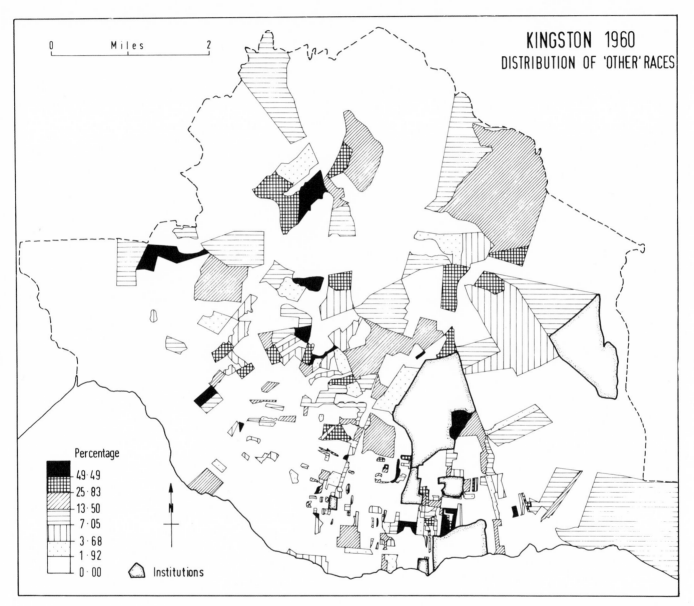

Figure 81. Kingston, 1960: Distribution of "other" races.

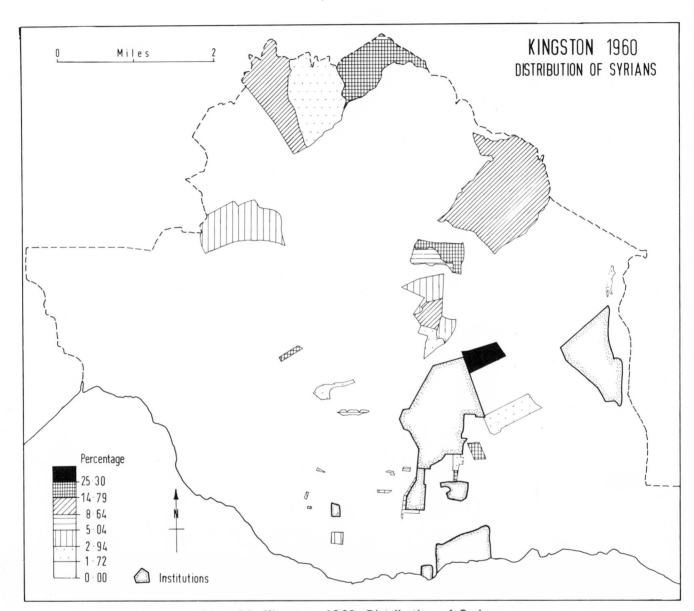

Figure 82. Kingston, 1960: Distribution of Syrians.

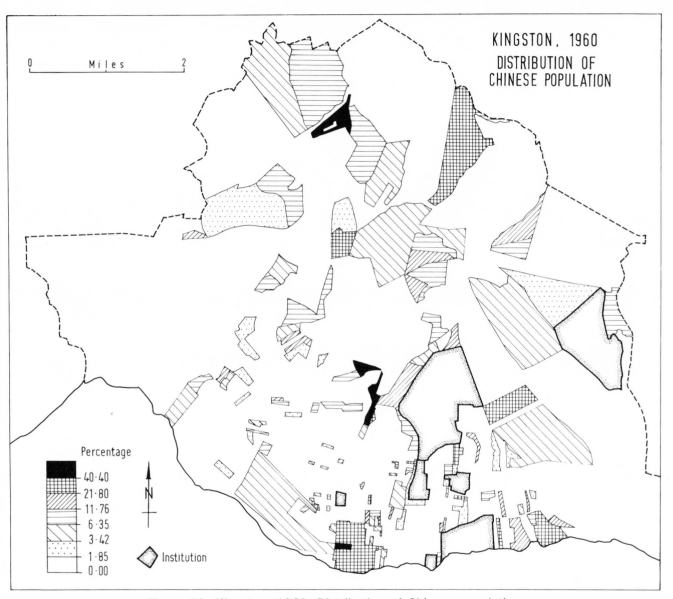

Figure 83. Kingston, 1960: Distribution of Chinese population.

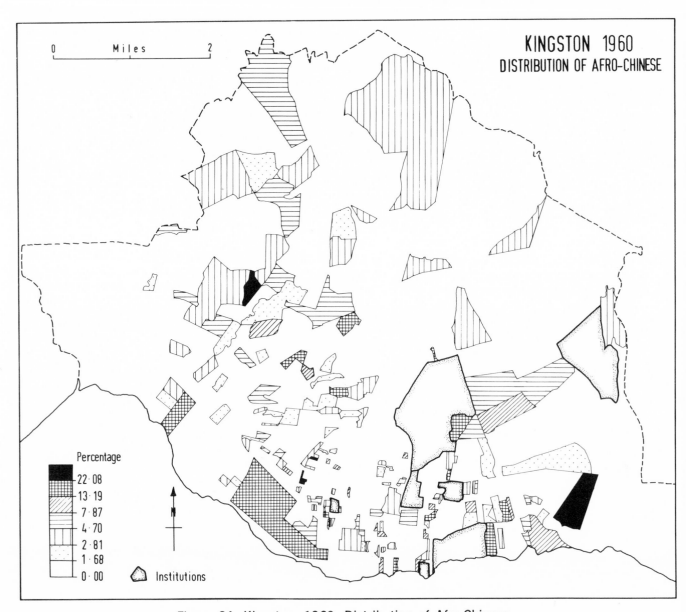

Figure 84. Kingston, 1960: Distribution of Afro-Chinese.

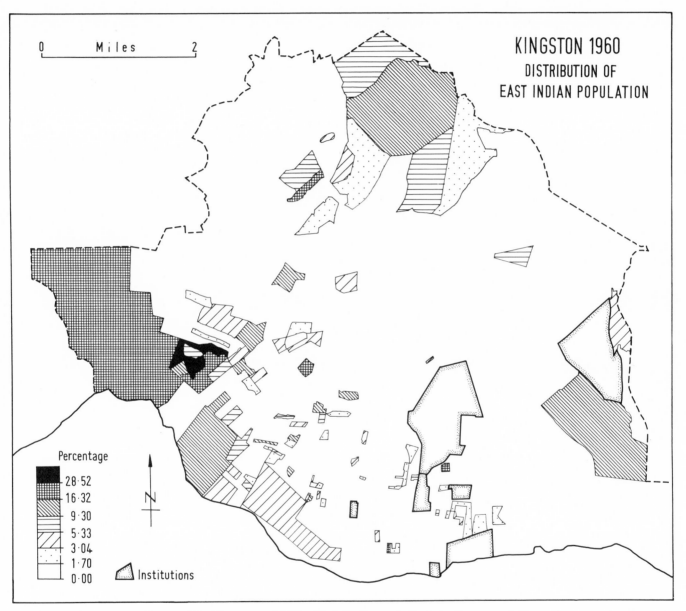

Figure 85. Kingston, 1960: Distribution of East Indian population.

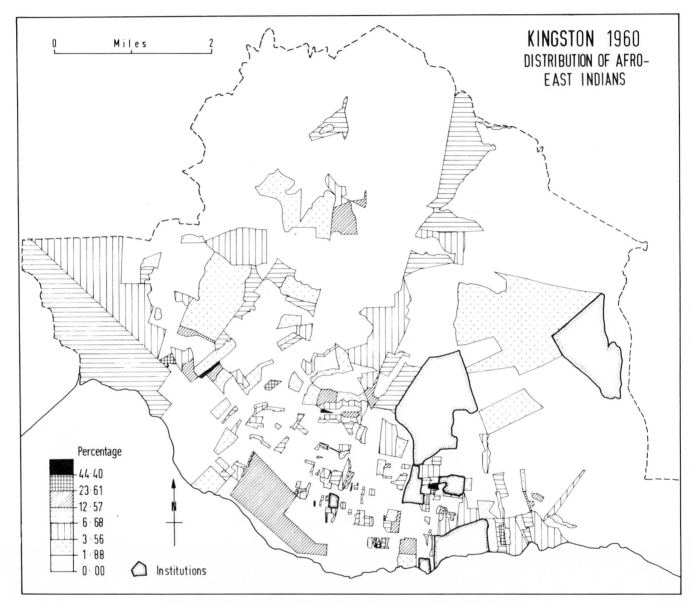

Figure 86. Kingston, 1960: Distribution of Afro-East Indians.

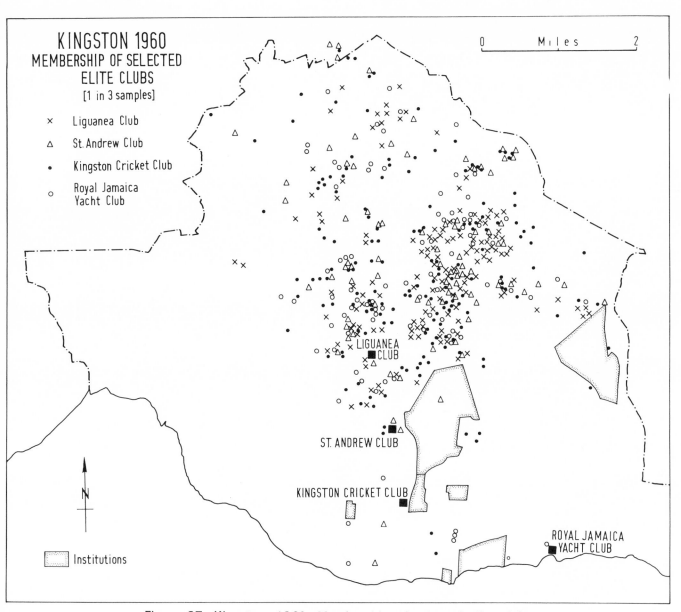

Figure 87. Kingston, 1960: Membership of selected elite clubs.

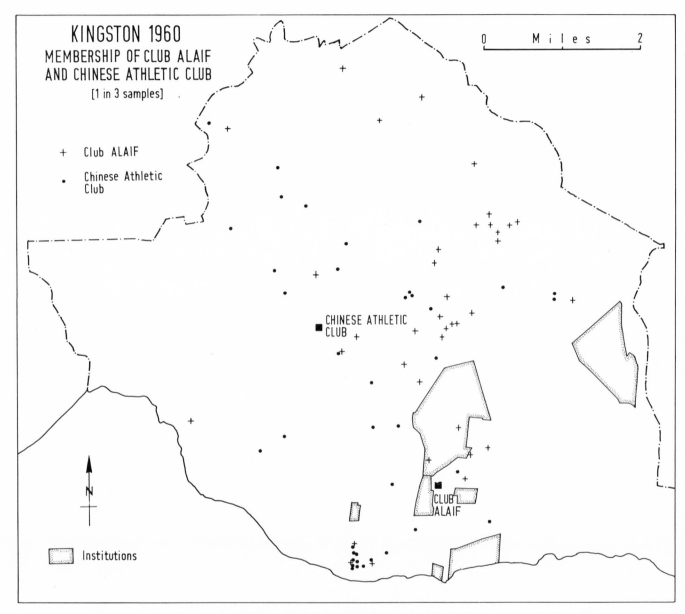

Figure 88. Kingston, 1960: Membership of Club Alaif and the Chinese Athletic Club.

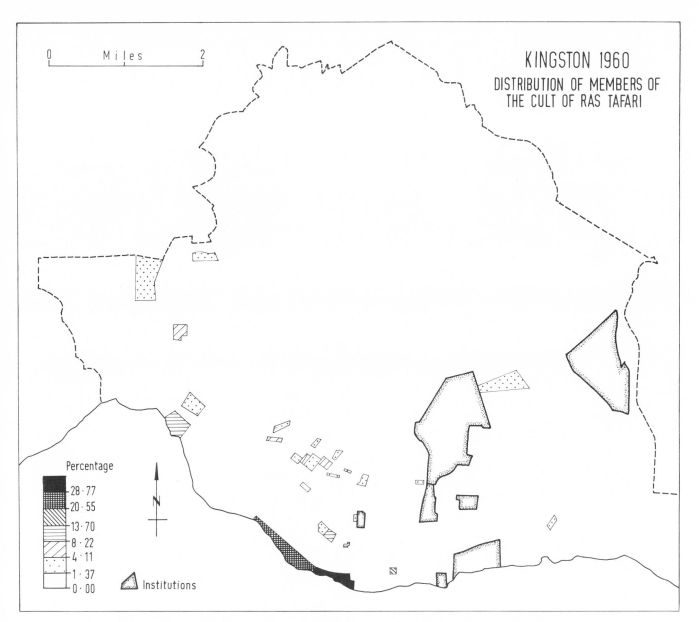

KINGSTON 1960
DISTRIBUTION OF MEMBERS OF
THE CULT OF RAS TAFARI

Percentage

- 28·77
- 20·55
- 13·70
- 8·22
- 4·11
- 1·37
- 0·00

Institutions

Figure 89. Kingston, 1960: Distribution of members of the Ras Tafari cult.

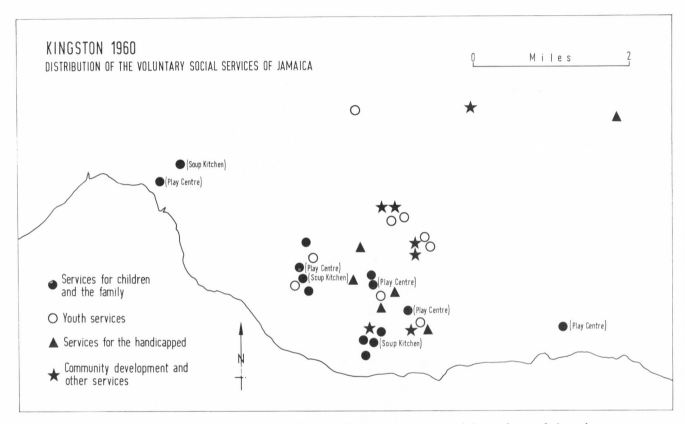

Figure 90. Kingston, 1960: Distribution of the voluntary social services of Jamaica.

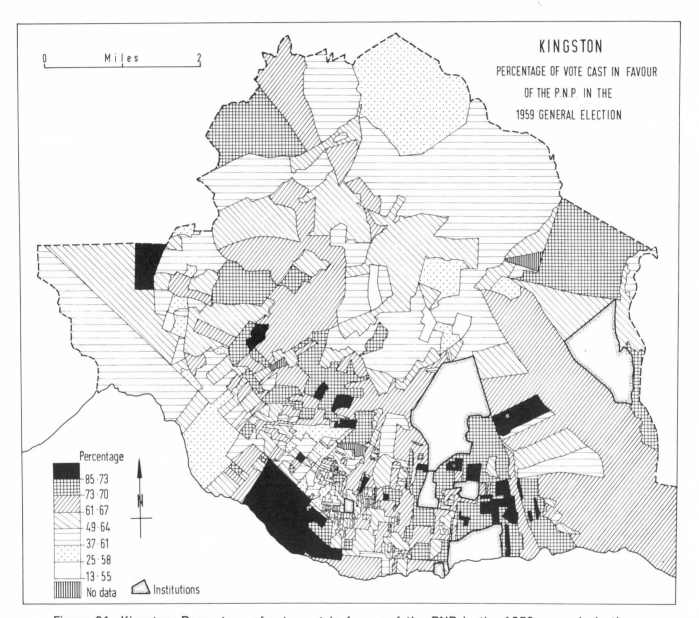

Figure 91. Kingston: Percentage of vote cast in favour of the PNP in the 1959 general election.

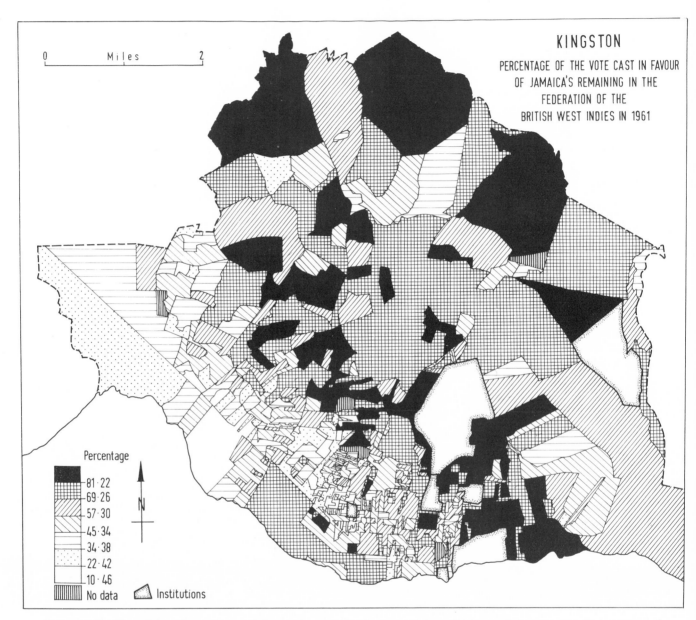

Figure 92. Kingston: Percentage of the vote cast in favour of Jamaica remaining in the Federation of the British West Indies in 1961.

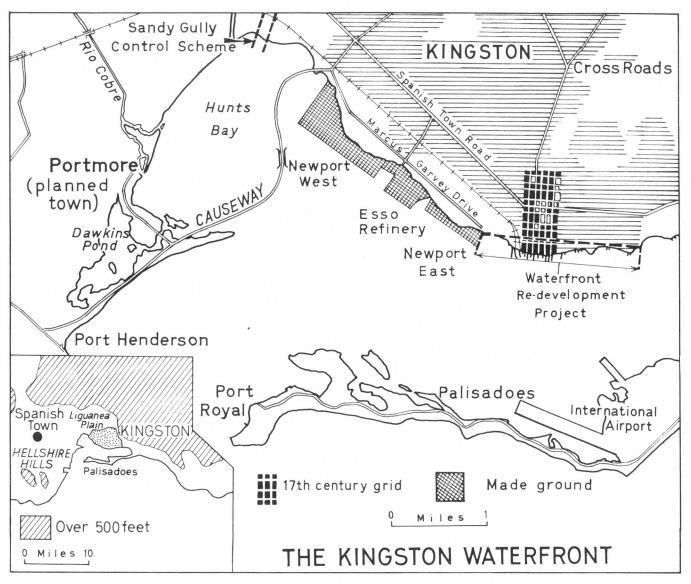

Figure 93. Kingston, 1961: Waterfront development.

Plate 1

Liguanea Plain in 1961 viewed from the east. In the foreground is the middle-income housing scheme of Harbour View, separated from the remainder of the city by Long Mountain. The course of the Hope River is visible in the bottom right-hand corner, and the cement factory is in the middle ground.

Plate 2

Washington Boulevard and the Sandy Gully on the north-western fringe of the city in 1961. The new housing estates and the sub-divisions of real-estate speculators are clearly visible. In the distance the foothills recede as the Plain of St. Catherine is entered. Here Caymanas Estate provides a green belt separating the expanding capital from Spanish Town.

Plate 3

A fine colonial town-house on Hanover Street in the north-eastern part of the eighteenth-century grid, now occupied by a ministry of government.

Plate 4

A house in East Kingston. Sash windows, shingled roof, deep verandah, and columns are typical of the period 1920 to 1940.

Plate 5

A house on the middle-income scheme at Mona Heights, built ca. 1960. Sash windows of the earlier period have been replaced by louvres.

Plate 6

King Street, the main shopping centre, showing the parish church on the corner with the Parade, and the piazzas. In 1961 this section of King Street was the most valuable in terms of real estate. Several stores were owned by Bombay Indians. Syrian property was concentrated on the opposite side of the road.

Plate 7

Shanties clinging to the banks of a controlled gully in central St. Andrew.

Plate 8

Kingston ca. 1838, showing the parish church and the colonial townscape of rectangular roads, dense buildings, high-pitched shingle roofs, jalousies, and piazzas. The foothills of the Blue Mountains are not true to scale. (From J. B. Kidd, **Forty Coloured Views of Jamaica**, London, ca. 1838.)

Plate 9

King Street ca. 1850. The formerly thriving port was in decline, the buildings dilapidated, and the street unpaved. Water carts were still in use. King Street succeeded Harbour Street as the main shopping centre. (From A. Duperly, **Daguerian Excursions in Jamaica**, Kingston, Jamaica [printed in Paris, ca. 1850].)

Plate 10

Detached, single-room dwelling with concrete walls and corrugated-iron roof of the type built in most Central Housing Authority schemes during the 1950s.

Plate 11

Shopping centre for the poor at Papine, a former estate market during slavery.

Plate 12

Syrian dry-goods shops and stalls of pots and pans at the junction between West Queen Street and Spanish Town Road. Donkey carts were still used for haulage between the port and the commercial area in the early 1960s.

Plate 13

A street-corner bar near the Spanish Town Road in West Kingston.

Plate 14

The Department of Education located on South Race Course. This highly controversial building was constructed to withstand earthquakes.

Plate 15

Gordon House, the new House of Representatives, situated on Duke Street in the eighteenth-century grid. The wooden houses that surround it are typical of the north-eastern part of the old city.

Plate 16

Nineteenth-century colonial buildings on East Street. These were survivors of the 1907 earthquake and fire but are now dilapidated.

Plate 17

Single storey tenements in one of the better parts of West Kingston. Dwellings have been built one behind the other until the entire lot has been almost completely covered.

Plate 18

A house typical of those built in central St. Andrew between the two world wars.

Plate 19

Modern house built on the northern edge of Long Mountain.

Plate 20

Neo-classical great house situated between Hope and Old Hope Roads.

Plate 21

Aerial view of Trench Town in 1961, showing the hurricane rehousing scheme and, on the left, the late 1930s redevelopment at Denham Town. Between the two and around Clock Circle are located a number of squatter camps. All three areas possess a distinctive morphology. The Boy's Town squatter settlement is located in the middle of photograph.

Plate 22

Heavily stockaded squatter settlement at Boy's Town.

Plate 23

Cardboard-and-newspaper shanty in the new and growing squatter camp at Moonlight City on the fore-shore in West Kingston.

Plate 24

Shack in Moonlight City constructed from packing cases and fish barrels.

Plate 25

New stand-pipe in the
squatter camp at Boy's Town
in 1961.

Plate 26

Broom makers at Majesty Pen.

Plate 27

The dungle in West Kingston. Squatters compete with John Crows for the contents of garbage carts.

Plate 28

A good example of a late nineteenth- or early twentieth-century house in East Kingston. The fretwork, shingles, and louvres are outstanding features.

Plate 29

Housing typical of many of the recent suburbs.

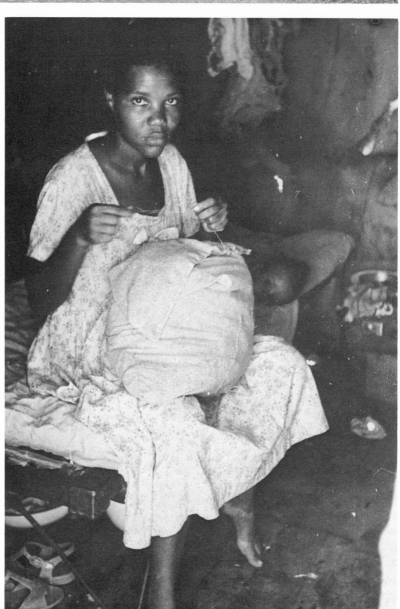

Plate 30

Female head of household in squatter settlement at Moonlight City. The poverty and hopelessness of her situation are only too clearly revealed.

Plate 31

Inhabitants of the Boy's Town squatter camp.

Plate 32

Hut of a member of the Ras Tafari movement in Moonlight City. Most of the words and symbols painted on the outside are readily intelligible, except for the circle painted green, yellow, and red, the colours of the movement. Green represents the pastures of Africa, yellow the wealth of that land, and red the Church Triumphant, while the black star at the centre of the circle stands for black supremacy and Garvey's back to Africa movement.

Abbreviations Used in Notes

A.A.A.G.	:	*Annals of the Association of American Geographers*
Amer. Anthrop.	:	*American Anthropologist*
Am. Soc. Rev.	:	*American Sociological Review*
Brit. Jour. Soc.	:	*British Journal of Sociology*
Caribb. Quart.	:	*Caribbean Quarterly*
Caribb. Stud.	:	*Caribbean Studies*
C.E.R.	:	*Caribbean Economic Review*
C.H.R.	:	*Caribbean Historical Review*
G.J.	:	*Geographical Journal*
G.R.	:	*Geographical Review*
I.B.G.	:	*Transactions of the Institute of British Geographers*
J.H.R.	:	*Jamaica Historical Review*
J.M.H.	:	*Journal of Modern History*
J.N.H.	:	*Journal of Negro History*
Soc. and Econ. Stud.	:	*Social and Economic Studies*

Notes

Preface

[1] E. W. Gilbert and R. W. Steel, "Social Geography and Its Place in Colonial Studies," *G.J.*, 106 (1945), 129.

[2] L. Broom, "Urban Research in the British Caribbean: A Prospectus," *Soc. and Econ. Stud.*, 1 (1953), 113.

[3] Both L. Braithwaite, "Social Stratification in Trinidad," *Soc. and Econ. Stud.*, 2 (1953), 5-175, and F. Henriques, *Family and Colour in Jamaica* (1953), couch their analysis in terms of colour-class.

[4] J. Lobb, "Caste and Class in Haiti," *Amer. Journ. of Sociology*, 46 (1940), 23-34.

[5] See especially M. G. Smith, *The Plural Society in the British West Indies* (1965), p. 82.

[6] *Ibid.*, p. 53.

[7] *Ibid.*, p. 88.

[8] V. Rubin, "Social and Cultural Pluralism in the Caribbean," *Annals New York Academy of Sci.*, vol. 83, Art. 5, January 1960, p. 783.

[9] C. Wagley, cited in V. Rubin, *op. cit.*, p. 778.

[10] R. T. Smith, review of V. Rubin, ed., "Social and Cultural Pluralism in the Caribbean," *op. cit.*, in *Amer. Anthrop.*, 63, 155.

Chapter 1: Physical Environment

[1] Frank Raw's editorial observations in Charles Matley, *The Geology and Physiography of the Kingston District, Jamaica* (Kingston, 1951).

[2] *Ibid.*, p. 70.

[3] V. J. Chapman, "The Botany of the Jamaica Shoreline," in "Sand Cays and Mangroves in Jamaica, Report of the Cambridge University Jamaica Expedition, 1939," *G.J.*, 96 (1940), 319.

[4] *Report on the Harbour of Kingston*, Ewbank and Partners Ltd. (Toronto, 1961).

[5] Chapman, *op. cit.*, p. 320.

[6] Vaughan Cornish, "The Jamaica Earthquake, 1907," *G.J.*, 31 (1908), 245-270.

[7] Charles Leslie, *A History of Jamaica* (London 1740), p. 20.

[8] J. F. Brennan, *The Meteorology of Jamaica*, Government Printing Office (Kingston, 1936), p. 8.

[9] A. R. Thomas, *Storm Water Drainage in Jamaica*, United Nations Technical Assistance Administration, 1959.

[10] Brennan, *op. cit.*, pp. 18-19.

[11] *Engineering Department of Water Commission, Annual Report for Year Ending 31st March, 1960* (Kingston, 1961), p. 6.

[12] Edward Long, *History of Jamaica*, 1 (1774), 103-104.

Chapter II: Kingston during Slavery, 1692-1820

[1] The church at Half Way Tree is marked on Fig. 4.

[2] S. A. G. Taylor, "Port Royal," in W. A. Roberts, ed., *The Capitals of Jamaica* (Kingston, 1955), p. 22.

[3] E. Long, *History of Jamaica*, 2 (1774), 140.

[4] *Ibid.*, p. 143.

[5] F. Cundall, *Historic Jamaica* (Kingston, 1915), p. 148.

[6] Roberts, *op. cit.*, p. 42.

[7] *Ibid.*, p. 43.

[8] Long, *op. cit.*, 1, 58.

[9] *Ibid.*, p. 532.

[10] G. Milroy, *Report on the Cholera Epidemic in Jamaica* (Kingston, 1852), p. 47.

[11] The ratio of the population of Kingston to Jamaica as a whole should be treated with caution since it may have been used as a constant when these populations were estimated.

[12] F. W. Pitman, *The Development of the British West Indies, 1700-1763* (1917), Appendix 1, 375 and 58.

[13] The Maroons were originally runaway slaves who had escaped from their Spanish masters. They were subsequently joined by other runaways and became a threat to the security of the island. In 1739 they were confined to a number of settlements in the mountains, and permitted a certain amount of autonomy in return for which they were expected to capture or kill escaped slaves.

[14] M. G. Smith, "Some Aspects of Social Structure in the British Caribbean about 1820," *Soc. and Econ. Stud.*, 1 (1953), 57.

[15] B. Edwards, *The History, Civil and Commercial of the British West Indies*, 2, (1788), 22.

[16] Long, *op. cit.*, 2, 320.

[17] Clinton V. Black, "Kingston in the 18th Century," *in* Roberts, *op. cit.*, p. 58.

[18] *The Return of Slaves for the Parish of Kingston in 1817*, manuscript in the Jamaica Archives at Spanish Town.

[19] G. W. Roberts, *The Population of Jamaica* (1957), p. 71.

[20] D. G. Hall, "The Social and Economic Background to Sugar in Slave Days," *C.H.R.*, 3-4 (1954), 150.

[21] The details associated with the operation of this law are listed in R. Renny, *An History of Jamaica* (1807), Appendix 1. This restriction did not apply to sellers of provisions, fruits, and other staples.

[22] G. W. Bridges, *The Annals of Jamaica*, 2 (1828), 348n; J. W. Stewart, *A View of the Past and Present State of the Island of Jamaica* (1823), p. 182.

[23] Stewart, *op. cit.*, pp. 190-191.

[24] B. W. Higman, *Some Demographic Characteristics of Slavery in Jamaica in about 1832*, Postgraduate Seminars, Department of History, University of the West Indies (1969), unpublished typescript, table 1, column 12.

[25] J. G. Young, "Who Planned Kingston?" *J.H.R.*, 1 (1946), 145-146.

[26] *Ibid.*, p. 149.

[27] F. Cundall, *Historic Jamaica*, p. 148.

[28] Young, *op. cit.*, pp. 145-146.

[29] *Ibid.*, p. 150.

[30] The original of Lilly's plan could not be located in 1961, 1964 or 1968, when the writer examined the map collection of the Institute of Jamaica.

[31] Young, *op. cit.*, p. 151.

[32] Long, *op. cit.*, 2, 103.

[33] Renny, *op. cit.*, p. 103.

[34] Anon. [J. Stewart], *An Account of Jamaica and Its Inhabitants by a Gentleman Long Resident in the West Indies* (1808), p. 14. This is usually attributed to J. W. Stewart whose later work, *A View of the Past and Present State of the Island of Jamaica* (1823), it closely resembles.

[35] Renny, *op. cit.*, p. 103. Headquarters House, standing at the corner of Duke Street and Beeston Street, still testifies to the wealth of its original owners, the Hibbert family. See also Wilma Williams "Old Kingston," *Jamaica Journal*, 5, 2-3 (1971) 3-9.

[36] M. Scott, *Tom Cringle's Log* (1917), p. 105.

[37] W. J. Gardner, *History of Jamaica* (1872), p. 267.

[38] Pitman, *op. cit.*, p. 40n.

[39] R.J. Ragatz, *The Fall of the Planter Class in the British Caribbean, 1763-1833* (1928), p. 238.

[40] Long, *op. cit.*, 2, 124.

[41] W. Beckford, *A Descriptive Account of the Island of Jamaica* (1790), 1, xxii.

[42] Long, *op. cit.*, 2, 124.

[43] Anon. [STEWART], *op. cit.*, (1808), pp. 11-12.

[44] Stewart, *op. cit.*, (1823), p. 28.

[45] Pitman, *op. cit.*, p. 20.

[46] Renny, *op. cit.*, p. 49.

[47] Long, *op. cit.*, 2, 120.

[48] Gardner, *op. cit.*, p. 162.

[49] *Ibid.* p. 162.

[50] *Ibid.*, pp. 327-328.

[51] *Ibid.*, p. 328.

[52] Long, *op. cit.*, 1, 138.

[53] Gardner, *op. cit.*, p. 329.

[54] Long, *op. cit.*, 2, 229.

[55] *Ibid.*, p. 229. One hogshead was equal to approximately 16 hundredweight.

[56] Gardner, *op. cit*, p. 320.

[57] *Ibid.*, p. 319.

[58] *Ibid.*, p. 319.

[59] Long, *op. cit.*, 1, 496.

[60] *Ibid.*, 2, 230.

[61] Pitman, *op. cit.*, p. 138.

[62] *Ibid.*, p. 236.

[63] C. P. Nettels, "England and the Spanish American Trade, 1680-1715," *J.M.H.*, 3, (1931), 5.

[64] R. Le Page and D. De Camp, "Jamaica Creole," *Creole Language Studies*, 1, (1960), 66-68.

[65] *Ibid.*, pp. 66-67.

[66] F. Armytage, *The Free Port System in the British West Indies* (1953), p. 7.

[67] Quoted in Armytage, *op. cit.*, p. 21.

[68] Pitman, *op. cit.*, p. 79.

[69] Armytage, *op. cit.*, p. 2.

[70] Long, *op. cit.*, 2, 497-499, 500-502.

[71] Gardner, *op. cit.*, p. 319.

[72] Quoted in Armytage, *op. cit.*, p. 113.

[73] *Ibid.*, 92, 123.

[74] Scott, *op. cit.*, pp. 104-105.

[75] Gardner, *op. cit.*, p. 163.

[76] Stewart, *op. cit.*, (1823), pp. 199-200.

[77] R. Bickell, *The West Indies, or A Real Picture of Slavery . . .* (1825), p. 66.

[78] S. W. Mintz and D. G. Hall, "The Origins of Jamaica's Internal Marketing System," *Yale University Publications in Anthropology*, 57 (1960), 17.

[79] Long, *op. cit.*, 2, 410-411.

[80] Edwards, *op. cit.*, 2, 162n.

[81] Many of the stores were owned by Jews, and this also probably influenced opening on Sundays (see Renny, *History of Jamaica* [1807], p. 328).

[82] Anon. [STEWART], *op. cit.*, (1808), p. 60.

[83] C. V. Black "Kingston in the 19th Century," *in* Roberts, *op. cit.*, p. 55.

[84] Long, *op. cit.*, 2, 106.

[85] Cundall, ed., *Lady Nugent's Journal* (1939), p. 37n.

[86] Long, *op. cit.*, 2, 116.

[87] F. L. Casserly, "Kingston in the 19th Century," *in* Roberts, *op. cit.*, p. 75.

[88] Long, *op. cit.*, 2, 114-115.

[89] Renny, *op. cit.*, p. 103.

[90] Black, *op. cit.*, p. 56.

[91] H. P. Silverman, *A Panorama of Jamaican Jewry* (Jamaica, 1960).

[92] Anon. [STEWART], *op. cit.*, (1808), p. 14.

[93] *Vestry Minutes for Kingston, 1744*, manuscript in Jamaica Archives at Spanish Town.

[94] H. P. Jacobs, "An Historical Analysis of City Centre Movements," *Jamaica Architect*, 1, 3 (1967/8), 73.

[95] Renny, *op. cit.*, pp. 107-108.

[96] T. Southey, *A Chronological History of the West Indies* (1827), 3, 18.

[97] Bridges, *op. cit.*, 2, 381.

[98] M. G. Smith, *op. cit.*, p. 68.

[99] Stewart, *op. cit.* (1823), p. 249.

[100] Long, *op. cit.*, 2, 321.

[101] *Ibid.*, p. 320.

[102] Edwards, *op. cit.*, 2, 24n.

[103] Hall, *op. cit.*, p. 150.

[104] Long, *op. cit.*, 2, 323.

[105] Anon. [Stewart], *op. cit.* (1808), pp. 302-303.

[106] M. G. Lewis, *Journal of a West India Proprietor*, ed. Mona Wilson (1929), p. 289.

[107] A. V. Long, *Jamaica and the New Order (1827-1847)*, Institute of Social and Economic Research, University College of the West Indies (1956), p. 5.

[108] M. G. Lewis, *op. cit.*, p. 289.

[109] Anon. [Stewart], *op. cit.* (1808), p. 14.

[110] Between 1655 and 1690 the Jews were subject to annual taxes imposed by the Jamaica Assembly (E. Long, *op. cit.*, 2, 293), and as late as 1693, £750 was levied on them to provide two sloops to defend Jamaica (R. A. Fisher, "A Note on Jamaica [Taxation of Jews, 1693]" *J.N.H.*, 28 [1943], 200). Later it became customary for the Jews to send bribes to the governor in return for which discriminatory taxation was allowed to fall into abeyance (Gardner, *op. cit.,* p. 199). Freedom of worship was permitted during the governorship of Molesworth, 1684-87 (E. Long, *op. cit.*, 2, 294).

[111] Gardner, *op. cit.*, p. 198.

[112] Southey, *op. cit.*, 2, 400.

[113] Edwards, *op. cit.*, 2, 25.

[114] Anon., *Marly: or the Life of a Planter in Jamaica* (1831), p. 94.

[115] Anon. [Stewart], *op. cit.*, (1808), p. 204.

[116] Edwards, *op. cit.*, 2, 24.

[117] Scott, *op. cit.*, p. 202.

[118] Anon., *Marly*, *op. cit.*, p. 195.

[119] E. Long (*op. cit.*, 1, preface, V) wrote "What I have said does not imply that a system of servitude ought to be introduced to any country." See also Lewis, *op. cit.*, p. 331.

[120] Stewart, *op. cit.* (1823), pp. 195-200.

[121] Anon. [Stewart], *op. cit.* (1808), p. 182.

[122] E. Long, *op. cit.*, 2, 288.

[123] Pitman, *op. cit.*, pp. 52-53.

[124] Stewart, *op. cit.* (1823), p. 161.

[125] Hall, *op. cit.*, p. 165.

[126] *Ibid.*, pp. 162-163.

[127] *Ibid.*, p. 157. In 1826 the 28,800 free people of colour in Jamaica were classified in the following manner: 400, rich; 5,500 in fair circumstances; and 22,900 absolutely poor.

[128] F. Henriques, *Jamaica, Land of Wood and Water* (1957).

[129] *Returns of Slaves for the Parish of Kingston in 1817*, manuscript in the Archives of Jamaica at Spanish Town.

[130] Anon. [Stewart], *op. cit.* (1808), p. 10.

[131] E. Long, *op. cit.*, 2, 296.

[132] Southey, *op. cit.*, 2, 421.

[133] *Jamaica Almanack* (1796), p. 108.

[134] Lewis, *op. cit.*, pp. 73-74.

[135] W. Beckford, *A Descriptive Account of the Island of Jamaica* (1790), 1, 389.

[136] E. Long, *op. cit.* 2, 261.

[137] J. A. P. M. Andrade, *A Record of the Jews in Jamaica, from the English Conquest to the Present Time* (Kingston, 1941), p. 29.

[138] Renny, *op. cit.*, p. 189.

[139] Anon., *Marly, op. cit.*, p. 194.

[140] Stewart, *op. cit.* (1823), p. 327.

[141] Anon., *Marly, op. cit.*, p. 97.

[142] Southey, *op. cit.*, 2, 400.

[143] *Ibid.*, p. 335.

[144] Lewis, *op. cit.*, p. 94.

[145] M. G. Smith, *op. cit.*, p. 72.

[146] Gardner, *op. cit.*, p. 182; E. Long, *op. cit.*, 2, 413.

[147] Edwards, *op. cit.*, 2, 98.

[148] *Ibid.*, p. 98.

[149] Cundall, *op. cit.* (1939), p. 118.

[150] Anon., *Marly, op. cit.*, p. 217.

[151] R. T. Smith, however, argues that "there are really three phases in the development cycle of the household" ("The Family in the Caribbean," in Vera Rubin, ed., *Caribbean Studies: A Symposium* (1960), p. 70).

[152] Beckford, *op. cit.*, 2, 323-324.

[153] Leslie, *op. cit.*, p. 303.

[154] Gardner, *op. cit.*, p. 351.

[155] *Ibid.*, p. 184.

[156] Edwards, *op. cit.*, 2, 109.

[157] J. J. Williams, *Voodoos and Obeahs: Phases of West Indian Witchcraft* (1932), 145-146.

[158] E. Long, *op. cit.*, 2, 416.

[159] P. D. Curtin, *Two Jamaicas* (1955), 36-37.

[160] Gardner, *op. cit.*, p. 352.

[161] Lewis, *op. cit.*, p. 138.

[162] Leslie, *op. cit.*, p. 35.

[163] E. Long, *op. cit.*, 1, 511.

[164] *Ibid.*, 2, 257.

[165] Stewart, *op. cit.* (1823), p. 335.

[166] Renny (*op. cit.*, p. 172) was one of the few to contradict this view.

[167] E. Long *op. cit.*, 2, 370.

[168] Southey, *op. cit.*, 2, 420. The italics are Southey's. At this period it was argued in Jamaica that the import of slaves from Africa represented a danger to the colony. Africans formed the most rebellious element in the island, and an import tax was eventually levied on them.

[169] M. G. Smith, *op. cit.*, p. 78.

[170] Cundall, *op. cit.* (1939), p. xxxii.

[171] Lord Olivier, *Jamaica, The Blessed Isle* (1936), p. 60.

[172] E. Long, *op. cit.*, 2, 455.

[173] *Ibid.*, p. 410.

[174] Southey, *op. cit.*, 2, 400.

[175] Gardner, *op. cit.*, p. 248.

[176] Stewart, *op. cit.*, (1823), p. 333.

[177] E. Long, *op. cit.*, 2, 332.

Chapter III: Social and Economic Change, 1820-1938

[1] D. G. Hall, *Free Jamaica 1838-1865* (1959), p. 7.

[2] F. L. Casserly, "Kingston in the 19th Century," *in* W. A. Roberts, ed., *The Capitals of Jamaica* (Kingston, 1955), p. 77.

[3] G. Eisner, *Jamaica, 1830-1930* (1961), p. 220, table XXXV.

[4] G. W. Roberts, *The Population of Jamaica* (1957), p. 52. The other figures relating to natural increase appear on this page, too.

[5] *Ibid.*, p. 141.

[6] *Ibid.*, p. 141.

[7] *Ibid.*, p. 43, table 7.

[8] *Ibid,,* p. 153, table 38.

[9] "Report of the Commission upon the Condition of the Juvenile Population of Jamaica," *Jamaica Gazette*, Supplement (Kingston, 1880).

[10] This interpretation of the role of the Negro was widespread among the whites. It was expressed in the infamous "Queen's Advice" which was despatched to Jamaica from London in June, 1865, on the eve of the Morant Bay rebellion. For the full text of letter which has been quoted here see Hall, *op. cit.*, pp. 244-245.

[11] G. E. Cumper, "Population Movements in Jamaica, 1830-1951," *Soc. and Econ. Stud.*, 5 (1956), 272-273; *idem*, "Labour Demand and Supply in the Jamaican Sugar Industry, 1830-1950," *Soc. and Econ. Stud.*, 2, (1954), 68.

[12] Roberts, *op. cit.*, 87, table 25.

[13] Lord Olivier, *Jamaica, the Blessed Isle* (1936), p. 335.

[14] In the Caribbean the term East Indian is applied to those persons who were born, or whose forebears were born, in India.

[15] G. Milroy, *Report on the Cholera Epidemic of Jamaica*, (Jamaica, 1852), p. 47.

[16] G. W. Roberts, *op. cit.*, p. 132.

[17] *Annual Report of the Protector of Immigrants* (1885), quoted in Roberts, *op. cit.*, p. 132.

[18] H. P. Jacobs, "An Historical Analysis of City Centre Movements," *Jamaica Architect*, 1, 3 (1967-68), 72-74.

[19] Smith Village, Hannah Town, Fletcher's Town, Kingston Gardens, Allman Town, Franklin Town, Brown's Town, and Rae Town.

[20] Eisner, *op. cit.*, p. 181.

[21] M. Scott, *Tom Cringle's Log* (1917), p. 105.

[22] Quoted in Olivier, *op. cit.*, pp. 145-146.

[23] W. G. Sewell, *The Ordeal of Free Labour in the British West Indies* (New York, 1861), p. 28.

[24] R. J. Ragatz, *The Fall of the Planter Class in the British Caribbean, 1763-1833* (1928), p. 37.

[25] Hall, *op. cit.*, p. 83, table 11.

[26] F. Armytage, *The Free Port System in the British West Indies* (1953), p. 128.

[27] Eisner, *op. cit.*, p. 280.

[28] *Ibid.*, p. 280.

[29] *Ibid.*, p. 238, table 40.

[30] *Ibid.*, p. 268.

[31] *Ibid.*, p. 269, table 50.

[32] E. G. Underhill, *A Letter Addressed to the Rt. Honourable E. Cardwell* (1865), p. 17.

[33] Quoted in Hall, *op. cit.*, p. 213.

[34] C.O. 137/326, quoted in Hall, *op. cit.* p. 214.

[35] Hall, *op. cit.*, p. 214.

[36] *Ibid.*, p. 214.

[37] C.O. 137/390, Dr. Bowerbank to Eyre, April 1865, quoted in Hall, *op. cit.*, p. 212.

[38] Hall, *op. cit.*, p. 221.

[39] W. P. Livingstone, *Black Jamaica: A Study in Evolution* (1899), p. 141.

[40] *A Review of Industrial Development in Jamaica, West Indies,* Jamaica Industrial Development Corporation (Kingston, 1961), p. 4.

[41] Eisner, *op. cit.*, p. 174.

[42] *Ibid.*, p. 174.

[43] *A Review of Industrial Development in Jamaica*, p. 4.

[44] *Ibid.*, p. 5.

[45] *Ibid.*, p. 5.

[46] *Report of the Commission of Enquiry into the Match Industry* (Kingston, 1955), pp. 4-5.

[47] W. A. Lewis, in foreword to Eisner, *op. cit.*, p. XXII.

[48] *A Review of Industrial Development in Jamaica*, tables 2, 7.

[49] Lewis in foreword to Eisner, *op. cit.*, p. XX.

[50] Eisner, *op. cit.*, p. 175.

[51] Milroy, *op. cit.*, p. 41.

[52] *Ibid.*, p. 41.

[53] Livingstone, *op. cit.*, p. 52.

[54] Eisner, *op. cit.*, p. 338.

[55] Milroy, *op. cit.*, p. 42.

[56] *Ibid.*, p. 43.

[57] *Ibid.*, p. 46.

[58] *Ibid.*, p. 47.

[59] Eisner, *op. cit.*, p. 341.

[60] *Ibid.*, p. 342.

[61] Livingstone, *op. cit.*, p. 188.

[62] *Ibid.*, p. 154.

[63] A Trollope, *The West Indies and the Spanish Main* (1860), p. 14.

[64] J. A. P. M. Andrade, *A Record of the Jews in Jamaica from the English Conquest to the Present Time* (Jamaica, 1941), p. 148.

[65] Lee Tom Yin, ed. *The Chinese in Jamaica (Kingston, 1957).*

[66] Milroy, *op. cit.*, p. 47.

[67] *Rough Sketch of the Country around Kingston*, Intelligence Division, War Office, 1:36, 206 (1891).

[68] R. M. Martin, *The British Colonies: Division VIII: British Possessions in the West Indies* (1853), p. 38.

[69] E. E. Williams, *Documents on British West Indian History, 1807-1833,* Historical Society of Trinidad and Tobago in collaboration with the Social Science Research Centre, University of Puerto Rico (1952), p. 208.

[70] D. G. Hall, "The Social and Economic Background to Sugar in Slave Days," *C.H.R.*, 3-4 (1954), 157. This quotation used by Hall was taken from a letter written in 1830 to the free-coloured newspaper, *The Watchman and Jamaica Free Press*, ed. Edward Jordan.

[71] Martin, *op. cit.*, p. 40.

[72] W. J. Gardner, *History of Jamaica*, (1872), p. 277.

[73] E. E. Williams, *Capitalism and Slavery* (1944), p. 207.

[74] Williams, *Documents of British West Indian History*, p. 249.

[75] Martin, *op. cit.*, p. 49.

[76] Williams, *Documents of British West Indian History*, pp. 171, 174.

[77] *Ibid.*, p. 171.

[78] Livingston, *op. cit.*, p. 166.

[79] *Ibid.*, p. 163.

[80] G. Price, *Jamaica and the Colonial Office* (1866), pp. 118-119.

[81] J. M. Ludlow, "A Quarter Century of Jamaica Legislation," *Jamaica Papers*, no. IV (1866), p. 7.

[82] C. A. Hughes, "Adult Suffrage in Jamaica, 1944-1955," *Parliamentary Affairs*, VIII (1955), 344.

[83] J. A. Froude, *The English in the West Indies* (1909), p. 6.

[84] B. M. Senior, *Jamaica as it was . . .* (1835), p. 300.

[85] Quoted in Olivier, *op. cit.*, p. 233.

[86] Livingstone, *op. cit.*, pp. 2, 166.

[87] *Ibid.*, p. 166.

[88] W. A. Roberts, *Six Great Jamaicans* (Kingston, 1951), pp. 17-20.

[89] Trollope, *op. cit.*, p. 74.

[90] *Ibid.*, p. 73.

[91] P. Blanshard, *Democracy and Empire in the Caribbean* (New York, 1947), p. 101.

[92] *Ibid.*, p. 101.

[93] *The Jamaica Watchman*, April 6, 1833, quoted in C. H. Wesley, "The Negro in the West Indies," *J.N.H.*, 17, (1932), 63.

[94] Wesley, *op. cit.*, p. 88.

[95] *Ibid.*, p. 82.

[96] Trollope, *op. cit.*, p. 73.

[97] *Report of the Committee on Alien Immigration*, Legislative Council Minutes (appendix 16/1941) (Kingston, 1931), p. 2.

[98] Livingstone, *op. cit.*, p. 163.

[99] Olivier, *op. cit.*, pp. 73, 298, 303.

[100] Trollope, *op. cit.*, p. 87.

[101] *Ibid.*, pp. 78, 81.

[102] R. H. Whitbeck, "The Agricultural Geography of Jamaica," *A.A.A.G.*, 22 (1932), 15-16.

[103] Livingstone, *op. cit.*, p. 206.

[104] Hall, *Free Jamaica*, p. 231.

[105] Sewell, *op. cit.*, p. 174.

[106] Hall, *Free Jamaica*, p. 231.

[107] Olivier, *op. cit.*, p. 206.

[108] Sewell, *op. cit.*, p. 283.

[109] *Report of the Commission on Unemployment*, Legislative Council Minutes (appendix 41/1936) (Kingston, 1936), p. 6.

[110] *Ibid.*, p. 6.

[111] Trollope, *op. cit.*, p. 56.

[112] Livingstone, *op. cit.*, p. 216.

[113] *Ibid.*, p. 217.

[114] *Ibid.*, p. 216.

[115] *Ibid.*, p. 95.

[116] P. D. Curtin, *Two Jamaicas* (1955), p. 168.

[117] Price, *op. cit.*, p. 5.

[118] Trollope, *op. cit.*, p. 24.

[119] Curtin, *op. cit.*, p. 169.

[120] *Ibid.*, p. 170

[121] W. W. T., *A Letter from Jamaica on the Subject of Religious Revivals* (London, 1860), quoted in Hall, *Free Jamaica*, p. 239.

[122] Gardner, *op. cit.*, p. 188.

[123] G. E. Simpson, "Jamaican Revivalist Cults," *Soc. and Econ. Stud.*, 5, (1956), 337.

[124] Gardner, *op. cit.*, p. 424.

[125] *Special Reports on the Systems of Education in the West Indies and in British Guiana* (1901), p. 663.

[126] The Mico Trust, for example, established the Mico College as an institution for training school teachers.

[127] Sewell, *op. cit.*, p. 255.

[128] Olivier, *op. cit.*, p. 364.

[129] Curtin, *op. cit.*, p. 159.

[130] Olivier, *op. cit.*, p. 31; Livingstone, *op. cit.*, p. 143.

[131] *Special Reports on the Systems of Education in the West Indies . . .*, p. 579; *Report of the Commission Appointed to Enquire into the System of Education in Jamaica* (1898).

Chapter IV: Kingston in 1943

[1] G. W. Roberts, *The Population of Jamaica* (1957), pp. 147, 148, tables 35, 36.

[2] *Memorandum Dealing with the Development of Trench Pen Township*, Central Housing Advisory Board (Kingston, 1936), p. 21.

[3] G. E. Cumper, *The Social Structure of Jamaica*, University College of the West Indies (1949).

[4] G. ST. J. Orde Browne, *Labour Conditions in the West Indies* (1939), p. 78.

[5] *Ibid.*, p. 42.

[6] *West India Royal Commission Report* (1945), p. 33.

[7] Orde Browne, *op. cit.*, p. 78.

[8] *Ibid.*, p. 84.

[9] *West India Royal Commission Report*, p. 174.

[10] *Memorandum Dealing with the Development of Trench Pen Township*, p. 21.

[11] *Ibid.*, appendix (Part A), p. 2.

[12] *The West India Royal Commission Report*, p. 175.

[13] Orde Browne, *op. cit.*, p. 76.

[14] *West India Royal Commission Report*, p. 174.

[15] Professional people comprised the only occupational group listed in the tabulated material for Kingston. This index of occupational status is therefore a blunt instrument for analysis.

[16] Unless otherwise specified these terms include both the pure and racially mixed groups of Indian and Chinese origin.

[17] F. Henriques, *Family and Colour in Jamaica* (1953), p. 157.

[18] *Ibid.*, p. 158.

[19] *Ibid.*, pp. 86-87.

[20] J. M. Stycos and K. W. Back, *The Control of Human Fertility in Jamaica* (Cornall, 1964), p. 171.

[21] Henriques, *op. cit.*, p. 87.

[22] *The West India Royal Commission Report*, p. 221.

[23] Henriques, *op. cit.*, p. 78.

[24] *Ibid.*, p. 78.

[25] G. E. Simpson, "Jamaican Revivalist Cults," *Soc. and Econ. Stud.*, 5 (1956), 321-442.

[26] Orlando Patterson, *The Sociology of Slavery* (1967), pp. 201-202.

[27] Simpson, *op. cit.*, p. 336.

[28] Henriques, *op. cit.*, pp. 92-93.

[29] *Ibid.*, pp. 50-63.

[30] Lee Tom Yin, *The Chinese in Jamaica* (Kingston, 1957).

[31] Henriques, *op. cit.*, p. 94.

[32] Yin, *op. cit.*

[33] *Ibid.*

[34] A. W. Lind, "Adjustment Patterns among the Jamaican Chinese," *Soc. and Econ. Stud.*, 7 (1958), 160-161.

[35] *Spotlight*, October 1952, Kingston, quoted in Lind, *op. cit.*, p. 162.

[36] *The West India Royal Commission Report*, p. 410.

[37] The following discussion does not relate to the small group of Bombay merchants, almost all of whom were Hindus. They maintained household religious ceremonies and arranged marriages through contacts in India.

[38] R. T. Smith, "A Preliminary Report on a Study of Selected Groups of East Indians in Jamaica," unpublished typescript (1955).

[39] Glory Robertson, *Members of the Assembly of Jamaica from the General Election of 1830 to the Final Session January 1866*, Institute of Jamaica (1965).

[40] M. G. Smith, "Politics and Society in Jamaica," unpublished typescript (no date); O. W. Phelps, "The Rise of the Labour Movement in Jamaica," *Soc. and Econ. Stud.*, 9 (1960), 433.

Chapter V: Social and Economic Change, 1944-1960

[1] G. W. Roberts, "Provisional Assessment of Growth of Kingston—St. Andrew Area, 1960-70," *Soc. and Econ. Stud.*, 12 (1963), 434, table 2.

[2] M. G. Smith, *A Report on Labour Supply in Rural Jamaica* (Kingston, 1956), p. 55.

[3] M. G. Smith, "Education and Occupational Choice in Rural Jamaica," *Soc. and Econ. Stud.*, 9 (1960), 338.

[4] "Survey of Squatters in Western Kingston, 1951," *House of Representatives Minutes*, Parliamentary Reports, (Kingston, 1951), appendix IX, no. LII.

[5] R. A. Swaby, *Report on Housing Conditions in Middle Income Areas in Kingston and St. Andrew* (Kingston, 1951), typescript.

[6] "Report of the Department of Housing" (Kingston, 1959), unpublished.

[7] In 1961 the Minister of Housing admitted to the House of Representatives that his department had no record of the number of houses that had been built by the government in Kingston.

[8] *A National Plan for Jamaica, 1957-1967* (Kingston, 1957), p. 38.

[9] *Ibid.*, p. 39.

[10] *Annual Report of the Ministry of Education*, 1958 (Kingston, 1961), p. 4.

[11] M. G. Smith, "Race and Politics in Jamaica" (1961), unpublished typescript.

[12] D. R. Manley, "Mental Ability in Jamaica," *Soc. and Econ. Stud.* 12 (1963), 65.

[13] C. A. Moser, *The Measurement of Levels of Living (with special reference to Jamaica)*, Colonial Research Studies, No. 24, H.M.S.O., 1957, Table 5b, 19.

[14] Smith, "Race and Politics in Jamaica."

[15] Smith, "Education and Occupational Choice in Rural Jamaica."

[16] W. A. Lewis, "The Industrialization of the British West Indies," *C.E.R.*, 2 (1950), 17.

¹⁷ *A Review of Industrial Development in Jamaica, West Indies*, Jamaica Industrial Development Corporation (1961), p. 15.

¹⁸ *Annual Report of the Jamaica Industrial Development Corporation* (1952).

¹⁹ M. C. Taylor, "Tax Exemption and New Industry in Puerto Rico," *Soc. and Econ. Stud.*, 4 (1955), 121-132.

²⁰ W. D. Voelker, *Survey of Industry in the West Indies*, Institute of Social and Economic Research, University College of the West Indies (1961), p. 36.

²¹ *Industrial Development in Jamaica, Trinidad, Barbados and British Guiana*, Report of the Mission of U.K. Industrialists, H.M.S.O. (1953), p. 8. A. R. Prest, (*A Fiscal Survey of the British Caribbean*, H.M.S.O. [1957], p. 102), argued that the government should give each firm a subsidy proportional to the number of persons who were employed.

²² *Jamaica Industrial Review*, Jamaica Industrial Development Corporation, vol. 1, no. 9 (December, 1959).

²³ Mining refers to the open-cast working of bauxite, and manufacturing embraces factory industry as well as the grinding of sugar cane and processing of alumina.

²⁴ *Report of the Commissioner of Income Tax* (Kingston, 1959), pp. 16-17.

²⁵ L. Broom, "The Social Differentiation of Jamaica," *Am. Soc. Rev.*, 19 (1954), 125.

²⁶ Reported in R. Nettleford, "National Identity and Attitudes to Race in Jamaica," *Race*, 7 (1965), 62.

²⁷ C. Peach, "West Indian Migration to Britain: The Economic Factors," *Race*, 7 (1965), 31-46.

Chapter VI: Urbanisation in Kingston on the Eve of Independence

¹ For the purpose of the 1960 census the city centre and suburbs were divided into 830 enumeration districts, a fourfold increase in the number employed in 1943. The tabulations for the enumeration districts published by the Department of Statistics in Jamaica were limited to information on age and sex, religion, education, house ownership, main economic activity, occupation, and industry. Most of the material used in mapping has therefore been derived from a special tabulation of census punch cards prepared for all individuals in 10 percent of the households in each enumeration district in Kingston. The average sample population was 50 in each enumeration district. The data have been checked against many sources; the maps derived from the sample correspond almost completely with the results of fieldwork carried out in Kingston in 1961, 1964, and 1968. Furthermore, the sample enables critical variables to be isolated, mapped, and compared. Without it a detailed geographical analysis of the city in 1960 would have been quite impossible.

² The terms central and East Kingston refer to the central and eastern sections of Kingston parish and the adjoining parts of St. Andrew. West Kingston denotes the slum area in the west of the city.

³ Newling argues that population growth takes place in Kingston only where the density falls below 30,000 per square mile. The central business district has experienced decreases since 1911 when the "critical density" of 30,000 per square mile was exceeded by almost 100 percent. Newling's calculations probably use constituency material and the notion of "critical density" is certainly not substantiated by the enumeration district data. The highest densities are recorded in the

tenements and not in the central business district. These densities certainly increased between 1943 and 1960 (B. E. Newling, "Urban Growth and Spatial Structure; Mathematical Models and Empirical Evidence," *G.R.*, 56 (1966), 220-221).

⁴ E. Paget, "Value, Valuation and the Use of Land in the West Indies,", *G.J.*, 127 (1961), 494.

⁵ "Report of the Factory Inspectorate" (Kingston, 1960), unpublished.

⁶ The statistics relating to unemployment have been taken from the *Report of the 1960 Census of Jamaica*, 1, (1964). The data for Kingston refer to the urban and suburban areas.

⁷ O. C. Francis, *The People of Modern Jamaica* (Kingston, 1963), pp. 8.2-8.3.

⁸ W. F. Maunder, *Employment in an Underdeveloped Area: A Sample Survey of Kingston, Jamaica* (New Haven, Conn., 1960), p. 8.

⁹ Francis, *op. cit.*, p. 7.11.

¹⁰ *Ibid.*, p. 6.17.

¹¹ The figure of 20,000 squatters is probably closer to the truth. It is known that the Ras Tafari brethren, most of whom were squatters, were under-enumerated in the census.

¹² E. E. Hoyt, "Voluntary Unemployment and Unemployability in Jamaica," *Brit. Jour. of Soc.*, 11 (1961), 129-136.

¹³ Although the household data relating to migration are particularly susceptible to sample errors, the clustering factor is relatively unimportant in this instance, since internal migration affected young, single adults rather than entire families (fig. 57).

¹⁴ G. E. Ebanks, "Differential Internal Migration in Jamaica, 1943-60," *Soc. and Econ. Stud.*, 17 (1968), 206-208.

¹⁵ G. E. Simpson, "Jamaican Revivalist Cults," *Soc. and Econ. Stud.*, 5 (1956), 322.

¹⁶ M. G. Smith, *West Indian Family Structure* (Seattle, 1962), p. 164.

¹⁷ *Ibid.*, p. 164.

¹⁸ H. Gordon, "Preliminary Report of a Socio-Economic Survey of Parts of West Kingston," Jamaica Social Welfare Commission, Kingston (1961), unpublished typescript.

¹⁹ G. W. Roberts and D. O. Mills, *Study of External Migration Affecting Jamaica, 1953-55*, Institute of Social and Economic Research, University College of the West Indies (1957), pp. 46-57.

Chapter VII—The Social Structure of Kingston on the Eve of Independence

¹ M. G. Smith, "The Plural Framework of Jamaican Society," *Brit. Jour. of Soc.*, 12 (1961), 251.

² *Ibid.*

³ M. G. Smith, *West Indian Family Structure*, p. 170.

⁴ Smith, "The Plural Framework of Jamaican Society," p. 251.

⁵ This may have been equivalent to concubinage, but it is denied as being such by respondents to the census. (F. Henriques, *Family and Colour in Jamaica* [1954], p. 92).

⁶ Smith, "The Plural Framework of Jamaican Society," p. 251.

⁷ M. Kerr, *Personality and Conflict in Jamaica* (1952), p. 135.

⁸ *Annual Report of the Ministry of Education for 1958* (Kingston, 1961), p. 4.

⁹ Kerr, *op. cit.*, pp. 81-82.

[10] C. A. Moser, *The Measurement of Levels of Living (with Special Reference to Jamaica)*, H.M.S.O. (1957), p. 19; E. P. G. Seaga, "Parent-Teacher Relationships in a Jamaican Village," *Soc. and Econ. Stud.*, 4 (1955), 289-302.

[11] Smith, "The Plural Framework of Jamaican Society," p. 252.

[12] Kerr, *op. cit.*, p. 83.

[13] Smith, *West Indian Family Structure*, p. 259.

[14] Roman Catholics and the high ranking Jews, who are discussed later, were included with the denominational Christians.

[15] The socio-economic index scores for the 100 sample enumeration districts have been used in this analysis: these scores were ranked from low status to high.

[16] W. Bell, *Jamaican Leaders* (Berkeley and Los Angeles, 1964), p. 63.

[17] C. Neita, *Who's Who in Jamaica* (Kingston, 1960), p. 5.

[18] W. H. Knowles, *Trade Union Development and Industrial Relations in the British West Indies* (Berkeley and Los Angeles, 1959), p. 26.

[19] R. Nettleford, "National Identity and Attitudes to Race in Jamaica," *Race*, 7 (1965), 69.

[20] *Ibid.*, pp. 66-67.

[21] *Ibid.*, p. 69.

[22] M. G. Smith, R. Augier, and R. Nettleford, *The Ras Tafari Movement in Kingston, Jamaica*, Institute of Social and Economic Research, University College of the West Indies, (1960), pp. 8-10.

[23] G. E. Simpson, "Policial Cultism in West Kingston," *Soc. and Econ. Stud.*, 4 (1955), 133.

[24] Smith, Augier, and Nettleford, *op. cit.*, p. 21.

[25] *Ibid.*, p. 24.

[26] *Ibid.*, p. 50.

[27] *Ibid.*, p. 25.

[28] *Ibid.*, p. 38.

[29] "Report of the Mission to Africa" (Kingston, 1961), p. 1.

[30] *Ibid.*

[31] For a further discussion of this and related problems see C. G. Clarke, "Problemas de Planeación Urbana en Kingston, Jamaica," *Union Geográfica International, Conferencia Regional Latinoamericana, Tomo I, La Geografía y los Problemas de Población*, Sociedad Mexicana de Geografía y Estadística (Mexico City, 1966), pp. 411-431.

Chapter VIII: Neocolonialism and Colonialism

[1] For a more detailed account of these changes see C. G. Clarke, "The Development and Redevelopment of the Waterfront in Kingston, Jamaica," *Geography*, 56 (1971), 237-240.

[2] *Economic Survey of Jamaica 1969*, Central Planning Unit, Jamaica (1970), pp. 46-50.

[3] G. W. Roberts, "Provisional Assessment of Growth of the Kingston-St. Andrew Area, 1960-70", *Soc. and Econ. Stud.*, 12 (1963), 434, table 2.

[4] *Jamaica Industrial Development Corporation Annual Report 1964-65*, (Jamaica, 1966), p. 4; supplemented by information given by J.I.D.C. officials and by *Ministry Paper*, no. 31 (1970).

[5] *Economic Survey of Jamaica 1964*, 91; *1966*, 77-78; and *1969*, 86-87.

[6] The sanitary survey is carried out each year by the Public Health Department of the Kingston and St. Andrew Corporation. Public health inspectors have a legal right to enter premises, and they compile an annual register of statistics dealing with population numbers, rooms, and sanitary facilities. The urban and suburban sections of the city are divided into 27 sanitary districts.

[7] Interview with an official at the Ministry of Housing in 1968.

[8] A. Barham, E. Davis, S. Graham, and H. McKenzie, *Survey of Trench Town and Victoria Town: A Preliminary Report*, Department of Sociology, University of the West Indies (Jamaica, 1965), p. 29. Their comparison of the present and previous accommodation of residents in the housing projects shows no sign of squatter backgrounds.

[9] L. E. Barrett, *The Rastafarians: A Study in Messianic Cultism in Jamaica*, Institute of Caribbean Studies, University of Puerto Rico (1968).

[10] W. Rodney, *The Groundings with My Brothers* (1969), p. 28.

[11] *Ibid.*

[12] *Ibid.*, p. 33.

[13] E. W. Burgess, "The Growth of the City: An Introduction to a Research Project," in R. E. Park and E. W. Burgess, *The City* (Chicago, 1925), pp. 47-62.

[14] H. Hoyt, *The Structure and Growth of Residential Neighbourhoods in American Cities* (Washington, 1939).

[15] G. Sjoberg, *The Preindustrial City: Past and Present* (Glencoe, Ill., 1960), pp. 95-96.

[16] Burgess, *op. cit.*, pp. 47-62.

[17] R. M. Marsh, "Comparative Sociology, 1950-1963," *Current Sociology*, 14 (1966), 25.

[18] K. Lynch, *The Image of the City* (Cambridge, Mass., 1967).

[19] N. A. Adams, "Internal Migration in Jamaica: An Economic Analysis," *Soc. and Econ. Stud.*, 18 (1969), 145.

[20] W. Mangin, "Latin American Squatter Settlements: A Problem and a Solution," *Latin American Research Review*, 2 (1967), 65-98.

[21] F. G. Cassidy, *Jamaica Talk* (1961), 394-404.

[22] M. G. Smith, *The Plural Society in the British West Indies* (1965), p. 174.

[23] G. E. Cumper, ed., *Report of the Conference on Social Development in Jamaica* (Kingston, 1962), p. 9.

[24] E. Braithwaite, "Jamaican Slave Society: A Review," *Race*, 9 (1968), 331-342. H. O. L. Patterson, "Slavery, Acculturation and Social Change: The Jamaica Case," *Brit. Jour. Soc.*, 17 (1966), 163.

[25] For an elaboration of this concept see O. Lewis, *La Vida* (1968), pp. xlii-lii.

[26] O. Lewis, *The Children of Sanchez, Autobiography of a Mexican Family* (1961).

[27] Lewis, *La Vida*.

[28] M. Kerr, *Personality and Conflict in Jamaica* (1952), p. 194.

[29] *Ibid.*, p. 113.

[30] *Ibid.*

[31] *Ibid.*, p. 105.

[32] G. Knox, "Political Change in Jamaica (1866-1906) and the Local Reaction to the Policies of the Crown Colony Government," in Fuat M. Andic and T. G. Mathews, eds., *The Caribbean in Transition*, Institute of Caribbean Studies, Puerto Rico, (1965), p. 143.

Bibliography

Books, Articles, Theses, and Reports

Abrahams, Peter. *Jamaica: an island mosaic*. London: H.M.S.O., 1957.

Adams, Nassau A. "Internal migration in Jamaica: an economic analysis," *Social and Economic Studies*, 18 (1969), 137-151.

Ahiram, E. "Income distribution in Jamaica, 1958," *Social and Economic Studies*, 13 (1964), 333-369.

Alleyne, Mervin C. "Communication between the elite and the masses," *in* Fuat M. Andic and T. G. Mathews, *The Caribbean in transition: papers on social, political and economic development, proceedings of the Second Caribbean Scholars' Converence, 1964*. Río Piedras: Institute of Caribbean Studies, 1965. Pp. 12-19.

Andic, Fuat M., and T. G. Mathews, eds. *The Caribbean in transition: papers on social, political and economic development, proceedings of the Second Caribbean Scholars' Conference, 1964*. Río Piedras: Institute of Caribbean Studies, 1965.

Andrade, Jacob A. P. M. *A record of the Jews in Jamaica from the English conquest to the present time*. Kingston: Jamaica Times, 1941.

Annual report of the collector general, 1958. Kingston: Government Printing Office, 1959.

Annual report of the commissioner of income tax, 1958. Kingston: Government Printing Office, 1959.

Annual report of the engineering department of the water commission, 1960. Kingston, 1961.

Annual report of the department of housing, 1959. Kingston: Department of Housing, 1961 (mimeo).

Annual report of Jamaica together with departmental reports for 1921. Kingston: Government Printing Office, 1922.

Annual report of the Jamaica industrial development corporation, 1952–. Kingston: Jamaica Industrial Development Corporation.

Annual report of the ministry of education, 1958. Kingston: Government Printing Office, 1961.

Anon. *Marly, or, the life of a planter in Jamaica*. Glasgow: Griffin, 2d ed., 1831.

Anon. (Stewart, J.). *An account of Jamaica and its inhabitants: by a gentleman long resident in the West Indies*. London: Longmans, 1808.

Armytage, Frances. *The free port system in the British West Indies: a study in commercial policy, 1766-1822*. London: Longmans, 1953.

Association of Elected Members. *Report on unemployment*, Kingston: Legislative Council Minutes, Appendix 23, 1944.

Augier, F. Roy. "The consequences of Morant Bay: before and after 1865," *New World Quarterly*, 2, 2 (Croptime 1966), 21-42.

Back, Kurt W., and J. Mayone Stycos. *The survey under unusual conditions: methodological facets of the Jamaica human fertility investigation*. Ithaca, N.Y.: Society for Applied Anthropology, 1959.

Barham, A., E. Davis, S. Graham, and H. McKenzie. *Survey of Trench Town and Victoria Town, a preliminary report*, Kingston, Department of Sociology, University of the West Indies, 1965.

Barrett, Leonard E. "The Rastafarians: a study in messianic cultism in Jamaica," *Caribbean Monograph Series*, no. 6. Río Piedras: Institute of Caribbean Studies, 1968.

Beche, Sir Henry T. de la. *Notes on the present condition of the negroes in Jamaica*. London: Cadell, 1825.

Beckford, G. L. "Toward Rationalization of West Indian Agriculture," in *Papers presented at the regional conference on devaluation*, Kingston: Institute of Social and Economic Research, University of the West Indies, 1968. Pp. 147-154.

Beckford, William. *Remarks on the situation of the negroes in Jamaica*, London: T. and J. Egerton, 1788.

–––-. *A descriptive account of the island of Jamaica*. 2 vols. London: T. and J. Egerton, 1790.

Beckwith, Martha Warren. *Black roadways: a study of Jamaican folk life*. Chapel Hill: University of North Carolina Press, 1929.

Belisario, I. M. *Sketches of character in illustration of the habits, occupation and costume of the negro population of the island of Jamaica*. Kingston, 1837-38.

Bell, Wendell. *Jamaican leaders: political attitudes in a new nation*. Berkeley and Los Angeles: University of California Press, 1964.

Bell, Wendell, ed. *The democratic revolution in the West Indies: studies in nationalism, leadership, and the belief in progress*. Cambridge, Mass.: Schenkman, 1967.

Benedict, Burton. "Stratification in plural societies," *American Anthropologist*, 64 (1962), 1235-1246.

Bennett, Louise. *Jamaica labrish*. Kingston: Sangster's Book Stores, 1966.

Bickell, Rev. R. *The West Indies, or, a real picture of slavery*. London: Hatchard and Relfe, 1825.

Bigelow, John. *Jamaica in 1850, or, the effects of sixteen years of freedom on a slave colony*. New York: George P. Putnam, 1851.

Black, Clinton V. "Kingston in the eighteenth century," *in* Roberts, W. Adolphe, ed. *The Capitals of Jamaica* Kingston: The Pioneer Press, 1955.

Blake, Judith, with J. Mayone Stycos, and Kingsley Davis. *Family structure in Jamaica: the social context of reproduction*. New York: Free Press, 1961.

Blanshard, Paul. *Democracy and empire in the Caribbean: a contemporary review*. New York: Macmillan, 1947.

Blaut, James M. et al. "A study of cultural determinants of soil erosion and conservation in the Blue Mountains of Jamaica: progress report," *Social and Economic*

Studies, 8 (1959), 403-420.

Bloch, Ivan, and Associates. *Electricity load survey for Jamaica.* Portland, Or., 1957.

Blome, Richard. *A description of the island of Jamaica.* London: Milbourn, 1672.

Bradley, C. Paul. "Mass Parties in Jamaica," *Social and Economic Studies,* 9 (1960) 375-416.

Braithwaite, Lloyd. "Social stratification in Trinidad: a preliminary analysis," *Social and Economic Studies,* 2, 2 and 3 (1953), 5-175.

———. "Social stratification and cultural pluralism," *Annals of the New York Academy of Sciences,* 83 (1960), 816-836.

Brathwaite, Edward. "Jamaican slave society, a review," *Race,* 9 (1967-68), 331-342.

———. *The development of creole society in Jamaica, 1770-1820.* London: Oxford University Press, 1971.

Breese, Gerald. *Urbanization in newly developing countries.* Englewood Cliffs, N.J.: Prentice Hall, 1966

Brennan, J. F. *The meteorology of Jamaica.* Kingston: Government Printing Office, 1936.

Brewster, Havelock. "Sugar-mechanizing our life or death," *New World Quarterly,* 5, 1 and 2 (Dead Season and Croptime, 1969), 55-57.

Bridges, Rev. George Wilson. *The annals of Jamaica.* 2 vols. London: John Murray, 1828.

Broom, Leonard. "Urban research in the Britich Caribbean, a prospectus," *Social and Economic Studies,* 1, 1 (1953), 113-119.

———. "The Social differentiation of Jamaica," *American Sociological Review,* 19 (1954), 115-125.

———. "Urbanization and the plural society," *Annals of the New York Academy of Sciences,* 83, (1960), 880-886.

Brown, G. Arthur. "Sugar without emotion," *New World Quarterly,* 5, 1 and 2 (Dead Season and Croptime 1969), 40-41.

Brown, Samuel E. "Treatise on the Ras Tafari movement," *Caribbean Studies,* 6 (1966), 39-40.

Burchell, William Fitzer. *Memoir of Thomas Burchell, twenty-two years a missionary in Jamaica.* London: Benjamin Green, 1849.

Burge, William. *Reply to the letter by the Marquis of Sligo to the Marquis of Normanby relative to the present state of Jamaica.* London: Calkin and Budd, 1838.

Burn, W. L. *Emancipation and apprenticeship in the British West Indies.* London: Jonathan Cape, 1937.

Burt, Arthur E. "The first instalment of representative government in Jamaica, 1884," *Social and Economic Studies,* 11 (1962) 241-259.

Callender, C. V. "The development of the capital market institutions of Jamaica," Supplement to *Social and Economic Studies,* vol. 14 (1965).

"Capitation tax rolls for Kingston, 1843." Spanish Town: Jamaica Archives, ms.

Cargill, Morris, ed. *Ian Fleming introduces Jamaica.* London and Jamaica: Andre Deutsch and Sangster's Book Stores, 1965.

Casserly, F. L. "Kingston in the nineteenth century," *in* Roberts, W. Adolphe, ed. *The Capitals of Jamaica.* Kingston: The Pioneer Press. Pp. 61-88.

Cassidy, Frederic G. *Jamaica talk: three hundred years of the English language in Jamaica.* London: Macmillan, 1961.

Census of Jamaica, 1844, 1861, 1871, 1881, 1891, 1911, 1921. Kingston: Government Printing Office.

Census of Jamaica 1943, population, housing and agriculture. Kingston: Central Bureau of Statistics, Government Printing Office, 1945.

Census of Jamaica 1960. Kingston: Department of Statistics, vols. 1 and 2 (1963-64).

Census of Jamaica population 1970: preliminary report. Kingston: Department of Statistics, 1971.

Central Housing Advisory Board. *Memorandum dealing with development of Trench Pen Township and improvement of Smith Village and surrounding districts.* Kingston: Government Printing Office, 1936.

Chapman, V. J. "The botany of the Jamaica shoreline," *in* "Sand cays and mangroves in Jamaica, report of the Cambridge University Jamaica Expedition, 1939," *Geographical Journal,* 96 (1940), 305-328.

Clarke, Colin G. "Population pressure in Kingston, Jamaica: a study of unemployment and overcrowding," *Transactions of the Institute of British Geographers,* 38 (1966), 165-182.

———. "Problemas de planeación urbana en Kingston, Jamaica," in *La geografía y los problemos de población,* Union Geográfica Internacional, Conferencía Regional Latinoamericana, Tomo I, México, Sociedad Mexicana de Geografía y Estadística (1966), pp. 411-431.

———. "Aspects of the urban geography of Kingston, Jamaica," D. Phil. dissertation. Oxford, 1967.

———. "An overcrowded metropolis: Kingston, Jamaica," in Prothero, R. Mansell, Leszek Kosinski, and Wilbur Zelinsky. *Geography and a Crowding World.* New York and London: Oxford University Press, 1970 and 1971.

———. "Residential segregation and intermarriage in San Fernando, Trinidad," *Geographical Review,* 61 (1971), 198-218.

———. "The development and redevelopment of the waterfront in Kingston, Jamaica," *Geography,* 56 (1971), 237-240.

———. *Jamaica in Maps.* London: University of London Press, 1974.

Clarke, Edith. "Land tenure and the family in four selected communities in Jamaica," *Social and Economic Studies,* 1, 4 (1953), 81-118.

———. *My mother who fathered me: a study of the family in three selected communities in Jamaica.* London:

George Allen and Unwin, 1957; 2 ed., 1966.

Cohen, Yehudi A. "The social organization of a selected community in Jamaica," *Social and Economic Studies*, 2, 4 (1954), 104-133.

———. "Four categories of interpersonal relations in the family and community in a Jamaican village," *Anthropological Quarterly*, 3, 4 (1955), 121-147.

———. "Character formation and social structure in a Jamaican community," *Psychiatry*, 18 (1955), 275-296.

———. "Structure and function: family organization and socialization in a Jamaican community," *American Anthropologist*, 58 (1956), 664-686.

Coke, Rev. Thomas. *A history of the West Indies*. 3 vols. Liverpool: Nuttall, Fisher and Dixon, 1808.

Collins, Sidney. "Social mobility in Jamaica with reference to rural communities and the teaching profession," *Transactions of the Third World Congress of Sociology*, 3 (1956), 267-275.

Comitas, Lambros. *Caribbeana 1900-165: a topical bibliography*. Seattle: University of Washington Press, 1968.

Committee appointed to enquire into and report upon the question of the immigration of aliens into Jamaica. Kingston: Legislative Council Minutes, appendix 16, Government Printing Office, 1931.

Cornish, Vaughan. "The Jamaica earthquake, 1907," *Geographical Journal*, 31 (1908), 245-271.

Cronon, Edmund David. *Black Moses: the story of Marcus Garvey and the Universal Negro Improvement Association*. Madison: University of Wisconsin Press, 1964.

Cross, Malcolm. "Cultural pluralism and sociological theory: a critique and re-evaluation," *Social and Economic Studies*, 17 (1968), 381-397.

Cumper, George E. *The social structure of Jamaica*. Kingston: University College of the West Indies, Extra-Mural Department, 1949.

———. "A modern Jamaican sugar estate," *Social and Economic Studies*, 3, 2 (1954), 119-160.

———. "Labour supply and demand in the Jamaican sugar industry, 1830-1950," *Social and Economic Studies*, 2, 4 (1954), 37-86.

———. "Population movements in Jamaica, 1830-1950," *Social and Economic Studies*, 5 (1956) 261-280.

———. "The Jamaican family, village and estate," *Social and Economic Studies*, 7 (1958), 76-108.

———. "Tourist expenditure in Jamaica, 1958," *Social and Economic Studies*, 8 (1959), 287-310.

———. "Labour and development in the West Indies," *Social and Economic Studies*, 10 (1961), 278-305; 11 (1962), 1-33.

———. "Preliminary analysis of population growth and social characteristics in Jamaica," *Social and Economic Studies*, 12 (1963), 393-431.

Cumper, George E. ed. *The economy of the West Indies*. Kingston: Institute of Social and Economic Research,

University College of the West Indies, 1960.

———. *Report of the conference on social development held at the University College of the West Indies, 1961*, Kingston: Standing Committee on Social Services (1961).

Cumper, Gloria. "New Pattern for Kingston," *Geographical Magazine*, 40, 7 (1967), 588-598.

Cumpston, I. M. *Indians overseas in British territories, 1834-1854*. London: Oxford University Press, 1953.

Cundall, Frank. *Historic Jamaica*. Kingston: Institute of Jamaica, 1915.

Curtin, Philip D. *Two Jamaicas: the role of ideas in a tropical colony, 1830-1865*. Cambridge: Harvard University Press, 1955.

Davenport, C. B., and M. Staggerda. "Race crossing in Jamaica," *Carnegie Institution Publication No. 395*, Washington, D.C., 1929.

Davenport, William. "The family system of Jamaica," *Social and Economic Studies*, 10 (1961) (special number on "Caribbean Social Organization," edited by Sidney W. Mintz and William Davenport), 420-454.

Davison, Betty. "No place back home: a study of Jamaicans returning to Kingston, Jamaica," *Race*, 9 (1967-68), 499-509.

Davison, R. B. *Labour shortage and productivity in the Jamaican sugar industry*. Kingston: University of the West Indies, Institute of Social and Economic Research (1966).

———. *Black British: immigrants to England*. London: Oxford University Press for the Institute of Race Relations, 1966.

Delatre, R. *A guide to Jamaican reference material in the West Indies reference library*. Kingston: Institute of Jamaica, 1965.

Demas, William G. *The economics of development in small countries with special reference to the Caribbean*. Montreal: McGill University Press for the Centre for Developing-Area Studies, 1965.

"Demographic and housing statistics," Public Health Department, Kingston and St. Andrew Corporation, 1960 and 1967, manuscript.

Dollard, John. *Caste and class in a southern town*. New Haven: Yale University Press, 1937.

Duncan, Otis Dudley, Ray P. Cuzzort, and Beverly Duncan. *Statistical Geography*. New York: The Free Press, 1961.

Duncker, Sheila J. "The free coloured and their fight for civil rights in Jamaica, 1800-1830," M.A. thesis. University of London, 1961.

Dunlop, W. R. "Queensland and Jamaica: a comparative study in geographical economics," *Geographical Review*, 16 (1926), 548-567.

Duperly, Alphonse. *Daguerian excursions in Jamaica*. Kingston, ca. 1850.

Ebanks, G. Edward. "Differential internal migration in Jamaica," *Social and Economic Studies*, 17 (1968), 197-214.

Economic survey of Jamaica, 1958- , Kingston: Central Planning Unit.

Edwards, Bryan. *The history, civil and commercial, of the British colonies in the West Indies.* 5 vols., 5th ed. London: Whittacker, Reid, Nunn, etc., 1819.

Edwards, David T. "An economic study of agriculture in the Yallahs Valley area of Jamaica," *Social and Economic Studies*, 3, 3-4 (1955), 316-341.

——. *An economic study of small farming in Jamaica.* Kingston: Institute of Social and Economic Research, University College of the West Indies, 1961.

——. "An economic view of agricultural research in Jamaica," *Social and Economic Studies*, 10 (1961), 306-339.

Eisner, Gisela. *Jamaica, 1830-1930: a study in economic growth.* Manchester: University Press, 1961.

Ellis, Robert A. "Colour and class in a Jamaican market town," *Sociology and Social Research*, 41 (1957), 354-360.

Equiano, Olaudah. *Equiano's travels* [1789]. Ed. Paul Edwards. London: Heinemann, 1967.

Ericksen, E. Gordon. *The West Indies population problem.* Lawrence: University of Kansas Publications, 1962.

Erickson, A. B. "Empire or anarchy, the Jamaican rebellion of 1865," *Journal of Negro History*, 44 (1959), 99-122.

Ewbank and Partners Ltd. *Report on the Harbour of Kingston.* Toronto, 1961.

Eyre, L. Alan. *Land and population in the sugar belt of Jamaica.* Kingston: Department of Geology and Geography, University of the West Indies, Occasional Papers in Geography, no. 1 [1965].

——. *Geographic aspects of population dynamics.* Boca Raton, Fla.: Atlantic University Press, 1972.

Fisher, Ruth A. "A note on Jamaica (taxation of the Jews, 1693)," *Journal of Negro History*, 28 (1943), 200-203.

Five year independence plan 1963-68: a long-term development plan for Jamaica. Kingston: Government Printing Office, 1963.

Floyd, Barry. "Jamaica," *Focus*, vol. 19, no. 2 (1968).

Francis, O. C. *The People of Modern Jamaica.* Kingston: Department of Statistics, 1963.

Froude, James Anthony. *The English in the West Indies, or, the bow of Ulysses.* London: Longmans, Green, 1888.

Furnivall, J. S. *Netherlands India: a study of a plural economy.* Cambridge: University Press, 1939.

——. *Colonial policy and practice: a comparative study of Burma and Netherlands India.* Cambridge: University Press, 1948.

Gardner, William James. *A history of Jamaica.* London: Elliot Stock, 1873.

Gilbert, Edmund W., and Robert W. Steel. "Social geography and its place in colonial studies," *Geographical Journal*, 106 (1945), 118-131.

Girvan, Norman. "Bauxite: why we need to nationalize and how we do it," *New World Pamphlet*, no. 6 (1971).

Gordon, Horace. *Preliminary report of a socio-economic survey of parts of West Kingston.* Kingston: Jamaica Social Welfare Commission, 1961, typescript.

Gordon, Shirley C. *A century of West Indian education: a source book.* London: Longmans, 1963.

Gordon, W. E. "Imperial policy decisions in the economic history of Jamaica, 1664-1934," *Social and Economic Studies*, 6 (1959), 1-28.

Goveia, Elsa V. *A study in the historiography of the British West Indies to the end of the nineteenth century.* Mexico, D. F.: Pan-American Institute of Geography and History, 1956.

——. "The West Indian slave laws of the eighteenth century," *Revista de Ciencias Sociales*, 4 (1960), 75-105.

Guérin, Daniel. *The West indies and their future.* London: Dennis Dobson, 1961.

Hakewill, J. *A picturesque tour of the island of Jamaica.* London: Hurst, Robinson and Lloyd, 1825.

Hall, Douglas G. "The apprenticeship period in Jamaica, 1834-1838," *Caribbean Quarterly*, 3 (1953), 142-166.

——. "The social and economic background to sugar in slave days (with special reference to Jamaica)," *Caribbean Historical Review*, nos. 3-4 (1954), 149-169.

——. *Free Jamaica 1838-1865: an economic history.* New Haven: Yale University Press, 1959.

——. "Slaves and slavery in the British West Indies," *Social and Economic Studies*, 11 (1962), 305-318.

——. "Absentee-proprietorship in the British West Indies to about 1850," *Jamaica Historical Review*, 4 (1964), 15-35.

——. "The colonial legacy in Jamaica," *New World Quarterly*, 4, 3 (High Season 1968), 7-22.

Hamilton, B. L. St. John. *Problems of administration in an emergent nation: a case study of Jamaica.* New York: Frederick A. Praeger, 1964.

Hammond, S. A. A. *Jamaican education: memorandum to development and welfare comptroller.* Kingston: Government Printing Office, 1941.

Handbook of Jamaica 1960 and *1966.* Kingston: Government Printing Office, 1961 and 1967.

Harris, R. N. S., and E. S. Steers. "Demographic-resource push in rural migration: a Jamaican case-study," *Social and Economic Studies*, 17 (1969), 398-406.

Hart, Richard. *The origin and development of the people of Jamaica.* Kingston: Education Department, Trades Union Congress, 1952.

——. "The life and resurrection of Marcus Garvey," *Race*, 9 (1967), 217-238.

Hartshorne, Richard. *The nature of geography.* 5th printing. Lancaster, Pa.: Association of American Geographers, 1956.

Henriques, Fernando. "The social structure of Jamaica (with

special reference to racial distinctions)," D. Phil dissertation. Oxford, 1948.

———. "West Indian family organization," *Caribbean Quarterly*, 2 (1952), originally published in *American Journal of Sociology*, 55, 1 (1949), 30-37.

———. "Colour values in Jamaican society," *British Journal of Sociology*, 2 (1951), 115-121.

———. *Family and colour in Jamaica*. London: Eyre and Spottiswoode, 1953; 2d ed., London: MacGibbon and Kee, 1968.

———. *Jamaica, land of wood and water*. London: MacGibbon and Kee, 1957.

Herskovits, Melville Jean. *The myth of the negro past*. London: Harper, 1941.

Hicks, J. R., and U. K. Hicks. *Report on finance and taxation in Jamaica*. Kingston: Government Printing Office, 1955.

Higman, Barry W. "Some demographic characteristics of slavery in Jamaica about 1832," Kingston, Department of History, University of the West Indies, Postgraduate Seminars, March, 1969.

———. "Slave population and economy in Jamaica at the time of emancipation." Ph. D. dissertation. Kingston: University of the West Indies, 1970.

Hirsch, G. P. "Jamaica—a regional approach," *Regional Studies*, 1 (1967), 47-63.

Hoetink, Hermannus. *Two variants in Caribbean race relations*. London: Oxford University Press for the Institute of Race Relations, 1967.

Hogg, Donald W. "The convince cult in Jamaica," *Yale University Publications in Anthropology, no. 58* (1960).

Hoyt, Elizabeth E. "Voluntary unemployment and unemployability in Jamaica," *British Journal of Sociology*, 11 (1960), 129-136.

Hoyt, Homer. *The structure and growth of residential neighbourhoods in American cities*. Washington: Federal Housing Administration, 1939.

Hughes, Colin A. "Adult suffrage in Jamaica, 1944-55," *Parliamentary Affairs*, 8 (1955), 344-352.

Inglis, William J. "The Jamaican reply to English criticism of slavery and its social implications," 1959. Unpublished typescript.

Innis, Donald Q. "The Efficiency of Jamaican peasant land use," *Canadian Geographer*, 5 (1961), 19-23.

International Bank for Reconstruction and Development. *The economic development of Jamaica*. Baltimore: The Johns Hopkins Press, 1952.

Jacobs, H. P. "From the earthquake to 1944," *in* Roberts, W. Adolphe, *The capitals of Jamaica*. Kingston: The Pioneer Press, 1955. Pp. 102-112.

Jamaica almanack, Spanish Town, 1796, 1801, and 1832.

Jamaica, an economic survey. London: Barclays Bank, 1959.

Jamaica, Department of Statistics. *Report on a sample survey of population, 1953*. Kingston: Government Printing Office, 1957.

Jamaica Industrial Development Corporation. *A review of industrial development in Jamaica, West Indies*. Kingston, 1961.

Jefferson, Owen. "Some aspects of the post-war economic development of Jamaica," *New World Quarterly*, 3, 3 (High Season 1967), 1-11.

———. *The post-war economic development of Jamaica*. Kingston: Institute of Social and Economic Research, University of the West Indies, 1972.

Jenks, George F. "Generalization in statistical mapping," *Annals of the Association of American Geographers*, 53 (1963), 15-26.

Johnston, R. J. *Urban residential patterns: an introductory review*. London: Bell, 1971.

Jones, Emrys. *A social geography of Belfast*. London: Oxford University Press, 1960.

Katzin, Margaret. "The Jamaican country higgler," *Social and Economic Studies*, 8 (1959), 421-435.

———. "The business of higglering in Jamaica," *Social and Economic Studies*, 9 (1960), 297-331.

Kerr, Madeline. *Personality and conflict in Jamaica*. Liverpool: University Press, 1952; London: Collins, 1963.

Kidd, J. B. *Forty coloured views of Jamaica*. London, ca. 1838.

Kingston and St. Andrew Corporation. *Official souvenir album of the city of Kingston*. Kingston, 1964.

Kingston churchwarden's accounts 1722-1846. Spanish Town: Jamaica Archives, manuscript.

Kingston common council minutes, 1815-1820. Spanish Town: Jamaica Archives, manuscript.

Kingston common council minutes 1834-1839. Spanish Town: Jamaica Archives, manuscript.

Kingston common council minutes 1862-1866. Spanish Town: Jamaica Archives, manuscript.

Kingston common council special committee minutes 1842-1850. Spanish Town: Jamaica Archives, manuscript.

Kitzinger, Sheila. "The Ras Tafari brethren of Jamaica," *Comparative Studies in Society and History*, 9 (1966), 33-39.

Knowles, W. H. "Social consequences of economic change in Jamaica," *Annals of the American Academy of Political and Social Science*, 305 (1956), 134-144.

———. *Trade union development and industrial relations in the British West Indies*. Berkeley and Los Angeles: University of California Press, 1959.

Knox, A. D. "Some general comments," *in* "The symposium on the Hicks' Report," *Social and Economic Studies*, 5 (1956), 32-38.

Knox, Graham. "Political change in Jamaica (1966-1906) and the local reaction to the policies of the crown colony government." *In* Fuat M. Andic and T. G. Mathews, eds. *The Caribbean in transition: papers on social, political and economic development, proceedings of the*

Second Caribbean Scholars' Conference, 1964. Río Piedras: Institute of Caribbean Studies, 1965.

Kuper, Leo and M. G. Smith, eds. *Pluralism in Africa.* Berkeley and Los Angeles: University of California Press, 1969.

Le Page, R. B., and David De Camp. *Jamaican Creole.* London: Macmillan, 1960.

Leslie, Charles. *A new history of Jamaica.* 2d ed. London: Hodges, 1740.

Lewis, Gordon K. *The growth of the modern West Indies.* London: MacGibbon and Kee, 1968.

Lewis, James O'Neil. "A comparison of the economic development of Puerto Rico, Jamaica and Trinidad, 1939-53," B. Litt. thesis. Oxford, 1956.

Lewis, M. G. *Journal of a West India Proprietor, 1815-17.* Ed. Mona Wilson. London: George Routledge, 1929.

Lewis, Oscar. *La vida: a Puerto Rican family in the culture of poverty—San Juan and New York.* New York: Vintage Books, 1968.

Lewis, S., and T. G. Mathews, eds. *Caribbean integration: papers on social, political and economic integration, Proceedings of the Third Caribbean Scholars' Conference, 1966.* Río Piedras: Institute of Caribbean Studies, Puerto Rico, 1967.

Lewis, W. Arthur. "The industrialization of the British West Indies," *Caribbean Economic Review,* vol. 2 (1950).

——. "Economic development with unlimited supplies of labour," *Manchester School of Economic and Social Studies,* 22 (1954), 139-191.

——. *The theory of economic growth.* London: George Allen and Unwin, 1955.

Leyburn, James G. *The Haitian people.* New Haven: Yale University Press, 1955.

Lind, Andrew W. "Adjustment patterns among the Jamaican Chinese," *Social and Economic Studies,* 7 (1958), 144-164.

Livingstone, W. P. *Black Jamaica: a study in evolution,* London: Sampson Low, 1899.

Lobb, J. "Caste and class in Haiti," *American Journal of Sociology,* 46 (1940), 23-34.

Long, Anton V. *Jamaica and the new order, 1827-1847.* No. 1. Kingston: Institute of Social and Economic Research, Special series, 1956.

Long, Edward. *The history of Jamaica, or, general survey of the antient and modern state of that island.* 3 vols. London: T. Lowndes, 1774.

Lowenthal, David. "The West Indies chooses a capital," *Geographical Review,* 48 (1958), 336-364.

——. "The range and variation of Caribbean societies," *Annals New York Academy of Sciences,* 83 (1960), 786-795.

——. "Race and colour in the West Indies," in "Colour and race," *Daedalus,* 96, 2 (1967), 580-626.

——. "Black power in the Caribbean," *Race Today,* 2, 3 (1970), 94-95.

——. *West Indian Societies.* London: Oxford University Press for the Institute of Race Relations in collaboration with the American Geographical Society (New York), 1972.

Lowenthal, David, ed. *The West Indies Federation: perspectives on a new nation.* New York: Columbia University Press for the American Geographical Society and Carleton University, 1961.

Ludlow, J. M. *A quarter century of Jamaica Legislation.* London: Jamaica Committee, Jamaica Papers, no. 4, 1866.

Lynch, Kevin. *The image of the city.* Cambride, Mass.: MIT Press, 1967.

Lynch-Campbell, H. *The Chinese in Jamaica.* Kingston, 1957.

McGee, T. G. *The urbanization process in the third world.* London: Bell, 1971.

McKenzie, H. I. "The plural society debate: some comments on a recent contribution," *Social and Economic Studies,* 15 (1966), 53-60.

Macmillan, W. M. *Warning from the West Indies: a tract for Africa and the Empire.* London: Faber and Faber, 1938.

Mangin, William. "Latin American squatter settlements: a problem and a solution," *Latin American Research Review,* 2, 2 (1967), 65-98.

Manley, Douglas, R. "Mental ability in Jamaica," *Social and Economic Studies,* 12 (1963), 51-71.

Marsh, R. M. "Comparative sociology, 1950-1963," *Current Sociology,* vol. 14, no. 2 (1966).

Martin, R. Montgomery, "British possessions in the West Indies," *The British Colonies,* Division VIII. London: John Tallis, 1853.

Mason, Philip. *Patterns of dominance.* London: Oxford University Press for the Institute of Race Relations, 1970.

Mathews, T. G. et al. *Politics and economics in the Caribbean.* Río Piedras, Institute of Caribbean Studies, University of Puerto Rico, Special Study No. 3, 1966.

Mathieson, William Law. *The sugar colonies and Governor Eyre, 1849-1866.* London: Longmans Green, 1936.

Matley, Charles. *The geology and physiography of the Kingston District, Jamaica.* Kingston: Government Printing Office, 1951.

Mau, James A. "The threatening masses: myth or reality?" *in* Fuat M. Andic and T. G. Mathews, *The Caribbean in transition: papers on social, political and economic development, proceedings of the Second Caribbean Scholars' Conference, 1964.* Río Piedras: Institute of Caribbean Studies, 1965. Pp. 258-270.

——. *Social change and images of the future: a study of the pursuit of progress in Jamaica.* Cambridge, Mass.: Schenkmann, 1968.

Maunder, W. F. "Kingston public passenger transport," *Social and Economic Studies*, 2, 4 (1954), 5-36.

——. "The new Jamaican emigration," *Social and Economic Studies*, 4, 1 (1955), 38-63.

——. *Employment in an underdeveloped area: a sample survey of Kingston, Jamaica*. New Haven: Yale University Press, 1960.

Merrill, Gordon C. "The role of Sephardic Jews in the British Caribbean area during the seventeenth century," *Caribbean Studies*, 4, 3 (1964), 32-49.

Miller, Errol L. "Body image, physical beauty, and colour among Jamaican adolescents," *Social and Economic Studies*, 18 (1969), 72-89.

Milroy, Dr. Gavin. *Report on the cholera epidemic in Jamaica*. Kingston, 1852.

Mintz, Sidney W. "The Jamaican internal marketing pattern," *Social and Economic Studies*, 4, 1 (1955), 95-109.

Mintz, Sidney W., and Douglas G. Hall "The origins of Jamaica's internal marketing system," *Yale University Publications in Anthropology, no. 57*, 1960.

Moes, J. E. "The creation of full employment in Jamaica," *Caribbean Quarterly*, 12 (1966), 8-21.

Moore, E. A. *Flood control and drainage problems of western expansion of Kingston*. Kingston, 1962.

Moore, Joseph G., and George Eaton Simpson. "A comparative study of acculturation in Morant Bay and West Kingston, Jamaica," *Zaire*, 9-10 (1957), 979-1019; 11 (1958), 65-87.

Mordecai, John. *The West Indies: the federal negotiations*. London: George Allen and Unwin, 1968.

Moser, C. A. *The measurement of levels of living (with special reference to Jamaica)*, Colonial Research Studies, no. 24. London: H.M.S.O., 1957.

Munroe, Trevor. *The politics of constitutional decolonization: Jamaica 1944-62*. Kingston: Institute of Social and Economic Research, University of the West Indies, 1972.

Naipaul, V. S. *The middle passage*. London: Andre Deutsch, 1962.

National plan for Jamaica 1957-1967. Kingston: Government Printing Office, 1957.

Neita, Clifton. *Who's who in Jamaica*. 10th ed. Kingston: *Who's Who* (Jamaica), 1960.

Nettels, C. P. "England and the Spanish American trade, 1680-1715," *Journal of Modern History*, 3 (1931), 1-32.

Nettleford, Rex. "National identity and attitudes to Race in Jamaica," *Race*, 7 (1965-66), 59-72.

——. "Poverty at the root of race issue," *in* "Jamaica: a special report," *The Times*, 14 September, 1970.

——. *Mirror, mirror: identity, race and protest in Jamaica*. London and Jamaica: William Collins and Sangster's Book Store, 1971.

Newling, Bruce E. "Urban growth and spatial structure:

mathematical models and empirical evidence," *Geographical Review*, 56 (1966), 213-225.

Norris, Katrin. *Jamaica, the search for an identity*. Oxford University Press for the Institute of Race Relations, 1962.

Norton, Ann. "The Kingston metropolitan area: a description of its land-use patterns," in *Essays on Jamaica*. Kingston: Jamaican Geographical Society and Geology and Geography Department, University of the West Indies, 1970. Pp. 34-44, mimeo.

Norton, Ann V., and George E. Cumper. " 'Peasant', 'plantation' and 'urban' communities in rural Jamaica: a test of the validity of the classification," *Social and Economic Studies*, 15 (1966), 338-352.

Nugent, Maria. *Lady Nugent's Journal*. Ed. Frank Cundall, 3d ed. London: West India Committee, 1939.

Olivier, Lord. *The myth of Governor Eyre*. London: Hogarth Press, 1933.

——. *Jamaica, the blessed isle*. London: Faber and Faber, 1936.

Opie, E. L. "Memorandum on the control of tuberculosis," Kingston: Legislative Council Minutes, Appendix 35, 1933.

Orde Browne, G. St. J. *Labour conditions in the West Indies*. London: H.M.S.O., 1939.

Paget, Ernest, "Land use and settlement in Jamaica." *In* Steel, Robert W., and Charles A. Fisher, *Geographical essays on British tropical lands*. London: George Philip, 1956. Pp. 181-223.

——. "Value, valuation and the use of land in the West Indies." *Geographical Journal*, 127 (1961), 493-498.

Paget, Hugh. "The free village system in Jamaica," *Jamaica Historical Review*, vol. 1 (1945); reprinted in *Caribbean Quarterly*, 10 (1964), 38-51.

Palmer, Ransford W. *The Jamaican Economy*. New York: Frederick A. Praeger, 1968.

Pares, Richard. *War and trade in the West Indies*. Oxford: Clarendon Press, 1936.

——. *Yankees and creoles: the trade between North America and the West Indies before the American Revolution*. New York: Longmans, 1956.

Park, Robert E., and Ernest W. Burgess. *The city*. Chicago: University of Chicago Press, 1925. (New ed. introduced by Morris Janowitz, 1967).

Parry, J. H., and P.M. Sherlock. *A short history of the West Indies*. London: Macmillan, 1956.

Patterson, H. Orlando. "The social structure of a university hall of residence," *Pelican*, 9, 3 (March 1962), 22-39.

——. "Slavery, acculturation and social change: the Jamaican case," *British Journal of Sociology*, 17 (1966), 151-164.

——. *The sociology of slavery*. London: MacGibbon and Kee, 1967.

–––. "West Indian migrants returning home: some observations," *Race*, 10 (1968-69), 69-77.

Peach, Ceri. "West Indian migration to Britain: the economic factors," *Race*, 7 (1965), 31-46.

–––. *West Indian migration to Britain: a social geography.* London: Oxford University Press for the Institute of Race Relations, 1968.

Peck, H. Austin. "Economic planning in Jamaica," *Social and Economic Studies*, 7 (1958), 141-163.

Phelps, O. W. "Rise of the labour movement in Jamaica," *Social and Economic Studies*, 9 (1960), 417-468.

Phillippo, J. C. *Jamaica: its government and its people.* Kingston, 1883.

Phillippo, J. M. *Jamaica, its past and present state.* London: John Snow, 1843.

Phillips, U. B. "A Jamaica slave plantation," *Caribbean Quarterly*, 1, 1 (1953), 4-13.

Pim, Bedford. *The Negro and Jamaica.* London: Trübner, 1866.

Pitman, Frank W. *The development of the British West Indies, 1700-63.* New Haven: Yale University Press, 1917.

Post, K. W. J. "The politics of protest in Jamaica, 1938: some problems of analysis and conceptualization," *Social and Economic Studies*, 18 (1969), 374-390.

Prest, A. R. *A fiscal survey of the British Caribbean.* London: H.M.S.O., 1957.

Price, George. *Jamaica and the colonial office: who caused the crisis?* London: Sampson Low, 1866.

Proudfoot, Malcolm J. *Population movements in the Caribbean.* Port-of-Spain, Trinidad: Caribbean Commission, 1950.

Proudfoot, Mary. *Britain and the United States in the Caribbean: a comparative study in methods of development.* London: Faber and Faber, 1954.

Ragatz, Lowell J. *The fall of the planter class in the British Caribbean.* New York: American Historical Association, 1928.

Renny, Robert. *An history of Jamaica with observations on the climate.* London: Cawthorn, 1807.

Report of the Chief Electoral Officer, *Jamaica General Election 1959.* Kingston: Government Printing Office, 1959.

–––. *Jamaica referendum.* Kingston, 1961.

Report of the commission upon the condition of the juvenile population of Jamaica. Kingston: *Jamaica Gazette,* Supplement, 1880.

Report of the commission of enquiry into the match industry. Kingston: Government Printing Office, 1955.

Report of the commission on unemployment. Kingston: Legislative Council Minutes, Appendix 41/1936, 1936.

Report of the committee on alien immigration. Kingston: Legislative Council Minutes, Appendix 16/1931, 1931.

Report of the factory inspectorate 1960. Kingston: 1960, typescript.

Report of the Mission of U. K. Industrialists. *Industrial development in Jamaica, Trinidad, Barbados and British Guiana.* London: H.M.S.O., 1953.

Report of the Mission to Africa. Kingston: Government Printing Office, 1961.

Report of the select committee of the House of Commons on the West India colonies. London: House of Commons, 1843.

Returns of slaves for Kingston parish, 1817 and 1820. Spanish Town: Jamaica Archives, manuscript.

Roberts, George W. *The population of Jamaica.* London: Cambridge University Press for the Conservation Foundation, 1957.

–––. "Provisional assessment of growth of the Kingston-St. Andrew area, 1960-70," *Social and Economic Studies,* 12 (1963), 432-441.

–––. "Urbanization and the growth of small towns in Jamaica," *Jamaica Architect*, 1, 3 (1967-68), 69-71.

Roberts, George W., and Donald O. Mills. "Study of external migration affecting Jamaica 1953-55," supplement to *Social and Economic Studies*, vol. 7 (1958).

Roberts, W. Adolphe. *Six great Jamaicans.* Kingston: The Pioneer Press, 1951.

–––, ed. *The capitals of Jamaica.* Kingston: The Pioneer Press, 1955.

Robertson, Glory. *Members of the assembly of Jamaica from the general election of 1830 to the final session January 1866.* Kingston: West India Reference Library, Institute of Jamaica, 1965.

Robinson, E., H. R. Versey, and J. B. Williams. "The Jamaica Earthquake of March 1, 1957, *Transactions of the Second Caribbean Geological Conference,* University of Puerto Rico, 1960. Pp. 50-57.

Robson, B. T. *Urban analysis: a study of city structure with special reference to Sunderland.* London: Cambridge University Press, 1969.

Rodney, Walter. *The groundings with my brothers.* London: Bogle-L'Ouverture Publications, 1969.

Rottenberg, Simon. "Entrepreneurship and economic progress in Jamaica," *Inter-American Economic Affairs*, 7, 2 (1953), 74-79.

Royal Commission. *Report into the public revenues, expenditure, debts and liabilities of Jamaica, Grenada, St. Vincent, Tobago, St. Lucia and the Leeward Islands.* London: H.M.S.O., 1884.

Rubin, Vera, ed. *Caribbean studies: a symposium.* Kingston: Institute of Social and Economic Research, University College of the West Indies, 1957.

–––. "Social and cultural pluralism in the Caribbean," *Annals of the New York Academy of Sciences,* vol. 83, art. 5 (1960).

Scott, Michael. *Tom Cringle's log.* London: *Daily Telegraph* Edition, 1917.

Seaga, Edward P. G. "Parent-teacher relationships in a Jamaican village," *Social and Economic Studies,* 4 (1955),

289-302.

———. "Revival cults in Jamaica," *Jamaica Journal,* 3, 2 (1969), 3-13.

Segal, Aaron, with Kent C. Earnhardt. *Politics and population in the Caribbean.* Río Piedras: Institute of Caribbean Studies, University of Puerto Rico, Special Study No. 7, 1969.

Select Committee of the Jamaica House of Representatives. *To consider measures for the immediate relief of the unemployed.* Kingston: Government Printing Office, 1950.

Semmel, Bernard. *The Governor Eyre controversy.* London: MacGibbon and Kee, 1962.

Senior, Bernard M. (sometimes attributed to B. Martin Snr.) *Jamaica as it was, as it is, and as it may be.* Kingston, 1835.

Senior, Clarence, and Douglas Manley. *Report on Jamaican emigration to Great Britain.* Kingston: Government Printing Office, 1955.

Sesqui-centennial anniversary of the granting of the charter to Kingston 1802-1952. Kingston: 1952.

Sewell, William George. *The ordeal of free labour in the West Indies.* New York: Harper and Bros., 1861.

Sibley, Inez Knibb. *The Baptists of Jamaica.* Kingston: Jamaica Baptist Union, 1965.

Siegel, Sidney. *Nonparametric statistics for the behavioural sciences.* New York: McGraw-Hill, 1965.

Silverman, Rev. H. P. *A panorama of Jamaican Jewry.* Kingston: 1960.

Simey, T. S. *Welfare and planning in the West Indies.* Oxford: Clarendon Press, 1946.

Simpson, George Eaton. "Begging in Kingston and Montego Bay," *Social and Economic Studies,* 3, 2 (1954), 197-211.

———. "Political cultism in West Kingston, Jamaica," *Social and Economic Studies,* 4 (1955), 133-149.

———. "The Ras Tafari movement in Jamaica: a study of race and class conflict," *Social Forces,* 34 (1955), 167-170.

———. "Jamaican revivalist cults," *Social and Economic Studies,* vol. 5, no. 4 (1956).

Sires, Ronald V. "Negro labour in Jamaica in the years following emancipation," *Journal of Negro History,* 25 (1940), 484-497.

———. "The Jamaican slave insurrection loan, 1832-65," *Journal of Negro History,* 27 (1942), 295-319.

———. "The Jamaican constitution of 1884," *Social and Economic Studies,* 3, 1 (1954), 64-81.

———. "The experience of Jamaica with modified crown colony government," *Social and Economic Studies,* 4, 2 (1955), 150-167.

Sjoberg, Gideon. *The preindustrial city past and present.* New York: The Free Press, 1960.

Sligo, Lord. *Letter to the Marquess of Normanby relative to the present state of Jamaica.* London: John Andrews, 1839.

Sloane, Sir Hans. *A voyage to the islands Madeira, Barbados, Nievis, S. Chistophers and Jamaica.* London, vol. 1, 1707; vol. 2, 1725.

Smith, M. G. "Some aspects of the social structure of the British Caribbean about 1820," *Social and Economic Studies,* 1, 4 (1953), 55-80.

———. "A framework for Caribbean studies" [1955], in his *The plural society in the British West Indies.* Berkeley and Los Angeles: University of California Press. Pp. 18-74.

———. *A report on labour supply in rural Jamaica.* Kingston: Government Printing Office, 1956.

———. "Community organization in rural Jamaica," *Social and Economic Studies,* 5 (1956), 295-314.

———. "Education and Occupational choice in rural Jamaica," *Social and Economic Studies,* 9 (1960), 332-354.

———. "Politics and society in Jamaica." Unpublished typescript, n. d.

———. "Race and politics in Jamaica," typescript, 1961.

———. "The plural framework of Jamaican society," *British Journal of Sociology,* 12 (1961), 249-262.

———. *West Indian family structure.* Seattle: University of Washington Press, 1962.

———. "Introduction." *In* Edith Clarke, *My mother who fathered me . . .* 2d ed. London: George Allen and Unwin, 1966. Pp. i-xliv.

———. *The plural society in the British West Indies.* Berkeley and Los Angeles: University of California Press, 1965.

———. *Stratification in Grenada.* Berkeley and Los Angeles: University of California Press, 1965.

Smith, M. G., and G. J. Kruijer. *A sociological manual for extension workers in the Caribbean.* Kingston: Department of Extra-Mural Studies, University College of the West Indies, 1957.

Smith, M. G., Roy Augier, and Rex Nettleford. *The Ras Tafari movement in Kingston, Jamaica.* Kingston: Institute of Social and Economic Research, University College of the West Indies, 1960.

Smith, Raymond T. "Jamaican society since emancipation," *Times British Colonies Review,* no. 17 (Spring 1955).

———. "A preliminary report on a study of selected East Indians in Jamaica," typescript 1955.

———. *The Negro family in British Guiana.* London: Routledge and Kegan Paul, 1956.

———. "Social stratification, cultural pluralism and integration in West Indian societies," in S. Lewis, and T. G. Mathews, eds. *Caribbean integration: papers on social, political and economic integration, Proceedings of the Third Caribbean Scholars' Conference, 1966.* Río Piedras: Institute of Caribbean Studies, Puerto Rico, 1967. Pp. 226-258.

Social welfare committee. *Report on Housing.* Kingston: House of Representatives Minutes, appendix 56, 1945.

Southey, Capt. Thomas. *A chronological history of the West Indies.* 3 vols. London: Longmans, Rees, Orme, Brown and Green, 1827.

Special reports on the systems of education in the West Indies and in British Guiana. London: H.M.S.O., 1901.

Stanslawski, Dan. "Early Spanish town planning in the new world," *Geographical Review*, 37 (1947), 94-102.

Steers, J. A. "The cays and palisadoes of Port Royal, Jamaica," *Geographical Journal*, 106 (1940), 279-295.

Stewart, J. *A view of the past and present state of the island of Jamaica; with remarks on the physical and moral condition of the slaves, and on the abolition of slavery in the colonies.* Edinburgh: Oliver and Boyd, 1823.

Stone, Carl. *Race, class and political behavior in urban Jamaica.* Kingston: Institute of Social and Economic Research, University of the West Indies, 1973.

Sturge, J., and T. Harvey. *The West Indies in 1837: being the journal of a visit to Antigua, Monserrat, Dominica, St. Lucia, Barbados and Jamaica.* 2d ed. London: Hamilton Adams, 1838.

Stycos, J. Mayone. *Human fertility in Latin America.* Ithaca: Cornell University Press, 1968.

Stycos, J. Mayone, and Kurt W. Back. *The Control of human fertility in Jamaica.* Ithaca: Cornell University Press, 1964.

Survey of squatters in Western Kingston, 1951. Kingston: House of Representatives Minutes, appendix 9, no. 52, 1951.

Swaby, R. A. "Report on housing conditions in middle income areas in Kingston and St. Andrew," Kingston, 1951, mimeo.

Sweeting, Marjorie M. "The Karstlands of Jamaica," *Geographical Journal,* 124 (1958), 184-199.

Szulc, Tad, ed. *The United States and the Caribbean.* Englewood Cliffs, N. J.: Prentice-Hall, 1971.

Taylor, Milton C. "Tax exemption and new industry in Puerto Rico," *Social and Economic Studies,* 4 (1955), 121-132.

Taylor, S. A. G. "Port Royal." *In* Roberts, W. Adolphe, ed. *The Capitals of Jamaica.* Pp. 18-37.

Tekse, Kalman. *Internal migration in Jamaica.* Kingston: Department of Statistics, 1967.

Theodorson, George A. *Studies in human ecology.* New York: Harper and Row, 1961.

Thomas, A. R. *Storm water drainage in Jamaica.* New York: United Nations Technical Assistance Administration, 1959.

Thomas, J. J. *Froudacity.* London: New Beacon Books, 1969.

Thompson, R. "The role of capitalism in Jamaica's development," *Caribbean Quarterly,* 12 (1966), 22-28.

Thorne, Alfred P. "The size structure and growth of the economy of Jamaica," supplement to *Social and Economic Studies,* vol. 4 (1955).

———. "An economic phenomenon (study of an apparent psychological trait and its probable effect on regional economic development)," *Caribbean Quarterly,* 6 (1960), 270-278.

Tidrick, Gene. "Some aspects of Jamaican emigration to the United Kingdom, 1953-1962," *Social and Economic Studies,* 15 (1966), 22-39.

Timms, D. W. G. *The urban mosaic: towards a theory of residential differentiation.* London: Cambridge University Press, 1971.

Timpson, George F. *Jamaican interlude.* London: Ed. J. Burrow, 1938.

Town and country planning (Kingston) development order, 1966, The. Kingston: Government Printing Office, 1966.

Trollope, Anthony. *The West Indies and the Spanish Main.* London: Chapman and Hall, 1860.

Underhill, Edward Bean. *Letter addressed to the Rt. Honourable E. Cardwell, with illustrative documents on the condition of Jamaica and an explanatory statement.* London: Arthur Miall, 1865.

"Unemployment," *New World Pamphlet.* Kingston, 1967.

Unemployment commission. Kingston: Legislative council minutes, appendix 41, 1936.

Vestry minutes for Kingston, 1744-49. Spanish Town: Jamaica Archives, manuscript.

Voelker, Walter D. *Survey of industry in the West Indies.* Kingston: Institute of Social and Economic Research, University College of the West Indies, 1961.

Wesley, Charles H. "The Negro in the West Indies: slavery and freedom," *Journal of Negro History,* 17 (1932), 156-172.

———. "The emancipation of the free coloured people in the British Empire," *Journal of Negro History,* 19 (1934), 137-170.

West India Royal Commission Report. London: H.M.S.O., 1945.

Whitbeck, R. H. "The agricultural geography of Jamaica," *Annals of the Association of American Geographers,* 22 (1932), 13-27.

Williams, Cynric R. *A tour through the island of Jamaica.* London: Hunt and Clarke, 1826.

Williams, Eric. *Capitalism and slavery.* Chapel Hill: University of North Carolina Press, 1944.

———. *Documents on British West Indian History 1807-1833.* Trinidad: Historical Society of Trinidad and Tobago in collaboration with the Social Science Research Centre, University of Puerto Rico, 1952.

Williams, Joseph J. *Voodoos and obeahs: phases of West Indian witchcraft.* New York: Dial, 1932.

———. *Psychic phenomena in Jamaica.* New York: Dial, 1934.

Williams, Wilma. "Old Kingston," *Jamaica Journal,* 5, 2-3 (1971), 3-9.

Yin, Lee T., ed. *The Chinese in Jamaica.* Kingston, 1957.

Young, Bruce S. "Jamaica's bauxite and alumina industries," *Annals of the Association of American Geographers,* 55 (1965), 449-464.

Young, J. G. "Who planned Kingston?" *Jamaica Historical Review,* 1 (1946), 144-153.

Index